Chinese American Transnationalism

In the series

Asian American History and Culture

edited by Sucheng Chan, David Palumbo-Liu, Michael Omi, K. Scott Wong, and Linda Trinh Võ

Antonio T. Tiongson, Jr., Edgardo V. Gutierrez, and Ricardo V. Gutierrez, eds., *Positively No Filipinos Allowed: Building Communities and Discourse*

Keith Lawrence and Floyd Cheung, eds., *Recovered Legacies: Authority and Identity in Early Asian American Literature*

Rajini Srikanth, *The World Next Door: South Asian American Literature and the Idea of America*

Linda Trinh Võ, *Mobilizing an Asian American Community*

Franklin S. Odo, *No Sword to Bury: Japanese Americans in Hawai'i during World War II*

Josephine Lee, Imogene L. Lim, and Yuko Matsukawa, eds., *Re/collecting Early Asian America: Essays in Cultural History*

Linda Trinh Võ and Rick Bonus, eds., *Contemporary Asian American Communities: Intersections and Divergences*

Sunaina Marr Maira, *Desis in the House: Indian American Youth Culture in New York City*

Teresa Williams-León and Cynthia Nakashima, eds., *The Sum of Our Parts: Mixed-Heritage Asian Americans*

Tung Pok Chin with Winifred C. Chin, *Paper Son: One Man's Story*

Amy Ling, ed., *Yellow Light: The Flowering of Asian American Arts*

Rick Bonus, *Locating Filipino Americans: Ethnicity and the Cultural Politics of Space*

Darrell Y. Hamamoto and Sandra Liu, eds., *Countervisions: Asian American Film Criticism*

Martin F. Manalansan, IV, ed., *Cultural Compass: Ethnographic Explorations of Asian America*

Ko-lin Chin, *Smuggled Chinese: Clandestine Immigration to the United States*

Evelyn Hu-DeHart, ed., *Across the Pacific: Asian Americans and Globalization*

Soo-Young Chin, *Doing What Had to Be Done: The Life Narrative of Dora Yum Kim*

Robert G. Lee, *Orientals: Asian Americans in Popular Culture*

David L. Eng and Alice Y. Hom, eds., *Q & A: Queer in Asian America*

K. Scott Wong and Sucheng Chan, eds., *Claiming America: Constructing Chinese American Identities during the Exclusion Era*

Lavina Dhingra Shankar and Rajini Srikanth, eds., *A Part, Yet Apart: South Asians in Asian America*

Jere Takahashi, *Nisei/Sansei: Shifting Japanese American Identities and Politics*

Velina Hasu Houston, ed., *But Still, Like Air, I'll Rise: New Asian American Plays*

Josephine Lee, *Performing Asian America: Race and Ethnicity on the Contemporary Stage*

Deepika Bahri and Mary Vasudeva, eds., *Between the Lines: South Asians and Postcoloniality*

E. San Juan, Jr., *The Philippine Temptation: Dialectics of Philippines-U.S. Literary Relations*

Carlos Bulosan and E. San Juan, Jr., ed., *The Cry and the Dedication*

Carlos Bulosan and E. San Juan, Jr., ed., *On Becoming Filipino: Selected Writings of Carlos Bulosan*

Vicente L. Rafael, ed., *Discrepant Histories: Translocal Essays on Filipino Cultures*

Yen Le Espiritu, *Filipino American Lives*

Paul Ong, Edna Bonacich, and Lucie Cheng, eds., *The New Asian Immigration in Los Angeles and Global Restructuring*

Chris Friday, *Organizing Asian American Labor: The Pacific Coast Canned-Salmon Industry, 1870–1942*

Sucheng Chan, ed., *Hmong Means Free: Life in Laos and America*

Timothy P. Fong, *The First Suburban Chinatown: The Remarking of Monterey Park, California*

William Wei, *The Asian American Movement*

Yen Le Espiritu, *Asian American Panethnicity*

Velina Hasu Houston, ed., *The Politics of Life*

Renqiu Yu, *To Save China, To Save Ourselves: The Chinese Hand Laundry Alliance of New York*

Shirley Geok-lin Lim and Amy Ling, eds., *Reading the Literatures of Asian America*

Karen Isaksen Leonard, *Making Ethnic Choices: California's Punjabi Mexican Americans*

Gary Y. Okihiro, *Cane Fires: The Anti-Japanese Movement in Hawaii, 1865–1945*

Sucheng Chan, *Entry Denied: Exclusion and the Chinese Community in America, 1882–1943*

A poem carved on a wooden barracks wall on Angel Island.
Photograph by Mak Takahashi. Courtesy of Philip P. Choy.
Translated by Sucheng Chan

This wooden house has kept me for tens of days
For the Mexican exclusion law also lassoed me
What a pity heroes cannot use their martial skills
And can only wait to hear the crack of Zu's whip

As I leave this building far behind
My fellow villagers and I together rejoice
Don't say everything here is Western-styled
Though it might have been built of jade it still becomes a cage

Chinese American Transnationalism

The Flow of People, Resources, and Ideas between China and America during the Exclusion Era

Edited by
S<small>UCHENG</small> C<small>HAN</small>

TEMPLE UNIVERSITY PRESS
Philadelphia

Temple University Press
1601 North Broad Street
Philadelphia PA 19122
www.temple.edu/tempress

Copyright © 2006 by Temple University
All rights reserved
Published 2006
Printed in the United States of America

⊗ The paper used in this publication meets the requirements of the American
National Standard for Information Sciences—Permanence of Paper for Printed
Library Materials, ANSI Z39.48-1992

Library of Congress Cataloging-in-Publication Data

Chinese American transnationalism : the flow of people, resources, and ideas
between China and America during the exclusion era / edited by Sucheng Chan.
    p.   cm. — (Asian American history and culture)
    Includes bibliographical references and index.
    ISBN 1-59213-434-3 (cloth : alk. paper) — ISBN 1-59213-435-1
(pbk. : alk. paper)
    1. Chinese Americans — Ethnic identity.   2. Chinese Americans — History.
    3. Transnationalism.   4. United States — Emigration and immigration —
Social aspects.   I. Chan, Sucheng.   II. Series.

    E184.C5C478 2005
    973'.04951—dc22

                                                        2005041834

2 4 6 8 9 7 5 3 1

Contents

Preface and Acknowledgments   ix

1. Defying Exclusion: Chinese Immigrants and Their
   Strategies During the Exclusion Era
   ERIKA LEE   1

2. Trading with Gold Mountain: *Jinshanzhuang* and
   Networks of Kinship and Native Place
   MADELINE HSU   22

3. Against All Odds: Chinese Female Migration and
   Family Formation on American Soil During the Early
   Twentieth Century
   SUCHENG CHAN   34

4. Chinese Herbalists in the United States
   HAIMING LIU   136

5. Understanding Chinese American Transnationalism
   During the Early Twentieth Century: An Economic
   Perspective
   YONG CHEN   156

6. Republicanism, Confucianism, Christianity, and
   Capitalism in American Chinese Ideology
   SHEHONG CHEN   174

7. Teaching Chinese Americans to be Chinese:
   Curriculum, Teachers, and Textbooks in Chinese
   Schools in America During the Exclusion Era
   HIM MARK LAI   194

8.   Writing a Place in American Life: The Sensibilities of
      American-born Chinese as Reflected in Life Stories
      from the Exclusion Era
      XIAO-HUANG YIN   211

      Notes   237
      About the Contributors   275
      Index   277

Preface and Acknowledgments

THIS BOOK IS the third volume in a loosely connected trilogy on the Chinese exclusion era. The first volume, *Entry Denied*,[1] published in 1991, contains eight essays, four of which analyze how the exclusion laws and the changing ways in which they were enforced affected Chinese communities in the United States. The other four essays document how members of those communities dealt with the constraints on their lives by relying on a complex institutional structure that enabled them to combat the laws while connecting them to larger developments in both China and the United States. In contrast to the focus on institutions in the first volume, the seven chapters in *Claiming America*,[2] the second volume published in 1998, explore the multidimensional consciousness of individuals. They examine how some first- and second-generation Chinese Americans claimed America as their own by forcefully asserting that they, too, believed in democracy and equality. They declared that Chinese were not simply earning a living in the United States as "sojourners," but were also self-consciously embracing the American creed despite the fact that their presence was not welcomed on American soil. In the present volume, *Chinese American Transnationalism*, the eight contributors dissect the many ways in which Chinese living in the United States maintained ties to China through a constant transpacific flow of people, economic resources, and political and cultural ideas, the exclusion laws notwithstanding.

At first glance, the conceptual frameworks in the three volumes may seem to contradict one another. That is, the overarching theme of *Entry Denied* is resistance against discrimination—the Chinese American version of the "minority" paradigm that chronicles the agency of oppressed groups as they struggle against oppression. In contrast, the studies in *Claiming America* highlight not only the desire of some Chinese Americans to assimilate, but also their determination to claim a rightful place in U.S. society as Americans, thereby illustrating the complex ways in which assimilation theory is applicable to Chinese Americans. The guiding concept in this book is transnationalism. The essays document the many ways that Chinese migrants used to maintain ties to their homeland even as they set down roots in America. But the contradictions among the three conceptual frameworks are more apparent than real: the twenty-three essays in this trilogy, taken as a whole, underline the fact that the lives and consciousness of the Chinese who came to the United States were multifaceted and far more complex than any single scholarly concept can encompass or explicate. During the exclusion era, Chinese *simultaneously* resisted exclusion and defended the communities they had established in the United States; claimed America by fighting for the same rights that other immigrants enjoyed; and maintained demographic, economic, political, social, and cultural ties to their ancestral land. Studies based on a unitary scheme, be it the long-lived European-immigrant model of assimilation; or the 1960s conglomerate of pluralism, multiculturalism, agency, and resistance; or the currently trendy notion of transnationalism, are all simplistic. Counterposing one against another misses the point because life is more layered, fluid, and contradictory than the concepts that scholars think up to capture, in words, people's lived experiences in the material as well as symbolic realms. Therefore, instead of playing intellectual one-upmanship by declaring, "My theory is more sophisticated than yours," I think it is more important to ask, "What aspects of human existence do studies guided by each framework illuminate?"

Looking back, I am delighted by how much the writing of Chinese American history has changed in fifteen years. Thus, an observation I made when I wrote the preface for *Entry Denied* in 1990 is no longer correct. I had said that "In a double sense, then, the six decades of exclusion are the 'dark ages' of Chinese American history. That period is shadowy because we know so little about it; it is also dark because it was characterized by immense suffering and deprivation." While the suffering and deprivation can never be erased, standing as grim monuments to those decades of extreme hardship met with steadfast courage and endurance, the exclusion period is no longer "dark" in terms of historiography. Some of the best work in Chinese American history published in the late 1990s and the early 2000s deals with the exclusion era. Much of it was written by the contributors to this volume. If faculty teaching Chinese American or, more broadly, Asian American history can choose only one book about the exclusion era to assign in their classes, this book is it.

Two other statements I made earlier also require correction. In the preface to *Entry Denied*, I had said that "the exclusion era has received almost no scholarly treatment, at least not in English, due in large part to the paucity of documentary sources on the period." In the preface to *Claiming America*, which I drafted and Scott Wong revised, we had stated, "Compared with European immigrants, Chinese immigrants and their American-born children have left relatively few historical records." In both instances, the "documentary sources" and "historical records" I had in mind were writings *by* Chinese immigrants and Chinese Americans in the form of letters, diaries, journals, newspaper articles, essays, and books. In that sense, the two statements remain true. However, I had failed to consider the immense collection of government files generated in the process of implementing the Chinese exclusion laws—a mountain of material whose existence I was aware of but had not yet plumbed myself at the time—or the extant Chinese-language sources, especially those published in the twentieth-century segment of the exclusion era. As the endnotes in this book reveal, the documentary evidence from the exclusion era is definitely not "thin," as I had erroneously characterized it, but is, in fact, so overwhelmingly voluminous that it will take dozens of scholars years to go through it all.

Not only do we know a lot more about the exclusion era as a whole, but the chapters in this book also illustrate the fact that treating the exclusion years as a single "era" camouflages the changes that occurred over six decades. The variations from one span of the "era" to the next were significant, as Erika Lee shows in Chapter 1. Author of an award-winning book, *At America's Gates*,[3] based largely but not solely on an analysis of immigration files and oral histories, Lee discusses the changing pattern of Chinese immigration and the different strategies that the aspiring immigrants used to get around the exclusion laws. She examines their socioeconomic class backgrounds, the relative proportion of women to men, what difficulties each group encountered, and how they surmounted those hurdles. Using many telling examples of individuals and their experiences, she paints a picture that foregrounds the admirable determination, resourcefulness, and ingenuity of the Chinese who sought admission into the United States. Lee concludes that "of the different strategies the Chinese tried, the most effective one was learning to negotiate their way *through* exclusion, instead of attempting to dismantle the laws altogether." Seeking and using information from immigration officials, attorneys, and fellow Chinese already in the United States, the aspiring immigrants defied exclusion and outsmarted the bureaucrats guarding America's gates. Some 300,000 of them entered during the exclusion era—a number that matches those who came between 1849 and 1882 when no restrictions existed. The fact that Chinese communities on American soil did not disappear is a testament to their success.

In Chapter 2, Madeline Hsu, author of another award-winning book, *Dreaming of Gold, Dreaming of Home*,[4] discusses a mechanism—*jinshanzhuang* (Gold Mountain firms)—that facilitated Chinese migration and enabled the migrants to maintain their lifestyle. In addition to the supportive kinship networks and white allies Erika Lee identifies, Hsu's study, based on an imaginative use of Chinese-language sources that have survived war, revolution, famine, and natural disasters in China—specifically, in Taishan District, Guangdong Province—reveals that Chinese overseas migration was, in fact, a well-organized *business*: "Overseas migration in the thousands was not accomplished by crossing the Pacific in fishing boats, wooden junks, or even clipper ships. Migration in such numbers demanded a level of technological development and the existence of global networks of trade more sophisticated and reliable than had existed in China before the nineteenth century." Jinshanzhuang began as exporters of Chinese groceries. They established a foothold in North America—Canada, the United States, and Mexico—as well as in Australia in the early 1850s. For a century, not only were they "instrumental in the growth of China's foreign trade routed through Hong Kong," but they also enabled Chinese living and working abroad to continue eating the food, using the medicinal herbs, wearing the clothes, and reading the newspapers and magazines to which they were accustomed. Equally important, the firms acted as a postal system that enabled the migrants to send letters and remittances to family and clan members left behind, and to receive mail from their relatives and friends in a period when China's postal system was not yet well developed.

Sucheng Chan turns to yet another hitherto untapped body of evidence in Chapter 3—the 1900 and 1910 manuscript census schedules—to track the changing patterns of Chinese female migration, marriage, and family formation. Dividing California into three sections—San Francisco, agricultural counties, and mining and mountain counties—she discovers that *where* Chinese immigrants and their American-born progeny lived affected what work they could find. Those occupations, in turn, correlated with differential rates of marriage among the men, while the percentage of men whose wives lived with them in the United States also varied by the occupational grouping to which they belonged. However, contrary to the common belief that it was mainly merchants who could enjoy the company of their nuclear families, men in a wide array of occupations also managed to live with their wives and children in America. Chan's findings indicate that the prevailing narrative of Chinese marriage and family formation must be modified significantly. Though China was indeed the main site of marriage and family formation, the United States was *also* such a site, not only among U.S.-born Chinese, but among immigrant men and women as well. Most intriguing of all, a large number of the China-born married women did *not* wed before they came to America; rather, about three-quarters of them had been in the United States for some years before they married. Questions about various aspects of these women's lives can be answered only by combining the information in the manuscript censuses with other bodies of evidence—research that will take years of intensive labor to complete.

Haiming Liu author of *The Transnational History of a Chinese Family*,[5] takes a close look at an interesting group of immigrants—practitioners of Chinese herbal medicine—who relied on transnational ties to establish their profession-cum-business in the United States. In

Chapter 4, using both Chinese and English sources, he discusses the history of herbal medicine in China, who the immigrant herbalists were, how they got their professional training, the manner in which they conducted their profession/business in the United States, the legal and social problems they confronted, and how they overcame the obstacles in their path. Focusing on this specific group, Liu argues more broadly that the nature of Chinese American culture was and is "open, engaged, and cosmopolitan." By telling stories about individual herbalists, he shows how adeptly they "crossed ethnic borders." He brings to life the strategies they used to expand their culturally transplanted practice and to make it economically viable by serving non-Chinese clients—many of whom came from well-to-do backgrounds—in addition to Chinese ones. Some of the non-Chinese clients performed an important advertising function on behalf of their Chinese healers by telling their friends about the effectiveness of Chinese herbal medicine. "Thus," Liu observes, "Chinese herbal medicine can be seen as an instance of reverse assimilation." Unlike most of the writings on Chinese Americans that assess whether they adapted to life in the United States, Liu's chapter spotlights the impact of a certain group of Chinese immigrants on those aspects of American culture related to health, illness, and healing.

In Chapter 5, Yong Chen, author of a compelling book that tapped both Chinese and English sources, *Chinese San Francisco*,[6] argues that "We cannot comprehend the Chinese American historical experience fully by concentrating on the U.S. setting alone. Though they were a politically discriminated against and economically exploited minority in the United States, Chinese Americans enjoyed a respected social status in China.... They participated actively in the national political discourse of China while simultaneously campaigning against America's racism." By examining the "flow of capital from America to China and the social and political significance of those transactions that facilitated the redefinition and expansion of the relationship of Chinese Americans to China," as well as the immigrants' willingness to act on their belief that "only a strong and rejuvenated China could protect its emigrants," Chen offers new insights into the seeming paradoxes that characterized Chinese America and the changing meanings of "Chinese-ness" and "American-ness." He is attentive to both the material and the ideological dimensions of ethnic identity formation. By telling the stories of individuals, he deftly demonstrates how scholars can "recognize the complexities of Chinese American transnationalism, rather than romanticize it in a simplistic way."

In Chapter 6, Shehong Chen focuses her analytical lens on three ideological strands originating in China that generated vigorous debate within Chinese communities in America. Drawing from her outstanding book, *Being Chinese, Becoming Chinese American*,[7] she discusses the various ways in which Chinese in the United States responded to and interpreted major events in China while articulating their own preferences with regard to republicanism, Confucianism, Christianity, and capitalism. Based on a close reading of three Chinese-language newspapers published in the United States—*Chinese World* (the mouthpiece of the reform movement in China), *Young China* (the organ of the revolutionary movement headed by Sun Yat-sen), and *Chung Sai Yat Po* (a newspaper founded by Ng Poon Chew, a Chinese immigrant Protestant minister who linked the fates of China and Chinese America)—Chen demonstrates that the Chinese in America did not adopt wholesale the ideological currents flowing across the Pacific. Rather, they melded their own American experiences with critical assessments of events in China. They strongly supported a republican form of government but were not ready to jettison the core values of Chinese civilization, as embodied in Confucianism, which they continued to cherish even as intellectuals and student activists in China launched a New Culture Movement to change fundamentally China's literary tradition, to promote the study of science, and to liberate women. Also, some Chinese in America converted to and embraced Christianity, in contrast to many Chinese in China who participated in an anti-Christian crusade. Finally, the Chinese in America expressed a strong preference for capitalism over Communism, in the process reflecting what their own economic interests were.

Him Mark Lai, often called the "father" or "dean" of Chinese American history, analyzes in Chapter 7 how Chinese-language schools in America attempted to socialize Chinese American children in order to make them "authentic" Chinese. Based on both research and his own experiences as a youngster attending such a school, he describes how the first schools were established, who the teachers were, the contents of textbooks used in various grades, and what extracurricular activities were available. These schools were very much affected by the cultural, literary, and language reforms taking place in China during the early decades of the twentieth century. In particular, the reformers advocated changing the old literary style called *wenyan* to a simpler style known as *baihua* or *yutiwen*. They also promoted an oral national language called *guoyu* that all educated Chinese were supposed to learn in addition to the myriad regional dialects they spoke. Similar changes could not be implemented easily in North America, however, for several reasons. The exclusion laws limited the influx of teachers trained in the new written and oral linguistic forms; a majority of the Chinese in America spoke dialects that differed significantly from guoyu; and the financial resources of the immigrant communities were limited. Not surprisingly, the Chinese who set up these schools attempted to use them to disseminate the ideologies they supported, in a manner akin to how newspapers served as the mouthpieces of various political factions.

Despite the efforts to maintain economic, ideological, cultural, and educational ties between China and America, a small but growing number of U.S.-born children of Chinese ancestry eventually adopted an agenda of their own, as Xiao-huang Yin illuminates in Chapter 8. Drawing upon his insightful analysis of Chinese American texts in *Chinese American Literature Since the 1850s*,[8] Yin explicates two classic Chinese American autobiographies, *Father and Glorious Descendant* by Pardee Lowe and *Fifth Chinese Daughter* by Jade Snow Wong. He places these books, which are like windows through which we may catch glimpses of the conflicted nuances of an emerging Chinese American consciousness, within the larger sociohistorical contexts in which they were written and published. As Yin puts it, "the American-born of the exclusion era shared a common characteristic: they were 'American' by culture and Chinese only by race." This was so, despite the efforts of Chinese-language schools to make them into "authentic" Chinese. Yin summarizes the dilemma faced by Lowe and, by extension, other American-born youth of Chinese ancestry as follows: "how should he interpret the contradictions between the social reality that confronted him and the ideal of the American dream if the very American democracy and equality he admires exclude him from full participation in all aspects of American life?" Both works have endured and continue to be read decades after their first appearance because they capture how an articulate Chinese American young man and an equally eloquent Chinese American young woman negotiated their way through difficult psychological and social terrain, thereby enabling us, who live in quite a different racial and social environment—in which prejudice and discrimination still exist, but not by any stretch of the imagination similar to what prevailed in the early part of the twentieth century—to see how far we have come even though we still have a long way to go. Reading Chapter 8 in tandem with Chapters 6 and 7, we hear a stereophonic rendition of the multiple voices that rang out from Chinese America during the first several decades of the twentieth century while the exclusion laws were in effect.

Finally, a word about transliteration: when Chinese-language sources are cited or when Chinese terms are used, they are transliterated according to the pinyin system with the exception of well-known personal and place-names like Sun Yat-sen and Hong Kong or Canton. The pronunciation in the pinyin system is based on *putonghua*—the Communist name for what used to be called guoyu or "mandarin." When referring to place-names in the regions whence a vast majority of the immigrants came, both the pinyin and the Cantonese or Taishanese transliterations are given, with one of them in square brackets. When citing English-language sources, proper nouns are reproduced as they appeared in the original texts, however haphazard the transliterations may be. When citing Chinese-language sources, personal names are written in the Chinese order, with family/last name preceding given/first name. When citing English-language sources, personal names are written in the Western order, with given/first name preceding family/last name.

ACKNOWLEDGMENTS

We thank K. Scott Wong, advisory editor for history manuscripts in the *Asian American History and Culture* book series published by Temple University Press, and an anonymous reviewer for his or her insightful comments and suggestions that improved our work. We are also grateful to Janet Francendese for guiding the manuscript so efficiently through the review process, Jennifer French of Temple University Press and Joanne Bowser of TechBooks, who coordinated the production process, and Melissa Messina, who copyedited the manuscript.

Sucheng Chan
Goleta, California

Chinese American Transnationalism

1 Defying Exclusion: Chinese Immigrants and Their Strategies During the Exclusion Era

Erika Lee

> The reason we Chinese come to the United States is because of... extremity at home, we have no other method by which we can keep our bodies and souls together. Should we be blocked in this... will our calamity not be inexpressible?[1]
>
> —*Chinese Six Companies, May 2, 1910*

During the Chinese exclusion era, prospective Chinese immigrants faced a most difficult dilemma. While largely prohibited from immigrating to the United States by the Chinese exclusion laws, they also faced increasing economic, political, and social instability at home.[2] As the Chinese Six Companies, the umbrella organization for Chinese immigrant kinship and mutual benefit organizations in America, made clear in 1910, migration to the United States was essential in "keeping body and soul together" and in sustaining families both in the United States and in China. Chinese were thus highly motivated to continue to gain entry into America. Because of the immigrants' determination and ingenuity, the Chinese exclusion acts failed to end Chinese immigration altogether. During the exclusion era (1882–1943), an estimated 300,955 Chinese successfully gained admission into the United States for the first time or as returning residents and U.S.-born citizens. In fact, the number of exclusion-era Chinese admissions was greater than during the pre–exclusion era, from 1849 to 1882, when 258,210 Chinese entered the United States.[3] That so many managed to enter despite the exclusion laws is truly significant. It raises questions about the efficacy of restrictive immigration laws and demonstrates the power of immigrant resistance and agency.

Once the original Chinese Exclusion Act of 1882 was passed, the restrictions on Chinese immigration grew increasingly rigid over the course of the entire exclusion period. New laws were passed and administrative regulations were strengthened to make entry even more difficult for the Chinese who continued to seek admission into the country. By the end of the exclusion period, immigration restriction had become the rule rather than the exception—not only for Chinese, but also for other Asian immigrants and southern and eastern European immigrants. Government statistics, immigrant testimony, and other records reveal that the exclusion laws erected barriers that cast a large shadow over all Chinese immigrants, dictating who could come, when, and under what conditions. They also influenced the types of lives Chinese would have once in America. Nevertheless, the exclusion laws were not insurmountable and Chinese were willing to go to great lengths to live and work in *Gam Saan* [*Jinshan*, which means Gold Mountain]. Gold Mountain men and women, merchants and laborers, U.S. citizens and aliens, legal and illegal immigrants all passed through America's gates, most of them successfully. They came for work and other opportunities in order to sustain their families, and they adapted to and even contested the exclusion laws in ways that American lawmakers could hardly have predicted. This chapter first examines the reasons that Chinese continued to migrate to the United States after the exclusion laws were passed. It then offers a detailed demographic portrait of the immigrants themselves. The last section analyzes the broad range of strategies that Chinese used to pass through America's gates.

COMING TO AMERICA FOR A "BOWL OF RICE"

The Chinese who migrated to the United States during the exclusion era were just one part of the immense international migration of labor accompanying the global expansion of capitalism during the nineteenth century.[4] The European and American presence in China set in motion important preconditions for large-scale migration abroad. In other words, the Chinese went to America because Americans went to China.[5] It is no coincidence that the Chinese who immigrated to the United States during the late nineteenth and early twentieth centuries originated almost exclusively from the Pearl River Delta in Guangdong province, a center of American and European trade in China.[6] Domestic factors such as civil and ethnic unrest, rapid population growth, and natural disasters all took their toll on Chinese families, but as historian Yong Chen makes clear, they alone do not fully explain why Chinese emigrated from the delta to the United States and elsewhere; he argues that European and American imperialism brought instability not only to the region but also to the entire country in the form of increased taxes and unequal economic and political relations between China and its European and American trading partners. At the same time, China's trade with the United States and European countries fostered a diversified market economy that benefited the region—albeit unevenly—and allowed venturesome individuals to migrate abroad.

Migration was a tool to accumulate additional wealth and to maintain their families' prosperity or even to enhance their status in future generations.[7]

Equally important, new steamship routes between Hong Kong and San Francisco (established by the Pacific Mail Steamship Company in 1867) made possible large-scale migration from China to the United States—another legacy of American expansion across the Pacific.[8] In addition, contact with American missionaries and merchants introduced the idea of America to local Chinese, establishing an important precondition for emigration.[9] Wong Lan Fong, for example, immigrated to the United States in 1927, but her knowledge and exposure to American customs and institutions had begun at least twenty years earlier. Living in Canton, the heart of European and American economic trade in China, the Wong family had converted to Christianity, learned English, and entered an American mission home soon after Wong Lan Fong was born in 1908. They stayed there until she turned ten. Wong's father developed close ties with American missionaries by teaching Chinese language, history, and literature in the missionary schools and giving private lessons to American missionaries and Japanese merchants. Wong herself attended an American missionary school for Chinese girls. Having been in close contact with foreigners—Americans, specifically—every day for a number of years, Wong's decision to come to the United States as a merchant's wife when she was twenty years old was in part based on the family's positive experiences with Americans in China. She remembered the missionaries as "remarkable," generous individuals who took care of orphans and introduced "modern," Western ways, including education for girls. When her stepmother proposed that Wong marry a *Gam Saan haak* [*Jinshan ke*], a Gold Mountain man (*haak* in Cantonese or *ke* in *putonghua* means "guest," implying that a man who went to the Gold Mountain was only a guest there), in order to go to the United States, Wong's first thought was that "going to America meant having a good time."[10]

Even Chinese who had little firsthand contact with Americans in China possessed distinct understandings of America itself. Tales of fantastic wealth in the United States had first drifted back to China during the California gold rush. The "world rushed in" to California's gold fields following the discovery of gold in 1848, and Chinese were among the crowds of people, mostly men, eager to try their hand at mining.[11] Long after the rush ended, Chinese still found reasons to go to Gold Mountain, especially as economic and political conditions grew more desperate in China during the early twentieth century. Mr. Low, who was born in the United States, but who returned to China for schooling in the 1920s, observed that many Chinese could find little or no paying work in the farming areas or in the surrounding cities. "You gotta remember that all

Chinese wanted to come to this country for a bowl of rice. That's the main thing. And in order to get a bowl of rice, you gotta have a job. And what jobs are open? Back then in those days, there's a lot of people that work for free," he explained.[12] Emigration was a logical choice for another emigrant, Mr. Yuen: "In those days, it's almost impossible to find a job," he explained. "So coming to America is one of the better ways perhaps to have a better future."[13]

For some, the exclusion laws did act as a major deterrent. Fong Ing Bong, an applicant for admission into the United States in 1907, explained to immigration officials that he "understood it was impossible to get in before," so he did not even try.[14] Many others, however, considered emigration as the only means available to improve their economic and social standing in an increasingly unstable and tumultuous environment. Frequently, migration to the United States was regarded as nothing less than a necessity for survival. Lee Chi Yet, orphaned at a young age in Poon Lung Cheng village in Toisan [Taishan] District, was "kill[ing] himself for nothing" as a farmer in the early 1900s. People were starving to death around him, and the situation in his village was desperate. He immigrated to the United States in 1917. More than eighty years later, he explained his decision: "What the hell kind of life I have? I suffer! My eye just looking for a way to get out. I got to look for a way to go. I want to live, so I come to the United States."[15] Conditions were equally bad in Kung Yick village, also located in Toisan [Taishan] District, where Jeong Foo Louie lived. That village sent 40 percent of its inhabitants to the United States in the early twentieth century.[16] Like Lee Chi Yet's and Jeong Foo Louie's villages, other villages in Guangdong province, and especially in the Pearl River Delta, were filled with talk about going to the United States. Most of the young men in the countryside tried to leave by the time they were of working age; in some villages as many as 80 percent of the men were overseas, with the remaining village population—mostly women, old people, and children—relying on them for support.[17]

The idea that the United States was Gam Saan, Gold Mountain, remained firmly entrenched throughout the exclusion era. Although Chinese migrated throughout the world, many prospective migrants believed that their best future could be secured in America. The large numbers of Chinese who continued to come to the United States after 1882 is perhaps the strongest evidence of the positive (if unrealistic) perceptions that Chinese continued to have of life in America. Letters and visits home by Chinese in America and contemporary popular culture all reinforced the enduring vision of America as a land of opportunity. Early twentieth-century Cantonese folk songs praised the "sojourner [from] Gold Mountain" who had at least "eight hundred," if not "one thousand in gold," but chastised the "uncle from the South Seas" (Southeast Asia).

"Just look at your money bag," the lyrics went. "It's empty, it's empty."[18] Letters sent from prospective migrants in China to their relatives already in the United States echoed similar perceptions. In a 1916 letter to his elder brother in San Francisco, Lee Young Sing wished him success living in "the land of beauty and finding the fountain of wealth."[19] Wong Ngum Yin, another aspiring emigrant, outlined a similar vision of America in a poem that was ironically later confiscated by the immigration authorities. His verse clearly spells out the belief that migration to America could enable hardworking peasants to make their dreams come true. For Wong, those dreams consisted of a temporary sojourn abroad to secure financial stability for his family in China. He imagined that "after years of planning and trading (in America), property (in China) is regained, hundreds of *mou* of fields acquired and a mansion for the use of my maiden (wife) and myself is built. I clothe myself in the finest of fur garments and mount a fat horse. Upon bended knees I care for my parents and freely provide for my family. All these [are] my desires!"[20]

The existing immigration records do not reveal whether Wong Ngum Yin was able to achieve his goals, but many other Chinese found plentiful work opportunities in the United States. Industrialization and the expansion of American capitalism, especially in the American West, in the late nineteenth century created an incessant need for labor in building and maintaining railroads, growing and harvesting crops, manufacturing various goods, and mining. Chinese laborers filled many of the available jobs. Even after the 1882 Chinese Exclusion Act was passed, American employers remained more than willing to hire Chinese laborers despite the exclusion laws. In 1905, Harold Bolce, a U.S. Bureau of Immigration investigator, reported that there was a marked scarcity of labor throughout the western United States and that labor contractors were eager to hire Chinese workers whenever possible. One contractor who employed men to construct tunnels, aqueducts, piers, and railways explained that if they could, they would "put to work every Chinaman [they] could get."[21]

The employment patterns of Chinese began to change around the turn of the century. Anti-Chinese violence had pushed many out of the rural areas and into urban Chinatowns. By 1920, the Chinese were concentrated in only a few occupations that they dominated. In 1920, 48 percent of the Chinese in California—home to the largest number of Chinese in the United States—worked in small businesses, laundries, restaurants, or stores. Twenty-seven percent were domestic workers. Only 11 percent worked in agriculture and 9 percent in manufacturing and various skilled crafts.[22] Mr. Low, who grew up in New York City's Chinatown, recalled that before World War II, the vast majority of Chinese earned a living in only three types of work: "In those days, it's the laundry, the restaurant business, or a store helper. That's it."[23]

Despite the limited occupational opportunities in the United States, Chinese migrants continued to come for work. The wages earned in the United States as a lowly laundryman were still better than what most could earn in China. During a good week in the 1920s, a laundryman could earn up to fifty dollars a week. He could generally support his family in China on that income if he was frugal. When the Great Depression caused a dramatic decrease in income (to only twenty-five dollars a week), a laundryman could still fulfill his responsibility to support his family. In fact, sociologist Paul Siu found that in the 1920s and 1930s, an immigrant with some savings was able to buy a laundry for the relatively low investment of $2,800 to $3,000.[24] Such opportunities continued to lure Chinese immigrants to the United States. Although they did not find streets paved with gold, they did find jobs that provided sustenance for their families better than what they could find in China.

The same promise of economic security also motivated many Chinese women to migrate to the United States, usually as the wife or daughter of a returning resident or exempt-class immigrant. Wong Lan Fong's experience was not uncommon. A lack of steady work plagued her family following the 1911 Revolution in China, and by the 1910s, they were forced to move around Canton [Guangzhou] in search of work and to sell the family possessions. "I remember moving every couple of years," Wong Lan Fong reflected. "The house would become smaller and not so nice. We would have to sell things . . . my father always said that this was the last thing he would sell, because he hated it, but he always had to do it again." After Wong Lan Fong's mother fell ill and died, her father and new stepmother urged her to look for a Gam Saan haak, a Gold Mountain man, to marry so that she could go to the United States. It was the only way to secure her economic future, they explained. In 1926, she married Lee Chi Yet and came to the United States a year later.[25] Law Shee Low's parents made a similar decision. After bandits destroyed the family's farmland and property in the 1910s, life became difficult. "My parents decided to marry me off to a Gam Saan haak from the next village," she explained to an interviewer. "We were poor and there was no other way."[26]

IMMIGRANT CHARACTERISTICS

The Chinese who came, like other immigrant groups in America, were likely not the poorest members of society, but rather, those who had enough money to cover the expense of migration. By the 1920s, transpacific steamship passage could cost up to four hundred dollars, although most Chinese traveled "down in the bottom" in steerage, which cost significantly less.[27] Still, there were other costs associated with migration, notably the fees paid to immigration attorneys who were indispensable in filing the correct papers, finding witnesses, and arguing their cases before reluctant and unsympathetic immigration officials in the United States. Those who came as "paper sons" or "paper daughters" using fake immigration papers could expect to spend several hundred more dollars.[28]

Of the exclusion-era Chinese who managed to come, 80 to 90 percent were young, able-bodied men from the farming and laboring classes who could work and send money home, but taken as a whole, the Chinese who journeyed across the Pacific had diverse backgrounds. They included men and women, young and old, laborers and exempt-class migrants, citizens and aliens. For example, from 1880 to 1932, 8 percent of the Chinese immigrants admitted into the country were either under the age of sixteen or older than forty-four. The former, whose numbers grew significantly beginning in the 1910s and continued through the 1930s, were most likely children joining their parents who were already in the United States. There was also an increase in the number of Chinese older than forty-four years admitted (or, more likely, readmitted) into the United States beginning in the 1910s, but that number dropped significantly by 1930.[29] These older Chinese were probably either long-term residents who routinely crossed the Pacific to visit their families or to conduct business, or sojourners who had returned to China, where their accumulated savings dissipated. Such was the case of Yuen Tim Gong, who after working for eight years in the United States as a laundryman, returned "triumphantly" to China in 1928 with a new suit and a new pair of shoes. In his home village, he hosted a big banquet, bought a large tract of farmland, and built a grand four-story house. But life as a "Gold Mountain man" in his home village did not live up to his expectations, and his savings were quickly spent. The turbulent political and economic conditions in China convinced Yuen to move back to the United States in 1930. This time, he brought his wife with him, opened a supermarket, and remained in America for the rest of his life.[30]

Not only did Chinese immigrants of various ages come, those who were admitted also represented a range of class and citizenship categories. Sociologist Paul Siu found that the Chinese he interviewed in Chicago who came during the 1920s included village storekeepers, Hong Kong merchants, office clerks, politicians, teachers, students, seamen, and others, all of whom sought their fortunes in the United States.[31] U.S. government statistics also provide evidence of the immigrants' varied class backgrounds and point to changes in their demographic composition over time. As Table 1.1 illustrates, Chinese of the merchant class (including new and returning merchants as well as merchants' sons) constituted a third of the total number of Chinese men admitted from 1910 to 1924. U.S. citizens made up 42 percent of the admissions, while returning

Table 1.1. Number and Percentage of Chinese Male Immigrants Admitted by Class, 1910–1924

Year	New Merchant	Returning Merchant	U.S. Citizen	Returning Laborer	Merchant's Son	Total Males Admitted Including Other Classes
1910	228 (4%)	869 (16%)	2,060 (37%)	1,037 (19%)	882 (16%)	5,606
1911	199 (4%)	1,092 (23%)	1,570 (33%)	1,113 (23%)	404 (9%)	4,778
1912	170 (3%)	1,093 (22%)	1,689 (34%)	1,092 (22%)	412 (8%)	5,029
1913	105 (2%)	986 (19%)	2,076 (40%)	1,035 (20%)	555 (11%)	5,220
1914	180 (3%)	881 (16%)	2,126 (40%)	994 (19%)	647 (12%)	5,372
1915	238 (5%)	958 (18%)	1,935 (37%)	882 (17%)	624 (12%)	5,267
1916	242 (5%)	859 (18%)	1,871 (39%)	689 (14%)	605 (13%)	4,815
1917	180 (4%)	689 (16%)	1,906 (44%)	610 (14%)	560 (13%)	4,365
1918	128 (5%)	520 (19%)	868 (32%)	487 (18%)	274 (10%)	2,737
1919	136 (5%)	512 (17%)	905 (31%)	411 (14%)	190 (6%)	2,963
1920	102 (2%)	525 (13%)	1,693 (41%)	313 (8%)	443 (11%)	4,128
1921	284 (4%)	702 (10%)	3,120 (42%)	353 (5%)	986 (13%)	7,427
1922	642 (7%)	762 (9%)	3,823 (43%)	1,423 (16%)	1,012 (11%)	8,859
1923	495 (5%)	978 (11%)	4,452 (48%)	1,410 (15%)	1,002 (11%)	9,350
1924	452 (5%)	1,226 (13%)	4,521 (48%)	1,298 (14%)	745 (8%)	9,410
Total	3,781	12,652	34,615	13,147	9,341	85,326

Sources: U.S. Department of Commerce and Labor, Bureau of Immigration, Annual Report of the Commissioner-General of Immigration, 1910–1911 (Washington, D.C.: Government Printing Office, 1910–1911); U.S. Department of Commerce and Labor, Annual Reports of the Commissioner-General of Immigration, 1912–1924 (Washington, D.C.: Government Printing Office, 1912–1924).

laborers composed 17 percent during the same period. By the 1920s, the class composition of Chinese who successfully gained entry had changed dramatically as a result of the proliferation of illegal immigration using false papers, usually individuals claiming U.S. citizenship. During the 1920s, Chinese entering the United States as U.S. citizens were almost half of all admissions, and from 1930 to 1940, they accounted for 79 percent.[32]

Most Chinese probably wished either to visit temporarily or to sojourn only long enough to accumulate sufficient savings to enable them to return home in triumph rather than to settle permanently, as was the case with many European and Mexican immigrants in the late nineteenth and early twentieth centuries. Despite their intentions, many stayed in the United States much longer than they had originally planned, and some never made it back to China at all. Moreover, they did not have the wherewithal to visit China as often as they might have wished. My survey of over six hundred immigrant files, documenting Chinese immigrant arrivals from

1884 to 1941, indicates that only 4 percent were able to make two visits home to China, while another 9 percent made only one visit during their years in America.[33]

Many first-time arrivals joined family members already in the United States. Indeed, family reunification was a common motivation for emigration. Family members not only provided solace to homesick immigrants, they also facilitated the accumulation of more wealth in a shorter period. Some families sent all of their able-bodied sons to the United States. Arthur Lem, who entered the United States in the 1920s, explained that his uncle, who had been recruited to work as a laborer in the United States in the early 1900s, worked for many years in order to bring Lem's father to the country. "Still later, my father provided the money to bring my third uncle here. So—all three brothers were here in the United States in the 1920s." The Lems pooled their money and sent much of it to their families in China.[34] Kaimon Chin's family acted in a similar way. Once his father was able to establish himself as a merchant in New York City, "he sent for his brothers, and their families, and he provided a lot of money for the passage and for buying the papers and things like that."[35]

As Arthur Lem's and Kaimon Chin's families illustrate, Chinese immigration during the exclusion era was multigenerational. In many cases, the burden of working overseas was transferred from one generation to the next while the family maintained a permanent home in China.[36] Brett de Bary Nee and Victor Nee found that most of the men they interviewed in San Francisco's Chinatown in 1970 belonged to the second or third generation of men their families had sent to work in America. The first ancestors had come in the 1850s and 1860s to mine for gold and to build railroads. In time, the families in China became dependent on wages earned in America for survival. So, a new cycle of migration began. As one immigrant explained, "from one generation to another, everybody tries to send a man overseas. That's the only way you can make things better."[37]

The multigenerational pattern of male sojourning helps explain why Chinese male immigrants outnumbered Chinese females throughout the exclusion era. But patriarchal cultural values that discouraged and even forbade "decent" Chinese women from traveling abroad, anti-Chinese legislation, and the expense and trouble associated with migration also discouraged Chinese women from joining their husbands, brothers, and fathers in the United States. Immigration officials' enforcement of the exclusion laws added even more barriers to female immigration. Convinced that all Chinese women were either probable or potential prostitutes, they subjected female applicants to added scrutiny.[38] Thus, when the first Chinese Exclusion Act was passed in 1882, women accounted for only 0.3 percent of the total number of Chinese admitted into the United States;

in 1900, they made up only 0.7 percent of the total number of Chinese entering the country.[39] Over the course of the exclusion era, changes in both China and the United States affected Chinese female immigration. Changing attitudes about gender roles and an easing of cultural restrictions on Chinese female emigration made it easier for more women to leave China. In America, the immigration of Chinese women was made slightly more feasible through favorable court decisions that allowed the wives and children of Chinese merchants and U.S. citizens to apply for admission. An increase in educational and employment opportunities for women in the United States also made migration an attractive option for Chinese women.[40] In total, an estimated forty thousand Chinese women were admitted into the United States from 1882 to 1943. Although their numbers never equaled those of male immigrants, immigration statistics do indicate a trend toward gender parity over time.[41] In 1910, women were 9.7 percent of the total number of Chinese immigrants entering the country. Ten years later, they were 20 percent, and by 1930, the proportion of women immigrants had risen to 30 percent.[42]

Chinese women had varied reasons for coming to the United States. A small number came to study or teach. Some were U.S. citizens reentering the country after a visit abroad. Women who came as wives of merchants or U.S. citizens, however, made up the bulk of Chinese female immigrants, in large part because of the class and gendered dimensions of the exclusion laws. The exempt categories listed in the exclusion laws—merchants, students, teachers, diplomats, and travelers—were professional categories that applied almost exclusively to men in nineteenth- and early twentieth-century China. Most women were simply not eligible to enter independently. Instead, they depended on male relatives to sponsor and support their admission into the country.[43] As Table 1.2 indicates, from 1910 to 1924, 2,107 women (27 percent) entered as independent immigrants and 5,702 (73 percent) were admitted as dependents.

Entering as a dependent was disadvantageous. Because most Chinese women derived their right to enter the country from their male relatives' immigration status, their decisions to migrate were largely in the hands of their male relatives. Moreover, without male sponsorship, some women could not come to the United States at all. Moy Sau Bik, for example, was eligible to enter the United States as a merchant's daughter, but her father was not the person who sponsored her entry into the country because he had sold or given her immigration slot to her male cousin. He was able to do this because the papers he had filed with the immigration service listed a son, not a daughter. Acting on the prevailing patriarchal Chinese attitude that privileged sons over daughters, Moy's father apparently believed that his nephew was more worthy of immigration than his own daughter. Ineligible to enter as an independent immigrant, Moy Sau Bik was

TABLE 1.2. Chinese Women Admitted, by Class, 1910–1924

Year	Merchant Wife No. (%)	Merchant's Daughter No. (%)	Wife of U.S. Citizen No. (%)	New or Returning Merchant No.	Returning Laborer No. (%)	U.S. Citizen No. (%)	Student No. (%)	Teacher No.	Total Chinese Women Admitted Including Other Classes
1910	120 (35%)	27 (8%)	110 (32%)	0	0	49 (14%)	3	0	344
1911	136 (41%)	19 (6%)	80 (24%)	0	0	69 (21%)	5 (2%)	0	329
1912	118 (32%)	28 (8%)	88 (24%)	0	0	67 (18%)	9 (2%)	2	367
1913	155 (35%)	28 (6%)	126 (29%)	0	1	95 (21%)	19 (4%)	0	442
1914	133 (33%)	27 (7%)	122 (30%)	0	6 (2%)	75 (19%)	11 (3%)	0	401
1915	107 (27%)	15 (4%)	106 (27%)	2	7 (2%)	55 (14%)	29 (7%)	0	394
1916	108 (29%)	28 (7%)	108 (29%)	0	1	61 (16%)	16 (4%)	0	378
1917	111 (27%)	23 (6%)	110 (27%)	2	8 (2%)	102 (25%)	2	0	409
1918	88 (20%)	28 (7%)	132 (31%)	1	4	78 (18%)	28 (7%)	3	429
1919	91 (24%)	24 (6%)	91 (24%)	2	7 (2%)	50 (13%)	33 (9%)	0	377
1920	166 (30%)	35 (6%)	141 (25%)	3	7 (1%)	68 (12%)	47 (8%)	5	562
1921	271 (30%)	59 (7%)	290 (32%)	3	15 (2%)	119 (13%)	59 (7%)	4	896
1922	301 (26%)	47 (4%)	396 (34%)	9	44 (4%)	221 (19%)	75 (6%)	3	1,166
1923	319 (26%)	56 (5%)	387 (32%)	4	43 (1%)	238 (20%)	52 (4%)	4	1,208
1924	273 (21%)	78 (6%)	396 (31%)	3	42 (3%)	233 (18%)	81 (6%)	8	1,284
TOTAL	2,756 (28%)	522 (6%)	2,848 (30%)	29	185 (2%)	1,580 (18%)	469 (5%)	29	9,565

Sources: U.S. Department of Commerce and Labor, Bureau of Immigration, *Annual Report of the Commissioner-General of Immigration* (Washington, D.C.: Government Printing Office, 1910–1911); U.S. Department of Commerce and Labor, *Annual Reports of the Commissioner-General of Immigration* (Washington, D.C.: Government Printing Office, 1912–1924).

effectively excluded from the country until she married a merchant and gained entry as his wife in 1931.[44] It is difficult to determine how many other families also chose male relatives over female ones; what is clear is that there were far more opportunities for males than for females to come to the United States.

Class biases in the laws structured Chinese immigration patterns as well. From 1910 to 1924, wives and daughters of merchants formed the largest group (34 percent) of Chinese female applicants. Wives of U.S. citizens were a close second, making up 30 percent of the total female applicants, and female U.S. citizens represented 18 percent. Female students made up only 5 percent. The rest of the women applied for admission as new or returning merchants (often taking over the businesses of deceased husbands), returning laborers, teachers, or miscellaneous other categories, as shown in Table 1.2.

By the second decade of the twentieth century, Chinese women not only immigrated in larger numbers, they also enjoyed a slightly higher admission rate than did their male counterparts. From 1910 to 1924, an average of 98 percent of all merchants' wives applying for admission were allowed into the country. Ninety-seven percent of all female U.S. citizens or wives of citizens were admitted, while 96 percent of all women applying as merchants' daughters were admitted. In contrast, 94 percent of new merchant applicants, 94 percent of male U.S. citizens, and 82 percent of merchants' sons succeeded in entering the United States during the same period.[45]

The increase in female migration during the second half of the exclusion era reflects a significant change in Chinese immigration patterns away from sojourning and toward settlement in America. This occurred despite the exclusion laws. The impact of exclusion in shaping immigration patterns and admission processes did not wane, however. Rather, Chinese succeeded because they grew increasingly adept at challenging the laws meant to exclude them.

IMMIGRATION STRATEGIES

The Chinese exclusion laws were not insurmountable barriers. Immigrants who successfully defied them did so by fashioning strategies to combat the increasingly rigid laws and system of enforcement. Some battled fiercely against the laws and the ways they were enforced, charging the U.S. government with racial discrimination and injustice. Others adeptly navigated their way through the bureaucratic maze through legal as well as illegal means.

During the first decades of the exclusion era in the late nineteenth century, Chinese first used the American judicial system to challenge the legality of the laws and to find ways to be admitted *within* the confines of exclusion. They also protested the exclusion policies individually and through community organizations. They hired lawyers and used the courts to affirm the rights of merchant families, returning laborers, and American citizens of Chinese descent and their families to enter or reenter the country. The Chinese consulate and the Chinese Six Companies sponsored many of the early court cases.[46] Chinese were extremely successful at using the federal courts to overturn denials by the immigration service.[47] At the same time, they also used the courts to challenge the policy of exclusion itself, including a failed Supreme Court challenge to the 1892 Geary Act, which extended the ban on immigration for ten years and insisted on the registration of all Chinese.[48]

Outside of the courts, Chinese protested American exclusion policies through a variety of forums. Individually, both Chinese diplomats and working-class immigrants became persistent and vocal critics of the discriminatory treatment Chinese immigrants received.[49] In 1892, Yung Hen, a poultry dealer in San Francisco, asked a newspaper reporter, "Why do they not legislate against Swedes, Germans, Italians, Turks and others? There are no strings on those people. . . . For some reason, you people persist in pestering the Chinamen."[50] In 1899, a Chinese woman told government investigator Oscar Greenhalgh that the Chinese "had as much right to land in America as the Irish, who [are] always drunk and fighting."[51] Even thirty years later, anger and a sense of injustice remained deeply ingrained among the Chinese in America. As Woo Gen, a Chinese merchant in Seattle, excitedly explained to interviewers in 1924, "We have *exclusion* law on Chinese. All other countries have what are called *immigration* laws."[52]

Chinese leaders sent petitions, memorials, and letters to Presidents William Howard Taft, Theodore Roosevelt, and Woodrow Wilson, arguing that the exclusion laws and their enforcement were unjust.[53] In 1900, Wu Ting-fang, the Chinese minister to the United States, complained to the American secretary of state that Chinese were "entirely at the mercy of inquisitors, who . . . are generally unfriendly, if not positively hostile, to them."[54] Chinese American organizations also fielded complaints about immigration officials and the draconian measures they used to enforce exclusion.[55]

In 1905, the U.S. Supreme Court barred the federal courts from hearing Chinese admission cases, a decision that left the regulation of Chinese immigration solely in the hands of immigration officials.[56] Following the ruling, Chinese anger and frustration over the exclusion policy and continued racial discrimination reached a climax. Combining their anger over racial injustice in the United States with growing Chinese nationalism, merchants in China staged a boycott of American goods in May of 1905.

In a demonstration and expression of a newfound transpacific Chinese nationalism, teachers, students, professionals, laborers, and women joined the merchants and the Chinese in the United States to protest the discriminatory immigration policies.[57] While the boycott did bring about some important changes in the United States' enforcement practices, the policy of Chinese exclusion itself remained unchanged and became firmly entrenched in American immigration law by 1906. There is no better symbol of its institutionalization than the new immigration station on Angel Island in San Francisco Bay, which processed its first immigrants in 1910 and quickly became characterized as a "prison" by those detained there.[58] Indeed, admission through the island station proved to be much more difficult than it had been in the past when aspiring Chinese immigrants were usually kept in a shed owned by the Pacific Mail Steamship Company located on one of San Francisco's docks. After the Angel Island station had been in operation for only a year, the number of rejected Chinese increased dramatically. The Pacific Mail Steamship Company's detention shed had been located near Chinatown, and earlier immigrants could easily rely on kinsmen, friends, and lawyers to facilitate their entry into the United States. On Angel Island, however, Chinese were kept under close surveillance, and a lack of regular ferry service from the city made it much harder to receive assistance from outsiders. According to the annual report of the commissioner-general of immigration, the ratio of rejections to admissions was approximately 73 percent higher in 1910 than in 1909, 92 percent higher than in 1908, 89 percent higher than in 1907, and 100 percent higher than in 1906.[59]

Chinese diplomats, Chinese-language newspapers, and Chinese and Chinese American organizations continued to be vocal critics of the U.S. immigration service and its enforcement procedures throughout the exclusion era. But by the early 1900s, it also became increasingly clear that legal, political, and economic attempts to repeal the laws were unlikely to succeed.[60] Given these failures, Chinese turned to a strategy that relied on negotiating their way *through* exclusion, instead of attempting to dismantle the laws altogether. They first educated themselves about the details, loopholes, and enforcement procedures of the laws. Chinese and their friends turned to federal immigration officials for information about admission and readmission standards and regulations. Hundreds of letters written by Chinese residents, their attorneys, ministers, neighbors, politicians, and friends poured in not only from San Francisco, Los Angeles, New York, and Boston, but also from Springfield, Massachusetts; Rochester, New York; Jersey City, New Jersey; New Brunswick, New Jersey; Baltimore, Maryland; Norfolk, Virginia; Augusta, Georgia; Peoria, Illinois; Memphis, Tennessee; Fairmont, Nebraska; Boise City, Idaho; Denver, Colorado; and East Las Vegas, New Mexico.[61]

Networks of family and kin proved to be essential in financing and facilitating the journey to the United States and helping an immigrant navigate his or her passage through the bureaucratic procedures. Families with aspiring emigrants commonly pooled their savings to pay for the latter's steamer tickets, attorneys' fees, and possibly false immigration papers. As Arthur Lem explained, "everyone was very willing to help another family member to come to the Gold Mountain."[62] The actual journey to the United States was also a family affair. In my survey of over six hundred files of immigrants applying for admission into the United States through the port of San Francisco (1884–1941), 25 percent claimed that they were traveling with a family member and 78 percent claimed that they had family members already in the United States.[63] Of the 25 percent of immigrants who were accompanied by a family member, slightly more than a third of them came with a sibling, 31 percent with a child, 21 percent with a parent, and 16 percent with a spouse.

The benefits of relying on family members throughout the immigration process were enormous. Prospective immigrants depended on a steady stream of information and advice from their relatives and clansmen already in America to assist them with the necessary paperwork, government interrogations, and strategies on how to withstand the scrutiny of immigration officials. While Wong Quong Ken was preparing to sail to San Francisco in 1917, for example, his clansman, Wong Gong Kim, sent news of his impending arrival to the latter's two brothers who were already settled in that city. "If he should write you for assistance," instructed Wong Gong Kim, "be sure to go to the immigration office and give him whatever assistance needed. If you have to spend a little money for him, it will be all right; he will give it back to you when he is landed."[64] Likewise, Lee Young Sing in Hong Kong wrote to his brother in San Francisco asking him to look after a fellow clansman about to arrive in San Francisco and to give advice to their young nephew who would also be sailing soon and who "knew very little about things in the world."[65]

Once in the United States, immigrants routinely relied on family members upon arrival and throughout the government's investigation and detention process. They could count on their relatives and fellow clan members to greet them when their steamers finally docked in San Francisco. In December of 1899, Wong Hong and Chew Dong Ngin were among a welcoming crowd waiting at the pier. They had made a special trip to the Pacific Mail Steamship Company's dock to welcome young Fong Tim, the son of one of their Chinatown friends and probably a fellow villager from Ting Ching village in Ying Ping [Enping?] District. Fong Tim, recognizing the two faces in the crowd, nodded his head and waved.[66] The family friends would later spend much time in the interrogation room filing affidavits and answering questions asked by the immigration officials about

Fong Tim's family and his trip from China. They were expected to know every minute detail about the Fong family and were carefully scrutinized. "What kind of feet has Fong Tim's mother?" (This question was meant to distinguish whether a Chinese woman had bound or natural unbound feet.) "Where were the children born?" "When were they born?" "Did the boy's mother ever have brothers or sisters?" If the witnesses could not give exact answers, the immigration officials immediately jumped on them. "Why should you remember the day of one [boy's birth] and not the other?" demanded the official when Wong Hong could only give the approximate date of birth of Fong Tim's brother. "Would you not know of uncles or aunts if the boy had them?" the official continued. Fortunately for Fong Tim and his father's friends, these small gaps in the testimony were considered minor, and Fong Tim was landed.[67] Immigrants detained by the U.S. government also relied on family and friends as their link to the outside world. In 1906, Wong Ngum Yin's uncles and cousins in San Francisco hired an attorney, gained his release from the detention shed, and provided clothes to protect him from the cold. "I will surely repay you [and not] bring shame unto our Tribe," he promised.[68]

That the Chinese willingly traveled great distances, invested many hours, and even put themselves at risk of investigation to help relatives, friends, and clansmen is evidence of the importance of family and kin networks in the immigration process. As sociologist Paul Siu bluntly explained, "all laundrymen have relatives in China, but only those who have money and have good connections are able to have them come."[69] Wen-hsien Chen, another sociologist, agreed: new arrivals without relatives or friends in America were at an inherent disadvantage. If denied entry, these immigrants "seldom made an effort to force entry." However, those who had relatives and friends in the United States possessed the financial and moral support to fight the decision and "make every effort to secure entry."[70]

Strong connections and supportive family members were just two tools Chinese immigrants and returning residents used to facilitate immigration during the exclusion era. Other strategies involved an adept negotiation around government policies and procedures that favored certain classes and categories of Chinese immigrants over others. For example, because the exclusion laws exempted merchants, Chinese applying for admission under this category learned to emphasize their class status whenever they dealt with immigration officials. They hoped that they would not have to endure as much scrutiny and would pass easily through America's gates. In 1899, merchant Lee Fook hired an immigration attorney who repeatedly referred to his client as a "capitalist" and a "gentlemen of means, of elegant leisure."[71] Likewise, knowing that immigration officials generally treated first-class passengers better than those in steerage, merchant Lee

Chi Yet went so far as to save his wages as a laundry worker for an extra year to bring his wife, Wong Lan Fong, over in first class. When she arrived in Angel Island in 1927, she was processed and admitted within a day.[72]

Chinese women, whom immigration officials routinely suspected of being prostitutes, adopted similar strategies and offered evidence of their "proper character" or class status. One of the first women to apply for admission through the port of San Francisco after the 1882 Chinese Exclusion Act was passed was Leong Cum, a U.S. citizen born in Lewiston, Idaho. Applying for readmission in May of 1884, Leong found it necessary to distinguish herself from less desirable female applicants. A garment maker by profession, she presented three affidavits to immigration officials. Each emphasized that she was "a woman of excellent reputation and irreproachable character." One of the affidavits was from Jerome Millian, a Chinese interpreter who likely worked for the immigration service. Both the affidavits and Millian's endorsement worked in Leong's favor. She was landed two days after she arrived.[73]

Because immigration officials expected merchant families to possess fine clothing, a respectable manner, and especially, in the case of women, bound feet—a marker of wealth and status in traditional China—women applying as merchants' wives learned to highlight those traits. In 1901, Gee See, a merchant's wife residing in Los Angeles, submitted an application for readmission upon her return from a trip to China complete with a full-length photograph and an X-ray of her feet. Her affidavit explained that she was "a small footed woman or bound-footed woman." The photograph showed Gee See sitting down and holding a small child. Her small feet were clearly displayed. The X-ray was described as showing "conclusively that the feet of this woman are what is known as 'small' or 'bound,' the position of the bones and their abnormally small size distinctly appearing."[74]

In addition to emphasizing clear markers of class status and morality to suspicious immigration officials, Chinese immigrants and returning residents also relied on sympathetic neighbors, friends, politicians, employers, attorneys, and Christian ministers from across the country to file affidavits, write letters, and even travel to the immigration office to testify on their behalf.[75] As the Bureau of Immigration valued (and at times required) testimony from whites over Chinese to substantiate claims of entry and reentry into the United States, this assistance and support was very valuable. In 1889, A. S. Schell, a longtime resident of Knights Ferry, California, asked a lawyer to assist his two neighbors—American-born citizens Jin Young and Charley Foo—in their attempt to reenter the United States. Schell's letter was full of compliments. He tried his best to sway the immigration service in favor of his friends: "I trust that with your assistance, backed up with this and perhaps other testimonials, he [sic]

will have no difficulty in landing. Both are excellent and good men."
Schell also circulated a petition to a dozen other non-Chinese residents
of Knights Ferry who signed it, corroborating his own judgment that the
two Chinese residents were men of good character who should be admitted promptly. Soon thereafter, Jin Young and Charley Foo were landed.[76]
Likewise, in 1890, McConnell Jenkins of Logansport, Indiana, wrote on
behalf of a longtime Chinese neighbor who desired to go to China to visit
his mother and then return to the United States. "He is a laundryman,
a good citizen, industrious, temperate, and highly esteemed by all who
have business relations with him," McConnell wrote.[77] Wong Let, a merchant in Riverside, California, astutely recognized that credible witnesses
from the middle and upper classes increased his chances of reentering the
country. Thus, he secured affidavits from a number of merchants, lawyers,
and even the city's marshal, postmaster, and ex-postmaster, confirming his
long-term residence in the city and the status of his business. J. S. Noyes, a
superior judge for the state, also filed an affidavit supporting the character
of both Wong and the witnesses for the case.[78]

In addition, Chinese turned to Christian organizations like the Young
Men's Christian Association (YMCA) and the Presbyterian Mission Home
in San Francisco to substantiate their claims. Both were active in the
Chinese American community and were well respected by the immigration
service. In 1915, the YMCA even had a full-time immigration secretary
in San Francisco. Both organizations frequently intervened on behalf of
Chinese immigrants and returning residents. In 1915, for example, Lee
Sue Ben, a returning student and former teacher at the YMCA in Canton
[Guangzhou], sought the organization's assistance while he was detained
on Angel Island. Frank B. Lenz, the YMCA's immigration secretary, wrote
a letter to the immigration inspector in charge and pointed to Lee's right to
enter the United States. He also urged a "speedy settlement of the case."[79]
Likewise, Lee Sue Ben himself wrote to influential Chinese newspaperman
Ng Poon Chew, editor of *Chung Sai Yat Po*, to ask for his assistance,
and to Samuel Backus, commissioner of immigration in San Francisco, to
"find out what the trouble is" regarding his own landing. Ng Poon Chew
urged that Lee be admitted as promptly as possible. After several days of
detention, Lee was landed the day after Commissioner Backus received
the letters.[80]

Donaldina Cameron, director of the Presbyterian Mission Home, a
"rescue" home for Chinese prostitutes, was another particularly important ally of Chinese immigrants attempting to enter the United States.[81]
Historian Judy Yung notes that "it was generally known that a supporting
letter from Donaldina Cameron...often helped get cases landed."[82] In
1916, Cameron came to the assistance of Lee Kan, a Chinese merchant
whose wife and two sons were being detained on Angel Island. In her letter

to the commissioner of immigration, Cameron stated that she had known Lee Kan for some years and that he was indeed a bona fide merchant. At Lee's request, Cameron even traveled to Angel Island to meet the family. In her letter, she asked that parole be granted for the wife and youngest child if the entire family could not be landed immediately. She also made an investigation herself into Lee's status and reported to the immigration service, "I have made special inquiry and investigation to further assure myself that Mr. Lee Kan's interests centered in the store...I have been assured from reliable sources that he has been at all times engaged in the mercantile business.... In view of these and other facts, I trust that in due course of time it will be deemed advisable to land the family of Mr. Lee Kan."[83] With Cameron's help, Lee Kan's entire family was finally landed. Such assistance from non-Chinese acquaintances, friends, and allies was essential in enabling Chinese to continue immigrating to the United States while the exclusion laws were in effect.

By far, Chinese immigrants' most valuable resource during the exclusion era was an organized network of immigration lawyers. Chinese had a long history of hiring the best American lawyers to challenge anti-Chinese legislation even before 1882. During the early years of the exclusion era, these lawyers helped spearhead the constitutional challenges to the exclusion policy itself. They also represented Chinese immigrants who sought entry through the judicial courts.[84] Legal representation in Chinese immigration cases continued into the exclusion era, especially as Chinese appealed to the courts to overturn immigration officials' decisions to deny them entry. Collector John Wise noted in 1895 that "the interests of the Chinese are looked out by a Chinese Consul and also by shrewd lawyers."[85] In 1899, the Treasury Department found that as a rule, the "very best attorneys in the city" represented the Chinese.[86] Although one might suspect that only those Chinese with the most financial resources could afford to hire lawyers, Chinese from all class backgrounds found it expedient to do so. By the early twentieth century, when immigration cases were heard solely by the administrative officers of the immigration service, lawyers were still instrumental in keeping track of the necessary paperwork, lobbying on behalf of clients, and facilitating entry and reentry in ways that would have been extremely difficult for Chinese to accomplish on their own. The number of immigration lawyers hired by the Chinese grew in direct relationship to the increasing severity and complexity of the exclusion laws and their enforcement. By the 1930s, sociologist Wen-Hsien Chen observed that "without exception," all cases of Chinese aliens arriving at the port for the first time with an application for permanent residence were looked after by lawyers, and that even returning Chinese residents secured the services of an attorney "as a safeguard" because of the precarious nature of the immigration investigation.[87] My survey of over six hundred Chinese who entered the United States from 1884 to 1941 revealed that 90 percent had hired immigration attorneys to process papers and to represent them before the immigration service.[88]

Immigration attorneys were not allowed to participate or be present in the initial hearings and interrogations conducted by the immigration service, but if a Chinese applicant was denied entry, he or she could then hire an attorney to examine the file in order to rebut the decision. Attorneys lacked access to the entire file, but, despite this handicap, they continued to be invaluable assets to new and returning immigrants.[89] They effectively and consistently pointed out flaws in the judgments and conclusions of immigration officials, oftentimes successfully forcing a reversal in their decisions. They also marshaled outside experts, previous rulings and court decisions, witnesses, and evidence to challenge the government's findings.[90] As Commissioner of Immigration John D. Nagle commented in 1927, attorneys remained "indispensable" allies to the Chinese.[91]

Most of the lawyers who represented Chinese clients in the first decades of exclusion were prominent attorneys in San Francisco who worked not only on behalf of individual Chinese clients, but also on behalf of the Chinese Six Companies and the Chinese Consulate. Thomas Riordan, for example, was the principal attorney representing the Chinese in the 1880s and 1890s and was retained by the Chinese Consulate to represent all high-profile cases. His successor, Oliver P. Stidger, also became a vocal critic of the exclusion laws and built a formidable practice based on the Chinese immigration business.[92] In 1915, Stidger was listed as the official attorney for the Chinese Chamber of Commerce as well, and the firm of Stidger, Stidger, and Kennah—made up of Oliver Stidger, his son, Jason, and former immigrant inspector Henry C. Kennah—became one of the leading law firms representing Chinese immigrants.[93] Other individuals representing the Chinese before the Bureau of Immigration acted more like brokers who arranged for witnesses to testify before the immigration service, filed witness affidavits, and secured more experienced counsel if necessary. Some had deep-rooted connections with the Chinese community; a few had even been former members of the Bureau of Immigration and found that their inside knowledge of the agency translated into well-paid work outside the service. That the business of immigration lawyers was a lucrative one cannot be doubted. In 1885, Treasury Department officials estimated that the attorney's fee for habeas corpus cases was no less than one hundred dollars per case.[94] Moreover, as long as the exclusion laws remained in effect, the demand for skillful lawyers remained high, and attorneys proved their worth in a variety of ways. Immigrants like Chin Sing, a U.S.-born Chinese returning from China to the United States, could count on his attorneys to file the necessary documents and arrange for witnesses to travel to Angel Island even while he was detained and largely powerless to lobby on his own behalf. When Chin Sing returned to the United States after a two-year absence in 1911, immigration officials denied him admission on the suspicion that he was not the real Chin Sing, but an impostor. Although Chin could speak English and demonstrated a "good knowledge" of his hometown of Dutch Flat, California, he had neither the necessary certificate of identity that proved his status as a "returning native" (it had been burnt in a fire) nor any witnesses (preferably white) who could identify him and confirm his birth in the United States. Chin hired attorneys George McGowan and Alfred Worley to appeal the decision and launch a search in Dutch Flat for any old acquaintances who could come and testify on his behalf. After a two-month search, the lawyers located two witnesses and brought them to Angel Island, where they and Chin immediately recognized each other. Chin was finally landed in July 1911, five months after he arrived back in the United States.[95]

CONCLUSION

The strategies adopted by Chinese immigrants and returning residents and citizens to adapt to and negotiate their way through the exclusion laws proved to be highly successful. Indeed, most Chinese men and women were admitted into the country. From 1910 to 1924, the average admission rate counting both men and women, under the exclusion laws was 93 percent,[96] though non-Chinese immigrants subjected to the general immigration laws did have a higher admission rate of 97 percent.[97] Nevertheless, considering the immense barriers that the Chinese exclusion laws posed to new immigrants, returning residents, and citizens alike, the fact that over 300,000 Chinese successfully defied exclusion is testament to their persistence and motivation. In their opinion, the exclusion laws were unjust and discriminatory. Relying on family, clansmen, white allies, and lawyers to help them navigate their way through the maze of bureaucratic procedures and policies, they mobilized all of the resources at their disposal to challenge the laws in the nation's highest courts and in countless U.S. immigration service interrogation rooms across the country. Insisting that they had the right to immigrate to the United States, they played a crucial role in ensuring that Chinese communities would not disappear on America soil.

2   Trading with Gold Mountain: *Jinshanzhuang* and Networks of Kinship and Native Place

MADELINE HSU

ON NOVEMBER 21, 1853, the *Daily Alta California* described a wide array of Chinese goods available in San Francisco's Chinatown. "The majority of the houses were of Chinese importation, and were stores, stocked with hams, tea, dried fish, dried ducks and other . . . Chinese eatables, besides copper pots and kettles, fans, shawls, chessmen, and all sorts of curiosities." The presence of such a wide variety of Chinese goods in the young state of California was due in no small part to a handful of businessmen who had fled the economic depression of 1847 in Guangzhou (often Anglicized as Canton) to start anew in California the following year. They established the first outposts of a Chinese network of trade that by 1930 would provide overseas Chinese with groceries, newspapers and magazines, clothing, and tools, as well as postal and banking services in urban centers throughout North America, including Honolulu, San Francisco, Los Angeles, San Diego, Portland, Seattle, Hobart, Chicago, Minneapolis, Boston, New York City, Newark, Philadelphia, Baltimore, Washington, D.C., and Houston in the United States, and Vancouver, Victoria, Calgary, Winnipeg, Toronto, and Montreal in Canada. Hong Kong–based import-export firms called *jinshanzhuang* (Gam Saan Chung in Cantonese, meaning Gold Mountain firms) formed the backbone of this extensive trade network.

Jinshanzhuang began as Chinese grocery exporters but grew in response to the desire of customers overseas to maintain contact with their families and native places. The businesses expanded their range of services to include postal, remittance, and banking activities in an age when government-run institutions did not yet provide connections across vast distances. Cantonese businessmen employed networks of native place and mutual trust to develop secure and reliable communications channels that bridged the Pacific Ocean long before the era of telephones, jet airplanes, or the Internet. An examination of the functioning and development of jinshanzhuang reveals the flexible nature of the social and cultural resources that Chinese brought to their encounters with Western cultures, the changes in their values and identities as they adapted to a capitalist world economy, and the role of village and family networks in directing or at least mediating such changes.

The expanding reach and multiplying services offered by jinshan-zhuang reflected China's intensifying integration into the global economy. Hong Kong was essential in this process: it was the central channel through which people and goods flowed to and from China and the many overseas localities to which Chinese had migrated. Fueled by an expanding volume of migration and the needs of Chinese overseas, the malaria-ridden fishing village of Hong Kong grew into a flourishing city and port by the end of the nineteenth century. Its present-day wealth and reputation as a cosmopolitan gateway to China are rooted in no small part in the ties to home felt and nurtured by generations of Chinese migrants. Even though jinshanzhuang flourished decades before Congress passed the first Chinese Exclusion Act in 1882, they remained in business throughout the exclusion era. Thus, they were a crucial aspect of Chinese American life during those difficult years. Without them, Chinese immigrants might have had an even harder time gaining entry into the United States and, after arrival, maintaining contacts with families left behind.

Although their presence in the United States was reliably recorded as early as the 1770s, Chinese did not start coming in significant numbers until the gold rush. The San Francisco customs house recorded the arrival of 325 in 1849, 450 in 1850, 2,716 in 1851, and a dramatic leap to 20,026 in 1852.[1] A confluence of economic stagnation and crop failures in Guangdong Province and the well-advertised prospect of fast fortunes to be had in California led to this tremendous increase in the number of Chinese coming to America. Even after the surface gold quickly ran out, leaving deposits that could be extracted only by such capital-intensive methods as hydraulic and deep-shaft mining, other forms of lucre continued to draw Chinese to the land of opportunity to farm, fish, and engage in all kinds of labor to build the western regions of North America. By 1890, the Chinese population in the United States had reached a peak of almost 110,000.

Overseas migration in the thousands was not accomplished by crossing the Pacific in fishing boats, wooden junks, or even clipper ships. Migration in such numbers demanded a level of technological development and the existence of global networks of trade more sophisticated and reliable than had existed in China before the nineteenth century. Such facilities rapidly developed in Hong Kong after it came under British rule at the end of the First Opium War. People in southeastern China had only to go to this nearby port to find shipping companies, labor recruiters, friends, or businessmen who could tell them about opportunities abroad, and enabled them to buy tickets on credit to get to North America and elsewhere.

Hong Kong supplied other links in the chain between the Chinese in China and those in America by providing a secure and reliable channel for the back-and-forth flow of people, remittances, information, capital, political ideas, Chinese groceries, and technology. As working abroad became an increasingly common economic option chosen by southern Chinese, the evolution of Hong Kong into an efficient and bustling entrepôt was essential in enabling them to stay in touch with people, places, events, and an entire way of life left behind in China.

The shipping industry was the first commercial service to develop.[2] In 1843, newly constructed piers witnessed the launching of the first of many ships. By 1857, dry docks designed to repair Western ships had appeared in Aberdeen, an area in Hong Kong where fishing boats docked.[3] These facilities drew business into Hong Kong. "Large numbers of emigrant ships were fitted, repaired, and provisioned in Hong Kong, stimulating the colony's general economy. Large ship-building companies were established one after another."[4] By 1864, Hong Kong had supplanted Guangzhou and Shantou as southern China's major import center. Chinese merchants purchasing foreign goods in Hong Kong frequently traveled directly back to their home districts without passing through Guangzhou.[5] By 1880, Hong Kong handled 21 percent of China's total export trade and 37 percent of its imports. It was also the center of the opium trade, which constituted about 45 percent of the total value of China's imports.[6]

Hong Kong evolved into a major trading center by developing close commercial relations with the neighboring trading centers of Xiamen, Shantou, Macao, Guangzhou, the Pearl River Delta, and the West River valley, from which came the coastal vessels, river boats, and junks carrying cargoes of passengers and provisions. A number of companies, such as the China Hong Nim Life Insurance Co., Ltd. [Zhongguo Kangnien renshou yanshu youxian gongsi] or the Wu Chow Receiving Agency, Ltd. [Wuzhou huidiao youxian gongsi], provided the myriad services needed in China's coastal and international shipping, including medical facilities, marine and property insurance, money exchange, and barristers' legal advice and assistance. Large international banking institutions were set up one after another. In addition, native Chinese banks financed the trade between China and Chinese communities overseas.[7]

With the introduction of regular shipping lines, in particular steamer services, and commercial institutions designed to support emigration, Hong Kong became the main point of departure for migration overseas. By the 1860s, passengers who passed through Hong Kong could travel from the coastal cities of Shantou, Xiamen, and Guangzhou by steamer to the islands of Singapore and Penang (two of the Straits Settlements under British colonial rule at that time). By 1873, steamers sailed regularly between Hong Kong and Bangkok, Thailand. In the 1870s also, regular traffic flowed from China to the Philippines, which was under Spanish colonial rule at the time; the Malay Peninsula and its offshore islands; the islands of Java and Sumatra, then under Dutch colonial rule; and British-colonized Burma and back.[8] Although regular passenger lines directly linked Xiamen to Manila and Singapore, as well as Shantou to Singapore, by 1870 Hong Kong had become the embarkation point of choice for most Chinese. Between 1855 and 1900, 1,830,572 Chinese emigrants embarked at the port of Hong Kong. In addition, Hong Kong became the major port serving Chinese returning from abroad.[9]

In 1860, the average cost of passage from Hong Kong to San Francisco was fifty dollars. By 1860, 73,890 Chinese had entered the United States through the San Francisco Customs House.[10] Between 1860 and 1874, 112,362 Chinese left Hong Kong bound for the United States paying some $5,618,100 in fare.[11] This was big business. Monthly transpacific steamship services began when the Pacific Mail Steamship Company launched the *Colorado* from Hong Kong to San Francisco on January 1, 1867. Demand was so high that the transpacific schedule doubled to twice a month in 1872.[12] Shipping companies and labor brokers contributed their share to the numbers of Chinese going overseas by spreading word of the various economic opportunities available abroad. In the early 1850s, notices appeared in Hong Kong newspapers reporting gold on the streets, and in 1867, similar commercials announced the availability of jobs in agriculture and on the railroads.[13] Between 1883 and 1893 alone, 991,568 Chinese departed Hong Kong bound mainly for North America, Australia, and various places in Southeast Asia.[14]

Migration was good business for Hong Kong. In particular, it benefited the British, American, and French shipping firms that took Chinese overseas and brought them home. E. J. Eitel noted that "for San Francisco alone as many as 30,000 Chinese embarked in Hong Kong in the year 1852, paying in Hong Kong, in passage money alone, a sum of $1,500,000." According to Charles Denby, a diplomat who served as the U.S. minister to China from 1885 to 1898, shipping companies made a 1,000 percent profit on passage to the United States. "To bring a Chinaman from Macao or Hong-Kong would cost less than five dollars, but the steamship companies would charge, as they used to, fifty-five dollars. There would be a clear profit of fifty dollars per head."[15] Between 1860 and 1874, 112,362 emigrants bound for the United States embarked in Hong Kong, spending some $5,618,100 in passage money, a sum that did not include the high rates of interest attached to tickets bought on credit.[16]

The Chinese who traveled overseas benefited shipping firms in more ways than simply buying tickets. Their demand for food and things

Chinese led to a thriving export trade in foodstuffs and sundries bound for Chinese communities throughout Southeast Asia and the Americas, as described by Jung-fang Tsai:

> The Chinese communities abroad clung to the Chinese way of life, and Hong Kong became the center of an international trade catering to their needs. The arrival of large numbers of Chinese immigrants to the United States in the latter half of the nineteenth century created a demand for rice, tea, foodstuffs, drugs, and sundries from China. Hong Kong developed a flourishing trade with the United States, where a Chinese merchant class prospered by selling Chinese imports.[17]

Import-export firms, known variously as *nanbeihang* (Nam Pak Hong in the Cantonese dialect, meaning north-south firms) or jinshanzhuang had sprung up to serve the needs of overseas Chinese by the 1850s.[18] Whereas shipping companies and labor recruiters channeled the flow of bodies overseas, jinshanzhuang and nanbeihang handled the goods and services demanded by Chinese émigrés in their lives abroad. In so doing, the import-export firms were instrumental in the growth of China's foreign trade routed through Hong Kong. This trade started by catering to the specific desires of overseas Chinese communities for Chinese foods and medicines. Some specialized in Chinese herbs alone; others acted as importers and exporters of other popular commodities such as beans, teas, wines, preserved food, and fertilizers; while others became dealers of bulk goods like rice and sugar.

Nanbeihang began by specializing in the transport of goods between northern and southern China. They later expanded operations to encompass Southeast Asia. During the 1850s, they began charging a 2 percent commission for selling goods to customers on behalf of their suppliers— hence, their nickname, *jiubahang* (Gau Bat Hong in Cantonese, meaning Ninety-eight Percent firms).[19] Yuen Fat Hong is an example of a nanbeihang founded by a family in Shantou. The original fortune was made in trade between Thailand and Shantou. By the 1850s, however, Kao Man-hua, a scion of the founder, realized that Hong Kong would make a good central operating base. So, he established Yuen Fat Hong there. Initially the business dealt mainly in imports of Thai rice but later began distributing "large quantities of Chinese products" throughout the principal ports of Asia as a major sideline. Yuen Fat Hong had branches in Kobe, Bangkok, and Singapore and later acted as an agent for several steamship companies among its many services.[20]

Jinshanzhuang were the import-export businesses that traded with North America, Australia, and Mexico. They began operating sometime during the 1850s and had close links to Chinese businesses abroad, which were often run by kinsmen or people from the same villages.[21] On behalf of overseas merchants, jinshanzhuang managers took orders for Chinese goods and arranged for their shipment. They exported rice, Chinese groceries, medicines, and tea to overseas Chinese communities and imported goods like flour, dried fish, and oil from the United States. Through the networks of exchange developed by these firms, Chinese trade with North America steadily grew in the last decades of the nineteenth century. American imports of rice from China, Hong Kong, and Hawaii rose annually from 18.7 million pounds in 1867 to 59.6 million pounds in 1876, and 61.1 million pounds in 1878. Trade between the two countries increased from $11.4 million in 1867 to $26.8 million in 1872.[22] By 1922, there were 116 jinshanzhuang based in Hong Kong doing business with North American firms. By 1930, business had become so good that the number had more than doubled to 290.[23]

Jinshanzhuang were intimately involved in the lives of overseas Chinese for they made it possible for them to buy a tremendous variety of Chinese goods, including Chinese books and magazines, herbal medicines, fruits like lychees, pineapples, and pears; other cooking ingredients such as ginger, water chestnuts, and water lily roots; sweets; seafood like flower fish, black fish, eels, and oysters, as well as large numbers of live ducks, fried rice birds, and quail.[24] The firms also supplied "dried oysters, shrimps, cuttlefish, mushrooms, dried bean curd, bamboo shoots, sweetmeats, duck liver and kidneys, [and] water chestnut flour" to Chinese in the United States.[25] Preserved ginger was such a popular item that in 1908 alone about 450,000 pounds were exported, mostly to San Francisco.[26] Gilbert Leong recalls that during the 1920s, his father did not need to go to China to get supplies for his Chinese restaurant in Los Angeles because everything he needed was available locally.[27]

Chinese-run businesses scattered throughout North America had connections with jinshanzhuang, thereby ensuring that in a large number of cities local Chinese could buy the items they wanted. The distribution lists of *Xinning Magazine*, which was published in Taishan County (Toisan in Cantonese) in Guangdong Province for overseas Taishanese consumption, give us some sense of the dispersion of Chinese grocery stores in North America. In 1927, Chinese could pick up their copy of *Xinning Magazine* and buy items like dried shrimps and canned water chestnuts from stores in Honolulu, Los Angeles, San Diego, Portland, Seattle, Hobart, Vancouver, Victoria, Calgary, Winnipeg, Chicago, Detroit, Toronto, Montreal, Boston, Pittsburgh, New York City, Newark, Philadelphia, Washington D.C., Baltimore, and Houston.[28]

This network extended from the hinterlands of Guangdong through Hong Kong across the Pacific to San Francisco and ended in a widely dispersed set of partners, some of whom were located in relatively remote parts of the American West. One example is the Wing On Wo firm, which served both Chinese and European American customers in Dutch Flat, Placer County, California, between 1884 and 1915. Wing On Wo obtained its wares from a variety of sources. It purchased groceries such as hams, canned tomatoes, and soda crackers from the Sacramento business of Hall-Luhrs and Co. while ordering biweekly shipments of Chinese products such as rice, peanut oil, and tea from Kwang Sick Company in San Francisco. It also ordered goods from businesses located in nearby Auburn and Wheatland in Yuba County.[29]

The networks of trade that linked jinshanzhuang in Hong Kong to points all over the world did more than bring salted fish and rice to Chinese overseas. They also made it possible for Chinese living in urban centers like San Francisco, Chicago, Havana, Melbourne, or Singapore to send letters, money, and information to villages located in the backwaters of rural Guangdong. To readers accustomed to the conveniences of twenty-first-century life, the problem perhaps seems simpler than it was. In the reality of nineteenth- and early twentieth-century China, however, there were no government postal agencies whose reach extended from a big city like New York to a village like Sanba tucked in the hills of Taishan. After 1876, when Hong Kong joined the postal union, it became possible to send mail to and receive it from most cities in the world.[30] After arriving in Hong Kong, letters would somehow have to get to the Chinese countryside. If a letter contained money, recipients in Chinese villages would somehow have to find a way to change foreign dollars into Chinese currency that they could spend at the local marketplace.[31]

During the nineteenth century, although it was possible to get money to China from places overseas, the four main methods were rather unreliable. Overseas Chinese could ask returning relatives or friends to take small amounts of cash to their dependents free of charge but such opportunities occurred irregularly. With payment of a 5 percent commission, they could hire a courier, also known as "water guests" [shuike] or "city-circuit horses" [xunchengma], to take money and letters, along with goods for import or export, to China. Water guests made deliveries in person and they would wait to bring letters written by recipients in reply to the senders. However, the overseas Chinese had to trust that the couriers would not run away with their money. The third method, in which people brought back money themselves, was less prone to risk but required that, while overseas, they exchange their foreign currency for Chinese yuan. A fourth method was to convey the remittance money in the form of marketable goods bought and sold at either end of the journey. During the 1920s and 1930s, both government officials and private merchants attempted to develop Western-style banks and postal systems to wrest the remittance business from jinshanzhuang. These challengers arose in the form of foreign banks, Chinese government banks (for example, the Bank of Canton, the Communications Bank, or the Bank of China), and the Chinese postal service.[32]

Jinshanzhuang solved a multitude of mail-related problems. From their base in Hong Kong, they developed well-established connections to businesses in Chinatowns around the world. Their transactions with others were guaranteed, not by contracts, but by relationships based on kinship or native-place ties.[33] As such, they were the best qualified and most accountable agents that Chinese overseas could find to ensure that money sent to Hong Kong would be dependably forwarded to designated recipients waiting at home in the villages. An additional convenience was that by sending letters through the closest Chinese store, Chinese overseas did not have to deal with the unfamiliar language and rules of banks and post offices in foreign lands.

To reach all the places not served by banks and post offices of the time, jinshanzhuang had to develop a network of partners, not only in places around the world but also in the Guangdong hinterland. Wah Ying Cheong, located at 290 Des Voeux Road in the central district of Hong Kong, is an example of a jinshanzhuang that handled large sums of remittances with the help of widely dispersed business connections. The firm was founded in the late nineteenth century and run by members of the Chen clan from Doushan District in Taishan County, Guangdong. Fictive kinship or native-place connections secured most of its transactions as many of its customers either were surnamed Chen or came from Doushan District.[34] Its overseas business partners included several firms located in Seattle, Portland, San Francisco, Los Angeles, and New York. Wah Ying Cheong also handled money sent from San Diego, Boston, Chicago, Victoria, Vancouver, Montreal, Singapore, Rangoon, Manila, Osaka, and New Zealand. Within Taishan County, Wah Ying Cheong's partners were based in market towns in or around Doushan District. The main Taishan County contact was the Yichang firm in Doushan. Almost twenty other partners were scattered around Doushan as well as the five districts of Nafu, Duhu, Guanghai, Xialang, and Chonglou.[35]

In the Guangdong hinterland, local partners ran a variety of other businesses with postal and remittance services as lucrative sidelines although some, like the Baochang Money Shop in Taishan City, were known only as money shops and specialized in the receipt of letters and remittances as well as money exchange. Other businesses, like the Wansheng Hao firm, for example, acted as a postal drop. The latter was a sideline to its main business of selling sundry goods like oil, rice, and sugar.[36] A wide range of businesses accepted letters and remittances for other people: gold stores, medicine firms, and even china shops, like Yu Lianhe's Zhenji Porcelain Store.[37] Before 1937, there were at least one hundred firms—either banks or stores—in Taishan that directly communicated with jinshanzhuang in Hong Kong regarding the transfer of funds.[38]

Money and letters sent to Taishan through the auspices of a jinshanzhuang required several steps. In the United States, frugal Chinese, usually men, would buy cashier's checks for the amounts they wished to send, write letters giving instructions, including the precise destinations and the names of the intended recipients, and send both via registered mail to their jinshanzhuang of choice in Hong Kong. Or, if they did not wish to deal with American banks, they could go to the nearest stores run by trusted connections and hand them the money and give them instructions for sending remittances on their behalf.[39] Storeowners would wait until a pile of such remittances had accumulated before purchasing a single cashier's check for the total amount to be sent along with a bundle of individual instructions.

Once the money arrived in Hong Kong, the accountant at the jinshanzhuang would cash the check at a bank, exchange it into silver or Hong Kong dollars, deduct service fees, calculate the amounts to be sent to business partners in Guangdong, then figure out how to get everything to the right place, usually by courier.[40] For carrying out these transactions, all jinshanzhuang charged the same nominal service fee of 2 percent. Jinshanzhuang owners liked to advertise this fact as a symbol of their devotion and generosity to overseas Chinese. However, they did manage to profit from the remittance business through their manipulation of exchange rates.

After the money arrived at branch stores in Guangdong, the proprietors would contact the designated recipients, usually by word of mouth, to come to town and fetch their mail. For example, one woman living in Tangmei village in Zhudong District walked along the road to the nearby market of Hua'nanchang to pick up her money.[41] Sending letters overseas followed much the same process but was enacted in reverse.

Besides helping to send money, jinshanzhuang provided their customers with services normally associated with banks. Some rented out safe-deposit boxes and administered savings plans with interest rates. The Bai'anlong Yinhao at 41 Bonham Strand in Hong Kong was a fairly typical jinshanzhuang of the 1930s. It was backed by capital of two hundred thousand yuan and helped customers with remittances, currency exchange, savings accounts, and the storage of valuables in U.S.-made metal security boxes. Rates of interests on savings accounts were set at four *li* for six months, five for one year, six for two years, and variable interest for deposits with no fixed terms.[42]

If they were successful, American Chinese would eventually have recourse to the full range of a jinshanzhuang's financial services, as did Chen Kongzhao of New York. Chen appears in the Wah Ying Cheong books over the course of thirty years, during which his status in life changed from that of a laborer sending back remittances in small amounts, to a businessman with large sums to invest, and eventually to a retiree comfortably living in Hong Kong on a sizeable income from dividends and interest payments on his savings accounts.[43] In 1905, Chen could afford to send only a total of 90 yuan to his mother and 42 yuan to a cousin. Ten years later, he was doing well enough to place 1,000 yuan in his savings account, send 60 yuan to yet another cousin, and donate money to build a school in the Six Villages. In 1920, he sent 350 yuan to one Chen Qinqing, 2 yuan per person to two cousins, and added yet another thousand yuan to his savings account. In 1929, he put 34.50 yuan into the Qinji Company, 2,500 yuan into his account, and collected 25.75 yuan in interest from the Qinji Company. By 1935, he had returned to live in Hong Kong and personally dropped by the Wah Ying Cheong Company, which had helped him invest in the Qinji Co., to collect 470.80 yuan in dividends he had earned from the latter, as well as a total of 1,818.88 yuan in income from his savings account and from relatives overseas.[44] Chen Kongzhao is one example of how sojourning in the United States made socioeconomic elevation possible.

For trusted customers, jinshanzhuang offered a special line of services. When short on cash and faced with a family crisis at home, these special customers could ask the jinshanzhuang to forward money to Guangdong with the understanding that the full amount would be repaid at the U.S. branch when the customer was able.[45] Jinshanzhuang also acted as trustees for their overseas customers. Those with sizable savings (several thousand up to ten thousand U.S. dollars) and unreliable sons, wives, or younger brothers could send a lump sum of money to the jinshanzhuang, which would then use the interest to provide a regularly disbursed allowance to their families in China.[46] Merchants and restaurateurs who could not leave their businesses to return and personally supervise the upbringing of their heirs could thus delegate responsibility to trusted firms as they sustained families in China.

Perhaps the most confidential business services offered by jinshanzhuang involved helping their clients negotiate the complicated process of entering the United States, especially after passage of the highly restrictive Chinese exclusion laws. Between 1882 and 1943, Chinese could legally enter the United States only if they could document their status as one of the tightly defined "exempt" classes: merchants, family members of merchants, diplomats and their dependents, tourists, and teachers and students. Chinese quickly discovered the loopholes in these laws and how they were enforced. By 1910, a majority was entering through some form of fraud.[47] Many claimed statuses unplanned for by a hostile Congress: U.S.-born citizens and their foreign-born sons and daughters who could enter as "derivative citizens." After 1921, the percentage of those claiming U.S. citizenship as the basis for their right to enter never dipped below 40 percent.[48]

A suspicious immigration bureaucracy attempted to catch would-be immigrant Chinese by subjecting them to extended confinement and arduously detailed interrogations and medical examinations before permitting them to land. Despite these challenges, most Chinese did gain entry, the exclusion laws and the Immigration Bureau notwithstanding. To come to America successfully, however, Chinese had to prepare carefully and possess two essential tools: the identity of a Chinese person legally eligible to enter the United States and evidence that they were in fact that person. Such identities and evidence were rare and valuable resources. For those who did not possess them, papers could be purchased but only from the most trusted relatives or friends. Chinese preferred to purchase these paper identities within their immediate circle of fellow villagers and kin, but if a "slot" matching the age of the aspiring emigrant could not be found locally, jinshanzhuang were often the next most reliable source. Some managers of Gold Mountain firms had access to paper identities. They were held accountable, to a certain extent, for whether such papers would pass inspection upon arrival in the United States because they depended heavily on unblemished reputations to attract and retain customers. Because they drew much of their clientele from within the tight networks of shared kinship or native place, jinshanzhuang had further inducement to deal honestly with all their customers. Nonetheless, buying and selling papers was a weighty business. According to Jiang Yongkang, a businessman who ran a jinshanzhuang in the late 1940s, some jinshanzhuang sold papers, but not his. At the time, he had just gotten started in his business and thought that potential customers would consider him too young to be trusted with such important matters.[49]

Jinshanzhuang personnel also helped the sons, nephews, cousins, wives, and daughters of their overseas customers to go abroad by buying tickets, arranging health examinations, preparing evidence of identity, and filling out forms at the U.S. consulate in Hong Kong. Liu Zanchen, located at 234 Des Veoux Road in Hong Kong, specialized in such services and claimed twenty years of experience bringing people from their villages in Guangdong to the United States.[50] The firms provided prospective emigrants with a place to stay for the two or three weeks they had to spend in Hong Kong waiting for paperwork to be processed and boats to arrive. Larger jinshanzhuang had offices complete with living rooms and bedrooms for the use of their clients.[51] They also sold emigrants the goods that would be needed at their destinations, such as comforters, food, leather trunks, soap, and mats.[52] For these reasons, jinshanzhuang like the Huaxin Ginseng Company became known as the Chonglou Courier

Station because everybody from Chonglou District who went abroad stayed there.[53]

Given the intimacy and completeness of services offered by jinshanzhuang to their customers, it is no wonder that jinshanzhuang were well able to withstand the attempts of government banks, such as the Bank of China and the Bank of Canton, and postal services to take control of overseas Chinese remittances during the 1930s.[54] Despite these challenges, jinshanzhuang continued to survive even during the Great Depression. Liu Zuoren, head of the Bank of Canton's Research Office during the 1930s, estimated that 70 percent of remittances entered China via jinshanzhuang.[55] A team of Fujian scholars estimated that in 1937, 35.1 percent of remittances entered China through banks, 1.1 percent through post offices, and 63.8 percent through jinshanzhuang.[56]

CONCLUSION

After almost a century of multifaceted service to the Chinese in America, jinshanzhuang lost the profitable niche in the global economy that they had served so nimbly for so long. Although they withstood the onslaught of institutionalized racism and legal exclusion, as well as competition from Chinese national banks, they could not survive the severing of diplomatic relations between the United States and the People's Republic of China during the cold war. It became illegal in both China and the United States to participate in the exchange of goods, money, letters, and people. Exchanges of any sort became grounds for accusations of disloyalty and political heresy. Chinese in the United States, aided somewhat by ameliorating laws and attitudes, responded to these political pressures by focusing more on becoming Chinese Americans. Although some maintained illicit contacts with relatives and causes in China, most took advantage of newly available employment and residential opportunities in the United States to claim their right to make the United States their home. The raison d'etre for jinshanzhuang disappeared once the regular back-and-forth movements were no longer possible. True to their business ethos, jinshanzhuang evolved into something else. During the 1950s, many rechanneled their capital and entrepreneurial talents to Hong Kong's promising new ventures of real estate development and light manufacturing. By the time substantial Chinese migration resumed as Sino-U.S. relations thawed in the late 1970s, the technological infrastructure of global banking and trade had caught up with the desires and priorities of transnational Chinese, thereby rendering obsolete the highly specialized services once offered so compatibly by jinshanzhuang.

3 Against All Odds: Chinese Female Migration and Family Formation on American Soil During the Early Twentieth Century

SUCHENG CHAN

THIS CHAPTER IS A PROGRESS report on a research project, "In Search of Chinese Women and Girls," that I started in 1975 and will not complete until 2006 or 2007. The research has spanned decades because few narrative sources can be found on Chinese women and girls who lived in the United States during the second half of the nineteenth century and much of what is available is about Chinese prostitutes. While non-narrative sources such as the manuscript schedules of the U.S. decennial censuses of population are available, they require enormous effort to dig up, collect, and analyze. Even after a scholar has done that, he or she faces the challenge of crafting engaging stories about the individuals whose existence he or she has unearthed. A federal law prohibiting the release of a manuscript census until seventy-two years after it was taken is the main reason that this research project has been so drawn out. When I began, the latest manuscript census available was the 1900 one. To see and analyze the changes that have occurred over time, I had to wait until 1983 to process the information in the 1910 manuscript census, until 1993 to gain access to the 1920 manuscript census, and until 2003 to see the 1930 one.

I have had to be patient for three reasons. First, my research method is inductive to an extreme degree. I believe that when one is studying a grossly underresearched group, it is best to start with as few preconceived notions as possible. Thus, even though I was trained as a social scientist and not a historian, I thought it would not be appropriate to use the positivist scientific method in this research project. That is why I did not begin by formulating hypotheses nor will I try to "test" whether they are correct. Instead, I am trying to collect all the evidence available and will analyze them statistically in order to see what patterns may emerge. Only then will I look for corroborating evidence that helps explain what those patterns may mean. Just because documents such as letters, diaries, and journals—the kind of documents used by many scholars of women's history—cannot be found for the Chinese women and girls in question, it does not mean we should ignore whatever other traces they may have left. As I discovered over the years, the historical sediments left by Chinese women and girls are in fact voluminous, and they can be excavated and analyzed to deepen our insight into how Chinese female pioneers lived and worked in America.

Second, unlike some scholars who believe that oral history can help us recover fully what Yuji Ichioka called our "buried past," I recognize that oral history is a suitable method only when people who had lived during a certain period are still alive to be interviewed. While oral history is a valuable tool, it is insufficient if we wish to reconstruct a history of the Asian American female past that is broader, more textured, and more *representative* than oral history allows. The story of a single life can, indeed, illuminate many aspects of an entire historical period, but I cannot help but ask, "How representative of other women is that particular woman's life story?"

Third, existing studies of Chinese women in nineteenth-century America have focused largely on Chinese prostitutes partly because documentary evidence on them—much of it sensational—has been more readily available than on other classes of Chinese immigrant women and girls.[1] To paint a more inclusive picture of all kinds of women, we must search for hitherto untapped sources and analyze or interpret them in ways that ground our interpretations or conclusions in the broadest empirical base(s) we can find. As far as I know, the manuscript censuses provide the most extensive database available.

THE MANUSCRIPT CENSUSES

The manuscript (unpublished) census refers to the large sheets of paper, called schedules, that census takers used to write down the information they collected. The enumerators went door-to-door asking the same questions of every individual they counted. The schedules had printed headings that facilitated the data collection. Because these schedules recorded information on individuals, they are far more useful for research than the published census volumes that contain aggregated figures. In my view, the information that can be culled from the manuscript censuses is indispensable if we wish to tell a fuller story about Chinese women and girls who appeared on the American historical stage almost a century and a half ago. My conviction that it *is* possible to do research that goes beyond Chinese prostitution, while accepting its existence as a historical fact that should not be hidden, minimized, or erased, has compelled me to keep returning every ten years to this project when another manuscript census is released for public use.

Of all the manuscript censuses available (the latest being the 1930 census), the 1900 and 1910 are the most useful for a study of Chinese female migration and family formation on American soil because they contain several questions that the other censuses did not ask. While all the censuses recorded the name, age, sex, race, birthplace, mother tongue, literacy, and occupation of each individual enumerated, the 1880 census was the first one to include information on the marital status and the relationship of each person living in a household to the head of the household. In other words, it was the first census to make a study of household composition and family relationships possible. The 1890 census added many questions, including how many years an immigrant had been in the United States and, in the case of women, how many children they had given birth to and how many of them were living. Tragically, the manuscript schedules of the 1890 census went up in flames when the building housing them burned down in 1921. This is an especially great loss for historians of Chinese America because the 1890 census was the first one taken after the 1882 Chinese Exclusion Law went into effect and the information contained in its unpublished schedules would have revealed many aspects of how the Chinese population changed as a result of the 1882, 1884, and the two 1888 exclusion laws. Fortunately, the 1900 and 1910 censuses are even more useful than the 1880 or 1890 one: they contain information on the year of immigration of foreign-born individuals as well as the number of years a person had been married. Even though the two censuses asked the marriage question in slightly different ways—the 1900 census asked the number of years a person had been married while the 1910 census asked how many years the "present marriage" had lasted—the same computations can be made from the information recorded. The 1920 census, however, dropped the questions on number of years married and the number of children each woman had given birth to. The 1930 census asked the question about marriage in yet another way: census takers wanted to know a person's age at his or her "first marriage." By subtracting a person's age at marriage from his or her age when the census was taken, we can calculate how many years he or she had been married. Moreover, if the number of years married differs for the two spouses who make up a couple, then we know one of them had been married before to someone else.

Year of immigration and number of years married are critically important for the study of Chinese female migration and family formation on American soil because, for the first time, it is possible to figure out whether a woman was married before she came to the United States or married only after her arrival. We can calculate how many years she had been married before she came or how many years she had been in the United States before she married. For these reasons, I analyze only the

1900 and 1910 manuscript censuses in this chapter even though I intend to examine the entire period from 1860, when the census bureau first enumerated a significant number of Chinese, to 1930, the latest manuscript census released for public use, in a future publication.

Data from the manuscript censuses show how the Chinese male and female populations in California were distributed geographically, how those patterns changed over time, what kind of work the Chinese did, their literacy rates, their household composition, ages, sex ratio, marital status, and the average number of children they had. In this study, I divide California into three regions: (1) the city and county of San Francisco, (2) agricultural counties, and (3) mining and mountain counties. (See Appendix A for how I group the state's fifty-eight counties.) This division reveals how geographic and economic regional differences affected the Chinese living in each region, not only in terms of their occupations but also in terms of how geography and economy correlated with marital status, family formation, and household composition. Space limitation prevents me from discussing my findings on the changing occupations of Chinese men but interested readers may refer to Tables 3.1A, 3.1B, 3.1C, 3.2A, 3.2B, and 3.2C for details. (All tables for this chapter are located in the Appendices at the end of the chapter.)

In the tables that concern family formation, I cross-tabulate the Chinese men's "rate of marriage," which I define as the percentage of married men among all men with known marital status, by the men's occupational categories. (See Appendix B for the broad categories under which specific occupations are grouped.) The same tables also show what percentage of "presently married men" (that is, not counting widowers and divorced men)[2] in each occupational category actually had wives living with them in the United States. (I call wives living with their husbands "resident wives" and husbands living with their wives "resident husbands.") We know that the exclusion laws allowed only "domiciled" merchants to bring their wives, children, and servants to live with them in the United States. Yet, the 1900 and 1910 manuscript censuses—the first ones still extant after the 1882 Chinese exclusion law and its subsequent amendments went into effect—show that men in many other occupations also had resident wives. How was this possible? Where were the resident wives born? If born in China, how old were they when they came to the United States? How old were they when they married? No other extant body of evidence allows us to answer these questions as clearly as can the information in the 1900 and 1910 manuscript censuses.

The census schedules further reveal that a significant number of Chinese women were heads of households, and that some single women, married women without resident husbands, widows, and a handful of divorcees lived alone. Such a habitation pattern deviated from the

Chinese cultural norm that generally frowned on women living without men in their households. In order not to weigh down this chapter with an indigestible amount of statistics, I shall put off answering questions such as the following: Where were the female heads of household born? Where in California did they live? Whom did they live with? How did they support themselves? For now, suffice it to say that the answers to these questions will call into question the historical veracity of prevailing stereotypes about immigrant Chinese men and women, U.S.-born Chinese American men and women, and the families they formed and sustained.

The prevailing master narrative of Chinese immigrant family life goes something like this: to ensure that young men who went abroad to work would retain strong bonds to the families they left behind, those families who could do so found brides for them before they departed. The men might leave immediately after their weddings or stay around only long enough to find out whether their wives were pregnant. Then, over the years they returned one or more times to China to sire additional children. When their sons became old enough to work, the absentee fathers tried to bring the boys to the United States so that the sons' earnings could help increase the collective income of the families in China. Men who were too poor to wed before they left China worked hard and lived frugally in order to save enough money to enable them to return to China to marry. They, too, would wait for signs that progeny was on the way before heading back to the United States to continue earning a living there. Such practices led to the existence of transpacific families.[3] In this stereotypical picture, China is always seen as the site of family formation even though we do have a vague notion that Chinese children were also born in the United States and that when they reached marriageable age, they, too, found mates and formed Chinese American families. Yet, for both the China-born and U.S.-born populations, who got married, when, and where have never been precisely documented. As I am discovering bit by bit, the actual process of family formation was considerably more complex than has been assumed.

Demographic Characteristics of the Chinese Male Population

The first two sets of tables (3.1A, 3.1B, 3.1C, 3.2A, 3.2B, and 3.2C) that cross-tabulate birthplace and marital status by occupational category show the differences between China-born and U.S.-born males in terms of marital status, occupations, and time periods. However, as the economic status or the occupational structure of Chinese-ancestry males living in America is not the main topic addressed in this chapter, I discuss only the demographic aspects of that population (as indicated in the bottom half of each table). There were at least 11,449 Chinese men and boys counted in San Francisco in 1900, 9,512 of whom were born in China (83.1 percent of the total) and 1,937 in the United States (16.9 percent). (I say "at least" because some pages of the microfilmed census schedules are illegible and there may have been Chinese listed on those pages.) Census takers failed to record the marital status of 314 of the China-born males and 12 of the U.S.-born males. Of the 9,198 China-born males whose marital status is known, 36.1 percent were single, 62.9 percent were married, and 1.0 percent were widowed or divorced. Among the 1,925 U.S.-born males whose marital status is known, 82.3 percent were single, 17.4 percent were married, and only 0.3 percent were widowed or divorced. There is such a big difference between the proportion of single males within the two groups because most of the U.S.-born single males in 1900 were still boys, indicating that the Chinese American population at the dawn of the twentieth century was a youthful one.

The agricultural counties, numbering thirty-seven, had a larger Chinese male population than did San Francisco in 1900, with 22,448 males born in China (94.8 percent of the total) and 1,225 born in the United States (5.2 percent). The number with known marital status stood at 22,045 for the former and 1,210 for the latter. Of the China-born male population with known marital status, 56.9 percent were single, 41.3 percent were married, and 1.7 percent were widowed or divorced. Thus, compared to San Francisco, a considerably larger proportion of the China-born males in agricultural California was single. Among the U.S.-born males, 88.6 percent were single, 11.1 percent were married, and 0.3 percent were widowed or divorced, which means that compared to the U.S.-born males living San Francisco, a slightly larger proportion in the farming regions was single and conversely a smaller fraction was married.

The mining and mountainous counties, of which there are twenty, are the most remote part of California in terms of their distance from major population centers. In 1900, almost half a century after the gold rush ended, many Chinese lingered there, a significant number of them still looking for gold. Of the 5,258 Chinese men and boys, 5,008 were born in China (95.2 percent) and 250 in the United States (4.8 percent). Thus, the percentage of China-born males in the mining and mountainous counties was larger than in either San Francisco or the agricultural counties. Many were men who had gone into the gold country during the first few decades of Chinese immigration into California and had never left, even after the surface gold had run out by the late 1850s. The marital status is known for 4,984 of the China-born and 246 of the U.S.-born males. Among the former, 62.7 percent were single, 35.0 percent were married, and 2.2 percent were widowed or divorced. The corresponding figures for the latter were 89.4, 10.6, and zero percent, respectively. As the percentage of single males was larger than in either San Francisco or the agricultural counties, these statistical patterns suggest that the more remote a region was, the fewer married men, boys, and American-born males lived there. Apparently, it was mostly intrepid China-born single men in search of work or aging miners refusing to give up their dream of gold who ventured into and inhabited such faraway localities on the northern and eastern peripheries of California.

Comparing the data culled from the 1910 census with the 1900 one, the most noticeable trend is the decline in the total Chinese male population in San Francisco between 1900 and 1910—falling from 11,449 in 1900 to 9,207 in 1910. However, the change affected the China-born and U.S.-born differently. The number of China-born men and boys in San Francisco had fallen to 6,489, but the number of U.S.-born men and boys had risen to 2,718. The main cause of the overall decrease, of course, was the 1906 San Francisco earthquake and fire that leveled and burned down Chinatown, whose inhabitants scattered to unaffected areas, but mainly across San Francisco Bay to Alameda County, thereby enabling the city of Oakland to develop a sizable Chinatown. There were only 5,294 China-born males with known marital status in San Francisco (compared to 9,512 ten years earlier), of whom 45.2 percent were single, 53.4 percent were married, and 1.4 percent were divorced or widowed, compared to 36.1, 62.9, and 1.0 percent, respectively, in 1900. It thus appears that relatively more married men than single ones left San Francisco after the earthquake because the unsettled conditions during the rebuilding of Chinatown must have been very hard on families. Though the San Francisco Chinese community rapidly rebuilt itself, the 1910 census was taken only four years after the devastation—that is, before a sense of normality was restored. A second noticeable trend was that the proportion of U.S.-born married men had jumped from 17.4 percent in 1900 to 41.1 percent in 1910, which indicates that family formation was occurring rapidly among U.S.-born men, the earthquake notwithstanding.

The Chinese population in the agricultural counties in 1910 had also fallen but by a smaller percentage than in San Francisco. China-born males now numbered 16,649 (84.7 percent of the total) and U.S.-born ones stood at 3,012 (15.3 percent). Of the 15,989 China-born males with known marital status, 51.2 percent were single, 46.5 percent were married, and 2.3 percent were widowed or divorced. Thus, the percentage of married men had increased slightly compared to 1900. Among U.S.-born males, the increase in the proportion of married men was almost three-fold, rising from 11.1 percent in 1900 to 30.6 percent in 1910, though single males still made up 68.7 percent and widowed or divorced males 0.8 percent of the total.

In the mining and mountainous counties, the total number of Chinese males fell from 5,258 in 1900 to 2,799 in 1910. Within this dwindling population, 2,454 were born in China (87.7 percent) and 345 were born in the United States (12.3 percent). Of the 2,408 China-born males with known marital status, 51.4 percent were single, 45.2 percent were married, and 3.4 percent were widowed or divorced. Among U.S.-born males, all of whose marital status was recorded by census takers, 77.1 percent were single, 21.4 percent were married, and 1.4 percent were widowed or divorced. What these numbers indicate is that remote though they be, family formation was also occurring in the mining and mountainous counties.

Rate of Marriage and Percent of Married Men with Resident Wives by Occupational Category

The next two sets of tables (3.3A, 3.3B, 3.3C, 3.4A, 3.4B, and 3.4C) compare the rate of marriage among men, both China-born and U.S.-born, who were engaged in different occupations. They also compute how many and what percentage of the married men had wives living with them. In San Francisco in 1900, in rank order, the largest percentage of China-born married men was found among agents and supervisors (83.3 percent), followed closely by merchants (82.2 percent), professionals (77.9 percent), clerks and shop assistants (77.2 percent), skilled artisans (73.9 percent), other businessmen (72.8 percent), and factory workers (65.2 percent). Despite differences in class status—with agents and supervisors, merchants, other businessmen, professionals, and skilled artisans forming an upper stratum, and clerks, shop assistants, and factory workers belonging to a lower one—all these occupations were sedentary. Hence, they were more dependable as sources of regular income that allowed more of these men to be financially secure enough to marry. Miners and agriculturalists also had high marriage rates—70.0 percent and 70.1 percent, respectively—but there were so few of them in San Francisco that no significance should be attached to those two large percentages. In contrast to China-born men, the marriage rates among U.S.-born men were much lower: 50.0 percent of other businessmen, 44.4 percent of professionals, and 33.8 percent of skilled artisans were married. Because the total number in each of these three groups is small, these percentages are not particularly meaningful, either.

The high marriage rates among certain occupational categories of men, however, did not translate into a correspondingly large number of families in which resident wives and children were present. As the numbers are small, the percentages of men with resident wives should be considered more suggestive than definitive. The only meaningful figures are the 142 merchants, 136 other businessmen, 73 professionals, 67 skilled artisans, 66 factory workers, and 59 nonagricultural laborers. The percentages of men with resident wives in those occupational categories are 18.1, 28.5, 20.3, 14.1, 7.1, and 13.2, respectively. The relatively large percentage of married men who had resident wives among merchants, other businessmen, and professionals are to be expected, given their more secure socioeconomic status and the "exemption" that the exclusion laws granted them, but the fact that a noticeable proportion of factory workers as well as nonagricultural laborers also had resident wives certainly contradicts conventional wisdom. Additional computations need to be made to see whether they married before or after the exclusion laws went into effect. Overall, 12.7 percent of the China-born married men had wives and, in most instances, children living with them in America. While there were only 736 China-born married men with resident wives, their significance cannot be dismissed: even though they were outnumbered by married men whose wives were *not* by their sides, the existence of these 736 men shows that California was also a site, albeit a secondary one, of family formation among U.S.-born Chinese *as well as* among China-born men and women.

Among U.S.-born men, agents and supervisors, other businessmen, professionals, clerks and shop assistants, and skilled artisans had the highest marriage rates. However, because their total numbers are small, the large percentages (71.4, 50.0, 44.4, 43.1, and 33.8, respectively) again are more suggestive than definitive. What is surprising is that the overall proportion of U.S.-born men with resident wives, 21.5 percent, is only 8.8 percent larger than among China-born men. In other words, almost four-fifths of the U.S.-born married men must have had wives in China whom they either did not wish to or could not, for whatever reason, bring to America. Up to this point, most scholars, including myself, have implicitly assumed that U.S.-born young men must have married mostly U.S.-born young women, but manuscript census data show this was not the case. (Tables 3.7A, 3.7B, 3.7C, 3.8A, 3.8B, and 3.8C, which reveal who married whom, will be discussed later and will demonstrate why such a facile assumption is incorrect.)

In the agricultural counties in 1900, not only were the marriage rates lower than in San Francisco (an overall 41.3 percent among China-born men versus 62.9 percent in San Francisco), but the percentage of men with resident wives was also lower. Overall, only 4.9 percent of China-born married men enumerated in agricultural California had wives living with them, while only 10.4 percent of U.S.-born married men had resident wives. Here, too, China-born merchants (69.4 percent) and professionals (69.1 percent) led in the rate of marriage. However, clerks and shop assistants, as well as agents and supervisors, were not far behind. The main difference from San Francisco is that there were 794 China-born agriculturalists (a term that includes farmers, orchardists, ranchers, vineyardists, truck gardeners who grew vegetables and small fruit, and poultry raisers) who were married (49.1 percent), but only 4.9 percent had wives living with them. Among U.S.-born men and boys, merchants, agriculturalists, and cooks had the highest marriage rates at 40.7, 38.5, and 33.3 percent, respectively. But the number of U.S.-born married men with resident wives was so minuscule that not much should be made of these percentages.

Though the overall marriage rate in the mining and mountainous counties is even lower (35.0 percent among China-born men and 10.6 percent among U.S.-born men) than those in both San Francisco and the agricultural counties, the 7.9 percent China-born husbands who had resident wives was larger than the comparable figure in the agricultural counties but smaller than that in San Francisco. Similarly, among U.S.-born husbands, the 15.4 percent with resident wives also stood halfway between the figures for San Francisco and agricultural California. More research is needed before an explanation for these statistical differences can be offered.

Another unexpected finding is that in all three regions, only a tiny percentage of laundrymen had resident wives, despite their sedentary occupation, which might have led one to believe they could support and house wives in the same quarters where they washed and ironed clothes, ate meals, and slept. But this was not the case—a warning to scholars that commonsense assumptions do not always turn out to be correct.

The data from the 1910 manuscript census reveal a fall in the overall marriage rate in San Francisco compared to 1900: only 54.4 percent of the China-born men were married, in contrast to the 62.9 percent in 1900. The percentage with resident wives had also decreased by 1 percent, from 12.7 in 1900 to 11.8 in 1910. Members of the same occupational groups as those in 1900—agents and supervisors (88.3 percent), merchants (75.9 percent), and other businessmen (74.3 percent)—again had the highest marriage rates, while 28.2 percent of merchants and 23.8 percent of agents and supervisors had resident wives. In contrast, both the number (1,103 in 1910 versus 335 in 1900) and percentage (41.1 in 1910 versus 21.5 in 1900) of married men among the U.S.-born male population had increased substantially—an indication that families were being formed and children were being raised by U.S.-born fathers.

Probably because so many Chinese moved out of San Francisco to agricultural counties in the aftermath of the earthquake, the overall marriage rate of China-born men in the agricultural counties in 1910 increased to 46.5 percent, compared to 41.3 percent a decade earlier. The percentage with resident wives also grew from 4.9 percent in 1900 to 6.8 percent in 1910. The marriage rate of U.S.-born men in the farming areas rose to

30.6 percent, compared to 11.1 percent in 1900, and the proportion with resident wives likewise grew from 10.4 percent in 1900 to 13.1 percent in 1910. Men engaged in commerce, professionals, and artisans again had the highest marriage rates, but that of clerks and shop assistants was also high (62.0 percent). It is probable, but not provable, that many of the clerks and shop assistants must have been former merchants who fled San Francisco in 1906 and were now trying to survive hard times by doing lower-status work in the agricultural counties, having lost everything during the quake.

Even though fewer of these "refugees from the earthquake" found their way to the more remote mining and mountainous counties, where the total Chinese-born male population had fallen by half in the intercensus decade, the overall marriage rate among the China-born men there increased by more than ten percentage points from 35.0 percent in 1900 to 45.2 percent in 1910. The percentage of China-born married men with resident wives declined slightly, however, from 7.9 percent in 1900 to 7.0 percent ten years later, but the percentage of U.S.-born married men with resident wives increased from 15.4 percent in 1900 to 24.3 percent in 1910—a reflection of the maturation of the U.S.-born male population. However, since there were only eighteen U.S.-born married men, the increase cannot be interpreted as a definitive long-term trend.

To sum up, it is clear that there was a causal chain in operation. The natural resources in a geographic region affected the kinds of jobs available there. The job opportunities, in turn, attracted self-selected Chinese males who were interested in or were willing to take the jobs open to them during that historical period. These men were self-selected because they did not represent a random sample of all Chinese male job-seekers in California, much less in the United States as a whole. The occupations that provided Chinese men a living determined, at least in part, the differential rates of marriage among various categories of Chinese male workers, as well as the relative likelihood that men in particular occupational categories would have resident wives and children in their households. In a derivative way, then, these factors also affected the characteristics of the Chinese female population.

DEMOGRAPHIC CHARACTERISTICS OF THE CHINESE FEMALE POPULATION

As a large number of women and girls had no recorded occupations, instead of cross-tabulating their birthplace and marital status by occupational category as I do for the men and boys, I cross-tabulate their birthplace and marital status by age in Tables 3.5A, 3.5B, 3.5C, 3.6A, 3.6B, and 3.6C. In San Francisco in 1900, there were 905 women and girls born in China and 1,196 born in the United States. Thus, the 43.1 percent of China-born females in the total population of women and girls of Chinese ancestry was much smaller than the 83.1 percent of China-born males within the total population of Chinese-ancestry men and boys, while the percentage of U.S.-born females (57.0 percent) among all Chinese-ancestry females was much larger than that of U.S.-born males (16.9 percent) among all Chinese-ancestry males. These numbers, of course, reflect the fact that Chinese immigrant men greatly outnumbered immigrant women. But the number of U.S.-born females (1,196) was *also* considerably smaller than U.S.-born males (1,937)—a difference that requires explanation.

At the present stage of my research, I can only conjecture that the Chinese in America either still practiced female infanticide, which is highly unlikely, given the greater value accorded girls in Chinese America—an environment where females were scarce—or that many families sent their girls back to China to be "properly" socialized in a thoroughly Chinese cultural environment. The latter reason seems more likely, based on what I found in the Chinese Arrival Investigation Case Files. Many of these files are of women and girls, a vast majority of whom claimed to have been born in the United States and to have been sent to China when they were quite young, where they stayed for a number of years before returning to America. While that fact may offer a plausible explanation for why there were considerably fewer U.S.-born girls and young women than U.S.-born boys and young men, it is still problematic because boys and young men born in the United States were also sent to China—in their case to receive a Chinese education—where they likewise stayed for some years before coming back to the United States. Only additional research can clarify the reasons for the skewed sex ratio among the U.S.-born population.

Among the 905 China-born females enumerated in San Francisco in 1900, the 166 single females composed 18.3 percent of the total, the 538 married women with resident husbands made up 59.4 percent, the 73 married women with no resident husbands represented 8.1 percent, and the 128 widows and divorcees formed 14.1 percent. (The census did list explicitly a number of divorcees, again contradicting a common assumption that Chinese couples did not divorce.) A reverse image characterizes the 1,196 U.S.-born females, 857 of whom (71.7 percent) were single, 289 (24.2 percent) were married and had resident husbands, 32 (2.7 percent) were married but were not living with their husbands, and 18 (1.5 percent) were widowed or divorced.

The 166 China-born single women and girls were considerably older than their U.S.-born counterparts: 10.2 percent were fifteen years old or younger, 77.1 percent ranged in age from sixteen to thirty, and 12.4 percent were thirty-one or older. In contrast, fully 71.8 percent of the 857

U.S.-born single females were fifteen and younger, 27.8 percent were between sixteen and thirty, while only 0.3 percent were thirty-one or older. The 538 China-born married women with resident husbands were also older than their 289 U.S.-born peers. None of the China-born married women with resident husbands was fifteen or younger, 3.3 percent were in the 16–20 age cohort, 29.4 percent were twenty-one to thirty years old, 33.8 percent were between the ages of thirty-one and forty, and 24.9 percent were forty-one to fifty. In contrast, among U.S.-born married women with resident husbands, one woman (0.3 percent) was fifteen or younger, 17.3 percent were aged sixteen to twenty, 60.9 percent were twenty-one to thirty, 19.7 percent were thirty-one to forty, and only 1.4 percent were between forty-one and fifty. The China-born married women without resident husbands were even older than those who had husbands living with them. These women were neither widowed nor divorced, but there is no way we will ever know where their husbands were at the time the census takers knocked on their doors. Widows and divorcees outnumbered them, but both groups had the largest clusters between twenty-six and sixty years of age.

Compared to San Francisco, the agricultural counties in 1900 had fewer women—981 versus 2,101 in San Francisco. Of the 981 women, 512 were born in China (52.2 percent of the total) and 469 were born in the United States (47.8 percent). That is, unlike the situation in San Francisco, China-born females were still a majority in agricultural California. Also, a smaller percentage of China-born women (15.0 percent) was single than their peers in San Francisco (18.3 percent). Conversely, the percentage of China-born married women with resident husbands was slightly larger (62.7 percent) than that in San Francisco (59.4 percent); so was the percentage of married women without resident husbands (13.1 versus 8.1 percent). However, the number and percentage of widows and divorcees in the agricultural counties were smaller than in the capital of Chinese America.

The 512 China-born women in the agricultural counties were older than those in San Francisco: 87.1 percent of the 77 single females were between twenty and sixty years of age, while 93.1 percent of the 321 married women with resident husbands were in the same age range. In contrast, among the 469 U.S.-born females, the 303 single girls and women composed 64.6 percent of the total, and of those, 90.1 percent ranged in age from newborn to fifteen years, compared to San Francisco's 71.8 percent. In other words, the immigrant females were older but the American-born ones were younger than their peers in San Francisco.

The mining and mountainous counties in 1900 had 220 females who were born in China (66.5 percent) and 111 who were born in the United States (33.5 percent). A larger percentage of the China-born was single

(21.4 percent) than in either San Francisco or agricultural California. Conversely, the percentages of married women, both with and without resident husbands, were smaller. The same pattern applies to U.S.-born females. The most notable characteristic of China-born women in these remote counties was their age: 80.9 percent were older than thirty. A set of computations I have made (but am not presenting in this chapter) indicates they had also been in the United States longer than their counterparts in San Francisco and the agricultural counties. Some of these older women were pioneers who had arrived in America in the 1850s and 1860s and apparently had chosen to stay and grow old in the locations to which they had grown accustomed. Some of them lived alone.

By 1910, there were living in San Francisco only 464 women and girls born in China and 865 women and girls born in the United States. Not only had men moved away, so had women in the aftermath of the earth's violent and destructive rumbles. The percentage of single females, both the China-born and the American-born, had fallen by 1910 to 16.8 and 63.7 percent, respectively, compared to 18.3 and 71.7 percent, respectively, in 1900. However, the proportion of 273 China-born married women with resident husbands (58.8 percent) was only a bit smaller than the 59.4 percent found in 1900. Among U.S.-born females, who as a group remained much younger than their China-born peers, the 246 married women with resident husbands made up 28.4 percent, compared to the 24.2 percent found among this group in 1900. For both subpopulations, the age distribution was more spread out, with smaller concentrations in each age cohort.

Unlike San Francisco, the agricultural counties saw a substantial increase in their Chinese female population between 1900 and 1910, just as the population of Chinese males had also increased. There were 1,627 women and girls there in 1910, compared to only 981 ten years earlier, of whom 527 were born in China (32.4 percent) and 1,100 in the United States (67.6 percent). A good portion of these women and girls probably would have been residing in San Francisco instead of in the agricultural counties had the 1906 earthquake not occurred. While the percentage of China-born single women decreased slightly, from 15.0 percent in 1900 to 12.7 percent in 1910, single females among the U.S.-born rose from 64.6 percent in 1900 to 68.3 percent in 1910. As was the case in San Francisco, both groups were more spread out across the entire age spectrum.

By 1910, the number of Chinese women and girls had become very small in the mining and mountainous counties. There were only 88 China-born women and girls (40.7 percent of the total) and 128 U.S.-born ones (59.3 percent). Given these small numbers, it serves little purpose to compare these numbers to those in the 1900 census except to note that only eight China-born single women, who ranged from thirty-one to over sixty years of age, still lived in this region. China-born married women with resident husbands numbered fifty-five, and 81.8 percent of them were older than thirty. Only ten married women with resident husbands were younger than thirty. No China-born single women, married women without resident husbands, or widows and divorcees were younger than thirty. Among the U.S.-born, 62.5 percent were single and none was older than twenty. The forty-one married women with resident husbands composed 32.0 percent of the whole. None of them was fifteen years or younger, four (9.8 percent) were between sixteen and twenty, while thirty-three (80.5 percent) were between twenty-one and forty years of age. Only four China-born married women with resident husbands (9.8 percent) were older than forty. There were six married women without resident husbands, who ranged in age from twenty-one to thirty, and only one widow or divorcee who was in her thirties. Thus, the more frontier-like a region was, the fewer Chinese girls (regardless of birth place), as well as U.S.-born women, lived there.

Marriage and Family Formation on American Soil

The next two sets of tables, 3.7A, 3.7B, 3.7C, 3.8A, 3.8B, and 3.8C, which cross-tabulate type of couple by the age gap between husbands and wives, indicate who married whom and what the age difference was in various combinations of husbands and wives. I divide couples with both spouses residing in the same households into four types: China-born men married to China-born women (type I), China-born men married to U.S.-born women (type II), U.S.-born men married to China-born women (type III), and U.S.-born men married to U.S.-born women (type IV).

In San Francisco in 1900, out of a total 829 coresident couples, type I households numbered 537; of these, 512 had older husbands (95.3 percent) and 25 had older wives (4.7 percent). Type I couples made up 64.8 percent of all couples with both spouses living in the same household. Couples made up of China-born husbands and U.S.-born wives (type II) numbered 228, of whom 224 (98.2 percent) had older husbands and only 4 (1.8 percent) had older wives. The third combination, U.S.-born husbands with China-born wives (type III), had barely made an appearance in 1900, with only eight couples in this category. This combination, however, would increase in coming years (such couples numbered seventy-three in 1910) for two reasons. First, older China-born men, who very likely had acquired more economic stability than their younger U.S.-born peers, apparently had a comparative advantage in winning the hands of U.S.-born young women. Second, U.S.-born men, who were American citizens by birth, could travel to China more easily than could China-born men to find wives because, theoretically at least, U.S. citizens had the right to reenter the United States after trips abroad. However, in reality, immigration officials placed many hurdles in their path despite their citizenship status. Still, the chances of U.S.-born men getting readmitted by immigration officials were greater than for those China-born men who did not belong to the exempted classes. But just because male American citizens of Chinese ancestry could wed in China did not mean they could bring their wives to the United States. That helps explain why relatively few of the U.S.-born married men had resident wives in the United States, as noted earlier. Couples made up of U.S.-born husbands with U.S.-born wives (type IV) numbered fifty-six, fifty (89.3 percent) of which had older husbands and six (10.7 percent) had older wives. Overall in San Francisco in 1900, 95.8 percent of all four types of couples combined had older husbands and 4.2 percent had older wives. In terms of birthplace, 766 husbands were China-born but only 544 wives were China-born. There were only 64 U.S.-born husbands but 284 U.S.-born wives, which means that a significant number of China-born men married U.S.-born women, in the process denying many U.S.-born men of potential U.S.-born mates.

Equally revealing is the age gap between husbands and wives. Among type I couples, 30.8 percent of the husbands, out of 512 couples in which the husbands were older, were more than fifteen years older than their wives. There was even one man who was more than forty years older than his wife. The largest age gap existed between China-born husbands and U.S.-born wives—that is, type II couples. Among them, 58.0 percent had husbands who were more than fifteen years older than their wives— that is, 20 percent higher than among type I couples. In type III and type IV couples, both of which had U.S.-born husbands, only one man was more than fifteen years older than his wife. The most likely explanation for the huge age gap among type II couples is that China-born single men, by the time they had saved up enough money to afford wives, were relatively old, but there were few immigrant women in their own age groups available. So, they married U.S.-born women and girls—who, as a group, were still very young.

The situation was only slightly different in the other regions of California. In the agricultural counties in 1900, 473 couples had both spouses residing in the same household. Of these, 322 (68.1 percent) were type I couples, 134 (28.3 percent) were type II couples, only 3 (0.6 percent) belonged to type III, and only 15 (3.2 percent) belonged to type IV. Even though there were approximately twice as many Chinese men in the agricultural counties as in San Francisco in both 1900 and 1910, the number of couples with both spouses present in the same household in the agricultural counties was less than three-fifths of the number in San Francisco. It appears that the urban environment of San Francisco facilitated spousal coresidence and family formation on American soil more than did conditions in agricultural California. Also, a larger fraction, 96.2 percent, of the husbands with resident wives in the agricultural counties were China-born, compared to 92.4 percent in San Francisco. As for wives, 325 (composing 68.6 percent) were born in China—a figure that is also slightly larger than the 65.7 percent in San Francisco.

The age gap among type I couples in agricultural California in 1900 was even larger than that in San Francisco: 36.4 percent of the husbands were more than fifteen years older than their wives, compared to 30.8 percent in San Francisco. However, among type II couples, only 53.1 percent of the husbands were more than fifteen years older than their wives, compared to 58.0 percent in San Francisco. The number of type III and type IV couples was so small as to make any calculations meaningless.

In the mining and mountainous counties in 1900, there were only 147 couples with both spouses present. Type I couples represented an even larger percentage (81.0 percent) of all couples in these remote areas than in San Francisco or the agricultural counties. The age gap was also slightly larger, with 37.9 percent of the husbands in type I couples being more than fifteen years older than their wives, compared to 30.8 percent in San Francisco and 36.4 percent in the agricultural counties. In contrast, among type II couples, fully 71.4 percent of the husbands were more than fifteen years older than their wives, which means that almost three-quarters of the aging China-born men had married very young U.S.-born girls. (I examine the women's age at marriage below.)

A decade later in San Francisco, the number of couples with both spouses present had fallen from 829 in 1900 to 512 in 1910—yet another reflection of the Chinese exodus as a result of the 1906 earthquake. The most significant change was an increase in the number of U.S.-born spouses, both men and women. Only 63.9 percent of the husbands were now China-born, compared to 92.4 percent ten years earlier, while 36.1 percent were U.S.-born, compared to 7.7 percent a decade earlier. As for the wives, 53.3 percent were China-born, compared to 65.7 percent in 1900, and 46.5 percent were U.S.-born, compared to 34.3 percent in 1900. Type I couples in 1910 represented only 38.5 percent of all couples, compared to 64.8 percent in 1900. The proportion of type II couples changed only a little: from 27.5 percent in 1900 to 25.4 percent in 1910. Type III and type IV couples showed the greatest growth—15.0 percent belonged to type III and 21.1 percent to type IV in 1910, compared to 1.0 percent and 6.7 percent, respectively, ten years earlier. No matter how one looks at the picture, members of the second generation who were coming of age represented a significant factor in family formation in San Francisco by 1910. The age gap remained large, however, in both type

I and type II couples. In the former, 29.6 percent of the husbands were more than fifteen years older than their wives, while in the latter, 53.1 percent were more than fifteen years older than their wives.

In the agricultural counties in 1910, there were 308 type I couples, representing 49.0 percent of all couples, in contrast to San Francisco, where only 38.5 percent of the couples belonged to type I in the same year. But compared to ten years earlier, the percentage of type I couples in the agricultural counties, which had stood at 68.1 percent in 1900, had declined significantly. Meanwhile, the proportion of type II couples had become slightly larger. Numbering 202, they made up 32.1 percent of all couples—a modest increase from the 28.3 percent in 1900. Both type III and type IV couples, in which the husbands were U.S.-born, also increased but to a far smaller extent than in San Francisco. Married immigrants with resident spouses, both men and women, therefore continued to form a majority of the couples among the Chinese population in agricultural California. China-born husbands still made up 81.1 percent of all husbands in the agricultural counties, compared to 63.9 percent in San Francisco the same year. The difference among women in the two regions, however, was much smaller: China-born wives formed 54.2 percent and U.S.-born wives 45.8 percent in the agricultural counties, compared to 53.5 and 46.5 percent, respectively, in San Francisco. In the intervening decade, the age gap narrowed somewhat in type I couples in the agricultural counties: only 31.4 percent of the husbands in 1910 (compared to 36.4 percent a decade earlier) were older than their wives by more than fifteen years. In contrast, the age gap between husbands and wives in type II couples had widened: 65.5 percent of the husbands were more than fifteen years older than their wives, compared to 53.1 percent ten years earlier. It appears that an even larger proportion of aging China-born men in agricultural California in 1910 were marrying very young U.S.-born girls than they had done in earlier years.

As the mining and mountain counties lost population in the interval between the 1900 and 1910 censuses, only ninety-three couples with coresident spouses were found there in 1910, 49.5 percent of whom belonged to type I, 31.2 percent to type II, 10.7 percent to type III, and 8.6 percent to type IV. As in the agricultural counties, China-born husbands and wives in the mining and mountain counties remained prominent, with 80.6 percent of the husbands and 60.2 percent of the wives being immigrants. Though these percentages are considerably smaller than those in 1900, they still included four-fifths of the men and three-fifths of the women. The age gap between husbands and wives in type I couples in these remote counties had decreased slightly: 33.4 percent of type I couples in 1910 were more than fifteen years older than their wives, compared to 37.9 percent a decade earlier. The age gap between spouses in type II couples, however, remained huge: 68.9 percent of the husbands were still more than fifteen years older than their wives.

Given the huge age gaps, I computed how old the women and girls were when they got married. The statistics in Tables 3.9A, 3.9B, 3.9C, 3.10A, 3.10B, and 3.10C, which cross-tabulate birthplace by age at marriage, confirm the picture painted in the last two sets of tables: a significant number of girls, especially those born in the United States, were married off at tender ages. However, perhaps unexpectedly, there was also a small number of women who did not marry until they were quite old. Age at marriage was not a question asked in the 1900 census; rather, the census enumerators wrote down how many years an individual had been married. But since the age of an individual was one of the things most consistently recorded, we can compute how old a person was when he or she married by deducting the number of years married from his or her age.

In looking at the number of presently married women (that is, women who were neither widowed nor divorced) in San Francisco in 1900, readers may be startled that thirty-two girls born in China were married *before* the age of thirteen, while thirteen U.S.-born girls were similarly wed. How was this possible? Did the census takers write down the wrong information? I do not think so because there was a culturally sanctioned practice in traditional China in which two families could betroth their children to one another when the children were still very young. For example, if a boy was born into a family and a girl was born into another family, around the same time or a few years later (and occasionally a few years earlier), the two families could negotiate to betroth the two young children to one another. The little girl would continue to live with her parents until she was six, seven, or eight years old—that is, until she was old enough to do housework. At that time, when she became useful as a little servant, she would be moved into the boy's home where she would be expected to help with household chores. After she began menstruating, her young husband would be encouraged—indeed, taught—to have sexual intercourse with her. If a baby was conceived, the girl could become a mother at age twelve or thirteen. This practice might have been transplanted to the United States by some Chinese, which offers a plausible explanation for the startling statistics.

In San Francisco in 1900, there were 621 China-born married women and 315 U.S.-born married women. (These numbers combine women with resident husbands and those without.)[4] They composed 66.3 percent and 33.6 percent, respectively, of all married women. Of the China-born wives, 17.3 percent married at age fifteen or younger; the comparable figure for U.S.-born wives is 26.7 percent. Thus, a larger proportion of U.S.-born girls than China-born ones married very, very young. In both groups, the most common age at marriage was between sixteen and twenty. Among

China-born wives, 44.2 percent married within that age interval. An even larger percentage of U.S.-born young women, 54.0 percent, married between the ages of sixteen and twenty. Combining the two age cohorts, 61.5 percent of China-born wives married before they turned twenty-one, while 80.7 percent of U.S.-born wives did so.

The median age at marriage of China-born young women was 18.5 years, which is not all that different from the American norm during that period of history. The median age of marriage for U.S.-born young women, however, was only 16.7 years—almost 2 years younger than their China-born peers. These figures, too, reflect the tremendous demand for nubile young women. Since it took a lot of money and effort to bring girls or brides from China during the exclusion era, it is not surprising that the pressure to marry young was exerted mainly on girls born in the United States. Were the older men who married them pedophiles? I do not think we can pass that judgment because it was necessity that led men who wanted resident wives to find brides wherever they could. In other words, neither the large age gap between spouses nor the existence of such a large percentage of very young brides among type II couples were manifestations of Chinese "culture." Rather, they reflect structural factors created by the exclusion laws.

As discussed earlier, in the agricultural counties in 1900 there were proportionately more China-born married women (71.5 percent) than was the case in San Francisco. Interestingly, the median age at marriage for both the China-born and American-born wives in the farming areas was older than those in San Francisco—20.5 years among the former and 17.3 years among the latter, compared to 18.5 and 16.7 years, respectively, in the big city. Only 14.8 percent of the China-born wives married at age fifteen or younger, compared to 17.3 percent in San Francisco. Among U.S.-born wives, 18.5 percent married at age fifteen or younger, compared to 26.7 percent in San Francisco. The percentage of China-born young women who married between the ages of sixteen and twenty was also smaller: 31.9 percent among China-born wives, compared to 44.2 percent in San Francisco. The percentages of U.S.-born young women who married between sixteen and twenty were about the same in the two geographic localities—53.5 percent in agricultural California and 54.0 percent in San Francisco.

Given that the percentage of China-born wives in the mining and mountainous counties in 1900 was larger (85.1 percent) than those in either San Francisco or the agricultural counties, and that China-born girls did not marry as young as U.S.-born ones did, it follows that the percentage of China-born wives who married at age fifteen or younger should be smaller than in the other two regions. Such indeed was the case. Of 181 married women, 85.1 percent were born in China and 14.9 percent were born in the United States. Only 9.7 percent of China-born wives living in the mining and mountain countries married at fifteen or younger, while 24.7 percent married between the ages of sixteen and twenty. That is, only slightly more than a third (34.4 percent) of China-born wives married before they turned twenty-one—a much smaller fraction than in either San Francisco or the agricultural regions. The median age at marriage was 26.0 years among China-born wives—an unexpected deviation from the situation in San Francisco or the agricultural counties. The "abnormality" of this group of women is fascinating and deserves more research.

Among U.S.-born wives in these remote mountainous areas, 25.9 percent were fifteen or younger when they married—a proportion similar to that in San Francisco (26.7 percent) but considerably larger than that in the agricultural counties (18.7 percent). However, 63.0 percent of U.S.-born wives married between the ages of sixteen and twenty, making a total of 88.9 percent who married before they turned twenty-one. Their median age at marriage was 16.7—fully ten years younger than their China-born sisters. Though they lived in a more isolated environment, it is apparent that American-born girls in the mining and mountainous counties did not escape the pressure to marry young.

Ten years later, the proportion of China-born wives living in San Francisco had decreased and that of U.S.-born wives conversely had increased. The most significant change between 1900 and 1910 is that the median age at marriage had increased for both groups. It was 20.3 years among China-born wives and 18.0 years among U.S.-born wives. Moreover, only 6.9 percent of China-born wives had married at age fifteen or younger, while only 7.5 percent of U.S.-born wives had married at the same tender ages. What had happened in the ten intervening years to bring about such a dramatic change? The 1911 Revolution and the 1919 May Fourth Movement in China, both of which led to significant changes in gender relations, had not yet occurred, so the change in Chinese America cannot be attributed to the influence of political and cultural developments emanating from China. Can structural factors in the United States help explain the change? Or did Chinese-ancestry families in America develop new attitudes regarding their daughters in terms of educating them, delaying their marriage, and even allowing young women to pursue careers? More research is required to come up with an empirically grounded answer. What did not change was the large cluster of young women, both China-born and U.S.-born, who married between the ages of sixteen and twenty: 51.3 percent among the former and 58.9 percent among the latter. That is, three-fifths or more of the young married women became wives before they turned twenty-one.

Changes in the agricultural counties were less dramatic. There, 11.8 percent of China-born wives and 15.1 percent of U.S.-born wives married at age fifteen or younger, compared to 14.8 and 18.7 percent, respectively, in 1900. The median age at marriage actually declined by a year among China-born wives (from 20.5 years in 1900 to 19.5 years in 1910), while that of U.S.-born wives remained almost the same (17.3 versus 17.6 years). Could it be that the women who remained in San Francisco after the earthquake tended to be those who had married at older ages while the girls who married young moved with their families across San Francisco Bay to the arable valleys and plains of California? Unless a substantial number of narrative sources are discovered in the future, this question can probably never be answered.

In the mining and mountainous counties, the median age at marriage of China-born wives had also decreased—by four years, a significant drop— from 26.0 years in 1900 to 22.0 years in 1910. However, the median age at marriage of U.S.-born wives increased a year, from 16.7 to 17.8 years. The reason(s) for this change, too, require(s) more research.

Now we come to the most interesting finding of all. If the prevailing master narrative of Chinese family formation is correct, then one would assume that type I couples, in which both husband and wife were born in China, must have married in China and that the husbands must have either brought their wives with them when they themselves crossed the Pacific Ocean or sent for them some years later. Census data indicate that was not what happened for a large majority of the women. In Tables 3.11A, 3.11B, 3.11C, 3.12A, 3.12B, and 3.12C, I separate those immigrant women who had married before they emigrated to America from those who had come to the United States *before* they married. Contrary to expectations, there were far more Chinese immigrant women who had come to the United States before they married—that is, they came as single women—than women who were already married when they arrived. This contradicts everything we have believed about this aspect of Chinese American history to date. I also separate the women with resident husbands from those without. There was little difference between the two groups, so I shall discuss them together.

In San Francisco in 1900, 62.3 percent of the married China-born women had come to the United States *before* they married, 10.7 percent had immigrated the same year as their marriage, while only 27.0 percent had married before they emigrated. Many of the women who entered the United States before they married had been in the United States for quite a number of years before they wed: 27.7 percent had been in the United States between one and five years before they married, 16.5 percent had been in the United States from six to ten years before they found husbands, and 15.2 percent had been in the United States for more than ten years before they became wives. In addition, 3.0 percent had been in the United States for an unknown number of years before they married—"unknown" because one of several figures needed to compute the number of years married or the number of years in the United States was not recorded by the census takers. In contrast, 13.4 percent of the wives had been married between one and five years before they came to the United States, 7.4 percent had been married from six to ten years before joining their husbands in America, while 6.3 percent had been married for more than ten years before coming to the United States. The median number of years in the United States before marriage is six, while the median number of years married before coming to the United States is 4.5 years.

Who were the single girls and women who braved more than a month of tossing waves to reach America? Under whose auspices did they come? Did they come of their own volition or were they brought here by family members or traffickers in women? What did they do after they landed? I know of no documentary evidence that will enable us to answer these questions systematically and definitively though a few scraps of anecdotal evidence may be found. At this point I can only hypothesize that some of these women, especially those who had been in the United States for many long years, had probably been brought to America when they were still young girls to work as prostitutes and *that* was how they managed to support themselves before they escaped from their bondage by running away, finding husbands, buying their freedom, or being discarded by their "owners," pimps, or madams because they had grown too old to lure enough customers to satisfy the greed of those who controlled and profited from their sexual labor. A small number even remained in prostitution after their marriage, usually as managers or owners of brothels. The manuscript censuses recorded the existence of quite a number of such women who ran brothels either on their own or with men whom census takers listed as their husbands or business partners. If I am correct, then the dichotomy that George A. Peffer has drawn between prostitutes and married women did not really exist.[5] In other words, quite a number of wives had once been prostitutes. So, when Peffer and others insist that we sing the praises of wives—women who finally brought a measure of respectability to Chinese American communities—they unwittingly are celebrating the tenacity and resourcefulness of former prostitutes. In short, the two groups of women form an overlapping continuum; they do not represent two distinct entities.

Turning to the agricultural counties in 1900, the percentage of married immigrant women who had been in the United States before marrying was even larger than that in San Francisco: 81.1 percent. Only 11.7 percent of the women were already married before they came to the United States. In these farming areas, only 7.3 percent of the women immigrated the same year as their marriage. Almost a quarter (24.9 percent) had been in the United States for one to five years before they wed, 21.2 percent had lived in America for six to ten years before finding husbands, 21.2 percent had been U.S. residents for more than ten years before they became wives, and

13.7 percent had been in America for an unknown number of years before marriage. In contrast, only 4.7 percent of married immigrant women had been married for one to five years before they came to the United States, 3.1 percent had been wives for six to ten years before crossing the Pacific Ocean, while 3.9 percent had been married for more than ten years before joining husbands in the United States.

The statistics for the mining and mountainous counties suggest a tangential answer to the question of who the China-born married women in the mining and mountain areas might have been. Fully 86.8 percent of them had come to the United States before marrying. The fact that their median age at marriage in 1900 was twenty-six years suggests that they had been working before they married. But what kind of work was available in those remote areas? Scholars who wish to minimize the prominence of prostitution in the history of Chinese women in America might argue, "They probably earned a living as seamstresses or laundresses." But the garment industry was centered in San Francisco, not in the foothills of the Sierra Nevada Mountains. It is highly unlikely that a woman could have survived by sewing or washing clothes in sparsely populated areas. The mining and mountainous counties include a vast swath of land contiguous to the northern and eastern borders of California. Just because we have countable numbers for those counties as a whole, in reality as few as one, or at most, a handful of Chinese women lived in each county. Not only were there few Chinese women, the entire population, male and female of all ethnic origins combined, in the mining and mountain counties was also small by 1900. To be sure, a Chinese woman might have earned a little money mending and washing the clothes of miners and lumberjacks, but could such a minimal income sustain her? I would argue not.

Thus, we are forced to the conclusion that these women most likely were originally taken to the mining camps to work as prostitutes. Though the surface gold ran out within a few years, Chinese miners remained in the mining areas for decades—far longer than members of any other ethnic group—reworking tailings (huge mounds of dirt and gravel that miners panning for gold removed from river beds and piled up along the banks of streams and rivers), combing through the morass with the hope of finding a little bit of gold dust still left there. So, when there was a sufficient number of these men, as was the case from the 1850s to the end of the nineteenth century, their visits to the lone Chinese woman or a handful of women in these remote areas easily could have sustained her or them. Not only Chinese men, but also men of other ethnic and racial origins, may have been customers. Taken to serve men who fanned out all over the areas where gold was found, some of these women apparently did not move to more urban settings or go back to China as they grew too old to ply their trade. Another small bit of evidence that suggests my hypothesis is at least plausible is that a number of the aging immigrant Chinese women enumerated in the mining areas were named "China Mary"—a generic name that European Americans gave all Chinese prostitutes.

Changes are discernible in all parts of California ten years later. The percentage of women who had been in the United States before they married had fallen to 49.9 percent in San Francisco in 1910, compared to 62.3 percent ten years earlier. Conversely, 39.9 percent of married immigrant women that year had been married before they arrived. That is, by the beginning of the second decade of the twentieth century, the picture began to conform more to the master narrative of Chinese family formation. Those who entered the United States the same year as their marriage amounted to 10.2 percent, only half a percent less than in 1900. The percentage of women who had been in the United States for one to five years before they wed had dropped to 11.7 percent, compared to 27.7 percent a decade earlier. The percentages of women who were U.S. residents for six to ten years, as well as those who had been in the United States for more than ten years before they married, had also declined to 9.0 percent and 6.3 percent, respectively. What increased greatly was the proportion of women, 22.8 percent, who did not tell census takers how many years they had been in the United States. So, it is not possible to calculate how many years they had resided in America before they married. These statistics reflect the fact that old-timers, both male and female, were dying out, while a fear of being deported very likely led many more women in 1910 than in 1900 to tell census takers as little about themselves as possible. Perhaps as a reflection of the increasing harshness with which the exclusion laws were implemented, a larger percentage of women, 12.6 percent in 1910 versus 6.3 percent in 1900, had to wait ten or more years after they married before emigrating to join their husbands in America.

The percentages of China-born women who came to the United States before they married remained considerably higher in the agricultural counties (65.0 percent), as well as in the mining and mountainous counties (77.4 percent), than in San Francisco. That means fewer already-married immigrant wives went to live in the state's hinterland after their arrival. Rather, it was women who were single when they arrived in the United States but later found husbands who settled in regions that did not have the hustle and bustle of San Francisco. In the former mining areas, in particular, perhaps they found a haven of sorts—modest little homesteads—where they preferred to live out their days.

WHERE DO WE GO FROM HERE?

Although my work on the census has taken years, the tantalizing statistical patterns and unanswered questions dictate that additional research in other bodies of documentary evidence be done. I have started going through Chinese Arrival Investigation Case Files on women and girls. So far, I have examined over a thousand files of both males and females detained for questioning in San Francisco from 1884 to 1889. As the files on Chinese men and women are placed in the same storage boxes, I have to examine those for the men and boys in order to discover whether there were differences between how Chinese females and males were treated. Like the other sources I am using, this part of the research is also time consuming. Erika Lee used a random sample of 600-plus files in her studies (see Chapter 1 in this volume and her award-winning book), but her data do not provide the exact ratio of females who were investigated relative to all the Chinese who were investigated. For the kind of specificity I seek, a 100 percent count is needed. To tease out the effects of the successive exclusion laws, a comparison of the statistical patterns before and after each law was passed must be done.

As I looked at the Chinese Arrival Investigation Case Files, I began to suspect that they did not include all the arriving Chinese because so many of the females and males investigated in the 1880s were still in their teens. There were also references such as "mother was landed" or "father entered on Custom House certificate number such and such" in the files of the youths, but no files existed for the older persons referred to. Surely, I conjectured, there must have been older individuals who also tried to enter. Therefore, I decided to examine both the arriving and departing Chinese passenger lists that all ship captains had to submit to immigration officials during the exclusion era, in order to compute what percentage of the arriving passengers was female. I discovered that those Chinese who were investigated, at least in the 1880s, constituted only a small fraction of all the Chinese passengers who came to San Francisco. To figure out what percentage of females was detained and investigated, I must tally the information in the passenger lists and compare it to the data culled from the Chinese Arrival Investigation Case Files.

The passenger lists are even more difficult to work with than the manuscript censuses. The standardized forms the captains used did not contain a column for sex. Consequently, one must rely on other clues to find the minuscule number of women and girls traveling back and forth between China and America. Among the clues is the fact that ship captains sometimes made notations, such as "Mrs.," "with her husband," "to join her husband," "with her mother," "with her father," "with her aunt," that enable researchers to ascertain that the individuals in question were female. But there very well could have been other women and girls with no notations alongside their names. Unfortunately, we cannot determine if a Chinese individual is male or female simply by looking at his or her given (first) name because Chinese do not use ready-made given names that reveal the sex of the person. Rather, parents, grandparents, or other elders choose Chinese characters they favor and bestow those names on newborn babies. While it is true that certain Chinese written characters have a feminine connotation, they do not always guarantee that persons bearing them are female.

Some, but not all, captains provided a statistical breakdown of the Chinese passengers on their ships. They usually gave the total number of Chinese who wished to land in San Francisco and the number who were in transit. They also usually summarized how many persons were allowed to land based on type of certificate or some other criteria. But only a small number of captains bothered to count the Chinese female and male passengers separately, which means that searching for and finding Chinese female passengers takes far more effort than locating Chinese women and girls in the manuscript censuses.

Transit passengers passing through the port of San Francisco were headed for other places in the U.S. hinterland, for Victoria in British Columbia, for Port Townsend, Tacoma, and Seattle in the Puget Sound area, for Honolulu (yes—Chinese bound for Honolulu had to come to San Francisco first, where they boarded other ships that would take them to Hawaii), Mexican ports (usually Guyamas and Mazatlan), and Panama, from which locality some transferred to yet other ships to get to Peru. Other Panama-bound passengers disembarked on the Pacific side of the isthmus and traveled overland to the Atlantic shore, whence they boarded other boats destined for Havana, Cuba. The passenger lists, when tabulated and analyzed, will provide the most extensive and systematic documentary evidence available on the transnational journeys of the Chinese living in the Americas. That is why this eyesight-destroying and mind-numbing task must be undertaken.

Thus far, I have looked through the microfilms containing the Chinese arriving passenger lists from 1884 (the earliest ones microfilmed) to 1889. Even a cursory look—that is, without doing an actual count—makes it obvious that the 1888 Scott Act, which abrogated the provision in the 1882 Chinese Exclusion Act that had allowed laborers who obtained certificates to be readmitted after visits to China, was a far more effective deterrent to Chinese immigration than any laws passed earlier. The number of Chinese destined for San Francisco per se plummeted in late 1888. That does not mean, however, that the Chinese passenger traffic ceased. In fact, it remained voluminous but a vast majority of the passengers after late 1888 were persons in transit.

Some Chinese Arrival Investigation Case Files contained the case numbers of individuals who petitioned for writs of habeas corpus with the hope of being admitted into the United States. The passenger arrival lists also show court case numbers. Unfortunately, these numbers were written on top of other information, making it well nigh impossible to read the second layer of writing superimposed on the first. However, the case numbers offer the only sure way to link the information found in one body of evidence to that in another. It is impossible to identity the same individuals listed in different databases simply by looking at their names because Chinese names were transliterated in the most haphazard manner. For example, one young woman was named Hawn Mok in one document but Hong Ah Mock in another. I can be certain the two names referred to the same person only because the court case number jotted down on the two types of documents was the same.

The unpublished records of cases filed in the district courts of northern and southern California and the Circuit Court of Appeals for the Ninth Circuit will reveal the outcome of writs of habeas corpus and other cases submitted by Chinese female petitioners. The unpublished court records are far more voluminous than the published ones that I analyzed in my essay "The Exclusion of Chinese Women, 1870–1943." Even though Christian Fritz and Lucy Salyer have discussed the relative success the Chinese enjoyed by counting who was landed, discharged, refused, denied, or disapproved (all terms used by immigration and court officials), they did not separate the female petitioners and plaintiffs from the male.[6] To arrive at an accurate count of how many females went to court and the outcomes of their efforts, it is necessary to go through the files for both men and women in order to pick out the ones pertaining to women.

Some colleagues will no doubt fault me for my "California-centric" study, but I focus on California out of necessity. The available nonnarrative sources are so voluminous that it is impossible (until someone gets a huge grant someday to input all the pertinent data into computers) to cover more ground. Even when the myriad bodies of documentary evidence have been computerized, given the random transliterations used for Chinese names, it will still be impossible to say definitively what documents in the various databases pertained to which individuals. However, confining my study to California is not as limited as it may seem because California is a large state with many regional variations. By dividing the state into several geographic regions, as is done in this chapter, and by comparing the changes from one census year to the next or from the passage of one Chinese exclusion law to the next, it is possible to show that the experiences of Chinese women in California were by no means homogeneous. There were variations across both space and time—a fact that will allow a more nuanced tale to be told. The statistics presented in this chapter indicate that much of the existing historical writings on Chinese women and girls need to be challenged and modified. Though wringing a story out of numbers is difficult, it does offer its own rewards.

Appendix A:
How California's Counties
Are Grouped

In this study, I divide California into three regions: the city and county of San Francisco, agricultural regions, and mining and mountain regions. Before the advent of what are now called "statistical metropolitan areas," the Census Bureau used counties, and within them, townships, cities, enumeration districts, or assembly districts to divide up the state for the purpose of census taking. However, the political boundaries of California's counties do not coincide neatly with its geographic and economic features, so there is a degree of arbitrariness in what counties I have grouped together under "agricultural" and "mining and mountain." Especially problematic are Tehama, Butte, Yuba, Placer, Madera, Fresno, and Tulare counties that had both gold mining and farming. The rule of thumb I use is to place those counties dominated by gold mining in the state's early history in the "mining and mountain" category even though they also contained arable land and no longer produce gold today. "Mountain" counties are contiguous with "mining" counties, so they are placed under the same category.

San Francisco The geographic boundaries of the city and county of San Francisco are coterminous. The tallies for San Francisco include all Chinese in the city and county and not just those living in Chinatown.

Agricultural Agricultural counties include all coastal counties (except Del Norte, which is grouped under "mining and mountain" because gold was mined there), those in the Sacramento Valley, the San Francisco Bay area, the San Joaquin Valley, and the interior counties south of the Tehachapi Mountains. The term *agricultural* refers to farming, animal husbandry, and lumbering. The thirty-seven counties lumped under "agricultural," in alphabetical order, are:

Alameda, Colusa, Contra Costa, Fresno, Glenn, Humboldt, Imperial, Kern, Kings, Lake, Los Angeles, Madera, Marin, Mendocino, Merced, Monterey, Napa, Orange, Riverside, Sacramento, San Benito, San Bernardino, San Diego, San Joaquin, San Luis Obispo, San Mateo, Santa

Barbara, Santa Clara, Santa Cruz, Solano, Sonoma, Stanislaus, Sutter, Tehama, Tulare, Ventura, and Yolo. Chinese there engaged in a variety of occupations.

MINING AND MOUNTAIN Mining and mountain counties sweep in an arc from Del Norte County in the northwestern corner of the state eastward across its northern border with Oregon and then southward along its eastern border with Nevada. The mining counties were very prosperous from the beginning of the gold rush until the late 1860s. The mountain counties are of little economic importance. Even though they are the most remote regions of California, Chinese were found in almost all of these counties. The twenty counties lumped under "mining and mountain," in alphabetical order, are:

Alpine, Amador, Butte, Calaveras, Del Norte, El Dorado, Inyo, Lassen, Mariposa, Modoc, Mono, Nevada, Placer, Plumas, Shasta, Sierra, Siskiyou, Trinity, Tuolumne, and Yuba.

Appendix B: Occupational Categories

THE CHINESE IN CALIFORNIA engaged in hundreds of occupations, which means it is impossible to list all of them in statistical tables. To make the "raw" data manageable, I created occupational categories that I first used in my book, *This Bittersweet Soil* (*TBS*),[1] which differ from those used by the Census Bureau (see *TBS*, p. 430–31, note 12, for a discussion of how my categories diverge from those used by the Census Bureau). The occupational categories used in this chapter, in turn, differ slightly from those in *TBS* because the goals of the two studies are not the same. *TBS* is primarily an economic study, whereas this chapter is a social-demographic study that focuses on marital relationships.

In the present study, I separate professionals from artisans, whereas I had grouped them together in *TBS*, in order to see whether men in the two occupational categories differed with regard to marital status and the presence of wives in the United States. Though I use the term *artisan*, I know it is problematic because in the late nineteenth and early twentieth centuries, the line between "artisans" and "factory workers" was not clear. I classify people who gain their skills through apprenticeships, work alone or with just a handful of others, and have some control over the social conditions of their labor as "artisans" and reserve the term *factory workers* for those employed in industrial environments where they work in large groups and have little control over their working conditions. The word *industrial* is also problematic in the California context because in addition to the manufacturing that occurs within factories, the agribusiness sectors of California agriculture are also organized industrially. Thus, I count fruit packers and cannery workers as factory workers even though the goods they handle are products of agriculture, but I count fruit pickers as agricultural laborers. When workers can or pack fruit, they are in fact processing them just as factory workers process or manufacture nonagricultural products. To take another example, I count brick makers, brick molders, and brickyard laborers as factory workers, but count brick masons as artisans as the latter build houses using bricks that others have made.

I divide individuals who carry on various kinds of business into "merchants" and "other businessmen" in this chapter because the Chinese exclusion laws and the immigration officials who enforced them defined "merchants" narrowly. According to immigration officials, only those who conducted business at fixed addresses under their own names could be considered "merchants." In contrast, in *TBS*, I had lumped all those who carried on some kind of business as merchants, which had a subcategory for what I call "providers of recreational vices" (brothel owners, gamblers, and opium dealers). In this chapter, I group providers of recreational vices, along with individuals buying and selling a wide array of merchandise and services, under "other businessmen" as their numbers were declining by the early twentieth century (the chronological focus of this chapter) and they no longer need to be singled out.

I put laundrymen and ironers into their own category as there were so many of them. The class status of laundrymen is amorphous: they can be counted as "entrepreneurs," as I did in *TBS*, because most of them were partners, and not wageworkers, in laundry shops (a kind of business enterprise), or as "nonagricultural laborers," because their lives of toil differed little from those of other laborers, or as "providers of personal services," because washing clothes served the daily needs of other people. I also place cooks into a category of their own, instead of listing them under "providers of personal services," as I did in *TBS*, again because their number was so large and many of them lived in the households of their employers and thus existed in a different kind of social milieu than did other Chinese. Cooks were true pioneers: they were often the only Chinese in remote areas.

I had grouped students, miscellaneous occupations, and no occupation into a single category in *TBS*, but in this chapter I give students a category of their own because they were among the "exempted classes" under the Chinese exclusion laws and I wanted to see how many immigrant students there were. (As it turns out, a vast majority of the students were American-born.) I place people who cannot be put into any of the occupational categories under "miscellaneous," separating them from those whose occupational column was left blank by census takers. I place the latter under "no occupation."

The statistics in this chapter do not coincide with those found in *TBS* for three additional reasons. First, in the present study I separate men and women because I am interested in gender, age, marital status, Chinese family formation on American soil, and the impact of female migration on these variables, while I had not segregated the Chinese population by sex in *TBS*. Second, I divide the Chinese by birthplace—something I did not do in *TBS*—in order to see how those born in China differed demographically and socially from the ones born in the United States. Third, the tallies in *TBS* were of selected counties only (the footnotes at the bottom of the tables in *TBS* identify what counties are included in each table) but the computations in this chapter cover all the counties of California.

PRIMARY PRODUCERS AND EXTRACTORS earn a living by working with the natural resources of the earth. They include agriculturalists (I use this word instead of "farmers" because agriculturalists is a broader term), agricultural laborers, fishermen, and miners.

Agriculturalists: chicken ranchers, farmers, fruit farmers or growers, gardeners (who were truck gardeners growing vegetables and small fruit and *not* individuals who took care of other people's lawns and yards), orchardists, poultry raisers, and vineyardists.

Agricultural laborers: bush choppers, farm laborers, fertilizers, fruit laborers, fruit pickers, hop laborers, sheepherders, vineyard laborers, winery laborers, and woodchoppers.

Fishermen: fishermen and shrimpers.

Miners: gold miners and miners of other metals and minerals.

PROFESSIONALS are people who gained their specialized skills through some kind of education. Some of the occupations used by census enumerators are redundant (for example, doctors and physicians or interpreters and linguists) but they are shown separately below in order to take into account the specificity of the terms that census takers used. Professionals include actors, bookkeepers, Buddhist priests, clergymen, copyists, dentists, doctors, drugstores (these refer not to modern American drugstores but to doctors practising Chinese herbal medicine), druggists, fortune-tellers, interpreters, journalists, letter writers, linguists, musicians, newspapermen, nurses, photographers, physicians, preachers, priests, teachers, temple keepers, and treasurers.

SKILLED ARTISANS are people who learned to make things by serving as apprentices of individuals already skilled in those crafts. They include bakers, bean cake makers, bed makers, block fixers, boot makers, brick masons, butchers, cage makers, candle makers, carpenters, chair repairers, coffin makers, dressmakers, dye and stencil cutters, electrical works workers, fishnet makers, glazers, harness makers, ivory turners, jewelers, lace makers, lantern makers, locksmiths, mechanics, overalls makers, painters, paper binders, pipe makers, plumbers, printers, railroad repairmen, roofers, rope makers, shoemakers, silversmiths, soap makers, solderers, stonemasons, tailors, tanners, tent makers, tinsmiths, umbrella makers, watchmakers, watch repairers, whip makers, and wood carvers.

ENTREPRENEURS AND THEIR ASSISTANTS are people who carry on various kinds of business for profit while their assistants help sell merchandise and keep the stores orderly. They include merchants, other businessmen (including factory owners), clerks and shop assistants, factory workers, and agents and supervisors.

Merchants: food merchants, dry-goods stores or merchants, grocers, merchants, stores, storekeepers, and traders.

Other businessmen: bankers, boarding house keepers, boot factory owners, bowling alley keepers, broom factory owners, brothel keepers, capitalists, chicken dealers, cigar dealers, cigar factory owners, cigar merchants, clothes peddlers, company officials or presidents, confectioners, crockery store owners, dealers (merchandise not specified), fish dealers, fish markets, fish peddlers, fowl dealers, fruit buyers, fruit dealers, fruit peddlers, furniture dealers, (professional) gamblers, garment factory owners, gymnasium keepers, joss dealers, junk merchants, labor contractors, landlords, leather dealers, liquor dealers, lodging house keepers, market men, moneylenders, opium cellar operators, opium dealers, opium merchants, pawnbrokers, peanuts dealers, peddlers, pimps, poultry dealers, real estate agents, restaurant owners or proprietors or keepers, sewing factory owners, shoe factory owners, shoe store owners, speculators, stationery men, tea stores, tobacco leaf dealers, undertakers, vegetable peddlers, and wood and charcoal dealers.

Clerks and shop assistants: cashiers, clerks, phone operators, salesmen, and secretaries.

Factory workers: box factory workers, brick makers, brick molders, brickyard workers, broom makers, broom factory workers, can makers, candle factory workers, canners, cannery workers, cigar box makers, cigar factory workers, cigar makers, coffee packing house workers, collar factory workers, cotton factory workers, factory workers, fish canners, fish cannery workers, flour mill workers, fruit canners, fruit cutters, fruit packers, fuse factory workers, gum factory workers, hair works workers, jute mill workers, machine operators, match factory workers, match makers, mill laborers, paper mill workers, powder works workers, sack sewers, sack factory workers, sawmill workers, sewing factory workers, shoe factory workers, sugar factory workers, sulphur dippers, tannery workers, woolen mill workers, and woolers.

Agents and supervisors: brokers, cannery bosses, collectors, contractors, foremen, gas company agents, head hoppers (men in charge of hop picking), inspectors, intelligence officers, managers, and vineyard overseers.

LAUNDRYMEN are people who wash and iron clothes. They include ironers, laundry helpers, laundrymen, and washers.

COOKS are people who prepare meals in restaurants, work sites of various kinds, and private homes. They include cooks, cook's helpers, farm cooks, and hotel cooks.

OTHER PERSONAL SERVICES PROVIDERS facilitate the daily living of others. They include barbers, dishwashers, errand boys, hotel laborers, janitors, porters, restaurant workers, saloon cleaners, servants, waiters, and watchmen.

NONAGRICULTURAL LABORERS are people who earn a living by using their muscle power. They generally do not acquire their occupational skills through education or long apprenticeships. They include animal gut cleaners, chair cleaners, coal heavers, day laborers, draymen, drivers, firemen, fowl cleaners, handymen, laborers, longshoremen, packers (merchandise not specified), railroad laborers, sailors, scavengers, scruffers, seamen, salt works laborers, sewer [cleaning] workers, ship [furnace] stokers, steamboat workers, teamsters, truck drivers, wagon drivers, and window washers.

MISCELLANEOUS include people listed as having their "own income," patients (in hospitals), and prisoners.

NO OCCUPATION are people for whom the census takers did not write down an occupation, children who were not listed as students, those who were "at home," and retirees.

STUDENTS include individuals "at school," pupils, and students.

Appendix C:
Numerical Discrepancies

ALERT READERS MAY NOTICE some discrepancies in the numbers shown in the various tables in this chapter. Since the differences are small and it would take several months to do a recount, I shall simply discuss the reasons for the differences. Even more importantly, a recount will not ensure that the new numbers are more accurate. In the past, while creating the tables in *This Bittersweet Soil*, I tallied some data three times, because the first and second counts did not agree, but I came up with yet another figure after doing the third tally. Anyone who has done research in the microfilmed manuscript censuses will understand why it is so difficult to get "hard" numbers. Extracting raw data from the microfilmed manuscript censuses is labor-intensive, tedious, and mind-numbing work because the handwriting of the various enumerators differs greatly and the ink on many pages had already faded so much by the time the books were microfilmed that many pages, sections of pages, lines, or words are illegible. Because eye fatigue develops within two or three hours of peering at murky microfilmed material, it is easy to miss a Chinese here and there. Another problem is that getting census information from the Chinese was a daunting task because of the language barrier between the Chinese, most of whom did not speak English well or at all, and census enumerators, who had no or only a minimal mastery of the Chinese language. Not only that, but many dialects of Chinese were spoken, which further complicated matters. Equally problematic, Chinese who lived during the exclusion era mistrusted outsiders, especially individuals representing various government agencies. Thus, some census takers either failed to ask for the needed information or the enumerated Chinese chose not to provide the requested information or, in some instances, really did not know the answers.

However, these problems do *not* render the manuscript censuses worthless despite the criticisms that scholars such as George A. Peffer have leveled at them. In my opinion, the manuscript censuses are, in fact, among the most important sources of historical information we have about the Chinese in the United States during the latter half of the nineteenth century and the first half of the twentieth. The loss of the 1890 manuscript census schedules in 1921 in a fire that burned down the building where they were stored is especially tragic—at least to scholars interested in studying the demographic effects of the 1882, 1884, and 1888 Chinese exclusion laws on the Chinese community in America. To be sure, we can compare the pictures painted in the 1880 and 1900 manuscript censuses, but a twenty-year gap is unfortunate for a period when the Chinese American world changed significantly as a result of the 1882 exclusion law and its successive amendments.

Having worked with census materials for three decades, I believe that the raw data culled from the manuscript censuses are generally reliable because the internal evidence is quite consistent. For example, if an individual enumerated in 1900 was 15 years old, and she or he was listed as having been born in 1885 or 1886, then we know the information on her or his age and year of birth must both be correct. (I say 1885 *or* 1886 because Chinese count a person's age from the time of conception, not birth. Some Chinese also add a year to a child's age when the baby greets his or her first Chinese New Year.) Even some information that I initially thought must be incorrect turned out to be plausible. For example, I noticed that some individuals who were listed as having been born in California or another locality in the United States also had information on their years of immigration. I assumed such information must be wrong as I was not fully cognizant of the extraordinary mobility of the Chinese. I foolishly assumed that if a person was born in the United States, he or she could not have been an "immigrant." However, when I started going through the Chinese Arrival Investigation Case Files for the 1880s (I have not yet plumbed the voluminous files generated in later years), I discovered that most of the individuals investigated in the 1880s, both male and female, were teenagers, who claimed to have been born in California or some other place in the United States and who said they were taken to China when they were young children and were now trying to reenter the United States as "natives." Thus, they did "immigrate" in that sense. In other words, they thought of themselves as being both "natives" and "immigrants."

Doing numerous cross-checks, I have pinpointed the reasons for the discrepancies in the data presented in the tables in this study. The totals in the various tables are off only a little, but the component parts of the tables sometimes vary more. The errors came from placing individuals in the wrong birthplace columns: apparently, some born in China were placed in the "born in U.S." column and vice versa. The number of China-born married men with resident wives in San Francisco in 1900 is given as 736 in Table 3.3A, plus 13 whom I did not include in the computations, making a total of 749. In addition, there were 72 U.S.-born married men with resident wives, giving a grand total of 821. Table 3.5A, which shows the number of married women with resident husbands, has 538

China-born women and 289 U.S.-born women, making a total of 827. Thus, the difference between the total number of husbands and the total number of wives is only six. One might initially assume there must have been a miscount, but that is not the only possible reason for the difference. There were Chinese, both male and female, who had non-Chinese spouses, most of whom were European Americans, but a handful had "Mexican" or "Spanish" wives while one Chinese woman was married to an African American man from Tennessee. Because I tallied only Chinese men and women and boys and girls in this study, I did not include their non-Chinese spouses. There were also men with two, and in a few cases, three resident wives. For that reason, the totals for men and women do not always coincide. Moreover, I left out individuals with missing data in some of the tables. For example, if an individual has information on her age, birthplace, and marital status but not the number of years she has been married, she is included in the table that cross-tabulates age by marital status, but not in the table that cross-tabulates birthplace by age at marriage.

In the agricultural counties in 1900, if we add the individuals who were not included in the computations in Tables 3.3B and 3.5B (their numbers are indicated in the footnotes to those tables), there is no discrepancy: 468 men (454 born in China and 14 born in the U.S.) with resident wives and 468 women (321 born in China and 147 born in the U.S.) with resident husbands. In the mining/mountain counties in 1900, the respective numbers are 143 for men (139 born in China and 4 born in the U.S.) versus 147 for women (122 born in China and 25 born in the U.S.) Similarly, in 1910, the discrepancy in San Francisco is 517 married men (335 born in China and 182 born in the U.S.) with resident wives versus 519 women with resident husbands (273 born in China and 246 born in the U.S.), the difference in the agricultural counties is 634 men (515 + 119) versus 633 women (341 + 292), while the difference in the mining/mountain counties is 94 men (76 + 18) versus 96 women (55 + 41).

To look at another seeming discrepancy, if we compare Tables 3.5A and 3.9A, the total number of married women (adding together those with resident husbands and those without) in San Francisco in 1900 is 932 (611 born in China and 321 born in the U.S.) in Table 3.5A, but 936 (621 born in China and 315 born in the U.S.) in Table 3.9A. That is to say, though there is a difference of ten between the number of China-born married women counted (611 in Table 3.5A versus 621 in Table 3.9A), and a difference of six between the number of U.S.-born married women counted (321 in Table 3.5A versus 315 in Table 3.9A), the differences partly cancel each other out, yielding an overall discrepancy of only four. In the agricultural counties in 1900, the discrepancy is 549 men (388 born in China and 161 born in the U.S.) shown in Table 3.5B versus 547 women

(392 born in China and 155 born in the U.S.) shown in Table 3.9B, a difference of only two. In the mining/mountain counties in 1900, the difference is 178 men (151 born in China and 27 born in the U.S.) in Table 3.5C versus 181 women (154 born in China and 27 in the U.S.) in Table 3.9C, a difference of only three. The discrepancies in the 1910 data are similarly small. The totals for San Francisco are 615 in both Tables 3.6A and 3.10A. However, their component parts differ: 327 + 288 versus 335 + 280, respectively. The corresponding totals for the agricultural counties in 1910 are 722 men (402 + 320) in Table 3.6B and 720 women (408 + 312) in Table 3.10B, a difference of only two. The mining/mountain counties show 109 men (62 + 47) in Table 3.6C and 110 women (62 + 48) in Table 3.10C, a difference of only one.

Other comparisons can be made, but this discussion should suffice to show that even though the total Chinese population was definitely undercounted for the reasons just discussed and small discrepancies exist in the individual tallies, we can nevertheless conclude that an analysis based on such numbers does offer a reliable demographic overview of the entire Chinese population in the early decades of the twentieth century in California.

TABLE 3.1A. Chinese Men and Boys: Birthplace and Marital Status by Occupational Category, Number and Percentage in Each Occupational Category

City and County of San Francisco, 1900

Occupational Category	Born in China								Born in U.S.								Oth BP	
	Single		Married		Wid/Div		MS Unk		Single		Married		Wid/Div		MS Unk		All MS	
	No.	%	No.	%	No.	%	No.	%	No.	%	No.	%	No.	%	No.	%	No.	%
Primary Producers and Extractors																		
Agriculturalists	19	0.6	47	0.8	1	1.05	0	0	3	0.2	0	0	0	0	0	0	0	0
Agric. laborers	64	1.9	65	1.1	7	7.4	5	1.6	6	0.4	0	0	0	0	0	0	0	0
Fishermen	31	0.9	27	0.5	0	0	13	4.1	0	0	0	0	0	0	0	0	0	0
Miners	5	0.2	14	0.2	1	1.05	1	0.3	0	0	0	0	0	0	0	0	0	0
Professionals	95	2.9	359	6.2	7	7.4	3	1.0	20	1.3	16	4.3	0	0	0	0	0	0
Skilled Artisans	162	4.9	476	8.2	6	6.3	12	3.8	43	2.7	22	6.6	0	0	0	0	0	0
Entrepreneurs and Their Assistants																		
Merchants	167	5.0	784	13.6	3	3.2	10	3.2	61	3.9	44	13.1	0	0	0	0	0	0
Other businessmen	178	5.4	478	8.3	1	1.1	6	1.9	22	1.4	20	6.0	0	0	0	0	0	0
Clerks and shop assistants	46	1.4	159	2.7	1	1.1	1	0.3	33	2.1	25	7.5	0	0	0	0	0	0
Factory workers	471	14.2	928	16.0	24	25.3	61	19.4	108	6.8	35	10.4	2	33.3	0	0	0	0
Agents and supervisors	11	0.3	65	1.1	2	2.1	0	0	2	0.1	5	1.5	0	0	0	0	0	0
Laundrymen	819	24.7	915	15.8	9	9.5	43	13.7	247	15.6	63	18.8	0	0	2	16.7	0	0
Cooks	489	14.7	628	10.9	10	10.5	53	16.9	106	6.7	39	11.6	1	16.7	0	0	0	0
Other Personal Services	390	11.7	355	6.1	12	12.6	10	3.2	151	9.5	37	11.0	2	33.3	2	16.7	0	0

City and County of San Francisco, 1900

Occupational Category	Born in China								Born in U.S.								Oth BP	
	Single		Married		Wid/Div		MS Unk		Single		Married		Wid/Div		MS Unk		All MS	
	No.	%	No.	%	No.	%	No.	%	No.	%	No.	%	No.	%	No.	%	No.	%
Nonagricultural Laborers	326	10.2	448	7.7	9	9.5	20	6.4	86	5.4	24	7.2	1	16.7	5	41.7	0	0
Miscellaneous	2	0.1	3	0.1	0	0	0	0	4	0.3	0	0	0	0	0	0	0	0
No Occupation	18	0.5	27	0.5	2	2.1	76	24.2	343	21.7	2	0.6	0	0	3	25.0	0	0
Students	28	0.5	4	0.1	0	0	0	0	349	22.0	3	0.9	0	0	0	0	0	0
Total	3,321	99.9	5,782	99.9	95	100.0	314	100.0	1,584	100.1	335	100.0	6	100.0	12	100.1	0	0

	Born in China	Born in U.S.	Total
Total number of Chinese males	9,512	1,937	11,449
Number with known marital status	9,198	1,925	11,123
Number who have ever been married (married + divorced + widowed)	5,877	341	6,218
Number who are presently married	5,782	335	1,117
Number who divorced/widowed	95	6	101
Number who are single	3,321	1,584	4,905

	Born in China	Born in U.S.
Presently married males as a percentage of those with known marital status	62.9%	17.4%
Divorced + widowed males as a percentage of those with known marital status	1.0%	0.3%
Single males as a percentage of those with known marital status	36.1%	82.3%
	100.0%	100.0%

Source: Author's tally and computation from the 1900 manuscript census of population. For a list of which occupations are grouped under each occupational category, see Appendix B at the end of Chapter 3.

Abbreviations: Wid = widowed; Div = divorced; MS = marital status; Unk = unknown; Other BP = birthplace other than China or the U.S.

TABLE 3.1B. Chinese Men and Boys: Birthplace and Marital Status by Occupational Category, Number and Percentage in Each Occupational Category

Agricultural Counties in California, 1900

Occupational Category	Born in China								Born in U.S.								Oth BP	
	Single		Married		Wid/Div		MS Unk		Single		Married		Wid/Div		MS Unk		All MS	
	No.	%	No.	%	No.	%	No.	%	No.	%	No.	%	No.	%	No.	%	No.	%
Primary Producers and Extractors																		
Agriculturalists	791	6.3	794	8.7	31	8.2	51	12.7	16	1.5	10	7.5	0	0	0	0	0	0
Agric. laborers	3,854	30.7	2,411	26.5	148	39.1	155	38.4	119	11.1	11	8.2	0	0	1	6.7	0	0
Fishermen	140	1.1	62	0.7	4	1.1	0	0	15	1.4	1	0.7	0	0	0	0	0	0
Miners	159	1.3	66	0.7	4	1.1	11	2.7	0	0	0	0	0	0	0	0	0	0
Professionals	54	0.4	134	1.5	6	1.6	0	0	10	1.0	5	3.7	0	0	0	0	1	33.3
Skilled Artisans	99	0.8	119	1.3	3	0.8	1	0.2	9	0.8	1	0.7	0	0	0	0	0	0
Entrepreneurs and Their Assistants																		
Merchants	330	2.6	777	8.5	13	3.4	11	2.7	15	1.4	11	8.2	1	25.0	0	0	0	0
Other businessmen	369	2.9	372	4.1	9	2.4	2	0.5	17	1.6	2	1.5	0	0	0	0	0	0
Clerks and shop assistants	84	0.7	135	1.5	3	0.8	0	0	17	1.6	2	1.5	0	0	0	0	0	0
Factory workers	227	1.8	84	0.9	5	1.3	1	0.2	16	1.5	1	0.7	0	0	0	0	0	0
Agents and supervisors	22	0.2	32	0.4	0	0	0	0	3	0.3	0	0	0	0	0	0	0	0
Laundrymen	1,253	10.0	1,070	11.7	15	3.9	25	6.2	106	9.9	25	18.7	1	25.0	1	6.7	0	0
Cooks	2,066	16.5	1,244	13.6	61	16.1	29	7.2	190	17.7	30	22.4	1	25.0	1	6.7	2	66.7
Other Personal Services	468	3.7	278	3.0	10	2.6	3	0.7	86	8.0	13	9.7	0	0	0	0	0	0

Agricultural Counties in California, 1900

Occupational Category	Born in China								Born in U.S.								Oth BP	
	Single		Married		Wid/Div		MS Unk		Single		Married		Wid/Div		MS Unk		All MS	
	No.	%	No.	%	No.	%	No.	%	No.	%	No.	%	No.	%	No.	%	No.	%
Nonagricultural Laborers	2,408	19.2	1,434	15.7	61	16.1	63	15.6	83	7.8	15	11.2	0	0	8	53.3	0	0
Miscellaneous	57	0.5	22	0.2	1	0.3	45	11.2	7	0.7	1	0.7	0	0	0	0	0	0
No Occupation	142	1.1	77	0.8	5	1.3	6	1.5	227	21.2	5	3.7	1	25.0	4	26.7	0	0
Students	28	0.2	4	0.04	0	0	0	0	136	12.7	1	0.7	0	0	0	0	0	0
Total	12,551	100.0	9,115	99.9	379	100.1	403	99.8	1,072	100.2	134	99.8	4	100.0	15	100.1	3	100.0

	Born in China	Born in U.S.	Total
Total number of Chinese males	22,448	1,225	23,673
Number with known marital status	22,045	1,210	23,255
Number who have ever been married (married + divorced + widowed)	9,494	138	9,632
Number who are presently married	9,115	134	9,249
Number who divorced/widowed	379	4	383
Number who are single	12,551	1,072	13,623
Presently married males as a percentage of those with known marital status	41.3%	11.1%	
Divorced + widowed males as a percentage of those with known marital status	1.7%	0.3%	
Single males as a percentage of those with known marital status	56.9%	88.6%	
	100.0%	100.0%	

Source: Author's tally and computation from the 1900 manuscript census of population. For a list of counties counted as "agricultural," and which occupations are grouped under each occupational category, see Appendixes A and B at the end of Chapter 3.

Note: The three males born elsewhere (not in China or the U.S.) are not included in these computations.

Abbreviations: Wid = widowed; Div = divorced; MS = marital status, Unk = unknown; Oth BP = birthplace other than China or the U.S.

TABLE 3.1C. Chinese Men and Boys: Birthplace and Marital Status by Occupational Category, Number and Percentage in Each Occupational Category

Mining and Mountain Counties in California, 1900

Occupational Category	Born in China								Born in U.S.								Oth BP	
	Single		Married		Wid/Div		MS Unk		Single		Married		Wid/Div		MS Unk		All MS	
	No.	%	No.	%	No.	%	No.	%	No.	%	No.	%	No.	%	No.	%	No.	%
Primary Producers and Extractors																		
Agriculturalists	124	4.0	66	3.8	9	8.0	4	16.7	2	0.9	0	0	0	0	1	25.0	0	0
Agric. laborers	293	9.4	191	10.9	11	9.8	0	0	11	5.0	1	3.8	0	0	0	0	0	0
Fishermen	1	0	0	0	0	0	0	0	0	0	0	0	0	0	0	0	0	0
Miners	1,273	40.7	518	29.7	36	32.1	3	12.5	12	5.5	2	7.7	0	0	0	0	0	0
Professionals	19	0.6	24	1.4	2	1.8	0	0	2	0.9	1	3.8	0	0	0	0	1	33.3
Skilled Artisans	50	1.6	12	0.7	0	0	0	0	1	0.5	0	0	0	0	0	0	0	0
Entrepreneurs and Their Assistants																		
Merchants	114	3.6	222	12.7	9	8.0	5	20.8	8	3.6	4	15.4	0	0	1	25.0	0	0
Other businessmen	49	1.6	59	3.4	1	0.9	0	0	3	1.4	0	0	0	0	0	0	0	0
Clerks and shop assistants	24	0.8	24	1.4	0	0	0	0	5	2.3	2	7.7	0	0	0	0	0	0
Factory workers	3	0.1	3	0.2	0	0	0	0	0	0	0	0	0	0	0	0	0	0
Agents and supervisors	7	0.2	5	0.3	0	0	0	0	0	0	0	0	0	0	0	0	0	0
Laundrymen	162	5.2	102	5.8	8	7.1	2	8.3	4	1.8	2	7.7	0	0	1	25.0	0	0
Cooks	438	14.0	229	13.1	15	13.4	2	8.3	37	16.8	8	30.8	0	0	0	0	2	66.7
Other Personal Services	41	1.3	17	1.0	0	0	0	0	6	2.8	1	3.8	0	0	0	0	0	0
Nonagricultural Laborers	488	15.6	241	13.8	16	14.3	7	29.2	16	7.3	2	7.7	0	0	0	0	0	0

76

Mining and Mountain Counties in California, 1900

Occupational Category	Born in China										Born in U.S.								Oth BP	
	Single		Married		Wid/Div		MS Unk		Total		Single		Married		Wid/Div		MS Unk		All MS	
	No.	%	No.	%	No.	%	No.	%	No.	%	No.	%	No.	%	No.	%	No.	%	No.	%
Miscellaneous	0	0	0	0	0	0	1	4.2			0	0	0	0	0	0	0	0	0	0
No Occupation	37	1.2	32	1.8	4	3.6	0	0			59	26.8	3	11.5	0	0	0	0	0	0
Students	3	0.0	1	0	1	0.9	0	0			54	24.5	0	0	0	0	1	25.0	0	0
Total	3,126	99.9	1,746	100.0	112	99.9	24	100.0			220	100.1	26	99.9	0	0	4	100.0	3	100.0

	Born in China	Born in U.S.	Total
Total number of Chinese males	5,008	250	5,258
Number with known marital status	4,984	246	5,230
Number who have ever been married (married + divorced + widowed)	1,858	26	1,884
Number who are presently married	1,746	26	1,772
Number who divorced/widowed	112	0	112
Number who are single	3,126	220	3,346
Presently married males as a percentage of those with known marital status	35.0%	10.6%	
Divorced + widowed males as a percentage of those with known marital status	2.2%	0	
Single males as a percentage of those with known marital status	62.7%	89.4%	
	99.9%	100.0%	

Source: Author's tally and computation from the manuscript 1900 census of population. For a list of counties counted as "mining/mountain," and which occupations are grouped under each occupational category, see Appendixes A and B at the end of Chapter 3.

Note: The three males born elsewhere (not in China or the U.S.) are not included in these computations.

Abbreviations: Wid = widowed; Div = divorced; MS = marital status; Unk = unknown; Other BP = birthplace other than China or the U.S.

TABLE 3.2A. Chinese Men and Boys: Birthplace and Marital Status by Occupational Category, Number and Percentage in Each Occupational Category

	City and County of San Francisco, 1910																	
	Born in China								Born in U.S.								Oth BP	
	Single		Married		Wid/Div		MS Unk		Single		Married		Wid/Div		MS Unk		All MS	
Occupational Category	No.	%	No.	%	No.	%	No.	%	No.	%	No.	%	No.	%	No.	%	No.	%
Primary Producers and Extractors																		
Agriculturalists	10	0.4	25	0.9	0	0	0	0	6	0.4	10	0.9	0	0	0	0	0	0
Agric. laborers	22	0.9	24	0.8	1	1.3	5	0.4	4	0.3	1	0.1	0	0	0	0	0	0
Fishermen	54	2.3	33	1.2	3	3.9	23	1.9	9	0.6	15	1.4	0	0	0	0	0	0
Miners	5	0.2	6	0.2	0	0	0	0	1	0.1	0	0	0	0	0	0	0	0
Professionals	72	3.0	195	6.9	4	5.3	5	0.4	23	1.5	58	5.3	1	4.3	0	0	1	3.6
Skilled Artisans	103	4.3	126	4.5	1	1.3	0	0	31	2.0	38	3.4	1	4.3	0	0	1	3.6
Entrepreneurs and Their Assistants																		
Merchants	85	3.6	280	9.9	4	5.3	15	1.3	21	1.3	89	8.1	3	13.0	4	12.1	0	0
Other businessmen	38	1.6	113	4.0	1	1.3	10	0.8	9	0.6	41	3.7	1	4.3	0	0	0	0
Clerks and shop assistants	359	15.0	533	18.9	8	10.5	9	0.8	91	5.8	140	12.7	3	13.0	7	21.2	1	3.6
Factory workers	210	8.8	145	5.1	6	7.9	1,032	86.4	61	3.9	39	3.5	0	0	1	3.0	13	46.4
Agents and supervisors	29	1.2	235	8.3	2	2.6	5	0.4	16	1.0	68	6.2	4	17.4	3	9.1	1	3.6
Laundrymen	354	14.8	365	12.9	5	6.6	10	0.8	166	10.6	187	17.0	1	4.3	2	6.1	2	7.1
Cooks	345	14.4	353	12.5	18	23.7	32	2.7	245	15.7	249	22.6	5	21.7	5	15.2	2	7.1
Other Personal Services	236	9.9	125	4.4	8	10.5	17	1.4	108	6.9	75	6.8	3	13.0	8	24.2	2	7.1
Nonagricultural Laborers	119	5.0	184	6.5	7	9.2	15	1.3	82	5.3	66	6.0	1	4.3	2	6.1	0	0

City and County of San Francisco, 1910

Occupational Category	Born in China								Born in U.S.								Oth BP	
	Single		Married		Wid/Div		MS Unk		Single		Married		Wid/Div		MS Unk		All MS	
	No.	%	No.	%	No.	%	No.	%	No.	%	No.	%	No.	%	No.	%	No.	%
Miscellaneous	0	0	0	0	0	0	1	0.1	0	0	0	0	0	0	0	0	0	0
No Occupation	344	14.4	83	3.0	8	10.5	16	1.3	677	43.4	27	2.4	0	0	0	0	0	0
Students	8	0.3	0	0	0	0	0	0	9	0.6	0	0	0	0	0	0	0	0
Total	2,393	100.1	2,825	100.0	76	99.9	1,195	100.0	1,559	100.0	1,103	100.0	23	99.6	33	100.0	28	99.9

	Born in China	Born in U.S.	Total
Total number of Chinese males	6,489	2,718	9,207
Number with known marital status	5,294	2,685	7,979
Number who have ever been married (married + divorced + widowed)	2,901	1,126	4,027
Number who are presently married	2,825	1,103	3,928
Number who divorced/widowed	76	23	99
Number who are single	2,393	1,559	
Presently married males as a percentage of those with known marital status	53.4%	41.1%	
Divorced + widowed males as a percentage of those with known marital status	1.4%	0.9%	
Single males as a percentage of those with known marital status	45.2%	58.1%	
	100.0%	100.0%	

Source: Author's tally and computation from the 1910 manuscript census of population. For a list of which occupations are grouped under each occupational category, see Appendix B at the end of Chapter 3.

Note: The twenty-eight males born elsewhere (not in China or the U.S.) are not included in these computations.

Abbreviations: Wid = widowed; Div = divorced; MS = marital status; Unk = unknown; Other BP = birthplace other than China or the U.S.

TABLE 3.2B. Chinese Men and Boys: Birthplace and Marital Status by Occupational Category, Number and Percentage in Each Occupational Category

Agricultural Counties in California, 1910

Occupational Category	Born in China								Born in U.S.								Oth BP	
	Single		Married		Wid/Div		MS Unk		Single		Married		Wid/Div		MS Unk		All MS	
	No.	%	No.	%	No.	%	No.	%	No.	%	No.	%	No.	%	No.	%	No.	%
Primary Producers and Extractors																		
Agriculturalists	354	4.3	481	6.5	25	6.9	6	0.9	34	1.7	28	3.1	1	4.3	0	0	0	0
Agric. laborers	2,566	31.1	1,301	17.5	92	25.5	98	14.8	165	8.1	35	3.8	2	8.7	0	0	14	100.0
Fishermen	61	0.7	70	0.9	2	0.6	115	17.4	23	1.1	6	0.7	3	13.0	8	25.8	0	0
Miners	22	0.3	8	0.1	0	0	0	0	0	0	1	0.1	0	0	0	0	0	0
Professionals	71	0.9	123	1.7	9	2.5	0	0	21	1.0	28	3.1	0	0	0	0	0	0
Skilled Artisans	62	0.8	131	1.7	9	2.5	1	0.2	19	0.9	18	2.0	0	0	0	0	0	0
Entrepreneurs and Their Assistants																		
Merchants	381	4.7	1,008	13.5	22	6.1	30	4.5	73	3.6	136	14.9	2	8.7	0	0	0	0
Other businessmen	325	4.0	655	8.8	24	6.6	3	0.5	58	2.8	107	11.7	1	4.3	1	3.2	0	0
Clerks and shop assistants	181	2.2	308	4.1	8	2.2	0	0	56	2.7	67	7.4	1	4.3	1	3.2	0	0
Factory workers	485	5.9	377	5.1	4	1.1	284	43.0	54	2.6	16	1.8	3	13.0	15	48.4	0	0
Agents and supervisors	44	0.5	99	1.3	5	1.4	3	0.5	18	0.9	20	2.2	1	4.3	0	0	0	0
Laundrymen	748	9.1	830	11.2	18	5.0	33	5.0	113	5.5	117	12.8	1	4.3	1	3.2	0	0
Cooks	1,131	13.8	1,095	14.7	69	19.1	8	1.2	318	15.5	213	23.4	7	30.4	1	3.2	0	0
Other Personal Services	499	6.1	266	3.6	13	3.6	5	0.8	145	7.1	61	6.7	1	4.3	1	3.2	0	0
Nonagricultural Laborers	508	6.2	396	5.3	24	6.6	17	2.6	48	2.3	29	3.2	0	0	0	0	0	0

Agricultural Counties in California, 1910

Occupational Category	Born in China								Born in U.S.								Oth BP	
	Single		Married		Wid/Div		MS Unk		Single		Married		Wid/Div		MS Unk		All MS	
	No.	%	No.	%	No.	%	No.	%	No.	%	No.	%	No.	%	No.	%	No.	%
Miscellaneous	22	0.3	51	0.7	5	1.4	5	0.8	2	0.1	2	0.2	0	0	0	0	0	0
No Occupation	633	7.7	237	3.2	32	8.9	52	7.9	818	40.0	26	2.9	0	0	0	0	0	0
Students	93	1.1	6	0.1	0	0	0	0	82	4.0	1	0.1	0	0	1	3.2	0	0
Total	8,186	99.9	7,442	100.0	361	100.0	660	100.0	2,047	99.9	911	100.2	23	99.6	31	99.9	14	100.0

	Born in China	Born in U.S.	Total
Total number of Chinese males	16,649	3,012	19,661
Number with known marital status	15,989	2,981	18,970
Number who have ever been married (married + divorced + widowed)	7,803	934	8,737
Number who are presently married	7,442	911	8,353
Number who are divorced/widowed	361	23	384
Number who are single	8,186	2,047	10,233
Presently married males as a percentage of those with known marital status	46.5%	30.6%	
Divorced + widowed males as a percentage of those with known marital status	2.3%	0.8%	
Single males as a percentage of those with known marital status	51.2%	68.7%	
	100.0%	100.1%	

Source: Author's tally and computation from the 1910 manuscript census of population. For a list of counties counted as "agricultural," and which occupations are grouped under each occupational category, see Appendixes A and B at the end of Chapter 3.

Note: The fourteen males born elsewhere (not in China or the U.S.) are not included in these computations.

Abbreviations: Wid = widowed; Div = divorced; MS = marital status; Unk = unknown; Other BP = birthplace other than China or the U.S.

TABLE 3.2C. Chinese Men and Boys: Birthplace and Marital Status by Occupational Category, Number and Percentage in Each Occupational Category

Mining and Mountain Counties in California, 1910

Occupational Category	Born in China								Born in U.S.								Oth BP	
	Single		Married		Wid/Div		MS Unk		Single		Married		Wid/Div		MS Unk		All MS	
	No.	%	No.	%	No.	%	No.	%	No.	%	No.	%	No.	%	No.	%	No.	%
Primary Producers and Extractors																		
Agriculturalists	97	7.6	120	11.0	11	13.3	2	4.3	7	2.6	2	2.7	0	0	0	0	0	0
Agric. laborers	174	14.1	114	10.5	8	9.6	0	0	12	4.5	3	4.1	0	0	0	0	0	0
Fishermen	0	0	0	0	0	0	0	0	0	0	0	0	0	0	0	0	0	0
Miners	258	20.9	114	10.5	13	15.7	0	0	7	2.6	0	0	0	0	0	0	0	0
Professionals	3	0.2	19	1.7	1	1.2	0	0	0	0	0	0	0	0	0	0	0	0
Skilled Artisans	5	0.4	4	0.4	0	0	0	0	2	0.8	0	0	0	0	0	0	0	0
Entrepreneurs and Their Assistants																		
Merchants	43	3.5	163	15.0	3	3.6	0	0	3	1.1	8	10.8	0	0	0	0	0	0
Other businessmen	28	2.3	51	4.7	3	3.6	0	0	5	1.9	11	14.9	2	40.0	0	0	0	0
Clerks and shop assistants	21	1.7	9	0.8	0	0	0	0	5	1.9	1	1.4	0	0	0	0	0	0
Factory workers	2	0.2	0	0	0	0	0	0	0	0	1	1.4	0	0	0	0	0	0
Agents and supervisors	4	0.3	11	1.0	0	0	0	0	1	0.4	0	0	0	0	0	0	0	0
Laundrymen	43	3.5	71	6.5	6	7.2	3	3.0	8	3.0	7	9.5	1	20.0	0	0	0	0
Cooks	283	22.9	235	21.6	17	20.5	35	76.1	69	25.9	33	44.6	0	0	0	0	1	100.0
Other Personal Services	48	3.9	31	2.8	2	2.4	3	6.5	18	6.8	1	1.4	0	0	0	0	0	0
Nonagricultural Laborers	157	12.7	133	12.2	15	18.1	2	4.8	10	3.8	5	6.8	2	40.0	0	0	0	0

Mining and Mountain Counties in California, 1910

Occupational Category	Born in China								Born in U.S.								Oth BP	
	Single		Married		Wid/Div		MS Unk		Single		Married		Wid/Div		MS Unk		All MS	
	No.	%	No.	%	No.	%	No.	%	No.	%	No.	%	No.	%	No.	%	No.	%
Miscellaneous	3	0.2	3	0.3	1	1.2	0	0	0	0	0	0	0	0	0	0	0	0
No Occupation	63	5.1	10	0.9	0	0	0	0	105	39.5	2	2.7	0	0	0	0	0	0
Students	5	0.4	0	0	0	0	0	0	14	5.3	0	0	0	0	0	0	0	0
Total	1,237	99.9	1,088	99.9	83	100.0	46	99.9	266	100.1	74	100.3	5	100.0	0	0	1	100.0

	Born in China	Born in U.S.	Total
Total number of Chinese males	2,454	345	2,799
Number with known marital status	2,408	345	2,753
Number who have ever been married (married + divorced + widowed)	1,171	79	1,250
Number who are presently married	1,088	74	1,162
Number who are divorced/widowed	83	5	88
Number who are singled	1,237	266	1,503
Presently married males as a percentage of those with known marital status	45.2%	21.4%	
Divorced + widowed males as a percentage of those with known marital status	3.4%	1.4%	
Single males as a percentage of those with known marital status	51.4%	77.1%	
	100.0%	99.9%	

Source: Author's tally and computation from the 1910 manuscript census of population. For a list of counties counted as "mining/mountain," and which occupations are grouped under each occupational category, see Appendixes A and B at the end of Chapter 3.
Note: The one male born elsewhere (not in China or the U.S.) is not included in these computations.
Abbreviations: Wid = widowed; Div = divorced; MS = marital status; Unk = unknown; Oth BP = birthplace other than China or the U.S.

TABLE 3.3A. Chinese Males with Known Marital Status: Number of Presently Married Men as a Percentage of All Males with Known Marital Status and Number of Married Men with Resident Wives in the U.S. as a Percentage of Presently Married Men by Occupational Category

City and County of San Francisco, 1910

Occupational Category	Born in China					Born in U.S.				
	Males with Known Marital Status	Presently Married Men		With Resident Wives in U.S.		Males with Known Marital Status	Presently Married Men		With Resident Wives in U.S.	
	Number	Number	As % of MKMS	Number	As % of PMM	Number	Number	As % of MKMS	Number	As % of PMM
Primary Producers and Extractors										
Agriculturalists	67	47	70.1	6	12.8	3	0	0	0	0
Agric. laborers	136	65	47.8	6	9.2	6	0	0	0	0
Fishermen	58	27	46.6	7	26.0	0	0	0	0	0
Miners	20	14	70.0	4	28.6	0	0	0	0	0
Professionals	461	359	77.9	73	20.3	36	16	44.4	7	48.8
Skilled Artisans	644	476	73.9	67	14.1	65	22	33.8	8	36.4
Entrepreneurs and Their Assistants										
Merchants	954	784	82.2	142	18.1	105	44	11.9	7	15.9
Other businessmen	657	478	72.8	136	28.5	40	20	50.0	6	30.0
Clerks and shop assistants	206	159	77.2	10	6.3	58	25	43.1	5	20.0
Factory workers	1,423	928	65.2	66	7.1	145	35	24.1	6	17.1
Agents and supervisors	78	65	83.3	27	41.5	7	5	71.4	4	80.0

City and County of San Francisco, 1910

	Born in China					Born in U.S.				
Occupational Category	Males with Known Marital Status	Presently Married Men		With Resident Wives in U.S.		Males with Known Marital Status	Presently Married Men		With Resident Wives in U.S.	
	Number	Number	As % of MKMS	Number	As % of PMM	Number	Number	As % of MKMS	Number	As % of PMM
Laundrymen	1,743	915	52.5	17	1.9	310	63	20.3	0	0
Cooks	1,127	628	55.7	78	12.4	146	39	26.7	5	12.8
Other Personal Services	757	355	48.9	12	3.4	190	37	19.5	8	21.6
Nonagricultural Laborers	783	448	57.2	59	13.2	111	24	21.6	11	45.8
Miscellaneous	5	3	60.0	1	33.3	4	0	0	0	0
No Occupation	47	27	57.4	21	77.8	345	2	0.6	2	100.0
Students	32	4	12.5	4	100.0	352	3	0.9	0	0
Total	9,198	5,782	62.9	736	12.7	1,925	335	17.4	72	21.5

Source: Author's tally and computation from the 1900 manuscript census of population. For a list of which occupations are grouped under what category, see Appendix B at the end of Chapter 3.

Note: In addition to the males listed above, six men married to non-Chinese wives and seven married men with resident wives whose occupations are illegible on the microfilm are not included in this table.

Abbreviations: MKMS = males with known marital status; PMM = presently married men.

TABLE 3.3B. Chinese Males with Known Marital Status: Number of Presently Married Men as a Percentage of All Males with Known Marital Status and Number of Married Men with Resident Wives in the U.S. as a Percentage of Presently Married Men by Occupational Category

Agricultural Counties in California, 1900

Occupational Category	Born in China						Born in U.S.					
	Males with Known Marital Status	Presently Married Men		With Resident Wives in U.S.			Males with Known Marital Status	Presently Married Men		With Resident Wives in U.S.		
	Number	Number	As % of MKMS	Number	As % of PMM		Number	Number	As % of MKMS	Number	As % of PMM	
Primary Producers and Extractors												
Agriculturalists	1,616	794	49.1	39	4.9		26	10	38.5	0	0	
Agric. laborers	6,413	2,411	37.6	34	1.4		130	11	8.5	0	0	
Fishermen	206	62	30.1	7	12.3		16	1	6.3	1	100.0	
Miners	229	66	28.8	2	3.0		0	0	0	0	0	
Professionals	194	134	69.1	22	16.4		15	5	33.3	4	80.0	
Skilled Artisans	221	119	53.8	10	8.4		10	1	10.0	0	0	
Entrepreneurs and Their Assistants												
Merchants	1,120	777	69.4	166	21.4		27	11	40.7	2	18.2	
Other businessmen	750	372	49.6	47	12.6		19	2	10.5	1	50.0	
Clerks and shop assistants	222	135	60.8	6	4.4		19	2	10.5	0	0	
Factory workers	316	84	26.6	4	4.8		17	1	5.9	1	100.0	
Agents and supervisors	54	32	59.3	11	34.4		3	0	0	0	0	

Agricultural Counties in California, 1900

Occupational Category	Born in China					Born in U.S.				
	Males with Known Marital Status	Presently Married Men		With Resident Wives in U.S.		Males with Known Marital Status	Presently Married Men		With Resident Wives in U.S.	
	Number	Number	As % of MKMS	Number	As % of PMM	Number	Number	As % of MKMS	Number	As % of PMM
Laundrymen	2,338	1,070	45.8	26	2.4	132	25	18.9	0	0
Cooks	3,871	1,244	36.9	37	3.0	221	30	13.6	2	6.7
Other Personal Services	756	278	36.8	5	1.8	99	13	13.1	0	0
Nonagricultural Laborers	3,903	1,434	36.7	21	1.5	98	15	15.3	2	13.3
Miscellaneous	80	22	27.5	0	0	8	1	12.5	0	0
No Occupation	142	77	34.3	10	13.0	233	5	2.1	0	0
Students	32	4	12.5	0	0	137	1	0.7	0	0
Total	22,045	9,115	41.3	448	4.9	1,210	134	11.1	14	10.4

Source: Author's tally and computation from the 1900 manuscript census of population. For a list of counties counted as "agricultural," and which occupations are grouped under what category, see Appendixes A and B at the end of Chapter 3.

Note: In addition to the males listed above, six men married to non-Chinese wives are not included in this table.

Abbreviations: MKMS = males with known marital status; PMM = presently married men.

TABLE 3.3C. Chinese Males with Known Marital Status: Number of Presently Married Men as a Percentage of All Males with Known Marital Status and Number of Married Men with Resident Wives in the U.S. as a Percentage of Presently Married Men by Occupational Category

Mining and Mountain Counties in California, 1900

	Born in China					Born in U.S.				
	Males with Known Marital Status	Presently Married Men		With Resident Wives in U.S.		Males with Known Marital Status	Presently Married Men		With Resident Wives in U.S.	
Occupational Category	Number	Number	As % of MKMS	Number	As % of PMM	Number	Number	As % of MKMS	Number	As % of PMM
Primary Producers and Extractors										
Agriculturalists	199	66	33.2	10	15.2	2	0	0	0	0
Agric. laborers	495	191	38.6	3	1.6	12	1	8.3	0	0
Fishermen	1	0	0	0	0	0	0	0	0	0
Miners	1,827	518	28.4	20	3.9	14	2	14.3	0	0
Professionals	45	24	53.3	4	16.7	3	1	33.3	0	0
Skilled Artisans	62	12	19.4	1	8.3	1	0	0	0	0
Entrepreneurs and Their assistants										
Merchants	345	222	64.3	60	29.7	12	4	33.3	2	50.0
Other businessmen	109	59	54.1	12	20.3	3	0	0	0	0
Clerks and shop assistants	48	24	50.0	1	4.2	7	2	28.6	0	0
Factory workers	6	3	50.0	0	0	0	0	0	0	0
Agents and supervisors	12	5	41.7	2	40.0	0	0	0	0	0

Mining and Mountain Counties in California, 1900

Occupational Category	Born in China					Born in U.S.				
	Males with Known Marital Status Number	Presently Married Men Number	As % of MKMS	With Resident Wives in U.S. Number	As % of PMM	Males with Known Marital Status Number	Presently Married Men Number	As % of MKMS	With Resident Wives in U.S. Number	As % of PMM
Laundrymen	272	102	37.5	2	2.0	6	2	33.3	1	50.0
Cooks	682	229	33.6	7	3.1	45	8	17.8	0	0
Other Personal Services	58	17	29.3	1	5.9	7	1	14.3	0	0
Nonagricultural Laborers	745	241	32.3	10	4.1	18	2	11.1	1	50.0
Miscellaneous	0	0	0	0	0	0	0	0	0	0
No Occupation	73	32	43.8	5	15.6	62	3	4.8	0	0
Students	4	1	25.0	0	0	54	0	0	0	0
Total	4,984	1,746	35.0	138	7.9	246	26	10.6	4	15.4

Source: Author's tally and computation from the 1900 manuscript census of population. For a list of counties counted as "mining and mountain," and which occupations are grouped under what category, see Appendixes A and B at the end of Chapter 3.

Note: In addition to the males listed above, one man with a resident wife is not included in this table because his occupation was illegible in the microfilm. He is not placed under "no occupation" in this table because he did have an occupation but it could not be deciphered.

Abbreviations: MKMS = males with known marital status; PMM = presently married men.

TABLE 3.4A. Chinese Males with Known Marital Status: Number of Presently Married Men as a Percentage of All Males with Known Marital Status and Number of Married Men with Resident Wives in the U.S. as a Percentage of Presently Married Men by Occupational Category

City and County of San Francisco, 1910

	Born in China						Born in U.S.					
	Males with Known Marital Status	Presently Married Men		With Resident Wives in U.S.			Males with Known Marital Status	Presently Married Men		With Resident Wives in U.S.		
Occupational Category	Number	Number	As % of MKMS	Number	As % of PMM		Number	Number	As % of MKMS	Number	As % of PMM	
Primary Producers and Extractors												
Agriculturalists	35	25	71.4	0	0		16	10	62.5	1	10.0	
Agric. laborers	47	24	51.1	5	20.8		5	1	20.0	0	0	
Fishermen	90	33	37.7	1	3.0		24	15	62.5	1	6.7	
Miners	11	6	54.5	1	16.7		1	0	0	0	0	
Professionals	271	195	72.0	30	15.4		82	58	70.7	15	25.9	
Skilled Artisans	230	126	54.8	22	17.5		70	38	54.3	11	28.9	
Entrepreneurs and Their Assistants												
Merchants	369	280	75.9	79	28.2		113	89	78.8	22	24.7	
Other businessmen	152	113	74.3	12	10.6		51	41	80.4	11	26.8	
Clerks and shop assistants	900	533	59.2	34	6.4		234	140	59.8	25	17.9	
Factory workers	361	145	40.2	10	6.9		100	39	39.0	5	12.8	
Agents and supervisors	266	235	88.3	56	23.8		88	68	77.3	29	42.6	

City and County of San Francisco, 1910

Occupational Category	Born in China					Born in U.S.				
	Males with Known Marital Status	Presently Married Men		With Resident Wives in U.S.		Males with Known Marital Status	Presently Married Men		With Resident Wives in U.S.	
	Number	Number	As % of MKMS	Number	As % of PMM	Number	Number	As % of MKMS	Number	As % of PMM
Laundrymen	724	365	50.4	3	0.8	354	187	52.8	1	0.5
Cooks	716	353	49.3	25	7.1	499	249	49.9	23	9.2
Other Personal Services	369	125	33.9	5	4.0	186	75	40.3	11	14.7
Nonagricultural Laborers	310	184	59.4	33	17.9	149	66	44.3	23	34.8
Miscellaneous	0	0	0	0	0	0	0	0	0	0
No Occupation	435	83	19.1	16	19.3	704	27	3.8	4	14.8
Students	8	0	0	0	0	9	0	0	0	0
Total	5,294	2,825	54.4	332	11.8	2,685	1,103	41.1	182	16.5

Source: Author's tally and computation from the 1910 manuscript census of population. For a list of which occupations are grouped under what category, see Appendix B at the end of Chapter 3.

Note: In addition to the males listed above, three men married to non-Chinese wives are not included in this table.

Abbreviations: MKMS = males with known marital status; PMM = presently married men.

TABLE 3.4B. Chinese Males with Known Marital Status: Number of Presently Married Men as a Percentage of All Males with Known Marital Status and Number of Married Men with Resident Wives in the U.S. as a Percentage of Presently Married Men by Occupational Category

Agricultural Counties in California, 1910

| | Born in China | | | | | Born in U.S. | | | | |
| | Males with Known Marital Status | Presently Married Men | | With Resident Wives in U.S. | | Males with Known Marital Status | Presently Married Men | | With Resident Wives in U.S. | |
Occupational Category	Number	Number	As % of MKMS	Number	As % of PMM	Number	Number	As % of MKMS	Number	As % of PMM
Primary Producers and Extractors										
Agriculturalists	860	481	55.9	35	7.3	62	28	45.2	4	14.3
Agric. laborers	3,959	1,301	32.9	19	1.5	202	35	17.3	2	1.5
Fishermen	133	70	52.6	5	7.1	32	6	18.8	1	16.7
Miners	30	8	26.7	0	0	1	1	100.0	1	100.0
Professionals	203	123	60.6	25	20.3	49	28	57.1	8	28.6
Skilled Artisans	202	131	64.9	17	13.0	37	18	48.6	6	33.3
Entrepreneurs and Their Assistants										
Merchants	1,411	1,008	71.4	163	16.2	211	136	64.5	33	24.3
Other businessmen	1,003	655	65.3	61	9.3	166	107	64.5	10	9.3
Clerks and shop assistants	497	308	62.0	24	7.9	124	67	54.0	12	17.9
Factory workers	866	377	43.5	6	1.6	73	16	21.9	2	12.5
Agents and supervisors	148	99	66.9	23	23.2	39	20	51.3	10	50.0

Agricultural Counties in California, 1910

Occupational Category	Born in China						Born in U.S.					
	Males with Known Marital Status	Presently Married Men		With Resident Wives in U.S.			Males with Known Marital Status	Presently Married Men		With Resident Wives in U.S.		
	Number	Number	As % of MKMS	Number	As % of PMM		Number	Number	As % of MKMS	Number	As % of PMM
Laundrymen	1,596	830	52.0	9	1.1		231	117	50.6	3	2.6
Cooks	2,295	1,095	47.7	40	3.7		538	213	39.6	14	6.6
Other Personal Services	779	266	34.1	11	4.1		207	61	29.5	3	4.9
Nonagricultural Laborers	928	396	42.7	33	8.3		77	29	37.7	8	27.6
Miscellaneous	78	51	65.4	15	29.4		4	2	50.0	1	50.0
No Occupation	902	237	26.3	19	8.0		844	26	3.1	1	3.8
Students	99	6	6.1	0	0		83	1	1.2	0	0
Total	15,989	7,442	46.5	506	6.8		2,981	911	30.6	119	13.1

Source: Author's tally and computation from the 1910 manuscript census of population. For a list of counties counted as "agricultural," and which occupations are grouped under what category, see Appendixes A and B at the end of Chapter 3.

Note: In addition to the males listed above, nine men married to non-Chinese wives and one man with a resident Chinese wife but whose occupation was illegible on the microfilm are not included in this table.

Abbreviations: MKMS = males with known marital status; PMM = presently married men.

TABLE 3.4C. Chinese Males with Known Marital Status: Number of Presently Married Men as a Percentage of All Males with Known Marital Status and Number of Married Men with Resident Wives in the U.S. as a Percentage of Presently Married Men by Occupational Category

Mining and Mountain Counties in California, 1910

	Born in China					Born in U.S.				
	Males with Known Marital Status	Presently Married Men		With Resident Wives in U.S.		Males with Known Marital Status	Presently Married Men		With Resident Wives in U.S.	
Occupational Category	Number	Number	As % of MKMS	Number	As % of PMM	Number	Number	As % of MKMS	Number	As % of PMM
Primary Producers and Extractors										
Agriculturalists	228	120	56.2	6	5.0	9	2	22.2	0	0
Agric. laborers	296	114	20.0	4	5.0	0	0	0	0	0
Fishermen	0	0	0	0	0	0	0	0	0	0
Miners	385	114	29.6	1	0.9	7	0	0	0	0
Professionals	23	19	82.6	5	26.3	0	0	0	0	0
Skilled Artisans	9	4	44.4	0	0	2	0	0	0	0
Entrepreneurs and Their Assistants										
Merchants	209	163	78.0	30	18.4	11	8	72.7	3	37.5
Other businessmen	82	51	62.2	9	17.6	18	11	61.1	4	17.6
Clerks and shop assistants	30	9	30.0	0	0	6	1	16.7	0	0
Factory workers	2	0	0	0	0	1	1	100.0	0	0
Agents and supervisors	15	11	73.3	1	9.1	1	0	0	0	0

Mining and Mountain Counties in California, 1910

Occupational Category	Born in China					Born in U.S.				
	Males with Known Marital Status	Presently Married Men		With Resident Wives in U.S.		Males with Known Marital Status	Presently Married Men		With Resident Wives in U.S.	
	Number	Number	As % of MKMS	Number	As % of PMM	Number	Number	As % of MKMS	Number	As % of PMM
Laundrymen	120	71	59.2	3	4.2	16	7	43.8	2	14.3
Cooks	535	235	43.9	8	3.4	102	33	32.4	4	12.1
Other Personal Services	81	31	38.3	0	0	19	1	5.3	0	0
Nonagricultural Laborers	305	133	43.6	5	3.8	17	5	29.4	3	60.0
Miscellaneous	7	3	42.9	0	0	0	0	0	0	0
No Occupation	73	10	13.7	4	40.0	107	2	1.9	2	100.0
Students	5	0	0	0	0	14	0	0	0	0
Total	2,408	1,088	45.2	76	7.0	345	74	21.4	18	24.3

Source: Author's tally and computation from the 1910 manuscript census of population. For a list of counties counted as "mining and mountain," and which occupations are grouped under what category, see Appendixes A and B at the end of Chapter 3.

Note: In addition to the males listed above, one man married to a non-Chinese wife is not included in this table.

Abbreviations: MKMS = males with known marital status; PMM = presently married men.

TABLE 3.5A. Chinese Women and Girls: Birthplace and Marital Status by Age Cohort, Number and Percentage in Each Age Cohort

	City and County of San Francisco, 1900																Other BP
	Born in China								Born in U.S.								
	Single		Married w/ Resident Husband		Married but No Resident Husband		Widowed/ Divorced		Single		Married w/ Resident Husband		Married but No Resident Husband		Widowed/ Divorced		
Age	No.	%	No.	%	No.	%	No.	%	No.	%	No.	%	No.	%	No.	%	No.
0–5	4	2.4	0	0	0	0	0	0	262	30.6	0	0	0	0	0	0	0
6–10	6	3.6	0	0	0	0	0	0	185	21.6	0	0	0	0	0	0	0
11–15	7	4.2	0	0	0	0	0	0	168	19.6	1	0.3	0	0	0	0	0
16–20	37	22.3	18	3.3	0	0	0	0	97	11.3	50	17.3	2	6.3	5	27.8	0
21–25	57	34.3	70	13.0	7	9.6	4	3.1	100	11.7	106	36.7	19	59.4	2	11.1	1
26–30	34	20.5	88	16.4	9	12.3	11	8.6	41	4.8	70	24.2	7	21.9	8	44.4	0
31–40	11	6.6	182	33.8	19	26.0	28	21.9	2	0.2	57	19.7	4	12.5	2	11.1	0
41–50	6	3.6	134	24.9	24	32.9	43	33.6	2	0.1	4	1.4	0	0	0	0	0
51–60	4	2.4	42	7.8	10	13.7	35	27.3	0	0	0	0	0	0	0	0	0
61+	0	0	3	0.6	4	5.5	7	5.4	0	0	1	0.3	0	0	0	0	0
Age Unknown	0	0	1	0.2	0	0	0	0	0	0	0	0	0	0	0	0	0
Total	166	99.9	538	100.0	73	100.0	128	99.9	857	100.0	289	99.9	32	100.1	18	100.1	1

City and County of San Francisco, 1900

	Born in China		Born in U.S.		Total	
	No.	%	No.	%	No.	%
Single females	166	18.3	857	71.7	1,023	48.7
Married women with resident husbands	538	59.4	289	24.2	827	39.4
Married women without resident husbands	73	8.1	32	2.7	105	5.0
Women who are widowed or divorced	128	14.1	18	1.5	146	6.9
	905	99.9%	1,196	100.1%	2,101	100.0%

Source: Author's tally and computation from the 1900 manuscript census of population.

Note: The one female with unknown birthplace listed above is not included in the computations in this table because it is impossible to determine which column she should be placed under. However, the one female whose age is not known is included in the computation because we have information on her marital status.

Abbreviations: w/ = with; Other BP = birthplace other than China or the U.S.

TABLE 3.5B. Chinese Women and Girls: Birthplace and Marital Status by Age Cohort, Number and Percentage in Each Age Cohort

Agricultural Counties in California, 1900

	Born in China								Born in U.S.									
	Single		Married w/ Resident Husband		Married but No Resident Husband		Widowed/ Divorced		Single		Married w/ Resident Husband		Married but No Resident Husband		Widowed/ Divorced		Other BP	
Age	No.	%	No.	%	No.	%	No.	%	No.	%	No.	%	No.	%	No.	%	No.	
0–5	0	0	0	0	0	0	0	0	130	42.9	0	0	0	0	0	0	0	
6–10	4	5.2	0	0	0	0	0	0	91	30.0	0	0	0	0	0	0	0	
11–15	2	2.6	1	0.3	0	0	0	0	54	17.8	0	0	0	0	0	0	0	
16–20	3	3.9	16	5.0	1	1.5	0	0	16	5.3	34	23.1	1	7.1	0	0	0	
21–25	13	16.9	36	11.2	6	9.0	0	0	6	2.0	48	32.7	6	42.9	1	20.0	0	
26–30	15	19.5	62	19.3	16	23.9	1	2.1	2	0.7	39	26.5	4	28.6	4	80.0	0	
31–40	12	15.6	107	33.3	14	20.9	10	21.3	4	1.3	20	13.6	2	14.3	0	0	0	
41–50	16	20.8	63	19.6	19	28.4	16	34.3	0	0	6	4.1	1	7.1	0	0	0	
51–60	11	14.3	31	9.7	9	13.4	15	31.9	0	0	0	0	0	0	0	0	0	
61 +	1	1.3	4	1.2	0	0	0	0	0	0	0	0	0	0	0	0	0	
Age Unknown	0	0	1	0.3	0	0	0	0	0	0	0	0	0	0	0	0	0	
Total	77	100.1	321	99.9	67	100.1	47	99.9	303	100.0	147	100.0	14	100.0	5	100.0	0	

Agricultural Counties in California, 1900

	Born in China		Born in U.S.		Total	
	No.	%	No.	%	No.	%
Single females	77	15.0	303	64.6	380	38.7
Married women with resident husbands	321	62.7	147	13.1	468	47.7
Married women without resident husbands	67	31.3	14	3.0	81	8.3
Women who are widowed or divorced	47	9.2	5	1.1	52	5.3
	512	100.0%	469	100.0%	981	100.0%

Source: Author's tally and computation from the 1900 manuscript census of population. For a list of counties counted as "agricultural," see Appendix A at the end of Chapter 3.

Note: In addition to the females listed above, four females born in China with unknown marital status and two females born in the U.S. with unknown marital status are not listed in this table because of space limitation. However, the one female born in China with known age is included in the computations in this table.

Abbreviations: w/ = with; Other BP = birthplace other than China or the U.S.

TABLE 3.5C. Chinese Women and Girls: Birthplace and Marital Status by Age Cohort, Number and Percentage in Each Age Cohort

Mining and Mountain Counties in California, 1900

| | Born in China | | | | | | | | Born in U.S. | | | | | | | | |
| | Single | | Married w/ Resident Husband | | Married but No Resident Husband | | Widowed/ Divorced | | Single | | Married w/ Resident Husband | | Married but No Resident Husband | | Widowed/ Divorced | | Other BP |
Age	No.	%	No.	%	No.	%	No.	%	No.	%	No.	%	No.	%	No.	%	No.
0–5	0	0	0	0	0	0	0	0	33	39.3	0	0	0	0	0	0	0
6–10	0	0	0	0	0	0	0	0	22	26.2	0	0	0	0	0	0	0
11–15	0	0	0	0	0	0	0	0	19	22.6	0	0	0	0	0	0	0
16–20	2	4.3	4	3.3	1	3.4	1	4.5	9	10.7	3	12.0	0	0	0	0	0
21–25	3	6.4	7	5.7	1	3.4	0	0	1	1.2	11	44	0	0	0	0	1
26–30	4	8.5	15	12.3	0	0	0	0	0	0	7	28.0	1	50.0	0	0	1
31–40	9	19.1	40	32.8	7	24.1	5	22.7	0	0	4	16.0	1	50.0	0	0	2
41–50	13	27.7	34	27.9	12	41.4	9	40.9	0	0	0	0	0	0	0	0	1
51–60	11	23.4	20	16.4	7	24.1	4	18.2	0	0	0	0	0	0	0	0	0
61+	5	10.7	2	1.6	0	0	0	0	0	0	0	0	0	0	0	0	0
Total	47	100.1	122	100.0	29	99.8	22	99.9	84	100.0	25	100.0	2	100.0	0	0	5

Mining and Mountain Counties in California, 1900

	Born in China		Born in U.S.		Total	
	No.	%	No.	%	No.	%
Single females	47	21.4	84	75.7	131	39.6
Married women with resident husbands	122	55.5	25	22.5	147	44.4
Married women without resident husbands	29	13.2	2	1.8	31	9.4
Women who are widowed or divorced	22	10.0	0	0	22	6.6
	220	100.1%	111	100.0%	331	100.0

Source: Author's tally and computation from the 1900 manuscript census of population. For a list of counties counted as "mining and mountain," see Appendix A at the end of Chapter 3.

Note: Two females born in China with unknown marital status and one female born in the U.S. with unknown marital status are not listed above because of space limitation. Five females born in China with unknown birthplaces are listed above but are not included in the computations in this table.

Abbreviations: w/ = with; Other BP = birthplace other than China or the U.S.

TABLE 3.6A. Chinese Women and Girls: Birthplace and Marital Status by Age Cohort, Number and Percentage in Each Age Cohort

City and County of San Francisco, 1910

| | Born in China | | | | | | | | Born in U.S. | | | | | | | | Other BP |
| | Single | | Married w/ Resident Husband | | Married but No Resident Husband | | Widowed/ Divorced | | Single | | Married w/ Resident Husband | | Married but No Resident Husband | | Widowed/ Divorced | | |
Age	No.	%	No.	%	No.	%	No.	%	No.	%	No.	%	No.	%	No.	%	No.
0–5	4	5.1	0	0	0	0	0	0	170	30.9	0	0	0	0	0	0	1
6–10	13	16.7	0	0	0	0	0	0	132	24.0	0	0	0	0	0	0	0
11–15	14	17.9	0	0	0	0	0	0	99	18.0	1	0.4	0	0	0	0	1
16–20	6	7.7	15	5.5	4	7.4	1	1.7	79	14.3	21	8.5	4	9.5	0	0	1
21–25	14	17.9	28	10.3	12	22.2	3	5.1	37	6.7	44	17.9	12	28.6	1	3.8	1
26–30	10	12.8	35	12.8	8	14.8	1	1.7	11	2.0	66	26.8	11	26.2	2	7.7	0
31–40	14	17.9	91	33.3	8	14.8	4	6.8	18	3.3	90	36.6	10	23.8	13	50.0	1
41–50	1	1.3	60	22.2	9	16.7	27	45.8	0	0	22	8.9	4	9.5	8	30.8	0
51–60	2	2.6	39	14.3	10	18.5	11	18.6	0	0	2	0.8	1	2.4	2	7.7	0
61+	5	1.8	1	1.9	11	18.7	7	5.4	1	0.2	0	0	0	0	0	0	0
Age Unknown	0	0	0	0	0	0	1	1.7	4	0.7	0	0	0	0	0	0	0
Total	78	99.9	273	100.0	54	100.0	59	100.1	551	100.1	246	100.0	42	100.1	26	100.1	5

City and County of San Francisco, 1910

	Born in China		Born in U.S.		Total	
	No.	%	No.	%	No.	%
Single females	78	16.8	551	63.7	629	47.3
Married women with resident husbands	273	58.8	246	28.4	519	39.1
Married women without resident husbands	54	11.6	42	4.9	96	7.2
Women who are widowed or divorced	59	12.7	26	12.7	85	6.4
	464	99.9%	865	100.0%	1,329	100.0%

Source: Author's tally and computation from the 1910 manuscript census of population.
Note: One female born in China with unknown marital status and four females born in the U.S. with unknown marital status are not listed above because of space limitation. However, the one widow born in China with unknown age and the four single females born in the U.S. with unknown age are included in the computations in this table.
Abbreviations: w/ = with; Other BP = birthplace other than China or the U.S.

TABLE 3.6B. Chinese Women and Girls: Birthplace and Marital Status by Age Cohort, Number and Percentage in Each Age Cohort

Agricultural Counties in California, 1910

| | Born in China | | | | | | | | Born in U.S. | | | | | | | | Other BP |
| | Single | | Married w/ Resident Husband | | Married but No Resident Husband | | Widowed/ Divorced | | Single | | Married w/ Resident Husband | | Married but No Resident Husband | | Widowed/ Divorced | | |
Age	No.	%	No.	%	No.	%	No.	%	No.	%	No.	%	No.	%	No.	%	No.
0–5	8	11.9	0	0	0	0	0	0	279	37.2	0	0	0	0	0	0	0
6–10	8	11.9	0	0	0	0	0	0	202	26.9	0	0	0	0	0	0	0
11–15	8	11.9	0	0	0	0	0	0	150	20.0	1	0.3	0	0	0	0	1
16–20	9	13.4	11	3.2	1	1.6	0	0	88	11.7	26	8.9	1	3.6	0	0	0
21–25	5	7.5	37	10.9	4	6.6	1	1.7	21	2.8	79	27.1	7	25.0	3	10.3	0
26–30	5	7.5	39	11.4	9	14.8	1	1.7	8	1.1	72	24.7	2	7.1	1	3.4	0
31–40	11	16.4	114	33.4	17	27.9	2	3.4	2	0.3	91	31.2	10	35.7	16	55.2	1
41–50	7	10.4	86	25.2	16	26.2	18	31.0	1	0.1	22	7.5	6	21.4	8	27.6	0
51–60	3	4.5	41	12.0	9	14.8	22	37.9	0	0	1	0.3	2	7.1	3	10.3	0
61 +	3	4.5	13	3.8	5	8.2	14	24.1	0	0	0	0	0	0	1	3.4	0
Total	67	99.9	341	99.9	61	100.1	58	99.8	751	100.1	292	100.1	28	99.9	29	99.8	2

| | Born in China | | Born in U.S. | | Total | |
	No.	%	No.	%	No.	%
Single females	67	12.7	751	68.3	818	50.3
Married women with resident husbands	341	64.7	292	26.5	633	38.9
Married women without resident husbands	61	11.6	28	2.5	89	5.5
Women are widowed or divorced	58	11.0	29	2.6	87	5.3
	527	100.0%	1,100	99.9%	1,627	100.0

Source: Author's tally and computation from the 1910 manuscript census of population. For a list of counties counted as "agricultural," see Appendix at the end of Chapter 3.
Note: Two females born elsewhere (not in China or the U.S.) with known ages are listed above but are not included in the computations in this table.
Abbreviations: w/ = with; Other BP = birthplace other than China or the U.S.

TABLE 3.6C. Chinese Women and Girls: Birthplace and Marital Status by Age Cohort, Number and Percentage in Each Age Cohort

	Mining and Mountain Counties in California, 1910																	
	Born in China								Born in U.S.								Other BP
	Single		Married w/ Resident Husband		Married but No Resident Husband		Widowed/ Divorced		Single		Married w/ Resident Husband		Married but No Resident Husband		Widowed/ Divorced		
Age	No.	%	No.	%	No.	%	No.	%	No.	%	No.	%	No.	%	No.	%	No.
0–5	0	0	0	0	0	0	0	0	31	38.8	0	0	0	0	0	0	0
6–10	0	0	0	0	0	0	0	0	24	30.0	0	0	0	0	0	0	0
11–15	0	0	0	0	0	0	0	0	18	22.5	0	0	0	0	0	0	0
16–20	0	0	1	1.8	0	0	0	0	7	8.8	4	9.8	0	0	0	0	0
21–25	0	0	3	5.5	0	0	0	0	0	0	10	24.4	3	50.0	0	0	0
26–30	0	0	6	10.9	0	0	0	0	0	0	6	14.6	3	50.0	0	0	0
31–40	1	12.5	11	20.0	3	42.9	3	16.7	0	0	17	41.5	0	0	1	100.0	0
41–50	3	37.5	18	32.7	1	14.3	2	11.1	0	0	3	7.3	0	0	0	0	0
51–60	1	12.5	12	21.8	2	28.6	5	27.8	0	0	1	2.4	0	0	0	0	0
61 +	2	25.0	4	7.3	1	14.3	8	44.4	0	0	0	0	0	0	0	0	0
Age Unknown	1	12.5	0	0	0	0	0	0	0	0	0	0	0	0	0	0	0
Total	8	100.0	55	100.0	7	100.1	18	100.0	80	100.1	41	100.0	6	100.0	1	100.0	0

(continued)

TABLE 3.6C. (continued)

	Born in China		Born in U.S.		Total	
	No.	%	No.	%	No.	%
Single females	8	9.1	80	62.5	88	40.7
Married women with resident husbands	55	62.5	41	32.0	96	44.4
Married women without resident husbands	7	7.9	6	4.7	13	6.0
Women who are widowed or divorced	18	20.5	1	0.8	19	8.8
	88	100.0%	128	100.1%	216	99.9

Source: Author's tally and computation from the 1910 manuscript census of population. For a list of counties counted as "mining and mountain," see Appendix A at the end of Chapter 3.

Note: Four females born in China with unknown marital status are not listed above because of space limitation. However, one single woman born in China with unknown age is listed above because we know her marital status.

Abbreviations: w/ = with; Other BP = birthplace other than China or the U.S.

TABLE 3.7A. Spouses Living Together: Type of Couple by Age Gap, Number and Percentage in Each Age Gap Cohort

City and County of San Francisco, 1910

Type of Couple

Husbands Are Older Than Their Wives

Age Gap in Years	Type I Couples China-born husband & China-born wife		Type II Couples China-born husband & U.S.-born wife		Type III Couples U.S.-born husband & China-born wife		Type IV Couples U.S.-born husband & U.S.-born wife		Birth-Place Unknown	Subtotal	
	Number	Percent	Number	Percent	Number	Percent	Number	Percent	Unknown	Number	%
0–5	142	27.7	17	7.6	5	62.5	35	70.0	(1)	199	25.1
6–10	121	23.6	34	15.2	1	12.5	10	20.0	0	166	20.9
11–15	91	17.7	44	19.6	2	25.0	4	8.0	0	141	17.8
16–20	83	16.2	58	25.9	0	0	1	2.0	0	142	17.9
21–25	41	8.0	42	18.8	0	0	0	0	0	83	10.4
26–30	26	5.1	20	9.0	0	0	0	0	0	46	5.8
31–35	5	1.0	5	2.2	0	0	0	0	0	10	1.3
36–40	2	0.4	3	1.3	0	0	0	0	0	5	0.6
41–45	1	0.2	2	0.4	0	0	0	0	0	2	0.3
Subtotal	512	99.9	224	100.0	8	100.0	50	100.0	(1)	794	100.1
Wives Are Older Than Their Husbands											
0–5	17	68.0	2	50.0	0	0	4	66.7	0	23	65.7
6–10	6	24.0	2	50.0	0	0	2	33.3	0	10	28.6
11–15	1	4.0	0	0	0	0	0	0	0	1	2.9
16–20	1	4.0	0	0	0	0	0	0	0	1	2.9
Subtotal	25	100.0	4	100.0	0	0	6	100.0	0	35	100.1

(continued)

TABLE 3.7A. (continued)

City and County of San Francisco, 1910

Type of Couple

Husbands Are Older Than Their Wives

Age Gap in Years	Type I Couples China-born husband & China-born wife		Type II Couples China-born husband & U.S.-born wife		Type III Couples U.S.-born husband & China-born wife		Type IV Couples U.S.-born husband & U.S.-born wife		Birth-Place Unknown	Subtotal	
	Number	Percent	Number	Percent	Number	Percent	Number	Percent	Number	Number	%
Total (older husbands + older wives)	537		228		8		56			829	
% in each type of couple		64.8		27.5		1.0		6.7			100.1
% of couples with older husbands		95.3		98.2		100.0		89.3			95.8
% of couples with older wives		4.7		1.8		0		10.7			4.2
		100.0%		100.0%		100.0%		100.0%			100.0%

	Born in China		Born in U.S.		Total	
	No.	%	No.	%	No.	%
Husbands	766	92.4	64	7.7	829	100.1
Wives	544	65.7	284	34.3	829	100.0

Source: Author's tally and computation from the 1900 manuscript census of population.

Note: In addition to the couples listed above, one couple with unknown birthplaces is listed above but that couple and another one with both spouses born in China but with unknown ages are not included in the computations in this table.

TABLE 3.7B. Spouses Living Together: Type of Couple by Age Gap, Number and Percentage in Each Age Gap Cohort

Agricultural Counties in California, 1900

	Type of Couple										Subtotal	
	Husbands Are Older Than Their Wives											
	Type I Couples China-born husband & China-born wife		Type II Couples China-born husband & U.S.-born wife		Type III Couples U.S.-born husband & China-born wife		Type IV Couples U.S.-born husband & U.S.-born wife		Birth-Place Unknown			
Age Gap in Years	Number	Percent	Number	Percent	Number	Percent	Number	Percent	Unknown		Number	%
0–5	62	21.5	6	4.5	1	33.3	7	50.0	0		76	17.4
6–10	61	21.2	17	13.6	2	66.7	5	35.7	0		86	19.7
11–15	60	20.8	38	28.8	0	0	2	14.3	0		100	22.9
16–20	45	15.6	26	19.7	0	0	0	0	0		70	16.1
21–25	29	10.1	21	15.2	0	0	0	0	0		49	11.2
26–30	17	5.9	13	9.8	0	0	0	0	0		30	6.9
31–35	11	3.8	7	5.3	0	0	0	0	0		18	4.1
36–40	3	1.0	3	2.3	0	0	0	0	0		6	1.4
41–45	0	0	1	0.8	0	0	0	0	0		1	0.2
Subtotal	288	99.9	132	100.0	3	100.0	14	100.0	0		436	99.9
Wives Are Older Than Their Husbands												
0–5	21	61.8	0	0	0	0	1	100.0	0		22	59.5
6–10	10	29.4	2	100.0	0	0	0	0	0		12	32.4
11–15	2	5.8	0	0	0	0	0	0	0		2	5.4
16–20	1	2.9	0	0	0	0	0	0	0		1	2.7
Subtotal	34	99.9	2	100.0	0	0	1	100.0	0		37	100.0

(continued)

TABLE 3.7B. (continued)

	Agricultural Counties in California, 1900										
	Type of Couple										
	Husbands Are Older Than Their Wives								Birth-Place Unknown	Subtotal	
	Type I Couples China-born husband & China-born wife		Type II Couples China-born husband & U.S.-born wife		Type III Couples U.S.-born husband & China-born wife		Type IV Couples U.S.-born husband & U.S.-born wife				
Age Gap in Years	Number	Percent	Number	Percent	Number	Percent	Number	Percent	Unknown	Number	%
Total (older husbands + older wives)	322		134		3		15			473	
% in each type of couple		68.1		28.3		0.6		3.2			100.2
% of couples with older husbands		89.4		98.5		100.0		93.3			92.2
% of couples with older wives		10.6		1.5		0		6.7			7.8
		100.0%		100.0%		100.0%		100.0%			100.0%

	Born in China		Born in U.S.		Total	
	No.	%	No.	%	No.	%
Husbands	456	96.2	18	3.8	474	100.0
Wives	325	68.6	149	31.4	474	100.0

Source: Author's tally and computation from the 1900 manuscript census of population. For a list of counties counted as "agricultural," see Appendix A at the end of Chapter 3.

Note: In addition to the couples listed above, three couples with both spouses born in China with unknown ages are not included in the computations in this table.

110

TABLE 3.7C. Spouses Living Together: Type of Couple by Age Gap, Number and Percentage in Each Age Gap Cohort

Mining and Mountain Counties in California, 1900

Type of Couple

Age Gap in Years	Type I Couples China-born husband & China-born wife		Type II Couples China-born husband & U.S.-born wife		Type III Couples U.S.-born husband & China-born wife		Type IV Couples U.S.-born husband & U.S.-born wife		Birth-Place Unknown	Subtotal	
	Number	Percent	Number	Percent	Number	Percent	Number	Percent	Unknown	Number	%
Husbands Are Older Than Their Wives											
0–5	21	20.4	0	0	1	25.0	1	33.3	0	23	17.7
6–10	19	18.4	0	0	1	25.0	0	0	0	20	15.4
11–15	24	23.3	6	28.6	1	25.0	1	33.3	0	32	24.6
16–20	10	9.7	5	23.8	0	0	1	33.3	0	16	12.3
21–25	15	14.6	4	19.0	1	25.0	0	0	0	19	14.6
26–30	9	8.8	2	9.5	0	0	0	0	0	11	8.5
31–35	2	1.9	3	14.3	0	0	0	0	0	5	3.8
36–40	2	1.9	1	4.8	0	0	0	0	0	3	2.3
41–45	1	1.0	0	0	0	0	0	0	0	1	0.8
Subtotal	103	100.0	21	100.0	4	100.0	3	99.9	0	130	100.0
Wives Are Older Than Their Husbands											
0–5	9	56.3	0	0	0	0	0	0	0	9	56.3
6–10	5	31.3	0	0	0	0	0	0	0	5	31.3
11–15	0	0	0	0	0	0	0	0	0	0	0
16–20	2	12.3	0	0	0	0	0	0	0	2	12.3
Subtotal	16	99.9	0	0	0	0	0	0	0	16	99.9

(continued)

TABLE 3.7C. (continued)

Mining and Mountain Counties in California, 1900

	Type of Couple								Birth-Place	Subtotal	
	Husbands Are Older Than Their Wives										
	Type I Couples China-born husband & China-born wife		Type II Couples China-born husband & U.S.-born wife		Type III Couples U.S.-born husband & China-born wife		Type IV Couples U.S.-born husband & U.S.-born wife				
Age Gap in Years	Number	Percent	Number	Percent	Number	Percent	Number	Percent	Unknown	Number	%
Total (older husbands + older wives)	119		21		4		3			147	
% in each type of couple		81.0		14.3		2.7		2.0			100.0
% of couples with older husbands		86.6		100.0		100.0		100.0			89.0
% of couples with older wives		13.4		0		0		0			11.0
% of couples with age unknown		0		0		0		0			0
		100.0%		100.0%		100.0%		100.0%			100.0%

| | Born in China | | Born in U.S. | | Total | |
	No.	%	No.	%	No.	%
Husbands	140	95.2	7	4.8	147	100.0
Wives	123	83.7	24	16.3	147	100.0

Source: Author's tally and computation from the 1900 manuscript census of population. For a list of counties counted as "mining and mountain," see Appendix A at the end of Chapter 3.

TABLE 3.8A. Spouses Living Together: Type of Couple by Age Gap, Number and Percentage in Each Age Gap Cohort

City and County of San Francisco, 1910

Type of Couple

Age Gap in Years	Type I Couples China-born husband & China-born wife		Type II Couples China-born husband & U.S.-born wife		Type III Couples U.S.-born husband & China-born wife		Type IV Couples U.S.-born husband & U.S.-born wife		Birth-Place Unknown	Subtotal	
	Number	Percent	Number	Percent	Number	Percent	Number	Percent	Unknown	Number	%
Husbands Are Older Than Their Wives											
0–5	62	32.1	13	10.0	43	58.9	50	47.6	0	168	33.5
6–10	45	23.3	27	20.8	14	19.2	26	24.8	0	112	22.4
11–15	29	15.0	21	16.2	11	15.1	19	18.1	(1)	80	16.0
16–20	27	14.0	27	20.8	4	5.5	7	6.7	(1)	65	13.0
21–25	16	8.3	24	18.5	0	0	3	2.9	0	43	8.6
26–30	11	5.7	12	9.2	0	0	0	0	(2)	23	4.6
31–35	3	1.6	5	3.8	1	1.4	0	0	0	9	1.8
36–40	0	0	0	0	0	0	0	0	0	0	0
41–45	0	0	1	0.8	0	0	0	0	0	1	0.2
Subtotal	193	100.0	130	100.1	73	100.1	105	100.1	(4)	501	100.1
Wives Are Older Than Their Husbands											
0–5	3	75.0	0	0	2	50.0	2	66.7	0	7	63.4
6–10	1	25.0	0	0	0	0	1	33.3	0	2	18.2
11–15	0	0	0	0	1	25.0	0	0	0	1	9.1
16–20	0	0	0	0	1	25.0	0	0	0	1	9.1
Subtotal	4	100.0	0	0	4	100.0	3	100.0	0	11	100.0

(continued)

TABLE 3.8A. (continued)

	City and County of San Francisco, 1910										
	Type of Couple										
	Husbands Are Older Than Their Wives										
	Type I Couples China-born husband & China-born wife		Type II Couples China-born husband & U.S.-born wife		Type III Couples U.S.-born husband & China-born wife		Type IV Couples U.S.-born husband & U.S.-born wife		Birth-Place Unknown	Subtotal	
Age Gap in Years	Number	Percent	Number	Percent	Number	Percent	Number	Percent	Unknown	Number	%
Total (older husbands + older wives)	197		130		77		108			512	
% in each type of couple		38.5		25.4		15.0		21.1			100.0
% of couples with older husbands		98.0		100.0		94.8		96.3			97.9
% of couples with older wives		2.0		0		5.2		2.8			2.1
		100.0%		100.0%		100.0%		100.0%			100.0%

	Born in China		Born in U.S.		Total	
	No.	%	No.	%	No.	%
Husbands	327	63.9	185	36.1	512	100.0
Wives	274	53.5	238	46.5	512	100.0

Source: Author's tally and computation from the 1910 manuscript census of population.

Note: In addition to the couples listed above, four couples in which one or both spouses with unknown birthplaces are listed above but they and the one couple with both spouses born in the U.S. with unknown ages are not included in the computations in this table.

114

TABLE 3.8B. Spouses Living Together: Type of Couple by Age Gap, Number and Percentage in Each Age Gap Cohort

Agricultural Counties in California, 1910

| | Type of Couple | | | | | | | | Birth-Place | Subtotal | |
| | Type I Couples China-born husband & China-born wife | | Type II Couples China-born husband & U.S.-born wife | | Type III Couples U.S.-born husband & China-born wife | | Type IV Couples U.S.-born husband & U.S.-born wife | | | | |
Age Gap in Years	Number	Percent	Number	Percent	Number	Percent	Number	Percent	Unknown	Number	%
	Husbands Are Older Than Their Wives										
0–5	85	29.0	8	4.0	18	54.5	32	39.5	0	143	23.4
6–10	72	24.6	22	11.0	8	24.2	24	29.6	0	126	20.8
11–15	44	15.0	39	19.5	4	12.1	17	21.0	0	104	17.2
16–20	36	12.3	48	24.0	3	9.1	5	6.2	2	92	15.2
21–25	25	8.5	49	24.5	0	0	1	1.2	0	75	12.4
26–30	16	5.5	21	10.5	0	0	1	1.2	0	38	6.3
31–35	10	3.4	11	5.5	0	0	1	1.2	0	22	3.6
36–40	3	1.0	2	1.0	0	0	0	0	0	5	0.8
41–45	2	0.7	0	0	0	0	0	0	0	2	0.3
Subtotal	293	100.0	200	100.0	33	99.9	81	99.9	(2)	607	100.0
	Wives Are Older Than Their Husbands										
0–5	11	73.3	2	100.0	0	0	5	100.0	0	18	81.8
6–10	1	0	0	0	0	0	0	0	0	1	4.5
11–15	0	0	0	0	0	0	0	0	0	0	0
16–20	2	13.3	0	0	0	0	0	0	0	2	9.1
21–25	1	6.7	0	0	0	0	0	0	0	1	4.5
Subtotal	15	100.0	2	100.0	0	0	5	100.0	0	22	99.9

(continued)

115

TABLE 3.8B. (continued)

Agricultural Counties in California, 1910

	Type of Couple										
	Husbands Are Older Than Their Wives										
	Type I Couples China-born husband & China-born wife		Type II Couples China-born husband & U.S.-born wife		Type III Couples U.S.-born husband & China-born wife		Type IV Couples U.S.-born husband & U.S.-born wife		Birth-Place Unknown	Subtotal	
Age Gap in Years	Number	Percent	Number	Percent	Number	Percent	Number	Percent		Number	%
Total (older husbands + older wives)	308		202		33		86		(2)	629	
% in each type of couple		49.0		32.1		5.2		13.7			100.0
% of couples with older husbands		95.1		99.0		100.0		94.2			96.5
% of couples with older wives		4.9		1.0		0		5.8			3.5
		100.0%		100.0%		100.0%		100.0%			100.0%

	Born in China		Born in U.S.		Total	
	No.	%	No.	%	No.	%
Husbands	510	81.1	119	18.9	629	100.0
Wives	341	54.2	288	45.8	629	100.0

Source: Author's tally and computation from the 1910 manuscript census of population. For a list of counties counted as "agricultural," see Appendix A at the end of Chapter 3.

Note: The two couples with unknown birthplaces are listed above but are not included in the computations in this table.

116

Table 3.8C. Spouses Living Together: Type of Couple by Age Gap, Number and Percentage in Each Age Gap Cohort

Mining and Mountain Counties in California, 1910

	Type of Couple												
	Type I Couples China-born husband & China-born wife		Type II Couples China-born husband & U.S.-born wife		Type III Couples U.S.-born husband & China-born wife		Type IV Couples U.S.-born husband & U.S.-born wife		Birth-Place Unknown	Subtotal	
Age Gap in Years	Number	Percent	Number	Percent	Number	Percent	Number	Percent	Unknown	Number	%
Husbands Are Older Than Their Wives											
0–5	9	23.1	2	6.9	6	60.0	1	12.5	0	18	20.9
6–10	9	23.1	3	10.3	2	20.0	3	37.5	0	17	19.8
11–15	8	20.5	4	13.8	2	20.0	0	0	0	14	16.3
16–20	2	5.1	5	17.2	0	0	2	25.0	(1)	9	10.5
21–25	6	15.4	6	20.7	0	0	1	12.5	0	13	15.1
26–30	4	10.3	7	24.1	0	0	1	12.5	0	12	14.0
31–35	1	2.6	2	6.9	0	0	0	0	0	3	3.5
Subtotal	39	100.1	29	99.9	10	100.0	8	100.0	(1)	86	100.1
Wives Are Older Than Their Husbands											
0–5	4	57.1	0	0	0	0	0	0	0	4	57.1
6–10	3	42.9	0	0	0	0	0	0	0	3	42.9
Subtotal	7	100.0	0	0	0	0	0	0	0	7	100.0

(continued)

TABLE 3.8C. (continued)

Mining and Mountain Counties in California, 1910

	Type of Couple										
	Husbands Are Older Than Their Wives										
	Type I Couples China-born husband & China-born wife		Type II Couples China-born husband & U.S.-born wife		Type III Couples U.S.-born husband & China-born wife		Type IV Couples U.S.-born husband & U.S.-born wife		Birth-Place Unknown	Subtotal	
Age Gap in Years	Number	Percent	Number	Percent	Number	Percent	Number	Percent	Unknown	Number	%
Total (older husbands + older wives)	46		29		10		8		(1)	93	
% in each type of couple		49.5		31.2		10.8		8.6			100.1
% of couples with older husbands		84.8		100.0		100.0		100.0			92.6
% of couples with older wives		15.2		0		0		0			7.4
		100.0%		100.0%		100.0%		100.0%			100.0%

	Born in China		Born in U.S.		Total	
	No.	%	No.	%	No.	%
Husbands	75	80.6	18	19.4	93	100.0
Wives	56	60.2	37	39.8	93	100.0

Source: Author's tally and computation from the 1910 manuscript census of population. For a list of counties counted as "mining and mountain," see Appendix A at the end of Chapter 3.

Note: one couple with unknown birthplaces is listed above but is not included in the computations in this table.

118

TABLE 3.9A. Presently Married Chinese Women: Birthplace by Age at Marriage

	City and County of San Francisco, 1910							
Age at Marriage	Born in China		Born in U.S.		Other BP		Subtotal	
	No.	%	No.	%	No.	%	No.	%
0–12	32	5.2	13	4.1	0	0	45	4.8
13	18	2.9	11	3.5	0	0	29	3.1
14	24	3.9	27	8.6	0	0	51	5.4
15	33	5.3	33	10.5	0	0	66	7.0
16	58	9.3	37	11.8	0	0	95	10.1
17	51	8.2	48	15.3	0	0	99	10.6
18	66	10.6	41	13.1	0	0	107	11.4
19	46	7.4	24	7.6	0	0	70	7.5
20	54	8.7	20	6.4	1	100.0	75	8.0
21	42	6.8	14	4.5	0	0	56	6.0
22	32	5.2	11	3.5	0	0	43	4.6
23	21	3.4	7	2.2	0	0	28	3.0
24	14	2.3	3	1.0	0	0	17	1.8
25	23	3.7	8	2.5	0	0	31	3.3
26	17	2.7	4	1.3	0	0	21	2.2
27	12	1.9	1	0.3	0	0	13	1.4
28	14	2.2	4	1.3	0	0	18	1.9
29	8	1.3	0	0	0	0	8	0.9
30	12	1.9	3	1.0	0	0	15	1.6
31–35	19	3.0	1	0.3	0	0	20	2.1
36–40	13	2.1	1	0.3	0	0	14	1.5
41–50	2	0.4	0	0	0	0	2	0.2
51–60	1	0.2	0	0	0	0	1	0.1
60 +	1	0.2	0	0	0	0	1	0.1
Age at marriage unknown	8	1.3	3	0.9	0	0	11	1.2
Total	621	100.1	315	100.9	1	100.0	937	99.9

Percent of married women born in China	66.3
Percent of married women born in U.S.	33.6
Percent of married women with unknown birthplace	0.1
	100.0%

Median age at marriage of women born in China	18.5 years
Median age at marriage of women born in the U.S.	16.7 years

	Born in China		Born in U.S.		Total	
	No.	%	No.	%	No.	%
Girls married at age 15 or younger	101	16.3	84	26.7	185	19.8
Girls married between ages 16 and 20	275	44.2	170	54.0	445	47.5

(continued)

TABLE 3.9A. (continued)

	Born in China		Born in U.S.		Total	
	No.	%	No.	%	No.	%
Women married at age 21 or older	237	38.2	58	18.4	295	31.5
Women whose age at marriage is unknown	8	1.3	3	1.0	11	1.2
Total	621	100.0	315	100.1	936	100.0

Source: Author's tally and computation from the 1900 manuscript census of population.
Note: The one female who was born elsewhere (not in China or the U.S.) is listed above but is not included in computing the percentage married in each age cohort.
Abbreviation: Other BP = birthplace other than China or the U.S.

TABLE 3.9B. Presently Married Chinese Women: Birthplace by Age at Marriage

Age at Marriage	Agricultural Counties in California, 1900							
	Born in China		Born in U.S.		Other BP		Subtotal	
	No.	%	No.	%	No.	%	No.	%
0–12	14	3.6	4	2.6	0	0	18	3.3
13	2	0.5	5	3.2	0	0	7	1.3
14	16	4.1	7	4.5	0	0	23	4.2
15	26	6.6	13	8.4	0	0	39	7.1
16	18	4.6	22	14.2	0	0	40	7.3
17	30	7.7	21	13.5	0	0	51	9.3
18	29	7.4	17	11.0	0	0	46	8.4
19	20	5.1	10	6.5	0	0	30	5.5
20	28	7.1	13	8.4	0	0	41	7.5
21	24	6.1	9	5.8	0	0	33	6.0
22	13	3.3	6	3.9	0	0	19	3.5
23	9	2.3	7	4.5	0	0	16	2.9
24	14	3.6	4	2.6	0	0	18	3.3
25	16	4.1	5	3.2	0	0	21	3.8
26	17	4.3	1	0.6	0	0	18	3.3
27	11	2.8	3	1.9	0	0	14	2.6
28	9	2.3	0	0	0	0	9	1.6
29	9	2.3	0	0	0	0	9	1.6
30	12	3.1	1	0.6	0	0	13	2.4
31–35	25	6.4	3	1.9	0	0	28	5.1
36–40	14	3.6	0	0	0	0	14	2.6
41–50	10	2.5	0	0	0	0	10	1.8
51–60	4	1.0	0	0	0	0	4	0.7
60 +	0	0	0	0	0	0	0	0
Age at marriage unknown	22	5.6	4	2.6	1	0	27	4.9
Total	392	100.0	155	99.9	1	100.0	548	100.0

TABLE 3.9B. (continued)

	Born in China		Born in U.S.		Total	
Percent of married women born in China	71.5					
Percent of married women born in U.S.	28.3					
Percent of married women with unknown birthplace	0.2					
	100.0%					
Median age at marriage of women born in China	20.5 years					
Median age at marriage of women born in the U.S.	17.3 years					

	Born in China		Born in U.S.		Total	
	No.	%	No.	%	No.	%
Girls married at age 15 or younger	58	14.8	29	18.7	87	15.9
Girls married between ages 16 and 20	125	31.9	83	53.5	208	38.0
Women married at age 21 or older	187	47.7	39	25.2	226	41.3
Women whose age at marriage is unknown	22	5.6	4	2.6	26	4.3
Total	392	100.0	155	100.0	547	100.0

Source: My tally and computation from the 1900 manuscript census of population. For a list of counties counted as "agricultural," see Appendix A at the end of Chapter 3.
Note: The one female born elsewhere (not in China or the U.S.) is listed above but is not included in computing the percentage married in each age cohort.
Abbreviation: Other BP = birthplace other than China or the U.S.

TABLE 3.9C. Presently Married Chinese Women: Birthplace by Age at Marriage

	Mining and Mountain Counties in California, 1900							
Age at Marriage	Born in China		Born in U.S.		Other BP		Subtotal	
	No.	%	No.	%	No.	%	No.	%
0–12	7	4.5	2	7.4	0	0	9	5.0
13	1	0.6	0	0	0	0	1	0.6
14	2	1.3	0	0	0	0	2	1.1
15	5	3.2	5	18.5	0	0	10	5.5
16	6	3.9	3	11.1	0	0	9	5.0
17	8	5.2	5	18.5	0	0	13	7.2
18	5	3.2	3	11.1	0	0	8	4.4
19	7	4.5	1	3.7	0	0	8	4.4
20	12	7.8	5	18.5	0	0	17	9.4
21	5	3.2	1	3.7	0	0	6	3.3
22	6	3.9	0	0	0	0	6	3.3
23	4	2.6	1	3.7	0	0	5	2.8
24	3	1.9	0	0	0	0	3	1.7

(*continued*)

TABLE 3.9C. (continued)

	Mining and Mountain Counties in California, 1900							
Age at Marriage	Born in China		Born in U.S.		Other BP		Subtotal	
	No.	%	No.	%	No.	%	No.	%
25	2	1.3	0	0	0	0	2	1.1
26	5	3.2	1	3.7	0	0	6	3.3
0–27	0	0	0	0	0	0	0	0
28	2	1.3	0	0	0	0	2	1.1
29	2	1.3	0	0	0	0	2	1.1
30	7	4.5	0	0	0	0	7	3.9
31–35	14	9.1	0	0	0	0	14	7.7
36–40	7	4.5	0	0	0	0	7	3.9
41–50	8	5.2	0	0	0	0	8	4.4
51–60	2	1.3	0	0	0	0	2	1.1
60 +	0	0	0	0	0	0	0	0
Age at marriage unknown	29	18.8	0	0	0	0	29	16.0
Total	154	99.5	27	99.9	0	0	181	100.0

Percent of married women born in China	85.1
Percent of married women born in U.S.	14.9
Percent of married women with unknown birthplace	0
	100.0%

Median age at marriage of women born in China	26.0 years
Median age at marriage of women born in the U.S.	16.7 years

	Born in China		Born in U.S.		Total	
	No.	%	No.	%	No.	%
Girls married at age 15 or younger	15	9.7	7	25.9	22	12.2
Girls married between ages 16 and 20	38	24.7	17	63.0	55	30.4
Women married at age 21 or older	72	46.8	3	11.1	75	41.4
Women whose age at marriage is unknown	29	18.8	0	0	29	16.0
Total	154	100.0	27	100.0	181	100.0

Source: Author's tally and computation from the 1900 manuscript census of population. For a list of counties counted as "mining and mountain," see Appendix A at the end of Chapter 3.

Abbreviation: Other BP = birthplace other than China or the U.S.

TABLE 3.10A. Presently Married Chinese Women: Birthplace by Age at Marriage

	City and County of San Francisco, 1910							
Age at Marriage	Born in China		Born in U.S.		Unkn. BP		Subtotal	
	No.	%	No.	%	No.	%	No.	%
0–12	4	1.2	7	2.5	0	0	11	1.8
13	2	0.6	2	0.7	0	0	4	0.6
14	1	0.3	3	1.1	0	0	4	0.6
15	16	4.8	9	3.2	0	0	25	4.1
16	26	7.8	34	12.1	0	0	60	9.7
17	33	9.9	42	15.0	0	0	75	12.2
18	38	11.3	41	14.6	0	0	79	12.8
19	34	10.1	20	7.1	0	0	54	8.8
20	41	12.2	28	10.0	1	50.0	70	11.3
21	16	4.8	13	4.6	0	0	29	4.7
22	17	5.1	10	3.6	0	0	27	4.4
23	10	3.0	8	2.9	0	0	18	2.9
24	7	2.1	5	1.8	0	0	12	1.9
25	6	1.8	8	2.9	0	0	14	2.3
26	10	3.0	4	1.4	0	0	14	2.3
27	5	1.5	5	1.8	0	0	10	1.6
28	9	2.7	5	1.8	0	0	14	2.3
29	1	0.3	2	0.7	0	0	3	0.5
30	3	0.9	4	1.4	0	0	7	1.1
31–35	9	2.7	3	1.1	0	0	12	1.9
36–40	3	0.9	0	0	0	0	3	0.5
41–50	1	0.3	0	0	0	0	1	0.2
51–60	0	0	0	0	0	0	0	0
60 +	0	0	0	0	0	0	0	0
Age at marriage unknown	43	12.8	27	9.6	1	50.0	71	11.5
Total	335	100.1	280	99.9	2	100.0	617	100.0

Percent of married women born in China		54.3
Percent of married women born in U.S.		45.4
Percent of married women with unknown birthplace		0.3
		100.0%

Median age at marriage of women born in China	20.3 years
Median age at marriage of women born in the U.S.	18.0 years

	Born in China		Born in U.S.		Total	
	No.	%	No.	%	No.	%
Girls married at age 15 or younger	23	6.9	21	7.5	44	7.1
Girls married between ages 16 and 20	172	51.3	165	58.9	338	54.8

(*continued*)

TABLE 3.10A. (continued)

	Born in China		Born in U.S.		Total	
	No.	%	No.	%	No.	%
Women married at age 21 or older	97	29.0	67	23.9	164	26.6
Women whose age at marriage is unknown	43	12.8	27	9.6	71	11.5
Total	335	100.0	280	99.9	617	100.0

Source: Author's tally and computation from the 1910 manuscript census of population.
Abbreviation: Unkn. BP = birthplace unknown.

TABLE 3.10B. Presently Married Chinese Women: Birthplace by Age at Marriage

	Agricultural Counties in California, 1910						
Age at Marriage	Born in China		Born in U.S.		Other BP		Subtotal	
	No.	%	No.	%	No.	%	No.	%
0–12	10	2.5	12	3.8	0	0	22	3.1
13	3	0.7	4	1.3	0	0	7	1.0
14	12	2.9	13	4.2	0	0	25	3.5
15	23	5.6	18	5.8	0	0	41	5.7
16	29	7.1	38	12.2	0	0	67	9.3
17	37	9.1	44	14.1	0	0	81	11.2
18	35	8.6	47	15.1	0	0	82	11.4
19	36	8.8	23	7.4	0	0	59	8.2
20	43	10.5	28	9.0	1	100.0	72	10.0
21	15	3.7	15	4.8	0	0	30	4.2
22	17	4.2	7	2.2	0	0	24	3.3
23	12	2.9	10	3.2	0	0	22	3.1
24	13	3.2	4	1.3	0	0	17	2.4
25	12	2.9	4	1.3	0	0	16	2.2
26	9	2.2	5	1.6	0	0	14	1.9
27	9	2.2	2	0.6	0	0	11	1.5
28	9	2.2	2	0.6	0	0	11	1.5
29	4	1.0	3	1.0	0	0	7	1.0
30	4	1.0	1	0.3	0	0	5	0.7
31–35	14	3.4	3	1.0	0	0	17	2.4
36–40	9	2.2	3	1.0	0	0	12	1.7
41–50	6	1.5	1	0.3	0	0	7	1.0
51–60	0	0	0	0	0	0	0	0
60 +	1	0.2	0	0	0	0	1	0.1
Age at marriage unknown	46	11.3	25	8.0	1	0	71	9.8
Total	408	99.9	312	100.1	1	100.0	721	100.2

TABLE 3.10B. (continued)

	Born in China		Born in U.S.		Total	
Percent of married women born in China	56.6					
Percent of married women born in U.S.	43.3					
Percent of married women with unknown birthplace	0.1					
	100.0%					
Median age at marriage of women born in China	19.5 years					
Median age at marriage of women born in the U.S.	17.6 years					

	Born in China		Born in U.S.		Total	
	No.	%	No.	%	No.	%
Girls married at age 15 or younger	48	11.8	47	15.1	95	13.2
Girls married between ages 16 and 20	180	44.1	180	57.7	360	49.9
Women married at age 21 or older	134	32.8	60	19.2	195	27.0
Women whose age at marriage is unknown	46	11.3	25	8.0	71	9.8
Total	408	100.0	312	100.0	721	100.0

Source: Author's tally and computation from the 1910 manuscript census of population. For a list of counties counted as "agricultural," see Appendix A at the end of Chapter 3. Abbreviation: Other BP = birthplace other than China or the U.S.

TABLE 3.10C. Presently Married Chinese Women: Birthplace by Age at Marriage

	Mining and Mountain Counties in California, 1910						
Age at Marriage	Born in China		Born in U.S.		Other BP		Subtotal
	No.	%	No.	%	No.	%	No.	%
0–12	1	1.6	0	0	0	0	1	0.9
13	1	1.6	0	0	0	0	1	0.9
14	0	0	4	8.3	0	0	4	3.6
15	4	6.5	5	10.4	0	0	9	8.2
16	3	4.8	2	4.2	0	0	5	4.5
17	6	9.7	4	8.3	0	0	10	9.1
18	4	6.5	11	22.9	0	0	15	13.6
19	4	6.5	2	4.2	0	0	6	5.5
20	3	4.8	5	10.4	0	0	8	7.3
21	3	4.8	0	0	0	0	3	2.7
22	2	3.2	2	4.2	0	0	4	3.6
23	1	1.6	1	2.1	0	0	2	1.8
24	5	8.1	2	4.2	0	0	7	6.4

(*continued*)

TABLE 3.10C. (continued)

Age at Marriage	Mining and Mountain Counties in California, 1910							
	Born in China		Born in U.S.		Other BP		Subtotal	
	No.	%	No.	%	No.	%	No.	%
0–25	3	4.8	1	2.1	0	0	4	3.6
26	3	4.8	1	2.1	0	0	4	3.6
27	0	0	1	2.1	0	0	1	0.9
28	2	3.2	0	0	0	0	2	1.8
29	2	3.2	0	0	0	0	2	1.8
30	1	1.6	1	2.1	0	0	2	1.8
31–35	7	11.3	3	6.3	0	0	9	7.2
36–40	1	1.6	1	2.1	0	0	2	1.8
41–50	3	4.8	0	0	0	0	1	0.9
51–60	0	0	0	0	0	0	0	0
60 +	0	0	0	0	0	0	0	0
Age at marriage unknown	3	4.8	3	6.3	0	0	6	5.5
Total	62	99.8	48	100.2	0	0	110	99.7

Percent of married women born in China	56.4
Percent of married women born in U.S.	43.6
Percent of married women with unknown birthplace	0
	100.0%

Median age at marriage of women born in China	22.0 years
Median age at marriage of women born in the U.S.	17.8 years

	Born in China		Born in U.S.		Total	
	No.	%	No.	%	No.	%
Girls married at age 15 or younger	6	9.7	9	18.8	15	13.6
Girls married between ages 16 and 20	20	32.3	24	50.0	44	40.0
Women married at age 21 or older	33	53.2	13	27.1	45	40.9
Women whose age at marriage is unknown	3	4.8	3	6.3	6	5.5
Total	62	100.0	48	100.0	110	100.0

Source: Author's tally and computation from the 1910 manuscript census of population. For a list of counties counted as "mining and mountain," see Appendix A at the end of Chapter 3.

Abbreviation: Other BP = birthplace other than China or the U.S.

TABLE 3.11A. Married Immigrant Women: Number of Years in the U.S. Before Marrying and Number of Years Married Before Coming to the U.S., by Years

	City and County of San Francisco, 1910							
	In U.S. Before Marrying				Married Before Coming to U.S.			
	With Resident Husband		Without Resident Husband		With Resident Husband		Without Resident Husband	
Years	Number	Percent	Number	Percent	Number	Percent	Number	Percent
0	58	14.9	7	13.2	0	0	0	0
1	30	7.7	4	7.5	20	13.8	2	10.5
2	33	8.5	4	7.5	17	11.7	2	10.5
3	25	6.4	5	9.4	13	9.0	2	10.5
4	30	7.7	2	3.8	11	7.6	0	0
5	32	8.2	3	5.7	13	9.0	1	5.3
6	17	4.4	2	3.8	8	5.5	2	10.5
7	20	5.1	1	1.9	9	6.2	0	0
8	9	2.3	3	5.7	5	3.4	0	0
9	16	4.1	2	3.8	8	5.5	0	0
10	25	6.4	5	9.4	11	7.6	2	10.5
11	16	4.1	0	0	4	2.8	1	5.3
12	10	2.6	3	5.7	6	4.1	2	10.5
13	9	2.3	1	1.9	3	2.1	0	0
14	12	3.1	1	1.9	5	3.4	0	0
15	8	2.1	1	1.9	5	3.4	0	0
16–20	19	4.9	3	5.7	1	0.7	2	10.5
21–25	4	1.0	0	0	2	1.4	2	10.5
26–30	2	0.5	0	0	0	0	0	0
31–40	2	0.5	0	0	0	0	1	5.3
41–50	1	0.3	0	0	0	0	0	0
Yrs. Unknown	12	3.1	6	11.3	0	0	0	0
Subtotal	390	100.1	53	100.1	145	100.0	19	100.1

	Number	Percent
Women (with and without resident husbands) who were in the U.S. before marrying	378	62.3
Women (with and without resident husbands) who married before coming to the U.S.	164	27.0
Women who married the same year as they came to the U.S. (listed as 0 year above)	65	10.7
Total	607	100.0%

	Number	Percent
Women who had been in the U.S. 1–5 years before they married	168	27.7
Women who had been in the U.S. 6–10 years before they married	100	16.5
Women who had been in the U.S. more than 10 years before they married	92	15.2
Women who had been in the U.S. for an unknown number of years before they married	18	3.0

(continued)

Table 3.11A. (continued)

	Number	Percent
Women who were married 1–5 years before they came to the U.S.	81	13.4
Women who were married 6–10 years before they came to the U.S.	45	7.4
Women who were married more than 10 years before they came to the U.S.	38	6.3
Total	607	100.2

Not counting the 65 women who married the same year as they came to the U.S. and the 18 without information on how many years they had been in the U.S. before marrying, the number of years used to compute the median year for women who had been in the U.S. before they married is 386 and the number of years used to compute the median year for women who married before they came to the U.S. is 146.

Median number of years in the U.S. before marrying	6.0 years
Median number of years married before coming to the U.S.	4.5 years

Source: Author's tally and computation from the 1900 census of population.

Table 3.11B. Married Immigrant Women: Number of Years in the U.S. Before Marrying and Number of Years Married Before Coming to the U.S., by Years

Agricultural Counties in California, 1900							
In U.S. Before Marrying				Married Before Coming to U.S.			
With Resident Husband		Without Resident Husband		With Resident Husband		Without Resident Husband	
Years	Number	Percent	Number	Percent	Number	Percent	Number	Percent
0	25	8.9	3	5.1	0	0	0	0
1	8	2.8	5	8.5	4	10.3	1	16.7
2	25	8.9	2	3.4	4	10.3	0	0
3	7	2.5	2	3.4	3	7.7	0	0
4	9	3.2	5	8.5	3	7.7	0	0
5	25	8.9	8	13.6	1	2.6	2	33.3
6	13	4.6	1	1.7	2	5.1	0	0
7	17	6.0	0	0	4	10.3	0	0
8	10	3.5	2	3.4	2	5.1	0	0
9	14	5.0	3	5.1	2	5.1	0	0
10	20	7.1	2	3.4	2	5.1	0	0
11	8	2.8	1	1.7	2	5.1	0	0
12	7	2.5	0	0	1	2.6	1	16.7
13	8	2.8	2	3.4	2	5.1	0	0
14	10	3.5	1	1.7	0	0	0	0
15	11	3.9	1	1.7	2	5.1	1	16.7
16–20	13	4.6	6	10.2	3	7.7	0	0

Table 3.11B. (continued)

	Agricultural Counties in California, 1900							
	In U.S. Before Marrying				Married Before Coming to U.S.			
	With Resident Husband		Without Resident Husband		With Resident Husband		Without Resident Husband	
Years	Number	Percent	Number	Percent	Number	Percent	Number	Percent
21–25	8	2.8	1	1.7	1	2.6	0	0
26–30	2	0.7	1	1.7	0	0	1	16.7
31–40	2	0.7	0	0	1	2.6	0	0
41–50	0	0	0	0	0	0	0	0
Yrs. Unknown	40	14.2	13	22.2	0	0	0	0
Subtotal	282	100.1	59	100.1	39	100.1	6	100.1

	Number	Percent
Women (with and without resident husbands) who were in the U.S. before marrying	313	81.1
Women (with and without resident husbands) who married before coming to the U.S.	45	11.7
Women who married the same year as they came to the U.S. (listed as 0 year above)	28	7.3
Total	386	100.1%

	Number	Percent
Women who had been in the U.S. 1–5 years before they married	96	24.9
Women who had been in the U.S. 6–10 years before they married	82	21.2
Women who had been in the U.S. more than 10 years before they married	82	21.2
Women who had been in the U.S. for an unknown number of years before they married	53	13.7
Women who were married 1–5 years before they came to the U.S.	18	4.7
Women who were married 6–10 years before they came to the U.S.	12	3.1
Women who were married more than 10 years before they came to the U.S.	15	3.9
Total	386	100.0

Not counting the 28 women who married the same year as they came to the U.S. and the 53 without information on how many years they had been in the U.S. before marrying, the number of years used to compute the median year for women who had been in the U.S. before they married is 260 and the number of years used to compute the median year for women who married before they came to the U.S. is 45.

Median number of years in the U.S. before marrying	7.3 years
Median number of years married before coming to the U.S.	6.5 years

Source: Author's tally and computation from the 1900 census of population. For a list of counties counted as "agricultural," see Appendix A at the end of Chapter 3.

TABLE 3.11C. Married Immigrant Women: Number of Years in the U.S. Before Marrying and Number of Years Married Before Coming to the U.S., by Years

	Mining and Mountain Counties in California, 1900							
	In U.S. Before Marrying				Married Before Coming to U.S.			
	With Resident Husband		Without Resident Husband		With Resident Husband		Without Resident Husband	
Years	Number	Percent	Number	Percent	Number	Percent	Number	Percent
0	10	8.5	1	3.2	0	0	0	0
1	5	4.2	2	6.5	3	33.3	0	0
2	9	7.6	2	6.5	1	11.1	0	0
3	5	4.2	0	0	1	11.1	0	0
4	7	5.9	0	0	0	0	0	0
5	3	2.5	2	6.5	0	0	0	0
6	0	0	0	0	1	11.1	0	0
7	2	1.7	1	3.2	0	0	0	0
8	0	0	0	0	1	11.1	0	0
9	5	4.2	2	6.5	0	0	0	0
10	5	4.2	3	9.7	1	11.1	0	0
11	1	0.8	0	0	0	0	0	0
12	1	0.8	0	0	0	0	0	0
13	1	0.8	1	3.2	0	0	0	0
14	0	0	1	3.2	0	0	1	100.0
15	4	3.4	2	6.5	1	11.1	0	0
16–20	9	7.6	0	0	0	0	0	0
21–25	3	2.5	3	9.7	0	0	0	0
26–30	5	4.2	0	0	0	0	0	0
31–40	2	1.7	0	0	0	0	0	0
41–50	0	0	0	0	0	0	0	0
Yrs. Unknown	39	33.1	10	32.3	0	0	0	0
Subtotal	118	100.0	31	100.1	9	99.9	1	100.0

	Number	Percent
Women (with and without resident husbands) who were in the U.S. before marrying	138	86.8
Women (with and without resident husbands) who married before coming to the U.S.	10	6.3
Women who married the same year as they came to the U.S. (listed as 0 year above)	11	6.9
Total	159	100.0

	Number	Percent
Women who had been in the U.S. 1–5 years before they married	35	22.0
Women who had been in the U.S. 6–10 years before they married	20	12.6
Women who had been in the U.S. more than 10 years before they married	34	21.4
Women who had been in the U.S. for an unknown number of years before they married	49	30.8

TABLE 3.11C. (continued)

	Number	Percent
Women who were married 1–5 years before they came to the U.S.	5	3.1
Women who were married 6–10 years before they came to the U.S.	3	1.9
Women who were married more than 10 years before they came to the U.S.	2	1.3
Total	159	100.0

Not counting the 11 women who married the same year as they came to the U.S. and the 49 without information on how many years they had been in the U.S. before marrying, the number of years used to compute the median year for women who had been in the U.S. before they married is 89 and the number of years used to compute the median year for women who married before they came to the U.S. is 10.

Median number of years in the U.S. before marrying	12.0 years
Median number of years married before coming to the U.S.	5.0 years

Source: Author's tally and computation from the 1900 census of population. For a list of counties counted as "mining and mountain," see Appendix A at the end of Chapter 3.

TABLE 3.12A. Married Immigrant Women: Number of Years in the U.S. Before Marrying and Number of Years Married Before Coming to the U.S., by Years

City and County of San Francisco, 1910							
In U.S. Before Marrying				Married Before Coming to U.S.			
With Resident Husband		Without Resident Husband		With Resident Husband		Without Resident Husband	
Number	Percent	Number	Percent	Number	Percent	Number	Percent
Years							
0	32	20.6	2	4.4	0	0	0	0
1	8	5.2	3	6.7	23	18.9	2	18.2
2	6	3.9	1	2.2	16	13.1	1	9.1
3	5	3.2	1	2.2	4	3.3	0	0
4	5	3.2	1	2.2	8	6.6	1	9.1
5	8	5.2	1	2.2	6	4.9	5	45.5
6	7	4.5	0	0	5	4.1	0	0
7	2	1.3	0	0	1	0.8	0	0
8	9	7.3	3	5.7	6	4.9	0	0
9	5	3.2	0	0	5	4.1	0	0
10	6	3.9	0	0	8	6.6	0	0
11	3	1.9	0	0	7	5.7	0	0
12	4	2.6	0	0	2	1.6	0	0
13	1	0.6	0	0	4	3.3	1	9.1
14	3	1.9	0	0	6	4.9	0	0
15	1	0.6	0	0	1	0.8	0	0

TABLE 3.12A. (continued)

	City and County of San Francisco, 1910							
	In U.S. Before Marrying				Married Before Coming to U.S.			
	With Resident Husband		Without Resident Husband		With Resident Husband		Without Resident Husband	
Years	Number	Percent	Number	Percent	Number	Percent	Number	Percent
16–20	5	3.2	0	0	13	10.7	0	0
21–25	1	0.6	1	2.2	5	4.1	0	0
26–30	1	0.6	0	0	2	1.6	1	9.1
31–40	1	0.6	0	0	0	0	0	0
41–50	0	0	0	0	0	0	0	0
Yrs. Unknown	42	27.1	34	75.6	0	0	0	0
Subtotal	155	99.9	45	100.0	122	100.0	11	100.1

	Number	Percent
Women (with and without resident husbands) who were in the U.S. before marrying	166	49.9
Women (with and without resident husbands) who married before coming to the U.S.	133	39.9
Women who married the same year as they came to the U.S. (listed as 0 year above)	34	10.2
Total	333	100.0%

	Number	Percent
Women who had been in the U.S. 1–5 years before they married	39	11.7
Women who had been in the U.S. 6–10 years before they married	30	9.0
Women who had been in the U.S. more than 10 years before they married	21	6.3
Women who had been in the U.S. for an unknown number of years before they married	76	22.8
Women who were married 1–5 years before they came to the U.S.	66	20.0
Women who were married 6–10 years before they came to the U.S.	25	7.5
Women who were married more than 10 years before they came to the U.S.	42	12.6
Total	333	100.1

Not counting the 34 women who married the same year as they came to the U.S. and the 76 without information on how many years they had been in the U.S. before marrying, the number of years used to compute the median year for women who had been in the U.S. before they married is 90 and the number of years used to compute the median year for women who married before they came to the U.S. is 133.

Median number of years in the U.S. before marrying	7.5 years
Median number of years married before coming to the U.S.	7.6 years

Source: Author's tally and computation from the 1910 census of population.

TABLE 3.12B. Married Immigrant Women: Number of Years in the U.S. Before Marrying and Number of Years Married Before Coming to the U.S., by Years

	Agricultural Counties in California, 1910							
	In U.S. Before Marrying				Married Before Coming to U.S.			
	With Resident Husband		Without Resident Husband		With Resident Husband		Without Resident Husband	
Years	Number	Percent	Number	Percent	Number	Percent	Number	Percent
0	29	11.7	1	2.1	0	0	0	0
1	16	6.5	6	12.8	12	12.8	4	22.2
2	8	3.2	3	6.4	8	8.5	2	11.1
3	15	6.1	0	0	5	5.3	2	11.1
4	7	2.8	3	6.4	9	9.6	0	0
5	13	5.3	3	6.4	11	11.7	0	0
6	8	3.2	3	6.4	2	2.1	1	5.6
7	6	2.4	1	2.1	4	4.3	0	0
8	13	5.3	1	2.1	5	5.3	1	5.6
9	5	2.0	1	2.1	2	2.1	1	5.6
10	8	3.2	2	4.3	4	4.3	1	5.6
11	7	2.8	0	0	8	8.5	1	5.6
12	8	3.2	0	0	2	2.1	2	11.1
13	4	1.6	0	0	1	1.1	0	0
14	6	2.4	0	0	3	3.2	1	5.6
15	4	1.6	0	0	3	3.2	0	0
16–20	10	4.0	0	0	11	11.7	1	5.6
21–25	3	1.2	0	0	4	4.3	1	5.6
26–30	6	2.4	0	0	0	0	0	0
31–40	0	0	0	0	0	0	0	0
41–50	0	0	0	0	0	0	0	0
Yrs. Unknown	71	28.7	22	46.8	0	0	0	0
Subtotal	247	99.8	47	99.9	94	100.1	18	100.0

	Number	Percent
Women (with and without resident husbands) who were in the U.S. before marrying	264	65.0
Women (with and without resident husbands) who married before coming to the U.S.	112	27.6
Women who married the same year as they came to the U.S. (listed as 0 year above)	30	7.4
Total	406	100.0

	Number	Percent
Women who had been in the U.S. 1–5 years before they married	74	18.2
Women who had been in the U.S. 6–10 years before they married	48	11.8
Women who had been in the U.S. more than 10 years before they married	49	12.1

(continued)

TABLE 3.12B. (continued)

	Number	Percent
Women who had been in the U.S. for an unknown number of years before they married	93	22.9
Women who were married 1–5 years before they came to the U.S.	53	13.1
Women who were married 6–10 years before they came to the U.S.	21	5.2
Women who were married more than 10 years before they came to the U.S.	38	9.4
Total	406	100.1

Not counting the 30 women who married the same year as they came to the U.S. and the 93 without information on how many years they had been in the U.S. before marrying, the number of years used to compute the median year for women who had been in the U.S. before they married is 231 and the number of years used to compute the median year for women who married before they came to the U.S. is 45.

Median number of years in the U.S. before marrying	9.4 years
Median number of years married before coming to the U.S.	6.0 years

Source: Author's tally and computation from the 1910 census of population. For a list of counties counted as "agricultural," see Appendix A at the end of Chapter 3.

TABLE 3.12C. Married Immigrant Women: Number of Years in the U.S. Before Marrying and Number of Years Married Before Coming to the U.S., by Years

	Mining and Mountain Counties in California, 1910							
	In U.S. Before Marrying				Married Before Coming to U.S.			
	With Resident Husband		Without Resident Husband		With Resident Husband		Without Resident Husband	
Years	Number	Percent	Number	Percent	Number	Percent	Number	Percent
0	7	14.3	1	14.3	0	0	0	0
1	1	2.0	1	14.3	0	0	0	0
2	2	4.1	0	0	0	0	0	0
3	4	8.2	0	0	0	0	0	0
4	3	6.1	1	14.3	0	0	0	0
5	4	8.2	0	0	1	16.7	0	0
6	0	0	0	0	1	16.7	0	0
7	1	2.0	0	0	1	16.7	0	0
8	2	4.1	0	0	0	0	0	0
9	3	6.1	0	0	0	0	0	0
10	5	10.2	0	0	0	0	0	0
11	1	2.0	0	0	0	0	0	0
12	0	0	0	0	0	0	0	0
13	1	2.0	0	0	1	16.7	0	0
14	0	0	0	0	0	0	0	0
15	0	0	1	14.3	1	16.7	0	0

TABLE 3.12C. (continued)

	Mining and Mountain Counties in California, 1910							
	In U.S. Before Marrying				Married Before Coming to U.S.			
	With Resident Husband		Without Resident Husband		With Resident Husband		Without Resident Husband	
Years	Number	Percent	Number	Percent	Number	Percent	Number	Percent
16–20	5	10.2	1	14.3	0	0	0	0
21–25	1	2.0	0	0	0	0	0	0
26–30	0	0	0	0	0	0	0	0
31–40	2	4.1	0	0	1	16.7	0	0
41–50	0	0	1	14.3	0	0	0	0
Yrs. Unknown	7	14.3	1	14.3	1	16.7	0	0
Subtotal	49	99.9	7	100.1	6	100.1	0	100.0

	Number	Percent
Women (with and without resident husbands) who were in the U.S. before marrying	48	77.4
Women (with and without resident husbands) who married before coming to the U.S.	6	9.7
Women who married the same year as they came to the U.S. (listed as 0 year above)	8	12.9
Total	62	100.0

	Number	Percent
Women who had been in the U.S. 1–5 years before they married	16	25.8
Women who had been in the U.S. 6–10 years before they married	11	17.7
Women who had been in the U.S. more than 10 years before they married	14	22.6
Women who had been in the U.S. for an unknown number of years before they married	8	12.9
Women who were married 1–5 years before they came to the U.S.	0	0
Women who were married 6–10 years before they came to the U.S.	3	4.8
Women who were married more than 10 years before they came to the U.S.	2	3.2
Total	62	99.9

Not counting the 8 women who married the same year as they came to the U.S. and the 8 without information on how many years they had been in the U.S. before marrying, the number of years used to compute the median year for women who had been in the U.S. before they married is 46 and the number of years used to compute the median year for women who married before they came to the U.S. is 6.

Median number of years in the U.S. before marrying	16.3 years
Median number of years married before coming to the U.S.	7.0 years

Source: Author's tally and computation from the 1910 census of population. For a list of counties counted as "mining and mountain," see Appendix A at the end of Chapter 3.

4 Chinese Herbalists in the United States
HAIMING LIU

THE PRACTICE OF HERBAL MEDICINE is a rare instance of a profession that allowed Chinese immigrants to make a living for a prolonged period using a truly ethnic skill. Herb stores opened as soon as Chinese arrived in America. Medical knowledge being popular in Chinese society, more and more practitioners came to serve the needs of their fellow countrymen as Chinese immigration increased. Herbal medicinal formulae use hundreds of herbs gathered on the mountains and in the valleys of China. That meant herbalists in America had to import herbs regularly from their homeland. Thus, herbal medicine involved a transpacific trade. As a transplanted cultural practice, the herbal medicine business provides an illuminating example of the transpacific flow of people, medical knowledge, and ethnic goods.

The history of herbal medicine in America also illustrates how an ethnic medical skill gained a foothold in a new setting. In their efforts to bypass unfair restrictions and cross ethnic boundaries to serve society at large, Chinese immigrant herbalists developed and expanded their careers in a Western society where most of their patients were not familiar with Chinese culture and the medical profession was increasingly standardized and regulated. Like a Chinese restaurant, herbal medical practice served the needs of both Chinese and non-Chinese. However, unlike Chinese cuisine, herbal medicine could not change its ingredients, flavor, or dispensation to suit the taste of mainstream Americans. Rather, it had to remain distinctively Chinese in order to be effective. The acceptance of and the respect for Chinese herbal medicine demonstrate how mainstream American patients adapted themselves to an Asian form of therapy. Thus, Chinese herbal medicine can be seen as an instance of reverse assimilation.

In this chapter, I document why and when Chinese herbal medicine arose in America, who the herbalists were, how they operated their businesses, the major challenges they faced, and the accomplishments they achieved in their medical/business careers. By examining the history of Chinese herbalists, I intend to expand our understanding of early Chinese immigrants, their social backgrounds, and the cultural practices they brought with them. Chinese herbalists worked in an anti-Chinese environment; despite that, they managed to do a thriving business from the mid-nineteenth century to the first half of the twentieth. Their history challenges U.S.-centered and nation-based perspectives in immigration studies and promotes a transnational, multilingual approach to the discourse on the Asian American experience.

THE MEDICAL KNOWLEDGE OF CHINESE IMMIGRANTS

Herbal medical practice began as soon as the Chinese arrived in the United States. In the pioneer days of the mid-nineteenth century, Chinese stores supplied their immigrant patrons with not only food and clothing but also herbal medicine and other health care items. By the mid-1850s, San Francisco's Chinatown had grown into a bustling place with more than eighty stores doing various kinds of business. Five of them were herb shops.[1] According to Paul Buell and Christopher Muench, "although there are no direct accounts of Chinese medical practice in the United States prior to the 1860s," it is likely that professional herbalists were among the earliest Chinese immigrants to come in the late 1840s and 1850s.[2] Fiddletown in Amador County, California, has preserved to this day the old Chew Kee Herb Shop established by pioneer immigrant Fung Jong Yee in 1851. This business remained in operation for fifty-three years. According to Charles Hillinger, during the gold rush, as many as five to ten thousand Chinese miners lived in Fiddletown.[3]

Like other Chinese retail services, an herb shop in the early days was a transplanted business that retained the style of operation long established in China. It sold formulated medicines and various herbs as well as hired a physician to diagnose symptoms through feeling pulses and prescribing herbal remedies. As in China, some stores hung a dried calabash over the counter to signify the availability of medical service. Patients could easily communicate with the physicians about their symptoms and purchase medicinal herbs or other curative items for minor diseases and injuries. Herbal tea or other healing methods were familiar treatments that have been used by the Chinese for several thousand years. In the gold rush days, Chinese immigrants realized that life in America was rough, mobile, and sometimes dangerous. Western medical facilities were inadequate and not always effective, which meant that medical care was an important need among Chinese immigrants. Herb stores existed not only in San Francisco's Chinatown but also in many Chinese communities in remote mining areas. According to Liu Pei Chi, every Chinese community had at least one or sometimes three to four herb stores, each of which had a physician to diagnose the clients' ailments and to provide therapy. As Chinese immigrants called themselves "Tang people," they referred to the physicians as "Tang doctors" and those who treated non-Chinese patients as "Tang Fan" doctors.[4]

The existence of numerous herb shops or general stores that sold herbs reflects the fact that medical knowledge was common among Chinese immigrants. Many of them knew what herbs or herbal formulations they might need for certain minor diseases or injuries. If they needed to consult a physician for a more serious symptom, they would see one; otherwise, they just purchased the herbs they thought they needed. In 1964, the Chinese Historical Society of America in San Francisco examined three subbasements containing personal belongings of Chinese pioneers who had left them for safekeeping in the Son Loy Company at the turn of the century. Almost all the boxes and trunks contained Chinese herbs or medicines.[5] The *Overland Monthly*, a San Francisco–based journal, carried an article in 1869 that observed: "The Chinese, wherever they go, are followed up pretty closely by men professing to be skilled in the healing art. . . . Judging from the number of their apothecary stores, one would suppose that the Chinese were large consumers of medicines."[6] The widespread use of herbal medicine by Chinese immigrants was what made it a significant transpacific trade. As early as 1878, there were eighteen wholesale herb companies in San Francisco's Chinatown, which imported herbs from China and distributed them to Chinese herbalists all over the United States.[7] To facilitate the passage of Chinese medicines through U.S. customs, San Francisco's Chinese Chamber of Commerce published a booklet showing the forms and names of twenty-three types of herbs. The book was entitled *Liang yao zhaozhi* (Food and drug labels).[8]

MEDICAL CULTURE IN CHINA

Chinese immigrants came from a society where medical knowledge was popular and medical care was convenient. In towns and cities, herb stores, physicians, and other practitioners were always available to serve the needs of the population. In his discussion of the health care system in Hangzhou City during the Song dynasty (960–1279), Jacques Gernet pointed out that in addition to doctors' shops, there were many pharmacies: "some selling medicinal plants in the raw, wholesale, others selling ready-made decoctions (these being probably the most numerous), and others nothing but herbs for curing children's stomach disorders."[9] Charlotte Furth's analysis of medical cases in the late Ming dynasty (1368–1644) documents how patients and their family members argued and debated with established doctors over diagnoses and therapies, thereby revealing how widespread medical knowledge was.[10] During both the Ming and the Qing (1644–1911) dynasties, well-known doctors compiled verses and rhymes about the nature and uses of drugs, including recipes for the treatment of various ills, so that people could learn them verbally. As Angela Ki Che Leung pointed out, "Any literate person in late imperial China could have easy access to a reasonable amount of medical knowledge by reading inexpensive texts including verses, primers, and textbooks, and could apply his or her knowledge on the sick. Some even did it for a living."[11] In his observation of a rural village in Guangdong Province in the early 1920s, Daniel Kulp noted that gathering medicinal herbs was an occupation based on the needs of the home. "People regularly scour the nooks and crannies of the hills and mountains in search of the wild plants reputed to possess curative properties." He observed that even though there was a doctor in the village, "most curative effort is exercised by the housewives themselves. Whenever the opportunity offers, the women go out into the fields and on the hills to collect medicinal herbs with which they manufacture salves and medicines."[12] Some Chinese families possessed not only medical knowledge but also their own herbal formulations for certain sicknesses. The widespread knowledge of herbal medicine in China challenges the stereotypical image of early Chinese immigrants as poverty-striven and illiterate individuals.

Another indication of how important herbal medicine has been as a component of Chinese culture is that Chinese often refer to themselves as descendants of Emperor Yan and Emperor Huang. While Yan is better known as Shen Nong, a legendary person who tasted all herbs and created an herbal pharmacology, Huang authored a classical internal medicine text. In the words of Ralph Croizier, Chinese medicine is "the oldest continuous surviving tradition, rivaled only [by] the Ayurvedic medicine in India.... The earliest surviving pharmacopoeia, the *Pen-ts'ao ching* [*Ben cao jing* in pinyin] attributed to Shen-nung [Shen Nong], was probably compiled in the first century B.C."[13] Through centuries of empirical experiments, Chinese medicine developed into a systematic body of medical knowledge with complex theories and such specializations as pharmacology, pulsology, acupuncture, and moxibustion. Diagnostic methods included visual observation, inquiries into case histories, assessing auditory symptoms, and taking the pulse.[14]

Patients in China had many options because there were no enforceable medical standards, which enabled a wide variety of alternative practices and practitioners to exist. Elite scholarly physicians were trained at the Imperial Medical College and served the royal family and high-ranking officials. Many government officials themselves pursued herbal medicine as a hobby and saw it as a benevolent skill that enabled them to take care of family members, relatives, and friends. A master-disciple relationship produced authoritative herbalists with confidential formulations. There were also self-trained herbalists in towns and rural areas. Some Buddhist monks and Taoist priests were simultaneously respected and specialized physicians. Thus, Chinese traditional medicine was transmitted from one generation to the next through formal education, apprenticeships, and self-study.

Writings about medicine were popular among ordinary Chinese as well.[15] In addition to the classical medical texts often available at scholars' homes, urban bookstores, or libraries, printed booklets or handwritten herbal recipes for laymen were also passed around among relatives and friends or shared in the community for both medical and charity purposes. Yi-li Wu has documented how handbooks based on herbal formulations for women's illnesses prepared by the Bamboo Grove Monastery in Zhejiang Province were widely circulated in the eighteenth and nineteenth centuries all over China.[16] The popularity of medical books and the free circulation of herbal recipes reveal important aspects of Chinese society. First, many ordinary Chinese not only could read and write, but also possessed some basic medical knowledge. Second, as the Chinese were always interested in herbal recipes, both old and new, they were fairly well-informed patients. Third, sharing medical knowledge was a common practice among ordinary Chinese, which was considered a charitable act since health issues were important to everyone. Thus, herbal medicine was not only a profession but also a benevolent art practiced in a charitable way. In light of this tradition, we can perhaps better understand why some early Chinese immigrants in Seattle shared with one another an herbal recipe book containing the best personal recipes known to members of the Chinese community in that city. The book originally belonged to Wah Chong Company, which was founded in 1868. In subsequent years, it became a community property and served everyone when no professional herbalists were available.[17]

CHINESE ATTITUDES TOWARD WESTERN MEDICINE

Herbal medical practice should not lead us to assume Chinese immigrants were conservative, inward-looking individuals who totally rejected Western medicine or doctors. Early missionary doctor John Kerr's book, *A Guide to the City and Suburbs of Canton* (Guangzhou), recorded many Western medical institutions in China including his own Po-chi (Boji) Hospital.[18] Having noticed the importance of medical culture in Chinese society, missionaries translated Chinese medical works into Western languages. Robert Morrison, the first British missionary who arrived in China in 1807, purchased and collected eight hundred volumes of Chinese medicine books.[19] To attract Chinese attention, many missionaries were medical professionals who often provided free services in order to compete for patients with Chinese doctors. Peter Parker was the first American missionary doctor who opened his famous Ophthalmic Hospital in Guangzhou on November 4, 1835. The building housing the hospital was provided by Wu Bingjian, also known as Howqua, a leading *hong* (*hang*) merchant of Guangdong. In the first twenty years of its existence, the hospital treated over 53,000 patients. Following Parker, John Kerr established his Po-chi Hospital in 1859 and worked as its chief physician until 1899.[20]

During this period, Western-trained Chinese doctors began to practice in China as well. Dr. Huang Kuan graduated from a British university and returned to practice in Kerr's Po-chi Hospital. He assisted Kerr in establishing a medical school in 1863 and began to train local Chinese in the practice of Western medicine.[21] Holt Cheng was another well-known Chinese doctor of Western medicine. Born in Zhongshan County, Guangdong Province, Cheng went to Hawaii when he was eight years old, completed his medical education in California, and obtained his medical license in 1904. He then returned to China and set up Guanghua Hospital in Guangzhou in 1909—the first Western-style hospital established by a Chinese.[22] According to Jonathan D. Spence, during the late Qing dynasty, *Shen Bao*, a major newspaper in Shanghai, carried numerous advertisements for Western medicine and the language of such advertisements was often modeled after the sales style of traditional Chinese herbalists. Spence provided a good example of how open and receptive ordinary Chinese were to Western doctors: a Chinese boatman readily let a male Western doctor help his wife deliver her baby through caesarean section when the Chinese midwife gave up the difficult case and a woman Western doctor was not available.[23] As the story occurred in the Guangzhou area in the 1880s, we can surmise that many Chinese immigrants in the United States might have held the same open-minded attitude with regard to Western medicine as this boatman did.

THE DENIAL OF MEDICAL SERVICES TO THE CHINESE IN THE UNITED STATES

When Chinese immigrants arrived in the mid-nineteenth century, public medical facilities in America denied them service and segregated them from other patients. Thus, herbal medicine was often the only treatment available to them. During those years, newspapers and health officials described Chinese immigrants arriving in both Hawaii and the United States as carriers of dreaded alien diseases. Chinese passengers were subjected to medical examinations upon their arrival and Chinese residential areas were frequently inspected for disease and quarantine. Shih-shan Henry Tsai noted that in 1881, when Hawaii was still an independent kingdom, the ship *Septima* arrived in Honolulu with 699 Chinese passengers. All of them were detained in quarantine. In December 1899, the Hawaiian Board of Health removed 4,500 Chinese to a quarantine camp and the

Chinese quarter was incinerated after two cases of bubonic plague were reported.[24] When San Francisco suffered from a smallpox epidemic outbreak in 1876, the city's health authorities had every house in Chinatown fumigated. But the epidemic continued to cause many deaths. Unable to account for its severity, the city's health officer blamed the "lying and treacherous Chinamen" who allegedly ignored "sanitary laws" for the problem.[25]

Mary Coolidge, a pioneer scholar on Chinese immigration, noted that during the smallpox epidemic, the death rate in Chinatown actually decreased by six per thousand.[26] The public health issue was thus merely a pretext to define the Chinese as an inferior race. In the local political campaign in 1885, the Board of Supervisors made a horrifying report about the sanitary conditions in Chinatown. Unable to account for the Chinese immunity from "filth diseases," they attributed it to opium smoking. To dispense with such a ridiculous conclusion, Coolidge pointed out that the Chinese were "exceptionally free from venereal diseases partly because of their generally cleanly habits of body; and from bacterial diseases because they rarely drank unboiled water."[27]

Though Chinatown was accused of threatening the health of European Americans, city and county public hospitals refused to take Chinese patients. By 1880, the Chinese population reached about 75,000 in California and constituted 8.7 percent of the state's total population of almost 865,000; the approximately 22,000 Chinese in San Francisco made up 9.3 percent of the city's total population of 234,000. But the number of Chinese admitted into the city's hospital or other public health facilities composed less than 0.1 percent of all patients admitted during the 1870–1897 period.[28] The sick Chinese were usually "shunted off to a smallpox or pest hospital or to a special building, originally operated exclusively for the Chinese and later designed as the Lazaretto or Lepers' Quarters."[29] Under these circumstances, the Chinese community had to take action on its own.

As established Chinese communities expanded in size and wealth, professional herbal doctors, herb stores, and dispensaries appeared. By the late nineteenth century, San Francisco's Chinatown had become the largest Chinese community in the United States. To meet the needs of its people, each clan or district organization set up a clinic for its own aged and ailing members. The Chinese Consolidated Benevolent Association and the Chinese consul-general in San Francisco also planned to establish a general hospital in Chinatown. But the city authorities repeatedly rejected the plan. Finally the Chinese were allowed to establish a hospital in 1899, but it closed down within a year because it hired only Western physicians and could hardly meet the needs of the non-English-speaking community. In 1900, the Chinese set up the Donghua (Tung Wah) Dispensary at 828

Sacramento Street and hired both Western and Chinese doctors. However, the Chinese doctors were only allowed to work in conjunction with licensed Caucasian physicians.[30]

CROSSING ETHNIC BORDERS

Though herbal medicine began by serving the Chinese community, it soon became known in the European American community as well.[31] As early as 1858, an herbalist named Wo Tsun Yuen (Hu Junxiao) in San Francisco's Chinatown put up English-language signs on his shop to attract Caucasian patients.[32] Even in Philadelphia, where the Chinese population was tiny, herbal shops also appeared. The article "Chinese Drug Stores in America," published in 1887, noted that herbalists were busy seeing patients, so they hired clerks for bookkeeping and for preparing and dispensing the medicine, paying them from twenty-five to thirty dollars a month. This wage was similar to what unskilled Chinese laborers earned even though the clerks' work was a lot lighter and sometimes they received additional compensation.[33] An article entitled "Chinese Physicians in California," published in *Lippincott's Magazine* in 1899, noted that Li Po Tai (Li Putai) was the first doctor to leave his countrymen to go boldly among whites, advocating his system of medicine and establishing a lucrative practice in the non-Chinese community. Li's son and nephew also became Chinese herbalists in Los Angeles. They spoke English readily and they practiced exclusively among English-speaking people. The author of the article was so impressed by this healing art that he claimed the herbalist was "the only professional man who has invaded our shores from the Flowery Kingdom."[34] According to Alexander McLeod, Li amassed a large fortune because many rich white men and women in San Francisco patronized him. He had an office on Washington Street in San Francisco and "his reception rooms were thronged with visitors of all conditions and nationalities, who came to consult him regarding their various ailments."[35] Historian Liu Pei Chi made a similar observation: he called Li the most famous herbalist in the late nineteenth century. "Li always had a completely booked schedule. Some of his patients came all the way from the East Coast. Li was one of the wealthiest Chinese in San Francisco with a yearly income of seventy-five thousand dollars."[36] Fong Wan was another well-known herbalist during the 1920s and 1930s. With a profitable business, his residence and office on 10th Street in Oakland was so glamorous that it attracted hundreds of visitors. One of his assistant's responsibilities was to provide a tour of the house.

Soon, other herbalists also marketed their profession in order to gain Caucasian clients. As a part of their promotional strategies, some herbalists actively used commercial advertising in local newspapers to attract non-Chinese patients. According to Ray Lou, commercial advertisements for Chinese physicians began to appear in English-language newspapers in Los Angeles in the early 1870s. By the 1880s, some advertisements contained sketches of herbalists taking the pulse of Caucasian patients. Some advertisements were as large as half a page.[37] Still others were printed in Spanish as the herbalists treated Mexican patients as well. When Sam Chang, a self-trained herbalist, went to practice herbal medicine in Utah in the late 1910s, he advertised in the Greek American community's newspapers.[38] During that period, Salt Lake City had a sizable Greek immigrant community.[39]

Famous herbalists in southern California like Tan Fuyuan, Tom Leung, or Yick Hong Chung all had more Caucasian clients than Chinese ones. Commenting on the company run by Li's nephew, Tan Fuyuan, Tisdale claimed that with the possible exception of one or two well-advertised doctors, Tan had more patrons than any of the 350 physicians in Los Angeles. Many of them were well-to-do people and their family members, including businessmen, lawyers, journalists, and even physicians.[40] Catering to upscale clients, some of the herbalists built offices that were spacious even by contemporary Californian standards. Moreover, they often had more than one office. To attract Caucasian patients, Los Angeles herbalist Yick Hong Chung established one office in Chinatown and another in a shopping center on 9th Street, which was essentially a white neighborhood though some Chinese and Japanese produce-distribution businesses and a number of middle-class Chinese families' residences were also located there. Chung mainly targeted Caucasian clients and only went to his Chinatown office in the evenings. His son Arthur recalled that Chung "had more Caucasian customers than Chinese."[41] His wife Nellie also said that in the first few years, her husband's patients were "mostly white. Hardly any Chinese came."[42] According to Rose Hum Lee, Chinese herb doctors in Montana served inhabitants of Welsh, Irish, French, Italian, and Slavic descent during the 1880s through the 1920s.[43] By treating non-Chinese patients, herbal medicine, as a transnational cultural practice, gained a foothold in America.

Working in partnership with Caucasian practitioners or hiring interpreters and receptionists was also a common practice among established herb physicians. In southern California, Chinese herbalists often hired young Mexican women as secretaries or nurses to aid in serving the considerable number of Spanish-speaking patrons.[44] When Yick Hong Chung started his business, he found a Caucasian partner, A. Z. Holmes, a chiropractor. On their calling card, Mr. Holmes advertised himself as the superintendent and Chung as the manager.[45] In the immigration files of Yick Hong Chung, however, Holmes was listed as a shareholder who invested two thousand dollars and functioned as the business secretary, treasurer, and manager of Chung's business. In addition to Holmes, there were three other Caucasian shareholders and a number of silent Chinese shareholders. Chung was only listed as an assistant manager.

Besides business functions, Holmes and another Caucasian partner offered witness testimonies on behalf of the Chung family in immigration proceedings. In 1911, Holmes testified in order to help Chung petition for his son's admission into America. He claimed that he had lived in Los Angeles for sixteen years and had practiced as a physician since 1909. Chung and Holmes were the only active members of the business among all the shareholders. Holmes also indicated that the store was leased in his name. He assured the immigration officials that Chung was a merchant, had another herb store in Chinatown, and had never performed manual labor of any kind outside of the stores in the past twelve months. This is probably the most crucial statement because another Caucasian shareholder made a similar statement, confirming that Chung had never been involved in the laundry, lodging house, restaurant, barber, or pawnshop businesses.[46] In general, however, Caucasian partners or employees knew little or no Chinese, let alone herbal medicine. Holmes' knowledge of Chinese was only good enough to allow him to greet Chinese clients in Cantonese.[47] Tom Leung's assistant, a Mr. Hallow, could not speak Chinese at all.[48] They functioned more as cultural intermediaries to attract non-Chinese patients than as interpreters for the herbalists. Equally important, they could help the herbalists as witnesses offering testimony during immigration proceedings, communicate with local newspapers for marketing purposes, with banks in order to obtain financing, or with attorneys who could fight in court when unfair charges were made against the herbalists.

The shrinking Chinese population due to the intensive anti-Chinese movement also pushed the herbalists to cater increasingly to Caucasian clients, rather than members of the Chinese community. Ing Hay in Oregon was a case in point. Jeffrey Barlow and Christine Richardson noted how Hay managed to continue his business by building up his clientele in the Caucasian community as the size of the Chinese community began to decline in the 1890s.[49] Chinese herbalists probably also had their own network though no record of any guild or association has yet been found. Since imports of herbs did not always arrive in time, a thoughtful herbalist usually had a variety of substitute formulae when a certain medicinal substance was not available. In addition, he very likely had a working relationship with other Chinese herb doctors so that he could get certain ingredients whenever he himself ran out of them. Being foremost businessmen, herbalists handled every aspect of the trade: advertising their practices, managing their offices, building business networks, and importing herbs.

TABLE 4.1. Chinese Herbalists in Los Angeles

Bow Sui Tong, Drugs	319 S. Marchessault St.
H. T. Chan, Physician	1045 S. Broadway
Chinese Herb Co.	433 S. Hill St.
Chinese Medical Co.	955 S. Hill St.
Chinese Tea & Herb Co.	1049 S. Main St.
Dai Sang Tong, Drugs	323 Marchessault St.
Din Au Tong, Drugs	306 Marchessault St.
Fong Sue Nom, Physician	208 Marchessault St.
Foo & Wing Herb Co., Medicines	903 S. Olive St. (its former address was 929 S. Broadway)
Gee Ning Tong, Drugs	514 Los Angeles St.
Hong Wo Tong, Drugs	212 Ferguson Alley
Kam Brothers & Co., Physicians	603 S Olive St.
Lum Wing Yue, Chinese Tea & Herb Co.	819 S. Hill St.
Mon Yick Tong, Drugs	304 Marchessault St.
Mon Yuen Tong, Drugs	319 Apablasa St.
Po Sang, Drugs	320 Marchessault St.
Po Sow Tong, Drugs	319 Marchessault St.
Quan Tong, Herb Company	716 S. Hill St.
Suey Gee Tong & Co., Drugs	757 N. Alameda St.
Sun Kam Lee & Co., Teas	418 W. 7th St.
Tom She Bin & Sons, Physicians	145-47 W. 22nd St.
Wah Young Herb Company, Drugs	936 S Broadway
Wing On Tong, Drugs	302 Marchessault St.
Wong Company Sanitarium	713 Main St.
Yee Sing & Co., Drugs	322 Marchessault St.
Yick Yuen Tong, Drugs	759 N. Alameda St.
Young Woo Tong, Drugs	315 Apablasa St.

Source: International Chinese Business Directory of the World (1913), 1413.[51]

The 1913 International Chinese Business Directory of the World shows that about half of the Chinese herb doctors' offices in Los Angeles were located in the white sections of the city if we assume that the Chinese mainly inhabited the following streets: Marchessault, Los Angeles, Ferguson, Alameda, and Apablasa.[50] The names and addresses of the herbal stores in Los Angeles are listed in Table 4.1 in alphabetical order.

The offices of herbalists were situated approximately one block apart in order to reduce the intensity of competition. But there is another possible explanation for the geographical location of these herb shops. Though some of the shops were clustered on the same street, each herbalist had his own formulations that had been passed from one generation to the next within the family. Therefore, geographical concentration was probably not a major concern to herbalists. As Ralph C. Croizier observed, "despite the large medical literature, much of Chinese medical knowledge was the private possession of the individual practitioner, who might transmit it to his son or disciple but would certainly not share it with his professional rivals."[52] The U.S. Census Bureau indicated that the Chinese population in the city of Los Angeles from 1890 to 1920 fluctuated around two thousand,[53] dispersed in several neighborhoods rather than concentrated in Chinatown. Based on the 1913 *International Chinese Business Directory of the World*, there were at least several dozen Chinese herbalists in the Los Angeles area, which was a fairly large number for a Chinese community with only about two thousand people. It can be surmised, therefore, that Caucasian patients greatly outnumbered Chinese ones.

Unfortunately, it is difficult to figure out the precise number of Chinese herbalists in California during that period. According to herbalist Garding Lui's estimate in 1948, there were more than 120 herbalists in California by then and one-third were in Los Angeles.[54] If we focus on southern California, the *International Chinese Business Directory of the World* listed twenty-eight Chinese herbal physicians in Los Angeles in 1913. This cannot be a complete number, as many of them were not listed for various reasons. For example, Yick Hong Chung's name was missing in the directory. A possible reason is that Chung was very careful about whether to publicize himself as a physician in order to avoid harassment from Western medical organizations, although he did advertise his herb business.

Authenticity in a Non-Chinese World

As in any other field, Chinese herbalists tried to prove their authenticity in the profession. Since their skill was inextricably tied to Chinese culture, many herbalists claimed that they were graduates of the Imperial Medical College. Others insisted that their skill was a family tradition that had existed for generations. Still others maintained that they learned the profession from a famous master. Herbalist Tan Fuyuan in southern California claimed to be an ex-official physician to the Emperor of China. His book, *The Science of Oriental Medicine*, contained a photo of him wearing a mandarin's hat and robe, as well as a certificate from Li Rongyao, the then Chinese consul-general in San Francisco, which indicated that Tan was indeed a graduate of the Imperial Medical College in Beijing.[55] His partner and later competitor, Tom Leung, claimed that his grandfather was a physician to the Emperor of China and that his father was also a doctor. Furthermore, he claimed that he had studied at the Imperial Medical College for three years.[56] However, even Tom Leung's children suspect the veracity of that claim.[57] Fong Wan, an herbalist in Oakland, wrote that he had passed the Chinese imperial literary examinations of the first degree in medicine.[58]

Such claims reflect how Chinese herb doctors were ranked in China. *Ru yi* (scholar-doctor) belonged to the top level of physicians. Moreover, there were official medical posts attached to the court bureaucracy and medical training was offered in the Imperial College of Medicine from the Tang dynasty onwards. Such doctors were scholars who acquired their knowledge from classical medical texts. They had to master such texts and pass tough examinations. Years of education were thus an important criterion for becoming doctors at this high level. The next level consisted of *Shi yi* (hereditary doctors). As a Chinese saying goes: *Yi bu sanshi, bo fu qi yao* (if a doctor does not have three generations in medicine, do not take his remedies). Hereditary doctors gained respect because Chinese believed that such doctors had reliable and secret herbal formulations handed down by their ancestors or special skills for treating difficult ailments.

Among the herbalists in America were descendants of families specializing in the herbal medical profession, medical students trained under famous masters, and individuals who obtained herbal knowledge informally. For example, Yick Hong Chung had already practiced herbal medicine in Guangzhou (Canton), China, before his arrival in the United States. Herbal medicine was a family tradition in his case.[59] But Tom Leung, equally famous in the Los Angeles area, probably acquired his herbal knowledge by working as a clerk for his cousin, Tan Fuyuan, and studying books about herbs.[60] Ing Hay of John Day, a small town in Oregon, learned the skill from another Chinese herbalist, Doc Lee, in that area. Hay turned his general merchandise store into an herb shop only after he had become established and had built up a clientele.[61] Chinese herbalists in America could hardly be at the *Ru yi* level because such high-class people usually did not migrate to another country to practice. Moreover, they constituted a tiny minority of the practitioners in China.

Medicine in China was an unregulated field where all kinds of practitioners coexisted. Patients consulted various doctors based on their reputations, made comparisons, and selected the ones they trusted. In America, Chinese immigrants also selected doctors according to the effectiveness of their skills and the herbs they prescribed. Alexander McLeod observed that it was common for Chinese immigrants to consult two or more doctors at the same time until they found the right one.[62] To illustrate their authenticity, some herbalists wore Chinese robes and round mandarin hats. Many others, however, dressed up in three-piece suits as they wished to look more like Western professionals. In their advertisements, photos of herbalists in traditional Chinese clothes often existed side by side with others garbed in Western suits. Claiming to be *Ru yi* or *Shi yi* indicates that the herbalists were fully aware that their profession had roots in China.

Regardless of which path they followed to become herbal doctors, it is clear that they based their professional authenticity on Chinese culture.

MARKETING THROUGH CLIENTS

Herbal medicine was popular in America because it met an important health need at the turn of the century for Chinese and non-Chinese alike.[63] Though American medicine began to be standardized during that period, it was still a profession that allowed different healing systems, which often competed with one another for market share, to coexist. Moreover, herbal medicine per se was not totally foreign to European Americans. Because of the influence of American Indian culture, botanical healing was popular from the colonial period until the mid-nineteenth century.[64]

To market their skills, famous herbalists published medical books probably at their own expense, printed commercial pamphlets, and distributed all kinds of flyers. Tan Fuyuan published *The Science of Oriental Medicine* in 1897. His former partner and later competitor, Tom Leung, published *Chinese Herb Science* in 1928. Fong Wan of Oakland in northern California published *Herb Lore* in 1933. Garding Lui, another Los Angeles herbalist, published *Secrets of Chinese Physicians* in 1943.[65] Written in smooth and straightforward English, such books were used not only to promote their authors' medical practices, but also to fight against the attacks on Chinese herbal medicine. Sensational newspaper articles often described Chinese herbal medicine as composed of sharks' fins, spiders' eggs, dried toads, or dragon bones. (I shall discuss the herbalists' resistance against racial discrimination later.) Those books used simple language to introduce Chinese culture, the tradition of herbal medicine in Chinese society, and the theories it was based on. The books also explained how herbal medicine dealt with various symptoms, giving numerous examples supported by appreciative letters from Caucasian patients. Such marketing skills on the part of herbalists seem similar to the circulation of the handbooks of the Bamboo Grove Monastery's formulations, which also contained letters from patients. Today, these books are valuable records that scholars can use as they research the history of herbal medicine in the United States.

The effectiveness of their medical skills enabled Chinese herbalists to build a stable and growing medical clientele. In his booklet, Tan Fuyuan wrote, "The Oriental system has cured thousands of cases of various forms of disease, which had been abandoned by other doctors. . . . As a rule, Caucasians have been unwilling to consult us until they tried every other form of medical treatment within their reach. Therefore, it may be said that all of the cures which we have made have been of cases given up by other doctors."[66] In his booklet *Herb Lore*, Fong Wan also claimed that "[t]he demand of Americans for Chinese Herbs has for several years been steadily on the increase. Consequently, whereas some forty years ago the sale of Chinese Herbs in the United States was confined almost wholly to the Chinese population, at the time of this writing, the American patrons far outnumber the Chinese."[67]

Contemporary American scholars have confirmed these claims. Buell and Muench wrote that "the traditional Chinese physicians were a vital part of the health care system for all of the frontier community. Chinese and non-Chinese alike employed their services, often preferring the Chinese medical approach to that of their Western doctors."[68] Journalist Carey McWilliams has also pointed out that "Chinese herb doctors still did a lively business when I first arrived in Los Angeles in 1922. . . . As late as 1870, Southern California had only one doctor in attendance at the annual meeting of the State Medical Society, and a local society was not formed until 1888. The vacuum created in the medical art was filled by Chinese herb doctors, faith-healers, quacks and a miscellaneous assortment of practitioners."[69] Here, McWilliams noted not only the medical market for Chinese herbalists, but also the existence of other nonorthodox practitioners.

That Chinese herbal medicine managed to break into the Caucasian community indicates that it was an effective therapy. As Barlow and Richardson noted, herbal medicine was far more successful in treating the ills and injuries of the frontier region than were conventional physicians at the turn of the century. While Western medicine "was helpless before the [winter] flu," herbal medicine kept Chinese road builders in Oregon from being bedridden and enabled them to complete the work on schedule. Moreover, none of the Caucasian patients of Ing Hay, the Chinese herbalist in the town of John Day, died during the 1915 and 1919 flu epidemics, which caused thousands of deaths in Portland. Ing Hay apparently also cured patients suffering from meningitis, lumbago, mumps, colds, stomach ailments, hemorrhaging, and influenza.[70] As herbalist Tan Fuyuan claimed, herbalists treated cases that Western-trained doctors had given up on.[71]

Chinese herbalists also treated European American women. Many of them indicated their ability to treat women's diseases in their promotional literature. In an advertisement in the *Los Angeles Times* on August 9, 1887, an herbalist stated that "diseases peculiar to women" was one of his specialties. Meanwhile, another herbalist listed the name of a supposedly well-known Caucasian lady in the local community as his reference.[72] In *Herb Lore*, Fong Wan included a brief testimony by a white woman who explained how she got rid of several lumps in her breast after taking his herbal medicine.[73] In both Tan Fuyuan's and Tom Leung's books, there are sections on women's diseases. Garding Lui even offered theoretical explanations of women's health problems. Frank advice to women, such as timely sex education in Lui's book and a sketch of a woman's body, reprinted from an ancient Chinese medical encyclopedia, in Fong Wan's book, demonstrate the professional attitude of herbalists toward their female patients.[74] The rational, objective, and nonmoralistic approach toward sexual matters probably helped make their female patients more comfortable as the women described their symptoms. In short, the herbalists were able to break into the European American female market because herbal medicine is effective, feeling the pulse is a noninvasive therapeutic method, and the confidential nature of their practice reduced the social distance between Chinese herbal doctors and their Caucasian clients.

As they expanded their profession in American society, the herbalists modified it to take new conditions into account. For example, many herbal physicians in China would only do diagnoses and leave it to the pharmacists to prepare and dispense medicines. But herbal medicine in the United States could not afford such specialization. An herbalist had to act as both a pulsologist and a pharmacist. Chinese herbalists did not charge for their diagnoses but billed the patients one to five dollars for a package of herbal medicine.[75] Because pulse diagnoses were free, herbalists relied on the sale of herbal medicine for the profits they made. Yick Hong Chung's wife, Nellie, remembered that it cost eight to ten dollars for a week's prescription, which consisted of seven packages.[76] This seems to have been the standard charge. According to *Herb Lore*, Fong Wan in Oakland charged the same price. Tom Leung in Los Angeles also charged ten dollars a week.[77] Some Chinese herbalists probably charged a higher fee to Caucasian patients than Chinese ones. The book by Barlow and Richardson, for example, tells of a letter written by a Chinese to his herbalist complaining about the unfair price charged to a Caucasian friend he had introduced to the herbalist. However, this incident also indicates that the herbalists obtained Caucasian clients through the recommendations of their Chinese patients.[78]

A FAMILY BUSINESS

Though the herb business is not a labor-intensive profession, an herbalist still needs assistants to prepare and dispense medicines. Some herbal practitioners in America, however, had to take care of everything, from ordering herbs to dispensing medicine, themselves. Because the herbalists belonged to the merchant class, most of them were able to bring their families with them during the Chinese exclusion period (1882–1943) and their wives or relatives often assisted them in the dispensary or in the manufacture of herbal pills, which was pretty hard work. As herbal medicine was a family business, usually the family's residence served as both a home and an office.

According to Yick Hong Chung, his business revenue was about eighty to ninety thousand dollars a year with a 20 percent profit. His Caucasian partner and he also each drew a monthly salary of sixty dollars. While seeing patients himself, Chung hired an assistant whom he paid around fifty dollars a month.[79] But the business became a family affair after he married Nellie Yee. An American-born Chinese woman, Nellie spoke and had a reading knowledge of both Chinese and English. In the room where herbs were stored, she could identify what herb was in which drawer in a room containing hundreds of drawers. In their house on Hill Street, the family lived upstairs, while the downstairs provided a spacious five-room office for Chung. Two were waiting rooms; one was an office where patients' pulses were taken; a fourth room was used by patients who were taking their brewed medicines; and in the fifth Chung wrote down the formulations needed by each patient. The stove in their big kitchen had six burners that could cook up to seventeen or eighteen pots of medicine on the same day. Nellie packed the week's prescription into seven paper bags for each patient. Medicine was cooked in a numbered pot for forty-five minutes and then served in beautiful porcelain bowls. A relative named Yee Pai helped pour the herbal tea and took it to the patients, to whom he also gave crackers. The patients drank the hot herbal tea like soup, spoonful by spoonful, swallowing it with the crackers so that it would not taste too bitter. Some patients picked up a whole week's prescriptions and brewed the medicine themselves. Chung, often through his wife's and children's interpretation, provided specific directions on how to cook it.[80] Nellie obviously played an indispensable role in Chung's business.

Immigrants' wives were able to get involved because herb medicine was part of Chinese culture, so they were familiar with it. For example, Chinese women often used certain herbs in preparing dishes on special occasions. In some exceptional cases, women even took charge of the business. Stella Louie of Los Angeles converted the family's grocery store into a gift shop that sold herbs when her husband went to China for a long visit.[81] Bing Woo Wong, wife of Tom Leung, took over the management of the herbal business after her husband passed away in 1931. While her eldest son, Taft, who was fluent in English, worked at the front desk, met the patients, and inquired about their sickness, she filled the prescriptions in the herb room. Because she was familiar with Tom Leung's formulae, she knew what to prescribe for various ailments after Taft relayed patients' problems to her.[82] Though the business did not last very long after Tom Leung died, this example demonstrates the active role of women in family businesses. When documenting the history of Chinese herbalists, we should not forget that women were an indispensable part of that story.

COMPETITION AND BIGOTRY

The business success of herbalists earned them intense envy and aroused bigotry. As an ethnic medical profession, herbal medicine was subjected to all kinds of distortion and prejudice. In his book *Herb Lore*, Fong Wan wrote, "In the United States of America due mainly to the persistency of the Chinese herbalists themselves and their willingness to endure persecution for the sake of their profession, the use of Chinese Herbal Remedies has been gradually introduced."[83] To protect their share of the American medical market, the herbalists fought continuously against distorted depictions of their profession. They published booklets, wrote to newspapers, and made extensive use of the testimonies given by their Caucasian patients as evidence to defend the effectiveness of herbal medicine. Dr. P. C. Remondino, the then president of the Southern California Medical Association, attacked Chinese herbal medicine viciously on several occasions. Expressing great resentment, Tan Fuyuan rebutted him in the *Los Angeles Times* on August 15, 1895, with an elaborate article defending herbal medicine. The article caused Remondino to write another offensive article, which Tan also refuted. The debate aroused a great deal of attention.[84] Ironically, this pen war gave Tan greater exposure and brought him more clients. It was after this debate that he published his booklet, *The Science of Oriental Medicine*, in 1897.

As herbal medicine was repeatedly distorted as a pseudoscience and suppressed harshly by mainstream medical organizations with government assistance, Chinese herbalists in the United States fought many battles in court. In "Chinese Physicians in California," Tisdale noted that Chinese herbal medicine was not recognized by law in California and that the judicial records of the state showed that its practitioners had often been arrested and fined. The pioneer herbalist, Li Po Tai, was subjected to serious persecution during the early years of his practice. Later, his friendship with Senator Leland Stanford and Governor Mark Hopkins gave him some protection.[85] Fong Wan of Oakland, who was known as the "King of the Herbalists" in the San Francisco Bay area and who had several thousand patrons from 1915 to mid-1930, said that a great campaign was conducted against the Chinese herbalists from 1929 to 1932 and people from all walks of life were involved. For example, the postmaster sent herbal doctors fraudulent orders in order to entrap them and examined their mail searching for information that might incriminate them. Fong Wan was repeatedly sued by Western doctors and had to appear in both local and federal courts. A federal court indicted him on sixteen counts on July 29, 1931. Pharmacologists, postmasters, professors, chemists, and physicians were all brought to the court to testify against him. But according to Fong, he was eventually found not guilty.[86]

During his career, he won dozens of court cases. In 1925, when an antiherb bill was introduced into the state assembly, Fong Wan went to Sacramento and presented the arguments and facts that were instrumental in getting the bill withdrawn.[87] Herbalist C. K. Ah-Fong of Idaho obtained his license as a physician/surgeon on February 21, 1901, after a series of appeals in the Idaho State Supreme Court. But he was probably the only herbalist in the United States who ever won such a victory.[88]

Chinese herbalists in the Los Angeles area also had to deal with extensive legal harassments. They used different strategies to resist the attacks against them. For example, Tom Leung, a very aggressive herbalist, was arrested many times on the charge of practicing medicine without a license. But he did not give up using the "doctor" title until the late 1920s. He also hired Thomas White and Paul Shenck as his attorneys to represent him in court. Both were famous lawyers in southern California.[89] The book *Sweet Bamboo*, by his daughter Louise Leung Larson, contains a vivid description of how Chinese herbal physicians in southern California were harassed in those days:

> Father did well as an herbalist, too well, in the opinion of the American Medical Association and the Board of Medical Examiners. He and the other Chinese herbalists in Los Angeles at that time were accused of practicing medicine without a license because they used the title "Doctor" and felt the pulse as one way of diagnosis. Papa was a special target and was arrested over 100 times on the misdemeanor charge. . . . The police, at times, used stool pigeons—people pretending to be patients—and would arrest Papa after the usual consultation. Sometimes a whole squad of police would arrive in a patrol car and raid our home. I came to view the AMA and the Board, as well as the police, as our mortal enemies. Papa was unflappable, even the time when he was hauled off in the patrol wagon. He had set up a routine for these crises. As soon as the police came, the secretary phoned A.C. Way of the First National Bank to arrange for bail.[90]

Only after Leung ceased to call himself a doctor and changed his company's name to "Leung Herb Company" did the harassment gradually subside.

Local medical organizations in Los Angeles also charged Yick Hong Chung for claiming to be a physician without an American medical degree; they demanded that he stop his medical practice in accordance with California law. He dealt with the harassments by keeping a low profile. His son Arthur recalled, "There were medical societies questioning father whether he treated patients or not. He always said that he was a herb seller. He never advertised his business. All his patients were sent to him by other patients. He did run into some trouble earlier but he managed to get out of it."[91] Chung's children remember that a big and tall policeman searched their home and frisked their father though no one was arrested. To carry on his herb business, Chung applied for a drugstore license. He also used a Caucasian partner who had a chiropractor's license so that the latter would be the one who took in patients. Seldom did he advertise his business in newspapers.[92] His business survived discrimination and persisted until the late 1940s.

The Chinese herb business shrank rapidly in the late 1940s and early 1950s because the federal government banned imports from China following the establishment of the People's Republic of China in 1949. Before and during World War II, the Japanese invasion of China had already disrupted the herbalists' businesses to a great extent. After Congress passed the Trading with the Enemy Economy Act in December 1950, thereby suspending the trade between the United States and China, many Chinese herbalists were forced to discontinue their businesses.

Conclusion

Chinese herbal medicine occupies a significant position in Asian American history because it was a vital part of the health care system in California and other parts of the American West for some nine decades. It was an ethnic skill that some Chinese used to resist being channeled into racially defined occupations such as laundries and restaurants. In contrast to the stereotypical image of the "docile" Chinese, the herbalists were a group of assertive, innovative, and well-informed medical practitioners. As a transplanted cultural tradition, herbal medicine reflects a close relationship between Chinese Americans and their homeland and allows us to place Chinese America into a larger historical context that transcends national boundaries. By examining the history of herbal medicine in America, we learn to appreciate the open, engaged, and cosmopolitan nature of Chinese American life.

5 Understanding Chinese American Transnationalism During the Early Twentieth Century: An Economic Perspective

YONG CHEN

IN HIS EARLY SIXTIES, Mr. Chang has led a life that spans the Pacific Ocean: he was born in central China, raised in Taiwan, and has spent most of his adult life in southern California, where he owns and runs several fast-food stores. His sense of identity is strongly associated with mainland China even though he is least familiar with it among the places where he has lived. He has long hoped to establish a school in central China; he has also hoped that his American-born children would go "back" to China to serve the "mother country." He still talks about these dreams, but none of them has come true. His businesses continue to keep him busy; he has bought a multimillion-dollar home in Los Angeles County; he has not yet made any investments in China; and his grown children are happily married and have prospering careers of their own in the United States.

The discrepancies in Mr. Chang's life story and the tensions between his sense of identity and the realities of everyday life, not uncommon among Chinese Americans, remind us that we must recognize the complexities of Chinese American transnationalism, rather than romanticize it in a simplistic way. Transnationalism has been a persistent and tenacious phenomenon throughout Chinese American history but it has also experienced serious constraints. Its extent and meaning in Chinese American life have shifted a great deal as circumstances changed from one historical moment to the next.

This chapter seeks to understand and to measure Chinese American transnationalism during the first half of the twentieth century. I do not consider transnationalism as a manifestation of ethnic consciousness per se. Rather, it also manifests itself in the everyday material world in which Chinese Americans have lived and continue to live. The movement of people, ideas, goods, and capital across the Pacific Ocean all helped delineate the physical boundaries of that world. Such movements reveal how Chinese Americans have negotiated their "Chinese-ness" and

"American-ness" as they defined the interwoven and dialectic meanings of "China" and "America" in a transpacific world[1] long before transnationalism became a trendy concept.

We cannot comprehend the Chinese American historical experience fully by concentrating on the U.S. setting alone. Though they were a politically discriminated against and economically exploited minority in the United States, Chinese Americans enjoyed a respected social status in China. As I discuss later, during the first half of the twentieth century they participated more actively than before in the national political discourse of China while simultaneously continuing to campaign against America's racism. Paradoxically, it was the American-ness of this numerically small community that gave its members an increasingly visible status in their country of origin. To a large degree, that American-ness was associated with the economic opportunities that lured most emigrants to America. Indeed, many Chinese Americans themselves viewed and articulated the meaning of their American experience in economic terms.

This study takes a close look at the flow of capital from Chinese America to China and its social and political significance. During the period under discussion, such capital flows grew to unprecedented levels and an increasing part of it arrived as direct investments and donations, helping to facilitate the redefinition and expansion of the relationship of Chinese Americans to China. Meanwhile, the Chinese government, which during the late 1860s and early 1870s had started to move away from its long-standing restrictive and hostile policies, became more and more sympathetic toward and supportive of the overseas Chinese. Modern Chinese nationalism, which emerged around the turn of the twentieth century as a viable political force, embraced them with enthusiasm. Reinforcing the Chinese-ness of Chinese Americans, such a redefined relationship with China encouraged them to fight racial prejudice in a transnational context. They believed, more consciously than before, that only a strong and rejuvenated China could help deliver them from America's anti-Chinese racism.

The Gold Mountain and Its Perils: The Meaning of America

To understand the importance of the economic dimensions of Chinese American transnationalism, we must first recognize the economic motive of Chinese immigration to the United States, a large-scale population movement triggered by the California gold rush.[2] That is why Chinese called California "Gold Mountain"—a notion that vividly captures the economic aspirations of Chinese Americans. An overwhelming majority of the emigrants were men, the traditional bread (or in this case, rice) winners. Thus, emigration can be seen as an economic strategy—an investment made by families for the sake of their collective future.

To get a glimpse of how heavily economic incentives mattered, all we need to do is to look at the income gap between the two countries. In the 1860s, for example, a Chinese working for the Central Pacific Railroad Company in the American West received a monthly wage of about thirty-one dollars.[3] Those working in other occupations and locations were paid less: labor recruiters in search of agricultural workers in the South offered only twenty-two dollars a month.[4] If Russell Conwell's estimate for 1870 is correct, rural workers in the immigrants' native land earned only eight to ten dollars a year,[5] which means that the average immigrant worker's income was twenty-six to forty-six times greater than that of his fellow villagers back in China. The money many were able to save enabled them, mostly young men, to fulfill their family responsibilities. According to the data gathered by Ta Chen and his research team during the 1930s for his study of emigrant communities in eastern Guangdong Province and southern Fujian Province, the remittances from immigrants in Southeast Asia "contribute an important part of the means available for the various purposes" their families might have.[6] That assessment applies as well to remittances sent by the Chinese in North America.

Even those who could not afford to send money back still enjoyed a more comfortable standard of living in comparison with that in the villages of South China. As a sixteen-year-old laundry worker in Chicago remarked before World War II, "People [Chinese] eat much better food here in America. In the native village, we did not eat chicken even once a month. But here we have chicken for dinner often—every Saturday. Soda water is a kind of rare treat in the native village. Here we drink it several times a day like water. I remember that it was a dream to have a drink of soda water when I was a little boy in the native village. It costs fifteen cents a bottle back there, but fifteen cents was too much money in those days."[7]

It is not surprising then, that Chinese immigrants continued to view the United States primarily in economic terms, which helped them to endure their maltreatment as culturally and physically inferior people and thus unsuitable to become a part of the social and political fabric of America. Racist legislation made it extremely difficult for Chinese Americans to have their families join them in America.[8] Indeed, for much of the period under discussion, many Chinese Americans who were married but did not have their families with them actually lived the life of "bachelors" in the United States.

Acknowledging the importance of economic issues for understanding the Chinese American experience does not mean that other kinds of issues are insignificant. Economically motivated immigrants encountered strong anti-Chinese ideologies that prevailed in America's political and socioeconomic landscapes. Racism took away the immigrants' fundamental political and social rights and was the most serious obstacle they encountered as they tried to achieve their economic goals. The infamous 1882 Chinese Exclusion Act suspended the immigration of laborers and stipulated that Chinese immigrants could not become naturalized citizens because they were not white, a stipulation that goes back to the 1790 Naturalization Act. By the early twentieth century, the ban on Chinese labor immigration became permanent. Anti-Chinese racism was also codified at the state and local levels. In California, for example, the 1913 Alien Land Law prohibited aliens who could not become naturalized U.S. citizens—a definition that included Chinese immigrants—to own land. Chinese were also not allowed to marry whites. Prejudice and violent riots drove Chinese away from rural areas and from manufacturing jobs. Increasingly concentrated mostly in a few urban settlements, such as New York, San Francisco, and Chicago, Chinese Americans found themselves employed increasingly in only a small number of service industries with the exception of San Francisco. Consequently, racism created dreadful constraints on the transnational world of Chinese Americans by severely limiting the flow of goods, capital, and people across the Pacific Ocean. Those who traveled to China for visits faced the risk of losing their right to reenter the United States.[9]

However, Chinese immigrants never remained passive victims of discrimination. They fought for their rights within the American legal and political arenas and even won a few significant battles. But overall, as a politically powerless, numerically small, economically oppressed, and socially segregated ethnic group, Chinese Americans did not have enough resources in the United States to win the war against racism. Therefore, they turned their struggle into a transpacific effort by getting involved in affairs in China. It was their financial resources that enabled them to do that.

COMING TOGETHER: CHINESE AMERICA'S CHANGING POLITICAL RELATIONSHIP WITH CHINA

In China, Chinese Americans found the social respect and political rights that were denied them in the United States. During the first half of the twentieth century, in particular, their political stature in their native land rose to an unprecedented level, significantly reinforcing the Chinese-ness in Chinese Americans' cultural consciousness.

Scholars of American immigration history have tended to view ethnic (national) consciousness as a product of the New World environment that transformed newcomers "from immigrants to ethnics" and submerged the parochialism that had "defined them by the place of their birth, the village, or else by the provincial region that shared dialect and custom."[10] The

Chinese American case, however, reminds us that it is equally important to recognize that the development of ethnic identity often has undeniably transnational dimensions. While Chinese American ethnic identity was undoubtedly influenced by American anti-Chinese hostility, it was not merely a result of racial formation and transformation in the New World environment; rather, it was a complex process that intersected with developments and dynamics taking place in a transpacific context. Therefore, the relationship of Chinese Americans with China is of fundamental importance for understanding the Chinese American experience. That relationship changed a great deal during the first half of the twentieth century, as they became intimately linked to the efforts to strengthen and modernize China.

First, the "China" with which Chinese Americans interacted expanded geographically during the early years of the twentieth century. Before then, the direct connections that Chinese Americans had with China had been focused primarily on the emigrant communities in the Pearl River Delta region. During the first half of the twentieth century, however, Chinese Americans established close and direct contacts with various national and provincial government agencies, political parties, social organizations, and various other groups in areas beyond Guangdong Province.

Second, the Chinese-ness of Chinese Americans also changed. Even though they had always identified themselves as Chinese, during the nineteenth century they articulated that Chinese-ness primarily in cultural terms—that is, through the practice and maintenance of cultural traditions and social customs, and the retention of historical memories. In the first half of the twentieth century, by comparison, the sense of "Chinese-ness" acquired a political dimension as they emerged as active participants and vital players in China's political events. They consciously placed their own futures within the folds of China, devoting tremendous energy to the revival of China and the protection of its dignity and sovereignty. They acted that way because they strongly believed that the discrimination they encountered in America was largely attributable to the weakness of China. In other words, they comprehended their experiences and negotiated their positions more often within a context of global geopolitics than in the context of American race relations. They believed that only a revitalized China could protect its emigrants when they saw how Japan, a rising world power, was able to better protect its immigrants in the United States than China could.[11]

Third, the legal and political status of Chinese Americans rose to an unprecedented level in the homeland during the first few decades of the twentieth century. The Chinese central government had long been hostile toward overseas emigration and trade activities: capital punishment awaited those who left and then dared to return, as stipulated by Article

225 of the Qing penal code established in the early years of the Qing dynasty. The Qing government saw emigration as an act of disloyalty and considered emigrants as outcasts because many of them remained loyal to the preceding Ming dynasty. The deliberations that led to the establishment of the first diplomatic missions overseas during the 1870s marked the beginning of a new attitude toward Chinese emigrants: they were now considered Qing subjects worthy of protection, rather than as social outcasts. The Qing government established a consulate in San Francisco and a legation in Washington, D.C. in 1878, but it did not officially abandon the policy of prohibiting migrants from returning home until 1894.[12] During the early twentieth century, the Qing Court and the subsequent governments in the new Republic of China all regarded the protection of the interests of overseas Chinese as an important policy issue. The 1911 Revolution, to which the Chinese in Southeast Asia and in North and South America made vital contributions, represented the beginning of a new chapter in Chinese Americans' relationship with the Chinese government. After the revolution, they were allowed to elect their own representatives to serve in China's legislature, thereby gaining direct representation in the central government for the first time. They no longer merely sought help from the Chinese government but instead became real players in issues of vital national importance to China.

The people in China also politically embraced their compatriots in America. Beginning early in the twentieth century, they took up the cause of Chinese Americans as a crucial issue intimately related to the future of the Chinese nation. In 1905, a massive boycott movement broke out throughout China, protesting against America's anti-Chinese immigration policy. That event signaled that the struggles of Chinese Americans would now take center stage in China's political arena and in the nation's consciousness.

The rise of modern Chinese nationalism shortened the distance between China and Chinese America, politically, during the twentieth century. Led by new urban elites with broad perspectives, it appropriated Western ideas, including social Darwinism, to reassess China's position in global geopolitics. Such ideas projected a strong sense of national crisis, intensifying the desire to "renew" China based on the model of Western nations in order to restore its national dignity. The plight of Chinese Americans received much public attention because some prominent leaders of the nationalist movement, such as Liang Qichao, had firsthand knowledge about it. People increasingly saw the mistreatment of Chinese Americans, the first large Chinese settlement in the West, as directly related to the humiliation inflicted upon their nation by the West. A popular pamphlet circulated during the 1905 boycott best captures the growing sense of nationalistic solidarity with Chinese Americans, now perceived as members of the same national community. "Although most Chinese laborers in America today are Cantonese," it stated, "they are like our brothers." "If we do not fight [against the mistreatment they now receive]," it concluded, "it will come to all of us."[13] In a letter urging the Chinese government to refuse accepting America's exclusion of Chinese immigrant laborers, a leading merchant boycott organization in Shanghai stated passionately: "if such exclusion happened to any western European country, its people would respond violently and bloodily."[14] Modern Chinese nationalism quickly crossed the Pacific Ocean and became the dominant political ideology of Chinese America. During the 1930s and early 1940s, it was Chinese America's turn to support their compatriots in China's war against Japanese aggression. Chinese Americans' participation in that war marked the climax of their expanding political connections with China. While strengthening their consciousness as Chinese, such connections also gave them a powerful leverage in fighting racism in America.

THE FLOW OF CHINESE AMERICAN CAPITAL TO CHINA AND ITS POLITICAL AND SOCIAL SIGNIFICANCE

An examination of the transpacific flow of capital between China and Chinese American communities helps us to appreciate more comprehensively the political changes discussed earlier. That capital flow, which remained by and large unidirectional (from overseas Chinese to China) until the late twentieth century, laid the foundation for these political changes, which reflected a growing appreciation of the enormous significance of the financial resources in the hands of the Chinese living outside China that could help rebuild a Chinese national economy that was in desperate need of foreign currency. A disproportionately significant part of the money that China received came from Chinese America. This numerically small community (under 90,000 persons in 1900 and slightly over 77,000 in 1940)[15] effectively used its resources as the most powerful vehicle at its disposal to negotiate the identity of its members and to improve their social and political status.

What follows is not a comprehensive history of Chinese Americans' economic activities. Rather, my goal is to provide an economic perspective on their changing relationship with China and their expanded Chinese consciousness through an examination of the trajectory of Chinese American capital, which crossed the Pacific as family-oriented remittances, investments, and charitable and political contributions, in order to analyze the meanings attached to Chinese American capital.

In the early years, Chinese immigrants sent money almost exclusively to their loved ones in the Pearl River Delta region, in accordance with the economic strategy that their families had devised before their emigration.

For many, it was in the emigrant communities that their hard-earned money would be most meaningfully spent. In other words, that practice was what gave meaning to Chinese Americans' existence and their labor in the New World.

The material apparatus that served to connect China and Chinese America remained frail during the first few decades of the Chinese presence in America. Those with money to remit often had to rely on fellow villagers and townspeople traveling back to China to carry the money to their families. One such immigrant was Ah Quin. The following are a few examples of the things he sent to his mother in 1879 and early 1880 (by that time he had been in the United States for more than sixteen years working as a laborer). In May 1879, Ah Quin sent a letter and thirty dollars. On October 4, 1879, he sent another letter and twenty dollars, which were given to "Ah Yaw [who] handed [it] to Hi Kowe [to] bring it to her." In December 1880, he recorded that he was sending "[a letter] to Yan Row and 10 dollars it gave to Tom send it to my Mother in Chi[na]." A few days later, he gave a letter and ten dollars to a fellow Chinese "to take back to my mother in person," along with one dollar for his grandmother.[16]

During the first half of the twentieth century, family-oriented remittances continued. Multiple channels emerged to handle them, combining traditional methods and modern banking techniques. Postal agencies, financial institutions, import-export companies known as *jinshanzhuang* (see Chapter 2 in this volume for a discussion of these firms), and individual couriers formed an extensive web for transporting and transferring Chinese diasporic capital, often by way of Hong Kong, to the hands of villagers in the Pearl River Delta.

Remittances brought overseas Chinese the kind of respect that had evaded them in their countries of settlement. Ta Chen's 1940 study quoted a social worker in an emigrant community who said, "When a son abroad earns substantial sums of money and sends them home, the father's attitude toward him is likely to depart somewhat from that customary in China. He will respect the wishes of the absent member of the family as to the ways in which the money is to be spent."[17] The existence of such a transnational space allowed numerous Chinese American laborers to possess more than one social class status. In his study of Chicago's Chinese laundrymen, Paul Siu discussed the trend among returned Chinese laborers who built houses first in villages and later in cities: "In the old days when the laundryman brought his fortune back to China, he built a house or bought a piece of land in the native village. He was then a typical 'home builder.' This still is a pattern. Or had been a pattern up to the time the Chinese Communists began to seize control of China. It then became a growing tendency to believe that purchasing property in the city is a wiser policy and gives a brighter outlook." They established enclaves in certain areas of the city, one of which was Tung Shan, "where the returned immigrants from America built Western-style houses, [and] their next-door neighbors are Westernized Chinese, government officials, and Europeans. Here the laundryman lives like a 'bourgeois.'"[18]

Perhaps as a measure of the respectability that they increasingly enjoyed within their families and communities, Chinese Americans also intervened assertively in local politics. For example, the placing of Enping District under the jurisdiction of another district prompted protests from Enping natives in San Francisco and Los Angeles in late 1906, and the governor had to explain his decision to appease them.[19] In another case, when a popular magistrate of Xinning District was forced to resign, expatriates from that district sent telegrams to the governor in 1908, demanding that he retain the magistrate.[20]

The significance of diasporic capital for the entire Chinese economy was also being recognized more and more. Late nineteenth-century promoters of a new policy toward overseas Chinese, such as high-ranking Qing officials Zhang Zhidong and Xue Fucheng, were already keenly aware of the financial contributions that overseas Chinese could make toward the modernization of China and believed that recognizing the legal status of emigrants and extending political protection to them would benefit China's economy.[21] Chinese diplomats stationed in foreign countries conveyed their knowledge of the wealth possessed by overseas Chinese communities to the Beijing government. Early in the twentieth century, the Qing Court adopted a series of new policies aimed at attracting investments from overseas Chinese. In 1902, for example, it allowed them to invest in the mining industry. In 1903 it established a commerce department for handling overseas Chinese investments. Around that time, it also started to reward overseas Chinese investors with official titles.

INVESTMENTS

Even before the Qing Court's new policies were announced, Chinese Americans were already investing directly in China. In the early years, like family-oriented remittances, such investments went to the emigrant communities to expand and modernize traditional industries. Between 1872 and 1895, for example, five of the first enterprises established by Chinese Americans were silk factories, located in the Pearl River Delta, which had been known for its exportable products for decades.[22] As early as the late nineteenth century, Chinese American investors also showed an interest in developing the economic infrastructure in their localities of origin. In 1890 a Chinese periodical named *Jiebao* published an interesting report: "soon the city of Guangzhou (Canton) will have electric lights.

A San Francisco Chinese merchant named Zhang Bingchang has raised money to form a corporation and has shipped all the necessary machinery to Guangzhou." The reports also mentioned that the governor-general of Guangdong Province, Li Hongzhang, and his predecessor Zhang Zhidong had both expressed their welcome and promised to offer protection.[23] Zhang Zhidong, serving then as governor-general of Hubei Province, had even invited Zhang Bingchang to go there. Li, meanwhile, instructed local officials to assist and protect Zhang Bingchang and his corporation. In this case, the Chinese American entrepreneur was seen not only as an investor but also as a pioneer in bringing modern technology to China. It was a role welcomed by Qing officials who aspired to modernize China.

Chinese American investments were not purely economic activities but often represented a material manifestation of their political ideology aimed at renewing China. Therefore, the first two decades of the twentieth century witnessed an increase not only in the volume of money invested but also in the greater attention paid to building China's economic infrastructure. The nature and scope of such investments reveal the extent to which Chinese American investors identified with China. The geographical locations and the industries to which such investments went, therefore, were in fact cultural sites where Chinese Americans' American-ness as well as their Chinese-ness came together. The former was represented by their American capital and knowledge of modern technology; the latter by their desire to help their native communities as well as China itself.

XINNING RAILROAD: INVESTMENT AND NATIONALISM

A case in point is the building of the Xinning Railroad in Xinning (later renamed Taishan) District, which had sent more emigrants than any other district during the first century of Chinese immigration to the United States.[24] From the initial capital-raising efforts in 1905 to its demise during World War II, the history of this railroad spans much of the period under discussion. Built with Chinese American expertise and capital, the railroad epitomized the union of Chinese Americans and modern Chinese nationalism. But the rise and fall of this venture also indicates the extents and limits of Chinese American transnationalism.

The project was started and orchestrated by a Chinese immigrant merchant named Chen Yixi. Coming to the United States in 1860 at the age of fifteen, he worked in two of the most important industries that employed Chinese immigrants. After briefly working in mining, he entered railroad construction, where he worked his way up from a laborer to a foreman. In the process, he made his fortune, acquired valuable knowledge about railroads, and became a small businessman and a community leader in Seattle.[25] During his long stay in the United States, he learned firsthand how Chinese Americans were victimized by racism and he participated in the struggles against it. As he stated in an open letter to stockholders of the Xinning Railroad Corporation in 1922, he had participated in demanding that the American government compensate the victims of anti-Chinese riots in the 1880s. He was also keenly aware of the new policies toward overseas Chinese adopted by the Qing Court, which had awarded him the title of a second-class official.[26] For people like Chen, China offered both opportunities and the personal dignity that American racism had denied them. Meanwhile, China also needed the resources accumulated by Chinese migrants abroad. In a memorial to the emperor requesting permission to start building the proposed railroad in 1906, the government's Commerce Department described Chen as a successful merchant who had extensive experience in building railroads in America. It also characterized him as a "patriotic" man, who cared deeply about the "vital importance" of a Chinese-owned and operated railroad in the effort to "strengthen China."[27]

Serving as the general manager and chief engineer of the Xinning Railroad Corporation, Chen started to raise money from Chinese Americans, especially his fellow Xinning people, in January 1905. Although immigrants from Xinning were among the poorest in Chinese America, they responded with great enthusiasm. Most of the money was raised from people with very modest means, many of whom could afford to buy only a few shares. However, their enthusiasm demonstrated not only a long-standing desire to help the emigrant communities but also a growing connection to the emerging nationalism in modern China. In the preceding two years, a national movement had broken out in China to try and take back the mines and railroads controlled by Westerners. That protest was followed by the 1905 boycott movement that spread within China as well as across the Pacific to Chinese America. Chen promoted the idea that his project would protect the rights and interests of China. Relying on nationalistic sentiments as a marketing tool, he exceeded his fund-raising goal in less than twelve months.

Chinese nationalism was also manifested in the way the company operated.[28] In its early years, it had a widely publicized "three no" policy: the company would have "no foreign stock holders, no foreign loans, and no foreign personnel." China's Commerce Department praised the policy and said it would ensure the protection of the national interests of China.[29]

Construction began in 1906.[30] In just three years the first line, about 60 kilometers long, opened for business. Shortly after 1911, when the second phase was completed, the company gradually saw an increase in passenger volume and in income. The historian Liu Pei Chi [Liu Boji] called it "one of the most successful enterprises built with the investment from Chinese immigrants in America."[31] It was so successful that an influential Chinese American newspaper, *Chung Sai Yat Po* [Chinese-Western Daily], called on the "Gold Mountaineers" to "exploit a gold mountain in China."[32] Their real future lay in China, the writer concluded, because not only did they face discrimination in America, but economic opportunities for Chinese workers in America were also diminishing. Later, the theme that Chinese Americans' future would be better in China than in America resonated with the thinking of U.S.-born Chinese as well. During the 1930s it became the topic of a national debate among second-generation Chinese Americans. At the same time, however, Chinese American transnationalism had its limits. Many American-born Chinese would find out, as the immigrant generation would as well, that "life in China perhaps had its difficulties too."[33]

The success of the railroad is best appreciated as a significant historical phenomenon. As an economic entity, however, the company experienced constant financial difficulties, which forced it to consider seriously seeking loans from Western banks in 1911. After 1920, when the last phase of the railroad was completed, the company's revenue virtually stopped growing while prices for parts and coal kept going up, causing its financial situation to deteriorate further. Meanwhile, it also experienced a mounting number of robberies by bandits, extortion by local and regional warlords, and labor disputes. In 1926 the provincial government took the company away from Chen and the board of directors. Chen was eventually forced to return to his native village and died there a few years later almost without a penny. Soon after Japanese troops crossed the Marco Polo Bridge and started an all-out war of aggression against China in July 1937, they bombed Taishan (formerly named Xinning) District. The war dealt the last blow to the besieged enterprise. The company ceased all operations in 1939, and all its assets were gone a few years after that.

In choosing to invest their money in building a railroad in Xinning District, Chinese Americans did not simply make a bold investment decision. Rather, the enterprise represented a proclamation of their connections to China. Constructing Xinning Railroad was an extremely risky business venture. The investors were well aware of the risk. As one of the least developed districts in the Pearl River Delta, Xinning did not have any important commodities to offer to markets outside its boundaries. In fact, during the years when the railroad was in operation, an overwhelming majority of its revenue came from transporting passengers, many of whom were returning emigrants. The "three no" policy also elevated the risk level. China's experience in independently financing, managing, and building railroads was extremely limited. By the end of the Qing dynasty in 1911, Chinese-owned railroads represented only 20 percent of all railroads in the country. The first railroad independently constructed by the Chinese was the Jing-Zhang (Beijing to the city of Zhangjiakou) Railroad

(1905–1909), which was located in the political center of China—a far more advantageous location than Xinning. Beginning in 1903, efforts started in numerous provinces to build railroads independent of Westerners, but few succeeded.

What made this highly risky venture appealing, above all, was the symbolic significance of railroads in the growing struggle for national sovereignty and dignity. Taking back the ownership of railroads from the Western powers was an important goal in the emerging modern Chinese nationalism. For many people, participating in the Xinning Railroad Corporation meant participating in the discourse of modern Chinese nationalism. Of particular importance was the "three no" policy, through which Chinese Americans unequivocally announced their identity as Chinese. In fact, nationalistic sentiments often outweighed economic considerations. Even when the company's finances plunged into a dire situation in 1911, for example, the attempt to borrow money from Westerners still generated significant controversy and objections in Chinese America and elsewhere.

Equally important, the willingness to take the risks associated with this enterprise demonstrated Chinese Americans' continued connections and commitment to their native communities. While their investments barely gave them any monetary return, the rewards they got in other ways were tremendously meaningful. The railroad gave underdeveloped Xinning District its first modern means of transportation, significantly improving the physical connections between two important sites in the Chinese American transpacific world: the emigrant communities and Chinese America.

The nationalistic sentiments and the commitment to the emigrant region, as embodied in the Xinning Rairoad, also constituted a dominant motive in many other investment ventures established with funds from overseas Chinese. In fact, the Xinning Railroad Corporation was only one of over 1,300 such ventures founded in Guangdong Province in the early years of the twentieth century.[34] Transportation was the sector that attracted most of these funds. During the 1920s and 1930s, overseas Chinese investments grew significantly in volume. In the 1920s, investments grew more than tenfold. The physical and economic infrastructure, including transportation, continued to attract investments. So did other sectors, such as financial institutions, which represented another important channel to cement Chinese America's connections with China.

Also like the Xinning Railroad, over 90 percent of these ventures failed by the time the Communists came to power in 1949. Almost all of the Chinese American investment ventures in transportation and financial institutions eventually collapsed. This sad outcome shows that the physical connectivity between China and Chinese America was frail. A critical reason for the frailty was the absence of political and financial stability in China. The Japanese invasion (1937–1945) dramatically decreased overseas Chinese investment activities and devastated existing enterprises. Almost equally brutal was the role played by what Chun-Hsi Wu has characterized as "post-war superinflation" in destroying the investment environment.[35]

POLITICAL DONATIONS

Compared to family-oriented remittances and regionally focused investments, Chinese American contributions to national causes articulated even more clearly their redefined identities and indicated broadened connections to the Chinese nation and modern Chinese nationalism. During his political exile in the United States around the turn of the twentieth century, Liang Qichao still found the mentality of Chinese America to be characterized by "the quality of the clansman, not that of the citizen," and "the village spirit, not the national spirit."[36] The influence of the Western model of nationalism and elitism may explain his failure to appreciate the nascent nationalistic feelings among Chinese Americans that coexisted with continued local loyalties. Beginning in the first decade of the twentieth century, a growing portion of the money that Chinese America sent to China reached people in areas beyond Guangdong Province.

First, they sent money for charity purposes. During a famine in 1907 that hit a vast area north of the Yangzi River in central China, Chinese Americans provided much needed financial assistance to the victims there. Interestingly, they saw such assistance as a way to repay their compatriots in China for the enormous moral support they had received during the 1905 boycott movement. Urging its readers to contribute to the relief effort, a Chinese newspaper in San Francisco stated in an editorial: "Those who receive help but do not repay are not gentlemen.... As we may recall, last year [after the earthquake] people in inland China generously helped with frequent remittances."[37] Many acted quickly and generously. A relief committee in San Francisco alone had collected $19,878.14 by early July.[38]

More important in volume and frequency were the donations of Chinese Americans for political causes, which started with money given to the political factions that established an extensive presence in Chinese American communities and competed for its resources around the turn of the twentieth century.[39] One Constitutionalist Party reformer reported in 1903, "I have since met the Chinese of half a dozen large American cities and find them devoted to the cause and willing to work for and give money to it."[40] Similarly, Chinese Americans also gave generously to the revolutionaries, whose leader, Sun Yat-sen, relied on his personal connections to his compatriots to raise money before the 1911 Revolution.

In fact, when the 1911 Revolution broke out, Sun was still traveling around Chinese American communities raising funds. In the early years of the Chinese republic, Chinese Americans responded generously to the call from the new government for financial help by buying government bonds.

In the following years, as the politically unstable and financially be-sieged nation once again faced growing foreign encroachments, Chinese Americans opened their wallets regularly and generously. Nothing ener-gized Chinese Americans more than the Chinese war against Japanese aggression. Shortly after the war broke out in 1937, Chinese Americans spontaneously started raising money for China. Soon, organizations mushroomed to handle fund-raising efforts in Chinese communities across the United States, with San Francisco, New York, Chicago, and Honolulu functioning as regional headquarters. Of particular importance was the Association to Save China located in San Francisco.[41] It became arguably the most visible of all such organizations. By the end of 1937, it had sent the equivalent of more than two million Chinese dollars to China.[42] The lists of donors frequently filled the news sections of Chinese newspapers. There were so many donors that the association and the five major Chi-nese newspapers issued a joint announcement in mid-November 1937 saying that donations less than one hundred dollars would no longer be publicly acknowledged. During the eight years of the Sino-Japanese War (1937–1945), the Association to Save China sent at least five million American dollars to China.[43] In those years, there was hardly a time when no fund-raising campaign was going on in the immigrant communities.

The enthusiasm evidenced in San Francisco was echoed in the rest of Chinese America. The economic difficulties of the United States during and after the Great Depression did not stop individual Chinese Americans from continuing to make financial sacrifices. In 1943 local and regional fund-raising organizations held a national meeting, at which it was an-nounced that donating to China's anti-Japanese war should be a monthly obligation for everyone over the age of sixteen. According to Him Mark Lai, Chinese America as a whole donated twenty-five million American dollars directly to China's war efforts during the Pacific war.[44]

THE VITAL IMPORTANCE OF OVERSEAS CHINESE CAPITAL

While we probably can never determine precisely the magnitude of the money China received from Chinese America and from the rest of the Chinese diaspora, its vital significance for China's economy is easy to appreciate. Overseas Chinese continuously sent so much money through so many different channels that individual investigators and various gov-ernment and financial organizations have reached different conclusions regarding its importance. C. F. Remer was one of the first scholars to study the subject by collecting and analyzing comprehensive empirical data. According to his estimate, the annual average of overseas Chinese remittances, including those from the United States, amounted to a hundred and fifty million Chinese dollars between 1902 and 1913. The annual average increased to two hundred million Chinese dollars between 1914 and 1930.[45] Even by Remer's estimate, which appears to be too conservative,[46] remittances from Chinese living outside of China equaled 80 percent of China's trade deficit. From 1914 to 1930, remittances were large enough to wipe out more than 70 percent of China's international trade deficit. For the same period, the remittances were more than 80 percent of the average revenue received by the Chinese central government.[47] During the eight years of the war against Japanese aggression, the importance of remittances from overseas Chinese communities became even clearer. From 1937 to 1939, for example, remittances were more than four times the size of the Chinese international trade deficit.[48]

It is important to note that a significant percentage of the remittances came from Chinese America, and that sum, as a percentage of the total amount remitted by Chinese living all over the world, grew during the course of the first half of the twentieth century. In most years during the 1930s, half of all remittances sent to China came from Chinese America.[49] Citing a report from the U.S. Postal Service, Xia Chenghua states that in 1939 alone Chinese Americans remitted thirty-five million dollars to China. This sum constituted half of the total remittances from the entire Chinese diaspora in that year.[50] The proportional importance of Chinese America's remittances is even greater when we consider that its population represented only about 2 percent of the entire Chinese diaspora.[51]

Signifying Chinese Americans' growing attachment to China, their remittances also played a critical role in motivating their homeland to embrace them. By the turn of the twentieth century, many people in China had become aware of Chinese Americans' contributions to the national economy.[52] During the 1905 boycott movement, a flyer circulated by participants reported that remittances from Chinese Americans in a period of less than five years amounted to fifty million Chinese dollars,[53] money that would be helpful for strengthening China. Chinese Americans themselves knew the political weight their economic resources carried. In a letter written in 1905, a Chinese merchant in San Francisco urged the Chinese government to stand up to America's anti-Chinese racist policies, pointing out that failure to do so would destroy an important source of revenue for China.[54]

As we have seen, the trajectory of funds Chinese Americans transported to China shows a significant growth in investments in the country's economic infrastructure and in direct political contributions. These contributions facilitated their participation in China's national political discourse, which, in turn, added a political dimension to their Chinese-ness. However, the transformation of Chinese American identity in the first half of the twentieth century cannot be seen as a simple and lin-ear process, one in which localism was replaced by nationalistic senti-ments. On the contrary, the very parochialism that Liang Qichao found disappointing around the turn of the century demonstrated a remarkable longevity in Chinese America as well as elsewhere in the Chinese dias-pora. For example, family-oriented remittances almost always accounted for an overwhelming majority of the money that overseas Chinese sent to China.[55] Even at their height, overseas Chinese direct investments never exceeded 4 percent of family-oriented remittances. Even though Chinese America as a whole donated twenty-five million American dollars to help finance China's war effort during the eight-year war against Japanese aggression,[56] that amount made up less than 9 percent of the total re-mittances that Chinese Americans sent to China.[57] Apparently, Chinese Americans were embracing modern Chinese nationalism without giving up their long-standing commitments to their loved ones in the emigrant communities.

The millions of dollars that traveled from Chinese America to China al-low us to appreciate and to measure the extent of the Chinese Americans' transnational world. This enormous amount helped their loved ones and injected much needed foreign currency into the Chinese economy. Mean-while, it empowered Chinese Americans and significantly improved their status in China as they found important allies in their struggles against racism in the Unites States. Despite its limitations, the repeal of Chinese exclusion in 1943 represents a landmark victory in that struggle. It ended the exclusion of many classes of Chinese immigrants and, for the first time in American history, allowed an Asian group to become naturalized U.S. citizens.[58] To a large degree, the repeal is a result of the Pacific war, a war in which Chinese Americans participated actively. It represents a victory won via the transnational practices of Chinese Americans. Their American resources enabled them to enlarge the boundaries of their Chinese-ness and increased their connections to China. That reinforced Chinese-ness, in turn, helped them to claim their political rights in the United States as Americans.

While the transpacific world has been an important context in which to understand the Chinese American experience, we must also remember that the conditions and relationships sustaining that world, which de-fined the meaning and direction of capital and human movements, varied in different historical periods. The extraordinary significance of Chinese remittances for the Chinese economy in the first half of the twentieth century is perhaps unthinkable for a man like Mr. Chang and his fel-low Chinese Americans in the twenty-first century. Similarly, the extent to which Chinese Americans' transnationalism has been a factor as they negotiated their identity and status has also changed over time. Moreover, transnational connections at any particular historical moment faced may constraints and threats. No one understood such constraints more clearly than individual Chinese Americans. However transnational they might have been in their perspectives and consciousness, the physical transnationality of individuals, especially laborers, has always faced high hurdles. During the period under discussion, most Chinese Americans remained in the United States because of the dictates of daily-life realities. Among those who were able to travel to China, few eventually found the opportunities that they had envisioned there. Shortly after World War II, most of the investments that Chinese Americans had made collapsed, thereby ending a chapter in the history of Chinese American transnationalism.

6   Republicanism, Confucianism, Christianity, and Capitalism in American Chinese Ideology

SHEHONG CHEN

THIS CHAPTER INVESTIGATES how Chinese immigrants in the United States (hereafter called American Chinese to differentiate them from U.S.-born Chinese Americans) envisioned a modern China and re-acted to developments in their homeland during the first three decades of the twentieth century.[1] In that period, educated Chinese debated about which model of political modernization China should adopt as it changed fundamentally from a monarchy to a republic. Chinese in the United States participated in these debates and contributed to the changes. What visions of a modern China did American Chinese come up with? What changes in China did they support or oppose? How did their experiences in the United States or their exposure to American values and ideologies affect their perspectives and actions?

U.S. IMMIGRATION LAWS, CHINA'S MODERNIZATION, AND AMERICAN CHINESE VISIONS

Large-scale Chinese migration to the United States started at the end of the 1840s. Widespread economic dislocation, caused mainly by Western ex-pansionism, pushed people out, while the discovery of gold in California lured them across the Pacific Ocean. Most Chinese who came to the United States in the nineteenth century were searching for economic betterment. The United States, which they called "Gold Mountain," was especially attractive because going there offered a chance to get rich. The desire to get rich was an important way in which Chinese immigrant communi-ties in the United States differed from traditional Chinese society, where merchants or businessmen had a low status and those who traded with for-eigners were regarded as treacherous and deserving of heavy punishment. In contrast, in American Chinese communities, merchants were not only admired but also shared the highest social status with Confucian scholars.

Anti-Chinese immigration legislation and practices also helped shape the character of the American Chinese population, in which merchants had, by the first decade of the twentieth century, become an increasingly large component.[2] The 1882 Chinese Exclusion Act barred Chinese laborers from entering the United States for ten years. The 1888 Scott Act prevented Chinese laborers who had returned to China for temporary visits from reentering the United States. The 1892 Geary Act extended the exclusion of Chinese laborers for another ten years and required them to carry registration cards at all times. Exclusion was extended indefinitely in 1904. These acts effectively reduced the American Chinese population from a high of 107,488 in 1890 to 61,639 in 1920.[3] In addition, economic depressions and the pressures exerted by white labor unions on capitalists to refrain from hiring "cheap Chinese labor" inhibited the growth of a Chinese working class. Meanwhile, racial discrimination limited the ability of American Chinese to accumulate capital, thereby making it impossible for them to provide a large enough number of jobs to American Chinese workers who might have formed a sizable Chinese immigrant working class had such jobs existed.[4]

Chinese in the United States were driven into urban areas during the first few decades of the twentieth century.[5] Many ran laundries and restaurants; some relied on other kinds of Chinatown businesses for employment; others worked as domestic servants in American families. By the turn of the twentieth century, only a small number of American Chinese continued to work as farm laborers, miners, railroad builders, cigar makers, and shoe manufacturers, as large numbers had done during the second half of the nineteenth century. Laundries, restaurants, and other retail businesses that helped sustain a Chinese lifestyle and culture in the United States were usually managed as partnerships. As a result, Chinese businessmen and professionals such as doctors, translators, and priests, who belonged to the "exempt classes" under the exclusion laws, composed more than 40 percent of the declining Chinese American population in the 1910s.[6] The term *merchant* was broadly used to include employees who owned shares in the businesses they worked in.[7]

Another characteristic prevalent among Chinese in the United States was their close connection with China. The fact that 79.1 percent of them in 1910 were born in China[8] suggests why they felt so close to the home country. Moreover, American legislation, which prevented the wives of Chinese laborers from coming into the United States, as well as Chinese tradition, which discouraged Chinese women from traveling far away from home, led most American Chinese to leave their families in China. The number of Chinese females (4,675 in 1910, including married and single women and girls, represented only 6.5 percent of the total American Chinese population) reveals that a majority of Chinese at this time still had families in China.[9] Therefore, it is not surprising that they were so concerned about China's well-being. In addition, U.S.

naturalization laws deprived Chinese of the right to become naturalized citizens, thus making it impossible for them to participate in American politics.

The close connection to the homeland fostered strong nationalistic feelings among Chinese in the United States. They recognized that China had become weak compared to the rapidly industrializing West. China's weakness was always mentioned in the same breath as the U.S. anti-Chinese immigration laws and practices. One of the poems carved on the walls of the Angel Island immigration station by detained Chinese reads, "For what reason must I sit in jail? It is only because my country is weak and my family poor." Another one stated, "If my country had contrived to make herself strong, this [banishing me to Island] never would have happened."[10]

This acute awareness made most Chinese in the United States supporters of modernization programs in China. One program they supported was Kang Youwei's reform movement. According to Kang, a Confucian scholar, the West could claim no superiority over China in moral terms, while the Six Classics provided the best discussion of the art of government. But China was lagging behind the West in scientific and technological developments, he warned. His prescription for modernizing the country was to catch up with the West in scientific and technological developments while preserving its own principles, institutions, and moral traditions as enunciated in Confucianism.[11]

Kang Youwei's student, Liang Qichao, joined him in the early 1890s to advocate for gradual and nonviolent reform in China.[12] With Kang Youwei providing the theoretical guidance, the reform movement, which was supported by Emperor Guang Xu and lasted one hundred days in 1898, centered on an effort to transform the existing absolute monarchy into a constitutional monarchy.[13] Known as the One Hundred Days Reform, the movement was suppressed by the conservative Empress Dowager Ci Xi. Kang and Liang escaped persecution by fleeing to North America with the hope of finding support there for their reform programs.

Such a reform-oriented modernization program fitted well with the mentality of most Chinese in the United States. In 1899, in order to get the widest support possible, Kang and Liang suggested that a Baoshanghui, Society to Protect Commerce, be organized to push for reforms in China. American Chinese community leaders, however, suggested naming the organization Baohuanghui, Society to Protect the Emperor. This suggestion reflected their willingness to uphold the position of the Chinese emperor while accepting the necessity of reforms in China.

Because its leaders showed respect for traditional Chinese values and advocated a moderate program to make China a strong and modern nation, the Baohuanghui commanded the loyalty of most Chinese in the United States during the first few years of the twentieth century. Most Chinatown organizations cooperated with the Baohuanghui and many businesses invested in Baohuanghui-sponsored banking and investment programs aimed at developing China's natural resources and commerce. They also helped finance the society's reform movement in China.[14] The most impressive feature of the Baohuanghui's success among Chinese in the United States was that it won the support of the Zhigongtang, a secret society[15] to which many Chinese laborers in the United States belonged, and of Wu Panzhao (Ng Poon Chew), the most respected American Chinese Christian. The Baohuanghui managed *Ta Tung Yat Po*, the Zhigongtang's newspaper, until 1904, and Wu Panzhao was a Baohuanghui "stalwart" until 1903.[16] The Baohuanghui also ran its own Chinese-language newspaper, *Chinese World*, which was financially supported by American Chinese.

The popularity of the reform movement among Chinese in the United States decreased as China continued its decline as a nation and as Chinese in the United States continued to suffer discrimination and exclusion. The failure of the reform movement to transform China into a strong and modern nation allowed more radical ideas for the salvation and modernization of China to emerge.

In sharp contrast to the reform-oriented program was Sun Yat-sen's revolutionary program, aimed at overthrowing the existing Qing rulers and changing China's century-old dynastic system to a modern democratic republic. In 1905, Sun established the Tongmenghui, the Revolutionary Alliance, in Tokyo, Japan. In 1910, the Tongmenghui set up its first branch office among Chinese in the United States. Its newspaper, *Young China*, a daily, articulated the organization's radical vision. The first issue declared that China was weak because "the barbarian Manchus" had ruled it. If China wished to become a strong nation, it "must overthrow the present tyrannical, dictatorial, ugly, and corrupt Qing government."[17]

The Tongmenghui's narrow concentration on anti-Manchuism failed to gain it much support among Chinese in the United States. However, its focus on the fact that the Manchus were foreigners, and not Han Chinese, and its principal goal of overthrowing the Qing dynasty fitted well with the Zhigongtang's political slogan, *fanqing fuming* (overthrow the Qing and restore the Ming). Yet, life in the United States played down the political nature of the Zhigongtang. Individuals became members more for protection, employment opportunities, or mutual aid for business purposes than for any political purpose. In addition, many Chinese valued conformity more than rebellion—a fact that hindered Sun's attempts to gain adherents for his revolutionary program in American Chinatowns.[18]

The ineffectiveness of the reform movement and the incompatibility of Sun's revolutionary vision with the prevailing mentality of American Chinese created ground for a third vision to be articulated. It was best expressed by Wu Panzhao and his newspaper, *Chung Sai Yat Po* (Chinese-Western Daily). Arriving in the United States as a Guangdong peasant boy of fifteen in 1881, a year before the passage of the Chinese Exclusion Act, Wu very quickly learned about the discrimination that Chinese suffered in the United States. He first attended a Presbyterian Church school and then the San Francisco Theological Seminary. In 1892, he was ordained as the first Chinese Presbyterian minister on the Pacific Coast. Wearing Western clothes, cutting off his queue, and preaching from his pulpit as a Protestant minister, he intended "to teach the Chinese to be at home in America" and "to teach Americans to appreciate the fine qualities of the precious and ancient civilization that had nurtured" individuals such as himself.[19]

Political developments in China and anti-Chinese discrimination in the United States made Wu realize that his original goals were insufficient if he truly wanted to help China and the Chinese in the United States. Living in an era in which "yellow journalism" was exerting significant influence on the American public, Wu decided to publish a Chinese-language daily newspaper to rally support from American Chinese for the reform programs in China, as well as to alert them to "the dangers of American immigration laws and the [imperative to] fight for civil rights and citizenship."[20]

Greeting the American Chinese public on the first Chinese New Year's Day of the twentieth century, *Chung Sai Yat Po*[21] announced that it would fight for "a modern strong Chinese nation and equal rights for Chinese both in immigrating to America and in settling there."[22] Wu's recognition of the necessity of reform and modernization in China made him a strong supporter of the Baohuanghui reform programs. Yet his particular background and vision shaped his own unique ideas for the salvation and modernization of China and for improving the lot of his fellow Chinese in the United States. *Chung Sai Yat Po* was thus born with a diasporic vision and served, in the years to come, as a strong American Chinese community voice in the search for ways to modernize China.

DEFENDING REPUBLICANISM AND OPPOSING MONARCHISM

Despite their penchant for reform rather than revolution, most Chinese in the United States supported the outcome of the 1911 Revolution, which ended the dynastic system and established the Republic of China. In the years to come, the three visions, as represented by *Chinese World, Chung*

Sai Yat Po, and *Young China,* merged in support of a republican form of government. *Chinese World* proclaimed, in October 1911, that the Qing government was too corrupt to be saved and encouraged American Chinese to support the rebels.[23] *Chung Sai Yat Po* called on all Chinese to support the emerging government for it represented democracy and promised happiness for all Chinese.[24] Those who identified with *Young China* achieved their aim of overthrowing the Qing dynasty and establishing a republic.

However, the Republic of China did not enjoy stability. Instead, the country suffered from internal political unrests such as the Second Revolution, waged by the Guomindang (GMD or the Nationalist Party) against Yuan Shikai's government, and external pressures such as the Twenty-one Demands imposed on China by Japan. By the middle of 1915, conservative forces in China launched a campaign to restore the monarchical system in the name of saving the nation. In late 1915, a Peace Planning Society was organized for the sole purpose of helping Yuan restore a monarchy. The society argued specifically that monarchism was better than despotism carried out under the name of a republic. It also argued that military men would be more faithful to an emperor because they hoped to secure wealth and positions for their offspring and that a devoted army could most effectively deter rebellions.[25]

Chinese in the Unites States were appalled by the possibility of a monarchical restoration in China. To an increasing number of them, republicanism was the world's most modern form of government. So, retaining it as China's political system would help improve their status in the United States. In their eyes, the establishment of the Republic of China had demonstrated to the world that China was once again a great Asian nation, comparable to the United States and France.[26] The retention of republicanism would thus help correct the Western image of China as a "backward and uncivilized" nation. Restoring the monarchical system, in contrast, would only reinforce the negative view of Chinese as a people too backward to appreciate the best form of government. If Chinese could not maintain a republican government in China, as the argument went, they might logically not be entitled to equal rights in the United States. American Chinese feared that political change in China might be used to justify further and more severe prejudice and discrimination against them.[27]

In late December 1915, Yuan Shikai declared that January 1, 1916, would be the first day of his Hong Xian dynasty. The monarchical movement triggered strong reactions from all three newspapers that represented a full spectrum of opinion in the American Chinese community. *Young China* called Yuan "the thief,"[28] accusing him of cheating all Chinese, stealing presidential power, and trying to destroy the republic in order to satisfy his own selfish ambition. The only way to stop Yuan from totally destroying the republic, the paper argued, was for all Chinese to rise up against him. It suggested that all Chinese should act as responsible citizens and refuse to recognize the Year of Hong Xian. It called on Chinese everywhere to support and donate money to the National Protection Army so that its military efforts could succeed.[29]

According to *Chung Sai Yat Po*, republicanism was the only political system that could guarantee freedom for and equality among all people. Moreover, it was also sthe only system that could gradually bring forth a middle-class society essential for the practice of democracy.[30] The paper admitted that China had become a backward and weak country compared to the fast-developing Western nations. To catch up and restore its status in the world, China had to reform and make progress. The establishment of the republic had transformed China from "a moribund feudal system" to a modern and progressive state, a definite step forward. Yuan's restoration of the monarchical system was seen as a retrogressive act, instigated by "a conservative party" in China.[31]

Chinese World argued that Yuan's monarchical restoration would bring disaster to China. When the paper had earlier advocated constitutional reforms and argued against revolution prior to the overthrow of the Qing dynasty, it had reasoned that China could not afford a radical revolution because that would provide opportunities for foreign powers to divide up the country and engulf it. But when the 1911 Revolution ended with no physical division of China and the establishment of a republic, the paper celebrated that result and became an advocate for protecting and maintaining the republic. According to *Chinese World*, Yuan's monarchical restoration caused chaos and opened the door to further changes that China could not afford. First of all, stated the paper, China was beset with domestic poverty, natural disasters, and especially rebellious forces. A further change in its political system would only deepen the poverty and open the way for more rebellions. Second, the world had finally recognized the Republic of China, and changing the form of government while she was still very weak would cause her to lose the precarious legitimacy she had gained.[32]

The preference for republicanism was expressed not only by the three newspapers but also by other organizations in American Chinatowns. In September 1915, the Chinese Consolidated Benevolent Association (CCBA) in San Francisco, on behalf of all Chinese in the United States, wrote a letter to President Woodrow Wilson, asking him to advise Yuan not to restore monarchism in China. The letter said that monarchical restoration was against the wishes of most Chinese people. Such an attempt would inevitably plunge China into chaos, which would not benefit American interests in China.[33] The CCBAs in Boston and New York

made their public announcements against Yuan's attempt in October
1915.[34] Chinese in the United States (including the relatively small communities in Chicago, Detroit, and Portland, Oregon), Canada, Cuba,
and Mexico all started to raise funds in preparation for military actions in China.[35] In San Francisco, a Chinese theater advertised benefit performances for the purpose of raising funds for the defense of
republicanism.[36]

Chinese communities all over the United States expressed support for
raising funds to enable the revolt against Yuan's monarchical restoration
to succeed. The CCBA led efforts to organize an All-American Overseas
Chinese Military Fund Raising Bureau for the National Protection Army
in May 1916.[37] This effort was supported by various American Chinatown organizations, including seven district associations, the GMD, the
Chinese American Citizens Alliance, the Zhigongtang, the Constitutionalist Party, the Chinese Church Alliance, *Young China*, *Chinese World*,
Chung Sai Yat Po, and *Ta Tung Yat Po*.[38]

Besides fund-raising activities, Chinese in the United States organized
their own volunteer corps to participate in the anti-Yuan military campaigns in China. Named Overseas Chinese Corps of Volunteers (Huaqiao
yiyong tuan), more than five hundred Chinese young men from the United
States and Canada "took upon themselves the responsibility for national
salvation" and vowed to wipe out national traitors and to restore the republic. The volunteers went to Japan for concentrated military training;
they arrived in Qingdao, China in May 1916. The corps had three airplanes, which distributed leaflets from the air to people on the ground,
with the hope of creating strong feelings among citizens against Yuan's
restoration attempt. After Yuan Shikai died on June 6, 1916, the Overseas Chinese Corps of Volunteers dissolved itself and its members all returned to North America, for none of them was "seeking personal fame
or gain" when he or she volunteered for the mission.[39] That effort clearly
expressed the preference of American Chinese for republicanism over
monarchism: they were ready to sacrifice their lives to defend the republican form of government in China. Meanwhile, they objected strongly
to proposals to eliminate a fundamental aspect of Chinese society—
Confucianism.

Preserving Confucianism

In mid-September 1916, Chinese in the United States cabled the Chinese
government to protest its proposal to abolish Confucianism in China.
One of the cables said, "Chinese civilization is rooted in Confucianism.
To abolish Confucianism is to commit national suicide, for such an act
cuts off the fountainhead for Chinese civilization. Education should make

Confucianism its principal content. We hereby beg you [the government] to keep it."[40]

Chinese World pointed out that China had stood in the world as a great civilization for thousands of years and had survived wars and natural disasters mainly because of "the four pillars of the nation."[41] These were *li* (decorum or rites), *yi* (righteousness or duty), *lian* (integrity or honesty), and *chi* (sense of shame), which represented the essence of the Confucian world order. According to Confucius and his disciples, if everyone under the heavens conformed to accepted standards of conduct, carried out his or her proper duties, maintained integrity, and subdued selfish desires, the expression of which was shameful, the world would be perfect. Confucianism prescribed a hierarchical society in which the refined and educated ruled and set the standards for moral and social conduct, while the inferior or common people obeyed and followed. In such a hierarchical society, men were superior to women and the old controlled the young. Rebellion or disobedience by inferior people constituted nonconformity to prescribed rules of conduct, negligence of one's duties, and a lack of integrity, and were thus shameful and punishable behaviors.

The cable sent to the Chinese government and the editorial in *Chinese World* highlighted the centrality of Confucianism in American Chinese life. Racial prejudice and cultural discrimination notwithstanding, American Chinese believed that their native culture provided the most appropriate framework for a rich and harmonious life and that nothing was superior to it. Alice Fong, who was born in California and reached adolescence in the 1910s, took pride in her Chinese cultural heritage. When she became a Christian, she did not see any conflict between what she had learned from her parents about Confucian virtues and Christian morals. In fact, she thought that the teachings of Confucius "contained all the virtues of Christian teachings, that only those who were unfamiliar with the heritage of China's wisdom failed to see that."[42] In *Fifth Chinese Daughter*, Jade Snow Wong described her experiences growing up in San Francisco's Chinatown. Her father firmly stated that nothing could replace "the practical experience of the Chinese, who for thousands of years have preserved a most superior family pattern."[43]

Chinese men and the Chinatown elite, in particular, supported Confucianism. CCBAs in American Chinatowns supported Chinese schools, which opened and concluded school semesters with ceremonies worshipping Confucius.[44] They also organized celebrations of Confucius' birthday.[45] Chinese men preferred to marry China-born girls because American-born girls had too much freedom and no longer knew their subordinate position within the Confucian hierarchy. According to Chin Cheung, an American-born Chinese man in Seattle, American-born girls were "too independent. Go out in the evening, dance, spend money, don't like stay home much. . . . Girls this country don't make so good wives as girls in China. Girls in China have more respect I think for husband. They look after husband better; look after children better; have more children." Chin Cheung thus wanted his children to receive a Chinese education first, because "If they don't have this old country education they no good."[46]

Chinese World directly opposed the women's liberation movement. It pointed out that the movement was sending women into teahouses and salons where they talked about politics with men. These women, with very little education and knowledge about the real world, were only making fools of themselves, the paper pointed out.[47] Women's appearance in teahouses and salons, until then strictly male social territory, and participation in politics were gross violations of Confucian propriety and a threat to male dominance.

Even the reform-minded Wu Panzhao told a newspaper reporter, "As for equality between men and women, and between their relative positions in the world, that need not enter into the discussion. There is no equality in nature. Everywhere, in physique, in intellect, in all her affairs, we find inequality. So the status of the woman is the home, and there is no excuse for her not being there and rearing a family. It is her province to raise the family, and that should settle the question."[48]

Another reality of life in American Chinatowns also shored up the desire to keep women subordinate to men. Many Chinese men had families in China; to ensure that such transpacific families stay together, the observation of female chastity, filial piety, female devotion to husbands, and subordination to in-laws were essential.

But Confucianism was under attack in China in the late 1910s. Led by Chen Duxiu, dean of humanities at Beijing University, and Hu Shi, who had studied with the pragmatist philosopher John Dewey at Columbia University and upon returning home became a professor of philosophy at Beijing University, Chinese intellectuals came to believe that the country's political problems were rooted in Chinese traditional culture in general and in Confucianism in particular. *New Youth*, a magazine edited by Chen, Hu, and other Chinese intellectuals, compared the health of Chinese society to a human body. According to *New Youth*, Chinese society was full of "old and rotten cells" that had accumulated for thousands of years. If the society were to flourish again, these cells had to be replaced by new and vital ones.[49] By "new and vital cells," they meant China's youth as well as "Mr. Democracy" and "Mr. Science." According to Chen, in order for "Mr. Democracy" to be introduced to China, "we are obliged to oppose Confucianism, the codes of rituals, chastity of women, traditional ethics, and old fashioned politics." To make way for "Mr. Science," Chen continued, "we have to oppose traditional arts and traditional religion."[50]

With such a theoretical foundation, China's intellectuals started campaigns to eradicate the roots of the country's problems. They launched a New Culture Movement. Chen attacked Chinese traditions and called for an ideological awakening among China's youth under the slogan "Down with Confucius and Sons." Hu concentrated on literary reform, deemphasizing literary Chinese (*wenyan*) in favor of writings in the Chinese vernacular (*baihua*), advocating writings that would reflect the contemporary spirit, and not imitations of ancient works.[51]

In response to the New Culture Movement, *Chinese World* argued that China did not have to borrow from the West because not only did Confucianism set moral standards, it also advocated civic participation in politics, emphasized economic development, and promoted humanitarianism. In fact, the paper said, so-called Western democracy had been practiced in China for thousands of years. An emperor's mandate to rule was based on the support of his subjects, without which the emperor, as well as the dynasty, would fall. One of the principal tasks of the governing body under Confucianism was to take care of the welfare of the people. In the modern world, that meant developing the national economy in order to enable China to survive. Confucianism was also humanitarian in nature, for it was against wars and the ill treatment of prisoners of war.[52] The paper further pointed out that Confucius was a great scientist who advocated reason against superstition. Confucius, on his own, had concluded that the earth could not be square, for its corners could not then be covered by heaven, which was believed to be round.[53] *Chinese World* worried that intellectuals in China had taken the wrong road and that their New Culture Movement was plunging China more and more deeply into trouble. People hated Confucianism, the paper pointed out, because it prescribed more duties than rights. Moreover, the attack on Confucianism played into the hands of corrupt politicians and despotic militarists and the movement would prolong the turmoil in China, eventually leading to the downfall of China as a nation.[54]

Such fundamental differences, however, did not suggest any lessening of patriotic or nationalist feelings for China among American Chinese. When, in May 1919, news came that the Versailles Peace Conference had agreed to transfer Germany's rights in China's Shandong Province to Japan,[55] Chinese in the United States responded rapidly and strongly. The San Francisco CCBA, Chinese Chamber of Commerce, Chinese Church Alliance, Chinese Language Newspapers Association, Chinese American Citizens Alliance, Confucian Society, and Constitutionalist Party cabled the Peace Conference and the Chinese delegation to the conference, urging them to reject that decision. Some of these organizations also cabled the president of the United States and the United States Congress, asking them to maintain justice and to refuse to recognize the decision concerning

Shandong.[56] Patriotic organizations were established and fund-raising activities followed. The San Francisco CCBA initiated the National Salvation Association (Jiuguo hui), which raised funds for the government to resist Japan's demands on Shandong.

The response in China to "the Shandong decision" showed that the kind of national awakening that the New Culture Movement intellectuals had been trying to arouse had become a reality. The Chinese government's arrest of student demonstrators in Beijing on May 4, 1919, triggered nationwide demonstrations and gave a new name, the May Fourth Movement, to the New Culture Movement. As student demonstrations turned into campus strikes and violence against authorities, *Chinese World* editorialized that there was a difference between the May Fourth demonstrations and the subsequent widespread student agitation throughout China. The former, the paper said, derived from students' patriotism while the latter was nothing but anarchism among young people that threatened China's educational system. The paper alleged that anarchists were using the young students to destroy Chinese culture and civilization.[57]

Chinese World's response seemed to represent the prevailing mentality among Chinese in the United States. *Young China*, for its part, emphasized the importance of education, which, it said, was being neglected in China because of the strikes, demonstrations, and assaults on professors. It reasoned that the best road to take in order to save China was to develop its national industries, and that education was the only way to prepare for industrial development.[58] *Chung Sai Yat Po* did not carry any comment at all on the New Culture and May Fourth movements. It supported the students' demonstrations on May 4, 1919, and accused the Chinese government of being corrupt and impotent.[59] The paper, however, used the term *anarchism* to describe the student demonstrations and other activities that occurred in late 1919, pointing out that patriotism and anarchism were incompatible.[60]

ADOPTING CHRISTIAN VALUES

Revering Confucius and preserving Chinese traditional culture did not preclude adopting Christian values. Although there were only about four thousand Christians among the Chinese in the United States in the early twentieth century, the Christian church played a significant role in the everyday lives of many American Chinese. While the hierarchical society prescribed by Confucianists was oppressive, in the eyes of women and youth, Christianity held out the promise of liberation. American Chinese women and youth used modern American concepts such as individual rights and gender equality to negotiate an escape from Confucian constraints. They turned to Christian churches and facilities for spiritual solace and intellectual and physical growth.

An increasing presence of women and the appearance of the second generation characterized American Chinese community development in the 1910s and 1920s. Christian churches facilitated the important role played by women in this development. The coming of age of an American-born second generation paralleled the growth of Young Men's Christian Associations, Young Women's Christian Associations, and other church-sponsored programs in American Chinatowns. The YMCA in San Francisco's Chinatown was established in 1912 and served as a model for Chinatown YMCAs in New York City, established in 1916; in Oakland, established in 1921; and in Seattle, established in 1923.[61] Chinatown YMCAs were designed to provide programs and facilities that included physical training, which would help raise a generation of healthy and strong Chinese Americans and help change the image of Chinese as "sick men"; practical or vocational training, which would bring education to ordinary Chinese in order to prepare them for modern life; and moral and ethical training, which would teach Christian love for all and a sense of duty as citizens of a republic.[62]

More specifically, YMCAs played a variety of roles. The YMCA in San Francisco's Chinatown sponsored lectures that taught Western ways of housekeeping. For example, in November 1912, the YMCA held a lecture on the hygiene of milk. Since dairy products were not part of a traditional Chinese diet, imparting such knowledge was important. At the lecture, pictures and drawings were shown to demonstrate how cows are milked and what harm that milk gone bad would cause.[63] According to *Chung Sai Yat Po*, part of the reason that Chinese were discriminated against was that they neglected exercise and personal hygiene as well as "human compassion for each other" (*renlei huxiang qinai zhi jingsheng*).[64] The YMCA, in an effort to address such issues, put on plays that encouraged martial qualities, disseminated ideas of civic responsibilities, and promoted patriotism.[65]

The Chinatown YMCA also played a significant role in transforming old Chinese customs and habits. *Chung Sai Yat Po* carried articles condemning Chinese traditions of encouraging early marriage, regarding women as property, allowing only arranged marriages, and permitting men to take concubines. Chinese in San Francisco established a Customs Reform Society (Gailiang fengsu hui). *Chung Sai Yat Po*, the YMCA, and the Customs Reform Society promoted marriages based on the free will of two mature adults, attacked wasteful Chinese wedding banquets, exposed superstitious beliefs about death, and introduced Western ways of conducting weddings and funerals.[66]

Chinatown YMCAs also served as meeting places for the growing number of second-generation Chinese Americans in the 1910s and 1920s. For Thomas Chinn, whose family moved to San Francisco from Oregon in 1919, when he was a teenager, the YMCA provided a place where he met and made friends with contemporaries he otherwise would not have been able to meet. The YMCA had a library and a lounge where people could "sit and converse." Young Thomas, a stranger in San Francisco, visited the Chinese YMCA daily, where he found Chinese people of his age who "spoke decent English."[67]

Because of its important role in Chinatown life, the YMCA in San Francisco's Chinatown expanded several times. In 1915, its headquarters moved to a much larger place to accommodate increasing demands for social, intellectual, religious, and vocational training. By mid-1922, $170,000 of a required total of $200,000 had been collected from Chinese in the United States for the construction of an entirely new YMCA building.[68]

Besides YMCAs, there were also Chinese Young Women's Christian Associations in American Chinatowns. At the YWCA in San Francisco's Chinatown, which was established in 1916, Chinese immigrant women studied English, learned American ways of housekeeping and baby care, and obtained help when they had problems at home or received unfair treatment at work.[69] Just like Chinese YMCAs, Chinese YWCAs aimed to help improve the public image of the Chinese people and to build bridges for Chinese immigrant as well as American-born women that would link Chinatowns and American mainstream society. Local residents enthusiastically supported the Chinese YWCA's programs. Within four years of its establishment, the YWCA in San Francisco's Chinatown had a membership of five hundred in 1920.[70]

Christian churches also offered English classes for Chinese immigrants. Christians even visited American Chinese homes to deliver English lessons and tutoring. In the early 1920s, when Law Shee Low, an immigrant woman in San Francisco's Chinatown, "had no time to take advantage of English classes offered by the churches," her husband "asked a 'Jesus woman' to come teach her English" at her home.[71]

As these examples suggest, by the early 1920s, many connections had developed between Christian churches and American Chinese communities, and Christian values had become an integral part of the lives of many American Chinese. In contrast, in March 1922, students and intellectuals at the forefront of the May Fourth Movement in China organized an Antireligious (also called Anti-Christian) Movement, whose adherents argued that religious teachings cultivated passivity and dogmatism and were obstacles to free, objective thinking and to the development of society.[72] The more practical argument of the movement centered on the

history of China in the preceding seventy years—a history full of humiliating experiences resulting from Western aggression. The manifesto of the
movement declared that Christianity was an instrument of imperialism.
Hence, Christianity was harmful to the development of a modern and
independent China.[73]

Chung Sai Yat Po opposed the Anti-Christian Movement. It argued
that philosophers throughout the world had acknowledged that "all human beings were religious animals" and to deny such a fact was just an
act of ignorance and ridicule.[74] If intellectuals embraced science at the expense of religion, they would develop the material part of a modern China
without developing its spiritual part. The paper added that the development of science depended on human intelligence and inspiration, both
of which were available only when the spiritual part of human life was
nurtured and given full play.[75] Neither *Chinese World* nor *Young China*
argued against the Anti-Christian Movement. *Ta Tung Yat Po* agreed with
Chung Sai Yat Po that religion was an undeniable part of human life. It
expressed a hope that there would be calm discussions about different re-
ligions and that the freedom to believe in whatever religion an individual
preferred would be protected in China.[76]

PREFERRING CAPITALISM OVER COMMUNISM

The split between the values Chinese in the United States embraced and
the overall situation in China widened even further as a result of political
developments in the 1920s. Sun Yat-sen, leader of the GMD in China,
became receptive to both the ideas expounded by the leaders of the New
Culture and May Fourth movements and the help offered by the Soviet
Union. Believing that China had to do away with its regional militarists,
whom the movement leaders accused of being remnants of the old culture and instruments of imperialism, Sun insisted on another nationalist
revolution to unify China under his leadership.

To carry out another revolution, Sun took several steps that further
alienated Chinese in the United States. In January 1923, he made a joint
declaration with Adolf Joffe, an agent of the Comintern, announcing a
formal alliance between the GMD and the Union of Soviet Socialist Republics. Determined to unite all progressive forces in China, Sun initiated a
reorganization of his party to include *sanda zhengce*, three major policies:
"to ally with the Soviet Union, to cooperate with the Chinese Communist
Party, and to help the workers and peasants." The ultimate goal of these
policies was to realize the three principles of the people (*sanmin zhuyi*),
namely, nationalism, democracy, and people's livelihood in China. Dele-
gates representing American Chinese at the GMD's reorganization conference in Guangzhou in 1924 spoke against the three policies, particularly

the alliance and cooperation with Communism. But their opinion was ignored.[77]

In the United States, the Chinese-language press voiced opposition to the alliance between the GMD and the Soviet Union and to Sun's projected revolution. *Chinese World* pointed out that Sun had allied with Communist Russia because he could not get diplomatic recognition for his government from other countries. The paper alleged that the radical, destructive Communist ideology complemented Sun's ambition to become China's president by overthrowing the existing government and that Sun's alliance with the Soviet Union was a "conspiracy."[78] In addition, the paper said, Sun's decision to launch another revolution, the Northern Expedition (so called because his troops planned to march from Guangdong Province northwards to conquer territory held by various warlords), would make that province a miserable and dangerous place in which to live. To recruit soldiers, Sun's men went among civilians, impressing young and able-bodied men—an act that would put family livelihood in jeopardy. Taking the workforce away from the fields, *Chinese World* claimed, would lead to the starvation of hundreds and thousands. Worse still, the military situation would destroy families when husbands, fathers, and sons were killed.[79]

Chung Sai Yat Po echoed the complaints carried in *Chinese World*. It referred to the Soviet Union's foreign policy as "socialist imperialism" aimed at instigating unrest in other countries for the purpose of taking control over them. The paper reminded all Chinese that the Soviet Union had stationed troops outside Manchuria in northeastern China, refused to recognize Mongolia as Chinese territory, and insisted on maintaining control over a railroad in northeastern China. The paper warned all Chinese not to be carried away by the Soviet Union's radical propaganda, which was only a shield for its imperialist ambitions in China.[80]

Chung Sai Yat Po carried a series of editorials describing a Guangdong beset with evil curses related to the existence of Sun's military government and his insistence on unifying the country by another revolution. The list included gambling, opium smoking, banditry, war, and a despotic and abusive government. The paper editorialized about each of these curses, explaining how the "current authorities," in reference to Sun's government, were plundering Guangdong's resources, blocking development of its industries and commerce, destroying its moral fabric, and bringing misery to its people.[81]

Using Guangdong as its base, the proposed revolution would directly affect American Chinese interests. The crisis over Ningyang Railroad is just one example. As discussed in Chapter 5 in this volume, the Ningyang Railroad Company (known as the Sunning [Xinning] Railroad Company before 1916) was established in 1905 by Chen Yixi, a Chinese who had

made a fortune in the United States first as a laborer and then as a foreman for the Central Pacific Railroad.[82] Having acquired some experience
in capitalist management and knowledge of railroad construction, Chen
returned to China to help develop its railroad system. One of China's
first railroads to be managed by Chinese themselves, the Ningyang Railroad was financed by money collected mostly from Chinese in the United
States. According to *Chung Sai Yat Po*, the company was worth more
than eight million Hong Kong dollars (about six million U.S. dollars) in
1918. In early 1923, Sun asked the company to support him financially,
and it contributed about 100,000 Hong Kong dollars, a rough equivalent of 75,000 U.S. dollars. When Sun asked for another 300,000 dollars
(about 225,000 U.S. dollars), Chen Yixi refused, replying that it was beyond the company's financial ability.[83] When Sun sent troops to take over
the railroad, Chen fled to Hong Kong, where he cabled stockholders in
the United States, asking them to help protect the company.[84]

This event touched many American Chinese, a large number of whom
were from Ningyang, a district in Guangdong Province. Ningyang people,
whether stockholders or not, were affected because the railroad had been
very beneficial to the economic life of their home region, where most of
their families still lived. Stockholders, whether they were from Ningyang
or not, were shocked by Sun's action and worked hard to protect their
immediate interests. Sun finally withdrew his troops from the railroad
when Chen Yixi agreed to lend more money to the government.

Although *Chung Sai Yat Po* had the reputation among Chinese in the
United States of being nonpartisan, the paper was very harsh in its attacks
on the Sun government. It called on all Chinese, especially stockholders
of the Ningyang Railroad Company, to unite in an effort to drive the Sun
government out of Guangdong.[85] It directly blamed the Sun government
for all the troubles and miseries in Guangdong. According to the paper,
Sun had done everything to harm China and humiliate the Chinese people except opening ancestral graves in search of valuables to finance his
military effort, selling Chinese women overseas to increase his revenues,
and eating human flesh and sucking human blood.[86]

Young China, the newspaper of the GMD in the United States, tried to
distinguish the GMD from Communism. The paper argued that whereas
Communism abolished private ownership of property, the GMD allowed
it; whereas Communism advocated working-class control over the means
of production and the distribution of wealth, the GMD advocated that
the government distribute land equally and retain control over capital;
whereas Communism advocated social revolution, the GMD emphasized political reforms and improving people's livelihoods.[87] According
to *Young China*, these were essential differences, visible in the GMD's
new political platform. The charge that the GMD had turned Communist

was nothing but a rumor, and a new alliance with the Soviet Union was only an expedient way to rejuvenate China.[88]

Such arguments indicated that *Young China* was, after all, a voice of American Chinese interests. Managed and supported by American Chinese who wanted to help build a strong and democratic republic in China, it had come, like the other papers, to represent the newly arisen petit bourgeois class. Its understanding of equality and democracy derived from prevailing ideologies in the United States. Communism was beyond what it could embrace or support.

The conflict between American Chinese and the reorganized GMD was further revealed in the Guangzhou Merchants' Association incident. In May 1924, the Guangzhou Merchants' Association, an organization of businessmen, directly confronted the Guangzhou municipal government when the latter imposed a special tax on all businesses in Guangzhou to be used for rebuilding streets in the city. The association called for a general strike to protest against the tax and put together a private army to deal with any government pressure. When the government repealed the special tax, the general strike was called off though the private army continued its existence.

In August 1924, the association's president, Chen Lianbo, who worked for the Hong Kong and Shanghai Banking Corporation in Hong Kong, applied for a license from the Sun government to import weapons for the association's use. Four days after Chen got the license from the government, more than nine thousand guns arrived in Guangzhou on a Danish ship. The number of guns was much greater than that allowed in the license, and the four-day period in which the purchasing, loading, and shipping were accomplished was unexpectedly short. Because the Sun government suspected a connection between Chen and the British colonial government in Hong Kong, it declared that the weapons had been smuggled into Guangzhou and so detained them.

Both *Chinese World* and *Chung Sai Yat Po* attacked the government's detention as a "despotic action" trampling the rights of the Guangzhou Merchants' Association.[89] They informed Chinese in the United States that the association's private army was protecting the people in Guangdong from the Sun government's forces and other bandits and looters. The weapons were legally purchased in order to strengthen the self-defensive forces organized by the association. Yet the Sun government was suppressing self-defense.[90]

Young China did not voice any direct opinion until two weeks after the government's detention of the weapons. When it did, though, the paper claimed that it stood together with the merchants in Guangdong but questioned the action of the president of the Guangzhou Merchants' Association. The paper believed that the merchants' private army should be used to help the local government and local police force maintain public security in Guangdong. The president of the merchants' association, the paper accused, was "an unscrupulous merchant" working for the militarists in north China. The paper then reported that most merchants in Guangdong, especially in the provincial capital, Guangzhou, wanted to end the dispute over the detention of the arms and return to normal business. The paper further pointed out that the business strike called by the association only hurt various businesses. The paper also hypothesized that if the local government were to be overthrown, anarchism would prevail, and there would be no safety or security for businesses. Once there was a political vacuum in Guangdong, the northern militarists would move in to take control. Would people in Guangdong welcome such an alternative?[91]

American Chinese interest in business development, their opposition to radical ideologies, and the desire for peace and stability in Guangdong all affected how Chinese in the United States reacted. They refused to support a military showdown between the Sun government and the Guangzhou Merchants' Association, which, it quickly became clear, was supported by the British in Hong Kong.[92] The San Francisco Chinese Chamber of Commerce, claiming to speak for all Chinese in the United States, cabled the association in Guangzhou, asking it to protect merchants, work for the good of the people, seek a peaceful resolution of the conflict, and not resort to military force.[93] A military showdown was indeed avoided. In September 1924, Sun decided to launch the Northern Expedition and leave Guangdong, where he had exhausted his support, and "to open a new field" for his nationalist revolution.[94]

CONCLUSION

U.S. anti-Chinese immigration laws, a desire for economic betterment, and acute nationalist feelings in support of a strong homeland all affected what visions American Chinese would have with regard to modernizing China. Their experiences in the United States and exposure to American values and ideologies influenced their reactions to political developments in China. They believed that only a combination of republicanism and capitalism could turn China into a strong and modern nation in the world. They did not see Confucianism as a barrier to the development of a modern China. They accepted Christianity as an important element in adapting and reforming China to enable it to take its rightful place in the family of nations.

The previous analysis shows that American Chinese selectively adopted both American and Chinese values and actively responded to the search for a modern China. They did not unthinkingly accept the ideologies espoused by political leaders in their homeland that found their way across the Pacific Ocean, but rather, arrived at independent conclusions based on their own assessment of events as well as on their interests as transnational migrants. They consistently worked to shape developments in China while battling discrimination in America. Their emerging identity as Chinese Americans—that is, they no longer saw themselves simply as American Chinese sojourning in the United States—resulted from a blending of American and Chinese cultures and ideologies.

7   Teaching Chinese Americans to Be Chinese: Curriculum, Teachers, and Textbooks in Chinese Schools in America During the Exclusion Era

HIM MARK LAI

SOON AFTER CHINESE IMMIGRANTS began raising families in the United States during the second half of the nineteenth century, they started teaching their children how to read and write the Chinese language. During the early years, when the population of school-age children was small, some parents probably hired private tutors to teach their progeny. Others sent their children to China for their schooling. In time, the number of Chinese in certain localities grew sufficiently large that schools had to be established. These schools were modeled after and influenced by China's educational system.

During most of the period from the founding of the first schools to World War II, Chinese in America faced hostility and discrimination. A series of exclusion acts severely limited their immigration and bred a sense of alienation among them, thereby fostering and sustaining a sojourner mentality that encouraged them to maintain ties with their homeland. Many pinned their hopes on the emergence of an internationally respected modern China that would help better their lot overseas. They also sought to pass on the ancestral heritage to their children by teaching them the Chinese language and culture so that the youngsters could function in a Chinese-speaking environment without too much difficulty either in the Chinatowns of America or in China. This chapter examines the relationship between Chinese-language schools in the United States and the educational system in China during the Chinese exclusion era.

ORIGINS OF CHINESE LANGUAGE EDUCATION IN AMERICA

Privately established Chinese schools first appeared in San Francisco, the principal port of entry for Chinese migrating to the continental United States. As a growing number of families with children of school age settled in that city, small private schools appeared, probably no later than the

1870s.[1] During this period, California's educational code did not make any provisions for the education of Chinese children. Close upon the heels of the passage of the Chinese Exclusion Act in 1882, the Chinese envoy in Washington, D.C. encouraged San Francisco's Chinese community, which was led by the Chinese Consolidated Benevolent Association (CCBA), to make plans for a school that would teach both Chinese and Western subjects. But progress on the project was slow in a Chinese immigrant community with limited resources, whose members were preoccupied with survival in an anti-Chinese environment. By the time the school was ready to open in 1888, the Chinese had already won a court judgment declaring that Chinese American children in San Francisco were entitled to a public school education. Thus, the San Francisco Board of Education was forced to establish a segregated Chinese primary school in 1885.[2] Given this new situation and because the community had only limited resources, CCBA restricted the curriculum in the Daqing Shuyuan—the school it had established—to classical Chinese literature, letter writing, and learning how to use the abacus.[3]

In Honolulu, Hawaii, then still an independent kingdom, there was also a Chinese community with a growing number of families. They started Chinese classes around the same time that private Chinese-language schools were being established in San Francisco. One difference was that the pioneering classes in Honolulu were sponsored by missionaries. Private schools sponsored by Chinese immigrants apparently did not enter the picture in Hawaii until around 1888.[4]

EDUCATIONAL REFORM IN CHINA AND ITS SPREAD ABROAD

During the second half of the nineteenth century, China, the immigrants' ancestral land, became a hapless victim of foreign aggression after its defeat by the British in the First Opium War (1839–42). Consequently, many Chinese searched for ways to strengthen and revitalize the nation. The prevalent thinking for several decades was that the acquisition of Western technology was all that was required. China's humiliating defeat in the Sino-Japanese War of 1894–95, however, exposed the inadequacy of this concept and led to demands for more basic reforms to modernize the nation. Japan, because of its successful efforts to learn from the West after the Meiji Restoration of 1868, became the model for many proposed institutional changes aimed at modernizing China. There was an extensive introduction of new terms associated with the proposed new institutions, mostly Japanese terms in *kanji* coined during that nation's modernization movement. These terms eventually became an integral part of the Chinese language.[5]

By this time, it had become apparent that the traditional Chinese educational system could no longer provide adequate training for confronting challenges of the modern world. Despite unstable political conditions, the imperial and succeeding republican governments made major changes in China's educational system, including language reform. The imperial government issued orders in 1902–03 that *xuetang* (schools) modeled after those in Japan and the West be established. In 1905, the government also abolished the imperial examination system, which for centuries had determined who would become officials and at what levels.[6] As part of such reforms, Liang Qinggui, an imperial commissioner, arrived in North America in 1908 to encourage Chinese communities in the United States and Canada to establish Chinese-language schools.[7]

In China itself, the Ministry of Education of the newly established republic issued temporary regulations in 1912 to change the term *xuetang* to *xuexiao* (the latter also means schools). School principals would henceforth be called *xiaozhang*. The primary grades could be coeducational—a truly radical departure from traditional norms of gender propriety. The regulations also abolished the study of Confucian classics in primary schools and promoted textbooks that supported the principle of republicanism. The minister of education declared that these textbooks should not attempt to foster loyalty to the sovereign nor encourage students to venerate Confucius. Such old practices, he said, conflicted with a republican form of government and the principle of religious freedom. To spread the new trend, the national government ordered its consulates abroad to collect information about schools that overseas Chinese communities had established on their own.

In 1913, the Duyin tongyi hui (Conference on the Unification of Pronunciation) adopted a phonetic alphabet, *zhuyin zimu*, which had thirty-nine symbols to specify how each Chinese written character should be pronounced in a national language. Three years later, the Guoyu yanjiuhui (National Language Research Association) advocated that a national language, *guoyu*[8] (also called mandarin or, after 1955 in mainland China, *putonghua*),[9] be introduced, and that it be used to bring written Chinese in line with its spoken form. Up to that point, the ability to read and write the classical form of Chinese, *wenyan*, was the mark of educated individuals.

Beginning in 1917, a movement developed to replace wenyan with a vernacular style, *yutiwen* or *baihua*. To implement these proposed changes, the Ministry of Education formally introduced a phonetic alphabet in 1918 and organized a Guoyu tongyi choubeihui (Society for Preparing a Unification of the National Language) in 1919. To make such reforms possible, during the early 1920s the ministry ordered textbooks written in guoyu to be printed, while the Society for Preparing a

Unification of the National Language announced in 1924 that the pronunciation used in Beijing, commonly called mandarin during that period, would become the national standard for spoken Chinese.[10]

After the Guomindang (GMD or Nationalist Party, also transliterated as Kuomintang) came to power in 1927 and made Nanjing the new capital, the central government required textbooks to reflect its own ideology; furthermore, all textbooks were subject to government review to ensure compliance. The GMD Central Committee passed a resolution changing the name of the phonetic alphabet from *zhuyin zimu* to *zhuyin fuhao* (phonetic symbols).[11] In 1931, the government issued additional regulations requiring schools established by Chinese living overseas to register with the central government in China. The following year, it reorganized the Overseas Chinese Affairs Commission, which included an Office for the Education of Chinese Overseas under its rubric, and mandated the latter to supervise and provide guidance to Chinese-language schools serving overseas Chinese, including those in the United States.[12] However, since the Chinese overseas were not under China's governance, the number of schools that registered was small.

Education reform as a means for modernizing China had many supporters among the intelligentsia, including some who emigrated or sojourned abroad either to work or to pursue higher education. The latter often became couriers who introduced some of the new concepts to Chinese overseas. Relatively easy access to the large Chinese communities in nearby Southeast Asia, which Chinese call Nanyang (Southern Ocean), had long enabled supporters of China's reform and revolutionary movements to be active in that region of the world. Its relative proximity to China also attracted many intellectuals seeking career opportunities abroad. These factors, together with the economic resources available in the affluent Southeast Asian Chinese communities facilitated the early adoption of China's education reforms in the schools established in those communities. The Chinese in Southeast Asia spoke many different dialects, but the abundant availability of imported teachers facilitated the early adoption of guoyu and yutiwen as the common spoken and written language, respectively, of instruction in Southeast Asian Chinese schools.

MODERN CHINESE SCHOOLS IN AMERICA

A different set of conditions in the New World forced a course of development different from what was occurring in Chinese communities in Southeast Asia. Liang Qinggui's 1907 visit to North America resulted in the founding of xuetang in eight cities. His first stop was San Francisco, where the Chinese community was still recovering from the disastrous 1906 earthquake and fire, all the while battling the oppressive Chinese exclusion laws and fending off hostile anti-Chinese actions. Eventually, however, the Chinese Consolidated Benevolent Association (CCBA) established Daqing Qiaomin Xuetang [Great Qing Overseas Chinese School], which began enrolling students in 1909. Because of insufficient funds and limited teaching talent in the community, the school focused on teaching only the Chinese language and selected subjects in social studies. Even though the school only offered classes at the primary school level, its students spent five hours a day, Monday through Saturday, studying the Confucian canon, classical literature, calligraphy, the history and geography of China, and the cultivation of moral character. On a lighter note, students also participated in choral singing, calisthenics, a military band, and other kinds of extracurricular activities.[13]

Commissioner Liang did not visit Honolulu during his journey, but at the turn of the century,[14] both the reform and revolutionary movements were active in the Hawaiian islands, where they found numerous sympathizers and supporters, especially among the Chinese Hawaiian middle class that had become important by then. Although the two movements differed in their visions for China's political future, as discussed in Chapter 6 in this volume, they agreed that education must play a fundamental role in the efforts to modernize China. Thus, supporters of both movements were already working in rival efforts during the 1900s to establish Chinese schools in Honolulu. Jackson Hee, an educator sympathetic to the revolutionaries, founded Jackson School in 1910.[15] Supporters of the reformers founded Mun Lun School in early 1911. A week later, Wah Mun School, sponsored by supporters of Sun Yat-sen and the revolution, also opened its doors.[16] Its name was changed to Chung Shan School in 1927 to honor the memory of Sun Yat-sen who had died two years earlier.

When Wah Mun School, a primary school, began operating, its curriculum was based on "national readers" imported from China. Students learned composition, letter writing, the history and geography of China, and the cultivation of moral character in classes that ran from 2:30 to 5:00 P.M., Monday to Friday, and from 9 A.M. to noon on Saturday. Students could also take elective courses in drawing and calisthenics. They engaged in many extracurricular activities, producing a weekly student newspaper, *Huawen xuesheng bao* (Chinese Language Students' Newspaper), in 1912; an annual magazine, *Huawen zazhi* (Chinese Language Magazine), from 1914 to 1916; and a newsletter, *Huawen xuesheng* (Chinese Language Students), in 1919. A student organization, Xueyi Hui (Society for Learning and the Arts), staged the first drama using vernacular Chinese in Hawaii in 1916.[17]

Mun Lun School, also established in 1911, had a curriculum that reflected the existence of classes at several levels of schooling. In the 1930s, when it offered classes at the lower primary, upper primary, and junior high levels, students learned calligraphy, vocabulary, social studies, and what Chinese educators call "common knowledge" in the lower primary grades. In the upper primary and junior high grade levels, students studied composition, letter writing, Chinese shorthand, the history and geography of China, public speaking, and choral singing. Initially, students in the junior high classes also learned guoyu, but that requirement was dropped in 1932. Mun Lun's students, like those in Wah Mun, participated in various activities. They put on stage performances, began publishing *Xuesheng yuebao* (Students' Monthly) in 1927, and founded *Alpha*, a wall bulletin in English and Chinese, in 1934. Mun Lun was in session from 3:00 to 5:00 P.M., Monday to Friday, and 9 A.M. to noon on Saturday.[18]

Because of the political activism of their supporters on the issue of women's rights, Mun Lun and Wah Mun schools accepted coeducation from the start. The first graduating class of thirteen in Mun Lun School in 1915 included three girls, while the graduating class of its rival, Wah Mun School, had twelve boys and ten girls. After Wah Mun staged a vernacular drama in 1916, a drama group also formed at Mun Lun in 1919. The productions of both schools often reflected a concern with current political developments in China. Both schools also established student and youth associations. A student self-governing organization appeared in Wah Mun in 1914. Mun Lun took a somewhat different tack by forming a youth self-governing organization that not only included students of the school but also reached out to youth outside the school.[19] Although other schools were established in the islands during the 1920s and 1930s, Mun Lun School and Wah Mun/Chung Shan School remained the leading Chinese-language schools in terms of resources and enrollment. In the 1930s they became the only schools in Honolulu to offer high school-level courses.[20]

In San Francisco, the CCBA board of directors was slow to act because board members belonged to different factions, but Daqing Qiaomin Xue-tang eventually became Zhonghua Qiaomin Gongli Xuexiao (Chinese Public School) around 1920.[21] Even though the CCBA revised the school's bylaws and discussed, in 1915, whether to expand its enrollment to include female students,[22] the board procrastinated and the school did not enroll girls until 1920.[23] Instead, a newcomer to the scene, Morning Bell School, led the way in introducing coeducation.

Guomindang sympathizers founded Morning Bell School in 1919, funding it with proceeds raised by theatrical performances of the Morning Bell Theatrical Society. Morning Bell became the first Chinese-language school in the community to enroll both male and female students. Its curriculum reflected the educational reforms in China. All students learned guoyu; those in the lower primary grades studied letter writing and drawing; students in the upper primary grades learned how to write essays for practical uses, the history and geography of China, cultivation of moral character, choral singing, and calisthenics. Morning Bell was one of the first Chinese-language schools to form a student government. Student activities included participation in student government, interschool athletic competitions, military exercises, drill teams, military bands, and public speaking. Every Friday evening students marched to Chinatown to make speeches on current political issues in China. They could also join Flip Flap Flop, a boys' club, and Vifee Vofee, a girls' club.[24] The school closed down after six years of operation because of a lack of funds, but other schools established during the second and third decades of the twentieth century in San Francisco adopted programs and activities similar to those that Morning Bell had pioneered.

Different groups led parallel efforts to develop other schools. In 1920 merchant leaders of Nam Hoy Fook Yum Tong founded Nam Kue School. In 1922 the Yeong Wo Association, which included among its constituency immigrants from the birthplace of Sun Yat-sen, started Yeong Wo School.[25] Guomindang supporters ran the school and it became one of the first schools to include the teachings of Sun Yat-sen, known as *sanminzhuyi* (Three People's Principles), and other Guomindang political doctrines in its curriculum. Students at Yeong Wo School, which had two years of junior high school in addition to primary school, learned guoyu, calligraphy, copying texts, writing and reciting texts from memory, composition, letter writing, the history and geography of China, common knowledge, civics (in the upper primary grades), sanminzhuyi, Guomindang ideology, and calisthenics. Its classes met for three hours a day, Monday to Saturday.[26]

Meanwhile, the CCBA-sponsored Chinese Public School reorganized itself. In 1929, it was renamed Chinese Central High School when it became the first Chinese school in America to include a high school-level curriculum.[27] In the 1930s the church-affiliated St. Mary's and Hip Wo schools also added high school-level curricula. Together with Chinese Central High School, they became the San Francisco Chinese schools with the largest enrollments.

During the first half of the twentieth century, schools also mushroomed in Chinese communities all over America. However, most cities usually had only one school, many of which were sponsored by local CCBAs. A few were sponsored by or used the facilities of other community organizations or churches. Practically all these schools had only primary-level classes.[28] Thus, San Francisco and Honolulu remained the major centers for Chinese-language schools in the United States.

THE FACULTY

A big factor affecting the development of Chinese education in America was the small population, which had decreased during the first forty years of exclusion to 85,702 in 1920 and then increased slowly to 106,334 in 1940 on the eve of World War II. This population had only limited financial resources compared to the large Chinese communities in Southeast Asia.

Another major factor that had an impact on the growth of Chinese schools was the extremely restrictive immigration policy of the United States that severely restricted the availability of Chinese-language educators in America. On occasion, schools in America had recruited teachers from abroad. For example, Honolulu's Mun Lun School hired Zheng Yun (also known as Wan Chang or Yum Sinn Chang) from Japan in 1911; Guan Shuyi came to San Francisco's Nam Kue School from Guangzhou in 1920.[29] However, most teachers had to be recruited from whoever was available in America. Teaching personnel most often were immigrants who had received a high school or an even higher level of education, or students who were in the United States to study at American universities. In some cases, such as in Honolulu, where a relatively small number of Chinese immigrants had settled, some schools had to turn to their own graduates. For example, Kong Chin Young from the first graduating class at Wah Mun School served as its principal from 1932 to 1960. In 1936, nine out of thirty faculty members in Mun Lun School were graduates of the school.[30]

Because teaching was usually part-time work and the remuneration was low, many teachers had to take up other work to support themselves and their families. In larger communities such as San Francisco, some teachers had second jobs, such as being an editor of a Chinese-language newspaper, a bank clerk, a marker of Chinese lottery tickets at a store, a sewing machine operator, a business manager, and so forth. Most of the teachers had no training in pedagogy and education. This, coupled with budgetary constraints and the fact that they often regarded their positions only as a means to earn some extra income or as short-term positions unconnected to their intended future careers, limited whatever motivation they might have had to improve the effectiveness of classroom instruction.

GUOYU AND YUTIWEN

Another aspect that differentiated Chinese communities in the New World from those in Southeast Asia was the fact that an overwhelming majority of the Chinese in the United States and Canada came from Guangdong's Pearl River Delta and spoke dialects that diverge greatly from guoyu. Nonetheless, many Chinese intellectuals in America, especially those sympathetic to the Guomindang, accepted educational reform as a key means to modernize China. They also generally subscribed to the concept of using guoyu as the national language for the sake of unifying the nation. Thus, Honolulu's Wah Mun School, led by Guomindang supporters, became one of the earliest Chinese schools in America to offer instruction in guoyu. In 1914, the school invited Guomindang leader Lin Sen, who had stopped by the islands on his way to the North American continent to supervise party affairs, to teach a guoyu class.[31] Morning Bell School on the mainland also started offering guoyu classes in 1919.[32] However, since an overwhelming majority of the people in local Chinese communities were Cantonese speakers, most of whom were not students and could neither speak nor understand guoyu, it was manifestly impractical to promote it as the common language in the schools and the community. Moreover, teachers who could speak guoyu were in extremely short supply in the Chinese communities. Thus, even though the schools were a step ahead of the community and some schools continued to try to offer guoyu classes sporadically, most students had, in fact, few opportunities to polish that skill except among themselves.

In San Francisco, where there was a significant number of speakers of the Sam Yup [Three Districts] and Zhongshan regional subdialects in addition to the subdialects spoken by the Sze Yup [Four Districts] majority, there was pressure to adopt Cantonese as it is spoken in Guangzhou as the language of instruction. Nam Kue School,[33] which was founded by immigrants from the vicinity of Guangzhou, was said to be the first school to do so. The CCBA-sponsored Chinese Public School followed suit in 1926, as did other schools. However, this standardization could only occur when teachers, such as educated immigrants or university students from Guangdong, were available. In areas such as Hawaii that had relatively few immigrants, which meant that locally available talent had to be used, instruction based on rural subdialects of Cantonese—in this case, that of Shiqi, Zhongshan's county seat—was still common.

Yutiwen, a writing style in which the vocabulary and syntax approximated that of the spoken language (unlike classical Chinese, in which the written language diverges widely from the spoken tongue) was probably introduced to schools in America at about the same time that guoyu classes began. However, when I examined student essays published in three school publications (a 1915 publication from Wah Mun School and a 1917 publication from Jackson School, both in Honolulu, and a 1922 publication from Morning Bell School in San Francisco), I found that despite the fact that all these schools were run by educators sympathetic to the Guomindang, and who, therefore, can be presumed to be sympathetic to the language reforms being carried out in China, all the essays were written in the classical style, wenyan. However, the Morning Bell publication did include a poem written by a teacher in the vernacular or colloquial style.[34] It is impossible to tell in retrospect whether the essays might have reflected the preferences of the teachers. Perhaps the teachers were catering to the wishes of the students' parents because the Chinese immigrant community as a whole was slow to accept the yutiwen writing style and most people still preferred to write in a simplified classical style. Articles in the newspapers were also mostly in wenyan. (It should be noted that yutiwen was derived from spoken guoyu and bore little resemblance to colloquial Cantonese.) Thus, for Cantonese speaking students, learning yutiwen would require them to learn another writing format, although a case could be made that yutiwen was easier to master than wenyan. Nonetheless, the use of yutiwen slowly made headway in China during the 1920s. Primary school textbooks from China began to be published in the yutiwen style. The emergence of the Guomindang government and a unified China in the late 1920s led to greater efforts to bring the curriculum of Chinese schools abroad more in line with the curriculum used in schools in China, including the use of guoyu and yutiwen.

In 1930 Honolulu's Chung Shan School (the former Wah Mun School) became one of the first schools in the Western hemisphere to register with the Overseas Chinese Affairs Commission of the Guomindang government. Student essays composed in yutiwen began to appear with greater frequency in school publications. In the school's 1934 yearbook, more than 90 percent of the essays written by students in the seventh to tenth grades were in the yutiwen style.[35] In contrast, in the more conservative San Francisco community, student essays in a 1932 yearbook from Yeong Wo School, the San Francisco institution run by supporters of the Guomindang, essays written in the colloquial or vernacular style composed less than 10 percent of the fifty-seven selections. All the student essays published in a 1934 publication of the CCBA-sponsored Chinese Central High School, the largest school in the community, were still in classical Chinese.[36]

During this period Japanese aggression was increasingly threatening the territorial integrity of China, ultimately resulting in the outbreak of the Sino-Japanese War in 1937. This march of events was accompanied by a corresponding rise in nationalist feelings among the Chinese in America. They frequently held rallies, often featuring visitors from China, who made speeches in guoyu encouraging resistance against Japanese aggression. The singing of patriotic songs with lyrics in guoyu and the writing of propaganda pieces in yutiwen all helped popularize the use of the national language. Toward the end of the decade, a number of immigrants from Guangdong, many the offspring of Chinese in America, arrived in the United States to seek refuge from the war. Many had attended school under the reformed educational system in China in which guoyu and yutiwen were important components. These developments greatly helped increase the usage and promote the acceptance of guoyu and yutiwen

204 HIM MARK LAI

among the Chinese in America. For example, the bulk of student essays published in the 1940 yearbooks of the Chinese Central High School and St. Mary's School were written in the yutiwen style.[37] The schools made greater efforts to establish guoyu classes; however, the dialect most commonly used in daily conversations remained Cantonese.

TEXTBOOKS

Chinese schools in America during the nineteenth century had used traditional texts published in classical Chinese that were widely used in China. For beginners there were titles such as *Sanzijing* (Trimetrical Classic), *Baijiaxing* (Surnames of the Hundred Families), *Qianziwen* (Thousand Characters Essay),[38] *Youxue shi* (Poems for the Young Student),[39] and *Youxue qionglin* (Jade Forest of Learning for Children).[40] More advanced students studied the *Sishu* (Four Books),[41] *Wujing* (Five Classics),[42] and other Chinese classics.[43]

As China began making efforts to modernize, the newly established Jiangnan Arsenal had created a department as early as 1868 to translate textbooks in the natural sciences and technology from Western languages into Chinese in order to teach its personnel such subjects. However, beginning in the 1860s and 1870s, when Christian missionaries were establishing schools in China to teach the Christian religion, ethics, mathematics, and Western history and geography, they found that no Chinese textbooks were available. In an 1877 Shanghai Conference attended by 142 Protestant missionaries, a School and Textbook Series Committee was formed to foster cooperation in the missionaries' educational efforts in China.[44] Many works published and distributed under the auspices of the committee were religious in nature, but there were also works on mathematics and the sciences. These publications became known as *jiaokeshu* (textbooks).[45] Their use was basically limited to the missionary-operated schools and some privately operated schools. In 1897 Commercial Press was founded in Shanghai and quickly became the leading publisher and distributor of textbooks.[46] However, it is doubtful that many of these new textbooks found their way to Chinese-language schools in the United States at a time when they still taught from traditional texts.

After the education reform of 1903, textbooks containing the new curriculum began to be published for the revamped educational system. Shanghai's Commercial Press continued to dominate the business of textbook publishing even after other competitors entered the field.[47] Because the Chinese composed a very small minority in America during the exclusion period and the school-age population was even smaller within a community dominated by bachelors and married men who had left their wives and children in China, there were really no economic incentives for the Chinese in America to edit and publish their own textbooks. Thus, when China began to modernize its educational system and published textbooks to accomplish its new goals, textbooks from China also came to be used in Chinese schools in America.

Many schools in the United States used the following types of textbooks: national readers (*guowen*), correspondence (*chidu*), common knowledge (*changshi*), history of China (*Zhongguo lishi*), geography of China (*Zhongguo dili*), cultivation of moral character (*xiushen*) and civics (*gongmin*).[48] National language readers were probably used by the largest number of students in primary schools since most students attended Chinese schools through the primary grades only and just a few went on to enroll in high school-level classes at schools that offered such instruction. However, since there was no central authority in America to help select textbooks, the choice was up to the administrators of each school. There was no particular edition that was universally used. Since I have not found the titles of textbooks used in various schools, the following discussion is based on textbooks that I myself had used at home or at Nam Kue School in San Francisco.

Textbooks were written with the objective of introducing the vocabulary and syntax of the Chinese language through graded readings. During the late 1920s my parents purchased at a San Francisco Chinatown bookshop a set of ten textbooks, *Dingzheng chudeng xiaoxue zuixin guowen jiaokeshu* (Lower Primary Schools New National Readers, Revised Edition), edited by Jiang Weiqiao and Zhuang Yu (Shanghai: Commercial Press, 1914), to start teaching me Chinese. My home instruction did not progress much beyond the first two readers before I enrolled at Nam Kue School. The contents in this set of books may be considered typical of Chinese school textbooks from the early 1910s to the late 1920s.

Each reader included sixty lessons. In the second reader the bulk of the lessons dwelled on topics in daily life such as the first day of school, writing implements, articles of clothing, cooking utensils, the mid-autumn festival, snow, winter, directions of the compass, the lotus, the chrysanthemum, the three winter companions (the pine, the bamboo, and the plum blossom), crickets, dragonflies, and so forth. Characteristically many lessons also introduced what the editors considered correct habits, attitudes, and standards of conduct for Chinese students. There were lessons discussing cleanliness and hygiene and lessons counseling against superstitious beliefs. One lesson that aimed to teach diligence told the tale of a slow-witted student who managed to place first in examinations by studying harder than his classmates. Still another reading impressed upon the student the fact that mankind is superior to animals only because humans can be educated. Other readings variously encouraged the pursuit of education, pointed out the folly of telling lies, and counseled against avarice.

Anecdotes such as that of Kong Rong voluntarily taking the smallest pear because he was the youngest sibling in the family, and the obedient filial son Huang, who cared for and served his old father while studying hard at school, were presented as models of correct ethical and moral behavior. Other readings were fables rewritten from Chinese classical works and from Aesop's collection, and anecdotes of historical personalities such as Sima Guang and Wen Yanbo—both historical personages of the Song dynasty—highlighting their abilities to cope with difficult situations when they were children, as well as easily understood folk songs.

Readings in more advanced readers pursued similar concepts. An increased number of lessons introduced anecdotes about historical personalities as well as easy-to-read classical works such as the Tang poems "In Sympathy with the Toiling Farmer" in the third reader, "Snow Song" in the eighth reader, and the "Poem of Mulan [the woman warrior]" in the ninth reader. Fables from Chinese literature added to the students' basic knowledge of the best in Chinese literature. Some selections were translations from Aesop's fables.[49] Beginning with the sixth reader, some lessons aimed to teach students basic concepts of modern science and technology, covering such subjects as the steam engine (sixth reader), the telegraph and the telephone (seventh reader), the water-steam cycle (eighth reader), the solar system (ninth reader), differences between the Chinese and Western calendars (tenth reader), and the telescope (tenth reader).

With the objective of instilling a national awareness and pride among the students, basic geographical information on China was included, beginning with the third reader that contained an essay on the Yangzi River valley as a prosperous part of China. This was followed in the fourth reader by a lesson describing China as a nation with a five-thousand-year history and another dwelling on the heroic deeds of Yu who controlled disastrous floods. The fifth reader told of Nanjing serving as a temporary capital when the republic was founded, followed by a description of Shanghai in which foreign powers governed concessions on Chinese soil. The northern metropolis, Tianjin, was discussed in the sixth reader, where it was pointed out that China's fortifications at Taku guarding the entranceway to Beijing were destroyed by allied troops in 1900 and China was prohibited from rebuilding those defensive structures. A lesson on Hankou followed, predicting that it would become a center for railway traffic. The same reader contained a brief account of the history of China, the story of the 1911 Chinese Revolution, a description of China's flag, a listing and description of unequal treaties imposed on China by foreign powers, as well as the mistreatment of Chinese in foreign countries. Lessons on Korea and India lamented their loss of independence to foreign aggressors, while another reading praised Japan (ninth reader) as a rising power after the Meiji Restoration, comparing it to China, which had been weakened by numerous diplomatic defeats inflicted by foreign powers (tenth reader). France under Louis XIV and Napoleon Bonaparte, England as an early constitutional monarchy (ninth reader), Prussia under Wilhelm I, and Russia under Peter the Great (tenth reader) were described positively as models for the revitalization of China. Students were also encouraged to use goods made in China as an act of patriotism.

There were also lessons based on the biographies of historical personalities such as Zhang Liang, who tried to assassinate the oppressive Qin emperor and later became an important advisor to the first emperor of the Han dynasty (ninth reader); Zhang Qian, who spread awareness of the power of the Han Empire to Central Asia (ninth reader); Su Wu, a Han envoy who was detained by the Xiongnu ("barbarians") for nineteen years but refused to surrender to them (tenth reader); and Yue Fei, who led the fight against the invading Nüzhen armies during the Song dynasty (tenth reader).

Shiyan guowen jiaokeshu (experimental national language textbooks) was a set of national readers for primary schools edited by Guan Zhihuai and Guan Youzhang and published in 1929 by the Shiyan jiaoyushe (Society for Experimental Education). By this time, the restructured educational system had reduced the number of readers to eight. I used some of these readers while attending Nam Kue School during the 1930s; some San Francisco schools continued to use them well into the 1940s. The revised set of national readers was similar to the earlier set in content except there were many more historical anecdotes and fables, some of which were rewritten versions of the same selections found in the earlier set. Apparently the drive to eradicate illiteracy in China led the editor to make the readings somewhat easier. Some texts for the lower grades were in colloquial rather than classical Chinese. Readings in the earlier set were also longer with about 160 characters in the seventh reader, compared to around 100 characters in the eighth reader of the later set. One change was that there were more readings on the Chinese Revolution, such as the celebration of National Day at school (fifth reader); the Mausoleum of the Seventy-two Martyrs of the Revolution at Huanghua Gang in Guangzhou (sixth reader); biographies of Sun Yat-sen, the leader of the revolution (eighth reader); and of Qiu Jin, a female martyr of the revolution (eighth reader); and a lesson on the overseas Chinese, the mistreatment they received abroad, and the contributions they made to the ancestral land with the hope that China would become a wealthy and strong nation (eighth reader). Another difference was that there were more selections about prominent individuals in the West, such as stories of George Washington chopping down the cherry tree (fifth reader); the hard work that brought success to the French potter, Palissy; Abraham Lincoln proclaiming emancipation for slaves (fifth reader); and Prussian Chancellor Otto von Bismarck's unruffled demeanor as he captured an assassin (seventh reader).

In class, the normal procedure was for the teacher to read a new lesson aloud to the students. After the teacher read each sentence, the class repeated it in unison in order to associate the pronunciation with the character in the text. The teacher then explained or interpreted the lesson. Teachers tested their students' mastery of a lesson by asking them to recite it by rote or write it from memory. Textbooks for courses in history, geography, civics, and common knowledge offered expanded coverage of topics already included in the national readers. In some cases the sequence of topics covered in the more advanced textbooks followed that in the national readers, but in other cases, particularly in more advanced classes, the teacher asked questions and students answered by writing short paragraphs.[50] The monotonous work required to memorize texts sometimes motivated less diligent students to cheat during tests.[51]

EFFECTIVENESS OF THE CURRICULUM

The objectives of the Chinese-language schools were to teach Chinese Americans the mechanics of the Chinese language, help them understand the world from a Chinese perspective, instill a sense of morality and responsibility to society according to Chinese moral standards, cultivate respect of and pride in China, a nation with ancient traditions and history, and sensitize students to foreign aggressions that had infringed on China's territorial integrity and sovereignty. The contents in the textbooks were often nationalistic in tone and many teachers had strong nationalist feelings.

An important question is whether youth growing up in American society could really relate to the instruction and the text materials based on concepts and phenomena in China—a society in which most Chinese American students had never lived. During the exclusion period, feelings of alienation and isolation from mainstream America engendered by racial discrimination were strong enough to motivate a number of students to become nationalists despite the fact that they had never lived in China. The teachers played an important role in inculcating facts and concepts. Classes in composition were a convenient platform used by the teachers since they could assign a wide range of topics to a class or to individual students for exposition. From essays written by students, but copyedited, sometimes heavily, by the teachers and published in yearbooks and other school publications, it can be seen that even though the titles of essays might have varied from school to school, the themes were broadly similar, many of which expressed nationalist sentiments.[52]

Some students in America managed to acquire a good working knowledge of Chinese and accepted elements of Chinese culture. Up to World War II, this had enabled a small but continuous stream of Chinese

Americans to go to China to seek further education. Others went to China to pursue careers in such fields as medicine, engineering, teaching, and the military, especially the Chinese Air Force. The study of this phenomenon remains a long neglected aspect of Chinese American history.

During this same period, however, Chinese Americans were also being continuously influenced by the public schools and church-related institutions in America. The United States, after all, was their native land where they were trying to gain acceptance and equal treatment. Thus, despite the best efforts of the Chinese schools, an increasing number of Chinese Americans adopted English and the practices of the larger society as time went on, while more and more of the students who went to Chinese-language schools picked up only the barest rudiments of the Chinese language and culture. However, this transformation occurred at different rates in different communities.

In communities with small Chinese populations, the Americanization process was rapid. But there was a difference even in the two major bastions of Chinese-language education, San Francisco and Honolulu. In Honolulu, even though discrimination did exist, Chinese had long lived in relative harmony with other ethnic groups. Thus, even while Chinese schools were thriving in Honolulu during the exclusion era, members of the younger generation were also rapidly adopting the ways of the larger society. By the mid-1930s, many in the younger generation were more proficient in English than in Chinese. In Mun Lun, the largest school, class meetings were being conducted in English, while in Chung Shan School, long supported by the nationalistic Guomindang, yearbooks included English sections with gossip and comments on fellow students just as in any school annual in mainstream schools.[53] The Chinese-language schools in San Francisco, where the Chinese had been forced by discriminatory measures and actions to live for an extended period under de facto segregation, were probably the most conservative in terms of preserving the Chinese language and culture of all the Chinese-language schools in America. Yearbooks of the CCBA-sponsored Chinese Central High School refrained from including English-language prose as late as the 1940s, even though many Chinese Americans were, by then, more proficient in English than in Chinese.

CONCLUSION

Taking an overall view, the effectiveness of the curriculum to ensure retention of the Chinese heritage and sensitize students to their ancestral land varied with time and place. From the perspective of the immigrants who established and supported the schools, the results were favorable during the earlier years; however, as Chinese Americans moved toward acculturation in American society, the gap between the curriculum and the stated objectives, on the one hand, and the results achieved in the classes, on the other, widened to a chasm, finally forcing a belated recognition, after World War II, of the reality that the curriculum and textbooks must be redesigned to suit American conditions if Chinese schools were to be effective as educational institutions. This evolution was inevitable in the open society of America despite its discrimination and inequities. Much as members of the first generation may regret the continuing loss of the ancestral heritage among their progeny, this was but a part of the process of becoming Chinese American.

8   Writing a Place in American Life: The Sensibilities of American-born Chinese as Reflected in Life Stories from the Exclusion Era

XIAO-HUANG YIN

> Jade Snow thought that he [Richard, a white boy] was tiresome and igno-
> rant. Everybody knew that the Chinese people had a superior culture. Her
> ancestors had created a great art heritage and had made inventions impor-
> tant to world civilization—the compass, gunpowder, paper, and a host of
> other essentials...Mama said they [white people] hadn't even learned how
> to peel a clove of garlic the way the Chinese did.
>
> —*Jade Snow Wong, Fifth Chinese Daughter*[1]

THE IMPACT OF THE CHINESE EXCLUSION ACTS on Chinese
Americans has long been a major topic in Asian American studies.[2] The
wide range of scholarly works on this issue, especially those published
since the late 1980s, has significantly enhanced our understanding of the
Chinese experience in this extremely difficult phase of Asian American
history. Most of the scholarship, however, tends to focus on the lives and
minds of Chinese immigrants; there is relatively little written about how
the views and sensibilities of American-born Chinese, or "ABC" as they
are more commonly called,[3] were shaped and affected by their unique
status during the exclusion era.

This lacuna is understandable because the population of American-
born Chinese in those years was very small due to legal barriers and discriminatory immigration acts such as the Page Law (1875), which specifically targeted "Mongolian women" and made it well nigh impossible for
Chinese immigrants to bring their families to the United States. The notori-
ous 1882 Chinese Exclusion Act further closed America's gates to Chinese
women.[4] As a result, the Chinese American community remained predominantly a "bachelor society" with an extremely unbalanced sex ratio in
subsequent decades. In 1900 the sex ratio of Chinese men to women was
12:1 in California, 36:1 in Boston, 50:1 in New York, and 19:1 in the
continental United States as a whole.[5] Lee Chew, a Chinese laundryman
in New York, complained bitterly in 1906: "In all New York there are less

than forty Chinese women, and it is impossible to get a Chinese woman out here unless one goes to China and marries her there, and then he must collect affidavits to prove that she really is his wife. That is in [the] case of a merchant. A laundryman can't bring his wife here under any circumstances."[6] Consequently, there was little family life among Chinese Americans until the post–World War II era. In reality, although Chinese had been born in the United States as early as 1825,[7] American-born Chinese remained an insignificant part of the Chinese community throughout much of the exclusion era.

With the decline of immigration from China, however, the population of American-born Chinese grew slowly but steadily from the early 1900s onward. They made up 30 percent of the Chinese American population in 1920. By 1940, three years before the exclusion acts were finally repealed, the figure had reached 52 percent in the continental United States.[8] Of course, the number of American-born in those years was actually smaller than that reported by the census bureau because the "native-born" category, as defined by the U.S. immigration service, also included descendants of American citizens born abroad. According to immigration laws, the children of the "native-born" could claim derivative citizenship in order to immigrate to the United States. In the case of Chinese Americans, however, the "native-born" category included some "paper sons"[9] and a few "paper daughters" who tried to enter fraudulently by purchasing paper identities. These "paper children" augmented substantially and misleadingly the number of "native-born" Chinese. Nevertheless, though "paper sons" artificially inflated the number of American-born Chinese, there is little doubt that the group had grown to a sizable population by the end of the exclusion era.

The emergence of a significant American-born population changed the characteristics of the Chinese community. As American-born, English-speaking U.S. citizens, they formed a distinct subgroup with its own subculture. They tended to think and act differently from immigrants who were China oriented and maintained close ties with the old country. Rejected by American society because of their "alien" background, the immigrants either indulged in the illusion that someday they would save enough money to return home to enjoy their accumulation or sought spiritual comfort by focusing on the superiority of Chinese culture.

The views and sensibilities of American-born Chinese, however, were different. Although they also felt "foreign" because of their "racial uniform"—a term coined by sociologist Robert E. Park to refer to a racial minority's distinct physical characteristics—few of them considered returning to China as a possible alternative to living in America. Born and raised in the United States, America was their only home: few emotional or personal bonds linked them to their parents' old country. As a result, no matter how distraught they might have felt about being excluded by American society, their lack of familiarity with a China they had never seen made them feel ambivalent about seeking their future there. At a time when the concept of multiculturalism was still a novelty, what they did in the face of racial prejudice was to redouble their efforts to win acceptance by mainstream society, sometimes even at the expense of abandoning their Chinese heritage.[10] In fact, the Americanization of second-generation Chinese Americans had become so complete and noticeable by the early 1920s that the public saw them as "Oriental in appearance but not in reality."[11]

As their numbers increased, "ABCs" produced a substantial body of autobiographical works. Representing a broad spectrum, these works provide fresh information about their lives and experiences, revealing their feelings and thoughts long before the civil rights movement reshaped the concepts of race and ethnicity in the United States. These authors' views and sensibilities differed widely, but their writings, placed within a historical context, suggest that the American-born of the exclusion era shared a common characteristic: they were "American" by culture and Chinese only by race.

In other words, what distinguishes their works is their strong quest for a place in American life. In contrast to the immigrants, the impact of American culture on American-born Chinese was unmistakable. They showed an intense desire to enter the mainstream world, a phenomenon that, to a great extent, was a result of their education in public schools. For many American-born Chinese children at the time, public school education provided not only a source of new ideas that enhanced their assimilation but also the social forces that uprooted them from the Chinese community. Contacts with their non-Asian peers in school made them dissatisfied with the thought of having to spend their entire lives in Chinatown ghettos and fostered their ambition to seek opportunities in the larger society in competition with their "American" peers.

Another interesting factor links the personal stories of the American-born: the authors had almost universally undergone a phase of "youthful rebellion" based on the ground rules of American culture—they sought independence and individuality. Such values certainly conflicted with those of Chinese culture, which stresses family ties, community interdependence, respect for patriarchal authority, and honoring traditions. While both sets of values existed in the minds of the American-born, their preferred goal was to achieve individuality rather than to live within the webs of family and community. This desire is reflected clearly in almost all their autobiographical works despite differences in their backgrounds and their individual personalities. For example, Pardee Lowe relates in his personal narrative that he openly rebelled against his father and broke away from the family; Jade Snow Wong mentions in her life story that she went to college as an act of defiance against her parents' will; and the heroine in Virginia Chin-lan Lee's quasi autobiography ran away with her Caucasian boy friend when their desire to marry was first opposed by her parents and then invalidated by California's antimiscegenation law. Although youthful rebellion against parents is nothing new among immigrant children, considering the strong family ties and patriarchal authority emphasized by traditional Chinese culture, the American-born youths' lack of filial piety is astonishing. They had indeed melted into the "American caldron."

In short, because the experience of U.S.-born Chinese was governed by a profound compulsion to be accepted in American society, their struggle to enter the mainstream world and their quest for a place in American life became the dominant themes of their autobiographical works and fictionalized life stories. These themes are expressed in terms of conflicts between the cultural values of East and West, the divergent views on interracial marriages held by their parents and themselves, the generation gap, the pursuit of the American dream, the imperative to assert their American-ness, and their anxiety to demonstrate patriotism as a "loyal minority" on the eve of America's entry into World War II.

Among the available writings, two books stand out. They deserve careful examination because the authors' self-portrayals are outstanding and the revelations in them are touching. Pardee Lowe's *Father and Glorious Descendant* and Jade Snow Wong's *Fifth Chinese Daughter* exemplify the sensibilities and feelings of American-born Chinese during the exclusion era. Lowe's personal narrative was the first published book-length literary work by an American-born Chinese, while Wong's autobiography, the most influential work by a second-generation Chinese American woman until the 1960s, illuminates the lives and emotions of those American-born who came of age before the repeal of the exclusion laws dramatically altered the landscape of Chinese America.

What were the views and sensibilities of the American-born in this critical phase in Chinese American history? In what ways did they differ from immigrants, particularly in terms of their attitudes toward China and America? What is the implication of their lives in the context of the overall Chinese American experience during the exclusion era? This chapter attempts to answer these questions based on a close reading of these two representative works.

FATHER AND GLORIOUS DESCENDANT: GROWING UP CHINESE AMERICAN IN THE EARLY TWENTIETH CENTURY

Published by the highly influential and mainstream publisher, Little, Brown and Company, Pardee Lowe's autobiography, *Father and Glorious Descendant*, was well received when it came out in 1943 while Congress was holding hearings on whether to repeal all the Chinese exclusion laws.[12] Critics found the work extremely rewarding to read and celebrated it as a "solid" and "significant" study of Chinese life, especially "a Chinese-American *Life with Father*."[13] While there is no documentary evidence that Lowe's personal story had any impact on the repeal of the Chinese exclusion laws, it can be argued that the enthusiastic reviews his book received reflected the American public's changing perceptions of China, as well as the Chinese in the United States.

When the United States got involved in World War II, China became an important ally and Chinese Americans were deemed a "loyal minority group" who consequently enjoyed unprecedented popularity.[14] The change in the American public's attitude toward the Chinese is indicated clearly in a critic's comment on Lowe's book: The "author's love for America and his respect for his Oriental roots...show an excellent blending of the two cultures [that] will contribute greatly toward better understanding of one of our loyal minority groups."[15] Using Lowe's personal story to shore up the public's vague notions about Chinese "loyalty" is shown even more conspicuously in the publisher's advertisement. To underscore his "American patriotism," Lowe's editors declared on the book jacket that the author had enlisted in the U.S. Army as soon as he had completed the manuscript. Indeed, what better proof of "Chinese loyalty" could there be than a willingness to fight on behalf of the United States on the battlefield?[16]

Undoubtedly, the American-style patriotism expressed in Lowe's autobiography contributed greatly to its popularity. But what the critics and publishers failed to perceive or chose to ignore is that the book also reveals frankly the formidable pressure placed on Chinese Americans to assimilate during the exclusion era. Seeking to assert his American-ness, Lowe articulates the notion that the only way for Chinese to gain respect in this country is to become a "real American," an idea also favored by many of his second-generation Chinese American peers. The quest for a place in American life is the dominating theme in Lowe's personal saga—a theme that also represents the feelings of most Chinese American youth during that period. His bitterness, rejoicing, and subtler moods were important aspects of the common experience of American-born Chinese during the very period when their existence began to catch the attention of mainstream society.

Born in San Francisco in 1905,[17] Lowe came from a well-established family. His father was a prominent figure in the San Francisco Bay area's Chinese community. In addition to owning several dry-goods stores that hired about fifty employees, the senior Lowe was the head of a large clan association and held a powerful position in the Chinese Six Companies. Since the clan owned more than one hundred chain stores in cities scattered along the Pacific Coast from San Diego to Seattle, the Lowe family's influence was widespread.

Unlike most of his contemporaries, Lowe grew up in a predominantly white neighborhood in East Belleville across the bay from San Francisco. The family's residence outside Chinatown is unusual during the exclusion era and indicates their high degree of acculturation and close relationship with mainstream society. Unlike the Lowe family, most Chinese in the United States were confined to Chinatown ghettos until the 1950s.

Indeed, Lowe's father's enthusiasm for American values clearly surpassed that of most Chinese immigrants. For example, instead of naming children in the traditional Chinese way as most of his countrymen insisted on doing, he gave them names of eminent American leaders at the time. Lowe was named after George C. Pardee as a gesture of respect for the then governor of California while his four sisters and brothers "bore the socially forbidding names" of Alice Roosevelt, Helen Taft, Woodrow Wilson, and Thomas Riley Marshall.[18]

Undoubtedly, the father's acceptance of certain American values and practices had a strong impact on the son. As a child, Lowe noted with pride that his father, with his "American dress and manners," was one of the few Chinese in San Francisco respected by whites. He recalls how his father was always greeted politely by whites who distinguished him from the rest of the Chinese passengers on the ferry that crossed San Francisco Bay: "Tall and brawny and queueless, Father resembled an American ... I could see it every morning when the conductor and the brakeman, without fail, nodded at Father graciously. They recognized him as an individual worthy of special notice, but their cordial greetings were never given to the others—who, I observed, wore sleek bowler hats, Chinese jackets, Western pants, padded slippers from Canton, and over all, dangling queues, streaked with vermilion braid—and whom they disparagingly called Ah John, Ah Charlie, or Ah Jim" (*Father* 34).

If Lowe's admiration for American values was deeply rooted in his childhood memory of his father's "unusual American qualities," it was further fostered by his public school education. Attending a suburban neighborhood school rather than a segregated classroom in Chinatown, Lowe caught an intense fever for the American dream early on. He identified himself consciously with mainstream society and "became a walking encyclopedia of American history" (*Father* 133). Legendary figures such as Buffalo Bill became shining heroes in his life. Even the names of American outlaws sounded more heroic and romantic than those of Chinese tong hatchet men: "Even though at the age of nine I was already an inveterate reader of the blood-and-thunder tales glorifying such fearless men as Buffalo Bill and Wild Bill Hickok, I found the tongs with their plots and counterplots, wicked schemes, scouting parties, ambuscades, armed nests, and the odd nicknames of their hatchet men—such as 'Big Queue,' 'Midget Pete,' 'Handsome Boy,' and 'Hot Stuff'—extremely sinister; they did not possess the flesh-and-blood qualities of my American heroes" (*Father* 93). When his father took him to a Chinese Lunar New Year's party, he found that "the entire performance struck me as being totally alien. Fed up, I informed Father: 'I like Yankee Doodle Dandy much better!' " (*Father* 45).

Of course, Lowe is not alone among non-white people whose fantasies reflect great admiration for mainstream culture. Bienvenido N. Santos, a prominent Filipino writer, describes sarcastically in his novel *The Man Who (Thought He) Looked Like Robert Taylor* how Solomon King, a Filipino butcher in Chicago, desperately wishes to look and behave like a white movie star.[19] Malcolm X also recalls in his *Autobiography* how some middle-class blacks "break their backs trying to imitate white people."[20] The reason is simple: although Americans today are more accepting of ethnic heritages other than their own, in Lowe's time anything not white American was drowned out. Educated in American public schools, Lowe and his peers learned and adopted many of the cultural values characteristic of mainstream society. They understood China less than they did the United States; consequently, they were less imbued with traditional Chinese ethics and morality. In light of this background, Lowe's fanatic admiration for American values is not exceptional, but is, rather, a typical example that demonstrates the powerful impact of mainstream culture on American-born Chinese during the exclusion years.

Amazingly, Lowe even nurtured a lofty illusion that he could become president of the United States like any other American child. In the chapter "Father Cures a Presidential Fever," Lowe gives a vivid account of how he believes America is a world of equality where everyone can participate fully in political life and be rewarded in accordance with his ability. The illusion is a scathing irony of the social reality. Until the repeal of the Chinese exclusion acts in 1943, Chinese immigrants were not even allowed to become naturalized U.S. citizens because of their alleged inability to assimilate. Caricatures such as power-hungry Chinatown despots, bloodthirsty tong hatchet men, sensual sing-song girls, or comical Oriental houseboys were all popular images of the Chinese drearily familiar to the public. Therefore, it is easily understandable why Lowe is met with cynical laughter when he proudly declares to his father's white business associates that his ambition is to be an "American President."

An innocent boy filled with bright hopes and the American dream, Lowe soon learns the hard way that the ideal "regardless of race, religion, or national origin" does not apply to everyone. No matter how American he may feel in his head, America will not treat him as an equal member of society because of the "racial uniform" he wears. This cruel, bitter lesson is unexpectedly brought home when Lowe tries for the first time, during his high school years, to find a summer job outside Chinatown. Although he is thoroughly "American" in name, birth, speech, manner, dress, and education—that is, in everything but appearance—Lowe painfully discovers that racial prejudice stands against him just as it does against all other "Orientals" throughout the exclusion period. While his white schoolmates find ample job opportunities, he is rejected in every place he applies, frequently not even given a chance for an interview.

In this respect, Lowe is by no means the only American-born Chinese who encountered obstacles in the mainstream job market. Edward C. Chew, the son of Dr. Ng Poon Chew—an eminent Chinese American journalist and leader of San Francisco's Chinese Christian community—was denied employment opportunities in numerous job applications despite his education at the University of California, Berkeley, and his distinguished service as one of only a few Chinese American officers during World War I.[21] To some extent, the more education the Chinese received, the fewer opportunities they found open to them. As a white scholar observed, "Those (American-born Chinese) who have graduated with honors from our best universities find it difficult to secure positions—the places which are open to them are of an inferior sort with but limited opportunities for advancement."[22] Indeed, statistics show that as late as 1940, only about 3 percent of the Chinese were engaged in professional and technical occupations. They usually either worked in small-scale, ethnic-oriented family enterprises or were confined to positions in Chinatown with little chance for promotion. Moreover, it is ironic that quite a few American-born Chinese got federal jobs in Lowe's time only because the immigration authorities needed their help to break the covers of illegal immigrants.[23]

Both the open and subtle racial prejudice present Lowe with a very real problem: how should he interpret the contradictions between the social reality that confronts him and the ideal of the American dream if the very American democracy and equality he admires exclude him from full participation in all aspects of American life? Historically, such a dilemma touched tender spots in the minds of all American-born Chinese. Depressed by rejection, they often felt disillusioned; many passed through a period of emotional disturbance. However, unlike those who solved the dilemma by staying within the Chinese community and its restraining influence, Lowe took a different course. Undoubtedly, the bitter lesson he learned while hunting for a summer job shatters his "Presidential dream." Returning home, he wakes up from his illusion and seems to understand better why his father chooses to identify with Chinese cultural traditions despite his adoption of American manners. Nevertheless, Lowe's experience does not dampen his stubborn devotion to American ideals.

He quickly dismisses the lesson and comforts himself that there are others whose fates are similar to his, and that he can at least study in an "American" public school: "I marched out of the house insouciant. When I wasn't whistling I was muttering to myself a Jewish slang phrase I had just picked up. It was 'Ishkabibble' and it meant that I didn't care. And I didn't until I reached the park where all my most vivid daydreaming periods were spent. There, I broke down and wept. For the first time I admitted to myself the cruel truth—I didn't have a 'Chinaman's chance' of becoming President of the United States. . . . But after a good cry I felt better—anyway, I could go to an American school again in the fall" (*Father* 147–48).

Being able to attend public school was, indeed, a significant symbolic progress for the Chinese, considering the formerly segregated educational system imposed on them. However, despite the "crash of the lofty hopes," Lowe obviously is not really convinced that he needs to account for the discrepancy between the promised equality of America and his experience of exclusion that makes him unequal. He still seems to think that becoming a part of mainstream society is his only choice: the optimal avenue for an American-born Chinese like himself when doors are closed is to redouble efforts to seek accommodation within American society.

Such an attitude today would surely be denounced as "Uncle Tomism." Nevertheless, it is an understandable response given the historical circumstances in which Lowe lived. That is, his behavior should not garner disapproval from readers today. As a U.S. citizen by birth, and American-made through public education, Lowe actually had few alternatives but to follow a common response to exclusion: working harder and seeking comfort in the fact that some people in the mainstream world did accept him. In addition, by demonstrating his resolve to participate in American life, Lowe in fact defied the then popular accusation that Chinese did not really wish to assimilate, thereby proving the falsity of that accusation against them.

Lowe's choice to adapt rather than challenge the racial prejudices confronting him is also a result of his alienation from the Chinese cultural tradition—an outcome of assimilation, unintended perhaps, but seemingly inevitable. In reality, his embitterment over being rejected by American society is much less than his frustration with and estrangement from his father. This again shows that he is more rooted in the mainstream world than the Chinese American community. In fact, throughout his personal narrative, his thorough assimilation is interwoven with and contrasted to his father's halfway acculturation. The troubled relationship between the father and the son constitutes another major theme running throughout Lowe's lengthy narrative.

While Lowe's autobiography is purportedly about "Father and Son," it is far from a neutral record of the son's reminiscences of the father. In general, Lowe's attitude toward his father vacillates between a "Glorious

Descendant" who is proud of his father's external American manners and a furious and rebellious son who is outraged by the old man's intrinsically Chinese mind. Although, in retrospect, Lowe acknowledges with gratitude that his father's strength, talent, and adaptability have given him substance and shaped and inspired his continuous pursuit of the American dream, he admits frankly that the old man's "stubborn Chinese mind" is a source of constant conflict between the patriarch and the son. As Lowe struggles to break away from the course his father designed for him and from the Chinese cultural heritage that he finds unacceptable in his Americanized mind, the subtle frictions on occasion escalate into open confrontations.

The opening of the book is poignant and indicative of Lowe's views on his father: "I strongly suspect that my father's life is a fraud"—a fraud in the sense that the old man has never become really Americanized despite his adoption of the external traits of American culture. Although the father had cut off his queue as an emblematic gesture to sever links with China,[24] he did not cast away the cultural heritage he brought from the old country. This is seen especially clearly in the father's distrust of individuality and emotional expression compared to his advocacy of sobriety and restraint of affection, which are traditional Chinese attitudes toward life.

The father's insistence that his son attend a Chinese-language school brings on the breaking point in their relationship. To be fair, the father's decision that Lowe "should undertake immediately the study of Chinese" is not really due to his fear of losing his son to "barbarian" culture; rather, it is motivated by practical considerations. He is fully aware that Lowe's illusion about American equality will cause his son to pay a dear price because no matter how American the latter may be, there is little chance for him to acquire a position other than menial work outside the Chinese community. Therefore, knowledge of the Chinese language would not only enable Lowe to preserve a cultural link with China, but also be "good job insurance" by providing him with an important means to enter a China-related profession. The intention is underscored by the fact that even though Lowe's father recognizes the necessity of assimilation and encourages it by giving his children names of prominent American politicians, he insists more vehemently that they accept Chinese cultural customs such as respect of traditions. This attitude also explains why he prevents Lowe in childhood from identifying himself entirely as an "American" and tells him he should eventually go to China for his college education.

Their disagreement over whether Lowe should receive a Chinese education is where the father meets the bitterest resistance from his son. Socially and culturally accustomed to the American way of life, Lowe considers Chinese education a major obstacle that would hamper his effort to become a "real American" and would "neutralize" his "excessive

Americanism." Thus, Lowe objects furiously to his father's plan: "What stood out in my mind then was that China was a remote and backward country with no redeeming features." Influenced by misleading concepts, which ignored the role of "the Orient" in world history, Lowe, like many of his peers in the exclusion era, was typically more enthusiastic about and familiar with the Anglo-American cultural heritage than that of China. According to a study done in several localities along the Pacific Coast in the 1920s, second-generation Asian Americans ranked much higher in their knowledge of American history than white children but knew little about the history of their parents' countries and cared even less.[25]

What further exemplifies the gap between the father and son is Lowe's critical attitude toward Chinese family life. Lowe argues that whereas in the mainstream world, affection, creativity, and personal feelings among family members are encouraged and welcomed, the same human expressions are restrained or even stifled by Chinese tradition. As a result, Lowe and his siblings all "longed to escape" from home. His criticism becomes more intense and bitter when he discusses parental authoritarianism and filial piety. As he points out, although Chinese immigrants are now in a new country, the influence of their old country's tradition hangs on tenaciously. Their demand for unquestioning acceptance of parental authority on the part of children is such an example. In Lowe's opinion, the custom thwarts the personal freedom of dutiful children who might otherwise pursue their own happiness in American life. Lowe is not entirely wrong on this issue, however: the reasons he gives for rejecting filial piety contain partial truth. In almost all the writings by American-born Chinese, we can find parents exerting unyielding patriarchal or matriarchal authority to force their children to take the course they have chosen for them. "Not when we were afraid, but when we were wide awake and lucid," Maxine Hong Kingston complained in her memoir three decades later, "my mother funneled China into our ears: Kwangtung Province, New Society Village, the River Kwoo, which runs past the village. 'Go the way we came so that you will be able to find our house.' I am to return to China where I have never been."[26] Clearly, the mentality of many Chinese immigrants remained unchanged long after the exclusion era ended.

Furthermore, Lowe epitomizes the experiences of the American-born: for them, assimilation is a process of alienation from traditional Chinese culture. Given the fact that he has so deeply acculturated, it is only natural that his feelings and attitude toward Chinese cultural heritage would be dramatically different from those of his father. The thoroughness of his assimilation is perhaps best evidenced by his marriage to a white woman from an old New England family during his attendance at the Harvard Graduate School of Business Administration. The wedding was held in a Protestant Evangelical Church in Germany in 1931. Lowe did not even inform his parents and Chinese friends of the event until two years after the wedding had taken place.

It is noteworthy that the marriage is mentioned only in a passing note in Lowe's autobiography. Although it is not unusual for an author to refrain from discussing his or her marital life, compared with Lowe's detailed and even meticulous description of many small events within his family, the scarcity of information he provides for such a significant issue appears rather suspicious and betrays a sense of uncertainty. Perhaps Lowe feared that a more personal and intimate account of his love story would embarrass his wife. Or, he might have been concerned that a detailed account of his romance with a white woman would give rise to a negative response from readers because public sentiment against interracial marriage was strong and an antimiscegenation law was in effect in California throughout the exclusion era. A study conducted by an eminent sociologist in 1927 shows only a mere 1 percent of white Americans would willingly accept a Chinese as a family member through marriage. As late as 1948, five years after the exclusion acts were repealed, 65 percent of white Americans still opposed marriages with Chinese.[27]

It is interesting to find that despite the tension and confrontations between Lowe and his father, they are reconciled in the end. The father finally realizes that his behavior is self-contradicting: having shorn his queue as a rebellious gesture against the Manchu court in China and no longer dreaming of returning to his village near the Pearl River, how could he still demand the absolute loyalty of his American-born son in accordance with Chinese tradition? In Lowe's case, one suspects it is practical considerations that prevailed. For one thing, Lowe's sense of his newly discovered "American freedom" from his father's control is predicated on his acceptance by mainstream society. Because he fails to find a job after graduating from Stanford and Harvard, he has to rely on his father's support to make ends meet. Thus, mainstream society's denial of his right to earn a living throws him, though unwillingly, back upon the Chinese community. On the occasion of his father's sixty-sixth birthday, Lowe lines up with his Caucasian wife and their three-year-old son, in accordance with their ranking within the family, and pays homage to his father. Curiously, despite all the traditional Chinese ceremoniousness and decorations at the party, including the father's enthroning on a *taishi* (an old-fashioned Chinese-style armchair), Lowe's father insists on wearing a Western suit rather than traditional Chinese "robes of longevity" expected in such an occasion. A bizarre and unharmonious picture is the result, yet it stands as a symbolic compromise between father and son, and between China and America. Such contending emotions and the message of the father-son relationship are skillfully superimposed in the autobiography's dramatic ending, which supplies the book's title: "Among our people, children are begotten and nurtured for one purpose—to provide for and glorify their parents." Indeed, although Lowe's father is more "American" than most Chinese immigrants of his era, it is an American-born son who eventually "glorifies" the father in the context of life in U.S. society.

As the first book-length personal narrative written by an American-born Chinese, the significance of *Father and Glorious Descendant* cannot be underestimated. It is a testimony that reveals the ardent desire of American-born Chinese to seek admission into mainstream society in the early twentieth century. Although Lowe sometimes disparages Chinese cultural traditions in order to display his quality as a "real American," we cannot totally dismiss the book's importance. The racial bias against the Chinese throughout the exclusion era effectively limited the degree to which Lowe could be integrated into American life. Therefore, alienation is a side effect of his acculturation. It is also the unfortunate price he must pay in the process of acquiring a place in American society during the specific historical period in question. Furthermore, despite his melting-pot mentality, Lowe was able to tell a story that the wider reading public could relate to, at a time when American-born Chinese were still a novelty and the public was unaware of their feelings and thoughts, especially their determination to be "American." In this concrete and limited sense, Lowe's sensitively written autobiography is a text well worth reading. It raises our awareness of the views and sensibilities of American-born Chinese who lived during the years of exclusion and increases our overall understanding of the Chinese American historical experience.

FIFTH CHINESE DAUGHTER: A YOUNG AMERICAN-BORN CHINESE WOMAN'S PATH TO SUCCESS

Not all American-born Chinese in the exclusion era were as critical as Pardee Lowe was of the cultural values of their immigrant parents. While Lowe represented those American-born who broke away from their "Oriental roots" to assimilate into the "melting pot," there were others whose search for the American dream took a different turn. These were members of the second generation who came of age around World War II when the American public shifted to a more favorable stance toward Chinese Americans. Realizing that their ethnic affiliation was no longer a liability, they were interested in looking for a thread that could link the American values to which they aspired with the Chinese culture into which they were born. Accepting attitudes popularly ascribed to the Chinese at the time, they strove to "utilize" their ethnic legacy by turning it into an advantage that might help them gain admission into the mainstream world. By introducing to the general audience the fine qualities in Chinese life, they hoped to create a new image of the Chinese in order to win acceptance in American society. Jade Snow Wong's *Fifth Chinese Daughter* is representative of such efforts.

Recommended by critics as "required reading for all those who are interested in the Sino-American experience," *Fifth Chinese Daughter* was perhaps the most widely read book by a Chinese American woman author before the publication of Maxine Hong Kingston's *The Woman Warrior* in 1976.[28] Narrated in the third person, Wong's autobiography captures vividly the life, aspirations, and triumphs of the first twenty-four years of her life in San Francisco's Chinatown. As soon as the book came out, it rose to the best-seller lists and stayed there for months—a feat for a book by any first-time author, and all the more amazing for a personal story of an ordinary Chinese daughter growing up in the exclusion era. It was selected as the Book of the Month and the Christian Herald Family Book in 1950, and awarded the Commonwealth Club's Medal for Non-Fiction in 1951. Since then, the book has undergone many printings, been translated into a dozen foreign languages, and reached a colossal circulation—nearly half a million copies have been sold.[29]

At first glance, Wong's personal background and her life story seem almost identical to those of Pardee Lowe. Like Lowe, Wong was born and grew up in San Francisco, and like him, she views the experience of being a second-generation Chinese American as a struggle to attain recognition by mainstream society. A closer examination reveals, however, that the similarities between these two representative works are not nearly as significant as the differences between them because each was greatly affected by the personal background of its author as well as the social milieu of the times in which they came of age.

While Lowe was an aristocrat of sorts and represented a small privileged segment of the "uptown" Chinese, Wong came from a humble background and belonged to the lower stratum of the Chinatown community—the "downtown" Chinese. Her father owned only a small sweatshop on the same scale as many tiny Chinese laundries or eating places in the early twentieth century. The family was constantly on the brink of bankruptcy. In contrast to the Lowe family, which lived a comfortable life in a suburban residential neighborhood, the Wong family could only afford to rent a basement apartment in the heart of San Francisco's Chinatown. Both of Wong's parents worked at sewing machines around the clock to save the family from starvation. Furthermore, in light of Chinese tradition that favors not only male children but also the primogeniture system, Wong's status as the "fifth daughter" was certainly no match for Lowe's place as the "number one son" in their respective families. While Lowe was fully supported in everything by his parents and studied at Stanford and Harvard, Wong had to take care of the housework from the age of fourteen—cooking, laundering, and buying the groceries for a family of seven. Later, because her parents were neither able nor willing to support her ambition for a college education, she worked as a housekeeper and cook in white families while attending San Francisco Junior College and then Mills College. The sharp contrast between the lives of Wong and Lowe shows how American-born Chinese differed profoundly in family background and experiences even though all of them taken together formed only a small group in the exclusion era.

The two authors also diverge in the content and style of their personal narratives. Although Wong shares with Lowe a sustaining desire to secure a place in American life, she takes a rather different approach toward that goal. To justify a position in the mainstream world, Lowe pursues an Anglo-American identity. Wong, in contrast, believing that the true American dream ought to include a Chinese daughter, assumes a role as a "model minority." Unlike Lowe, who exposes and attacks the conservative aspects of Chinese tradition in order to display his qualities as an American-born, Wong remains keenly aware of the opportunities her Chinese heritage can offer and uses this unique vantage point to win acceptance in the larger society. Discovering through her own experience that her ethnic background has "created a great deal of favorable interest...and [can] be accommodated in the widening knowledge of the Western world," she decides to promote, rather than play down, her Chinese ethnicity, in the process turning her knowledge of Chinese life into a source of inspiration to achieve success in the mainstream world. As she recounts: "Jade Snow found that the [white] girls were perpetually curious about her Chinese background and ideologies...she began to formulate in her mind the constructive and delightful aspects of the Chinese culture to present to non-Chinese."[30]

Ironically, while Lowe's strenuous efforts to demonstrate his Americanness failed to win him much acceptance, Wong's retention of Chinese ethnicity brought her wide recognition. However, the differences between the approaches of Wong and Lowe as they sought entry into the mainstream world and the respective outcomes are not entirely related to their personal backgrounds. Rather, they reflect the impact of the general public's changing social consciousness with regard to Chinese Americans during different phases of the exclusion era.

Although their books were published only seven years apart, the two authors are separated by almost a generation. While Lowe was born in 1905 and grew up in the years when anti-Chinese prejudice was still prevalent, Wong, born in 1922, reached maturity at a time when the American public had become more sympathetic to the Chinese. The World War II era, as noted earlier, directly boosted their position as a "loyal minority." As a result, Chinese Americans, once regarded as subhuman and unassimilated, now became known for their ability to withstand hardship and were praised for their loyalty to the United States. Through the mass media, the American public endowed them with many admirable characteristics, including being "patriotic," "patient," "hardworking," and "charming." Even popular magazines, such as *Life* and *Time*, joined the effort to enhance the Chinese image.[31] Supporting the Chinese had become very much a process of going with the flow at a time when the Chinese exclusion acts were about to be repealed.

The improved status of the Chinese and the more sympathetic reception given them by mainstream society since the early 1940s thus opened new doors into American life for an American-born Chinese daughter such as Wong. For one thing, she found what had been considered "negative" elements in her ethnic background became "favorable" conditions as aspects of her Chinese identity now drew great interest among white Americans. As Wong discovered, "her grades [in college] were constantly higher when she wrote about Chinatown and the people she had known all her life" (*FCD* 132). A term paper she wrote on a Chinese classic, *Chin Pin Mei* (*Jinping mei*, meaning "golden vase plum"), was even recommended by her professor for presentation at an academic conference. Of course, the interest in her essay may well be attributed to Wong's choice of this particular novel. Unlike other Chinese classics, *Chin Pin Mei* is a romance known for its exposure of sexual scandals in a merchant family in sixteenth-century China, and would surely stimulate curiosity about the traditional Chinese family and the society formed by such families.

For the most part, however, Wong's autobiography portrays the common aspects of Chinese American life rather than exotic elements of Chinese culture. Publications at the time, such as Nobel Prize winner Pearl S. Buck's trilogy (*The Good Earth*, 1931; *Sons*, 1932; *A House Divided*, 1935) with its depictions of the down-to-earth ways of Chinese peasants, not only produced popular sympathy for the Chinese but also had a compelling impact on the American public.[32] Thus, readers had shifted their attitude toward the Chinese and now showed a new receptivity, which initiated a strong interest in the more realistic aspects of the Chinese American community. This explains why Wong could entertain readers with familiar things in her life such as cooking, rice washing, child rearing, and folk customs.

To be fair, Wong not only tells a good story, but also tells it well. Her lucid and carefully researched accounts of daily activities in Chinatown deftly paint a fascinating picture. She examines in detail such varied but typical experiences as the elaborate preparations required to carry out a traditional Chinese wedding, the treatment of people with herbal medicine, and the staging of annual funeral services. She can be humorous and visually acute, as in the portrayal of how she learned the differences among human races. At the birth of her younger brother, her mother taught her that babies were "roasted in the hospital ovens" and brought out to the parents by "a lady doctor." There were three different sorts, her mother told Wong—the nearly done ones, which are the white babies; the slightly overdone ones, which are the black babies; and the golden brown ones, which are the Chinese (*FCD* 24). Such stories run throughout Wong's autobiography, making various minor details memorable and reading the book a pleasant experience.

However, Wong's coverage of Chinese life, no matter how fascinating and emblematic, does not mean that she has embraced wholeheartedly her Chinese heritage. That disposition serves only as a means to accomplish her goal—to paint a portrait of the "model minority." As she says, "What I intend to do is to help people understand Chinese Americans and show them how good and honest we are."[33] The intention is underscored in her effort to filter her personal stories in order to create various "positive" stereotypes of Chinese Americans. Her explanation of the Chinese attitude toward welfare programs is a case in point.

According to Wong, "being poor did not entitle anyone to benefits" and "the only way to overcome poverty is to work hard." During the Great Depression, even though her parents were under severe strain and faced extremely grim times, they refused to apply for relief. To make ends meet, the family cut down further their already meager spending and put the children to work: "He [Wong's father] leased sewing equipment, installed machines in a basement where rent was cheapest, and there he and his family lived and worked. There was no thought that dim and airless quarters were terrible conditions for living and working, or that child labor was unhealthful. The only goal was for all in the family to work, to save, and to become educated."[34]

Wong's self-defined notions about the welfare system and her family's determination to find a solution to their economic predicament certainly fit in with the popular belief that "Orientals never or rarely used welfare facilities." Unfortunately, the portrait of "Puritans from the Orient" Wong painted is not always true in real-life situations. If, historically, Chinese Americans in general underutilized available governmental relief, it is due to their ignorance, fear of the authorities, and statutory discrimination, rather than simply a spirit of self-reliance.

Because of the intention to create a positive Chinese image, Wong's depiction is inevitably restricted and defined by the social acceptance of Chinese in American life. This means that she has to satisfy the expectations that mainstream readers held about a "model minority." Therefore, Wong is highly selective in her portrayal of Chinese American life and she identifies only those elements that may help her win a place in American society. In this sense, *Fifth Chinese Daughter* parallels works by Chinese immigrant authors during the exclusion era. For instance, Wong seems to follow in the footsteps of Lee Yan Phou, author of *When I Was a Boy in China* (1887), in devoting a large portion of her work to discussing Chinese food. Like Lee, she finds that the topic can help her bring out charming features of Chinese life. Chinese food is indeed the first thing that helped Wong gain a foothold in the mainstream world: "Jade Snow considered a moment before answering. Certainly she could cook Chinese food, and she remembered a common Chinese saying, 'A Chinese can cook foreign food as well as, if not better than, the foreigners, but a foreigner cannot cook Chinese food fit for the Chinese.' On this reasoning it seemed safe to say 'Yes' " (*FCD* 123). To satisfy the curiosity of readers, Wong describes beautifully all the little details that make Chinese food unique. Considering the popularity of Chinese food in American society, this treatment of food would surely make her work more attractive to potential readers.

The similarity between Wong and immigrant authors during the exclusion era is and is not accidental. Wong is tied to them by the common desire to correct the distorted image of the Chinese even though Wong had no knowledge of the immigrant authors' work.[35] Moreover, while immigrants writers such as Lee Yan Phou dwelled on the experiences of the first generation and tended to look to their homeland when rejected by American society, Wong's emphasis falls on the courage and efforts of the American-born to seek admission into the mainstream world. Racial bias only reinforces her determination to acquire a place in American life. "Despite prejudice, I was never discouraged from carrying out my creed;" Wong makes it clear, "because of prejudice, the effort is ongoing" (*FCD* xi). When told by a bigoted placement officer at Mills College to give up her attempt to find employment outside Chinatown, Wong remarks, "No, this was one piece of advice she was not going to follow, so opposed was it to her experience and belief. She was more determined to get a job with an American firm" (*FCD* 189).

The gap between Wong and the immigrant authors of her era is further reflected in their different views on residence in Chinatowns. In general, as an immigrant scholar pointed out, despite many problems in the ghetto, a majority of Chinese immigrants at that time preferred life in Chinatown because living there provided certain conveniences as well as a sense of community: "Most of us can live a warmer, freer and a more human life among our relatives and friends than among strangers. . . . It is only in Chinatown that a Chinese immigrant has society, friends and relatives who share his dreams and hopes, his hardships, and adventures. Here he can tell a joke and make everybody laugh with him; here he may hear folktales told which create the illusion that Chinatown is really China."[36] But for an American-born Chinese like Wong, contacts with mainstream society made them dissatisfied with the idea of spending their entire lives within the Chinese community. Working in white families, Wong feels that her visions have been greatly broadened and that she is exposed to a new world shunned by the insular Chinese old-timers. The new world is one in which individuals have more freedom and recognition than she could ever have imagined. She acknowledges openly that it is in the larger society that she had her "first complete privacy . . . and inner peace" and concludes: "It was a home [the home of a white family in which she lived] where children were heard as well as seen; where parents considered who was right or wrong, rather than who should be respected; where birthday parties were a tradition . . . where the husband kissed his wife and the parents kissed their children . . . where the family was actually concerned with having fun together . . . where the problems and difficulties of domestic life and children's discipline were untangled perhaps after tears, but also after explanations; where the husband turned over his pay check to his wife to pay the bills; and where, above all, each member, even down to and including the dog, appeared to have the inalienable right to assert his individuality—in fact, where this was expected—in an atmosphere of natural affection" (FCD 113–14). Such longing and passionate admiration for the kind of life found in the mainstream world make Wong's writing distinct from the viewpoint of immigrant authors who speak chiefly for the first generation.

The attempt to bolster a positive Chinese image also prompts Wong to eulogize the unselfish white Americans who dedicate themselves to the improvement of the Chinese. Discussing her experience in college, Wong says: "She had a glimpse of the truth, that great people of any race are unpretentious, genuinely honest, and non-patronizing in their interest in other human beings" (FCD 173). To show that she appreciates the kind assistance given by white Americans, Wong frequently quotes Chinese maxims such as "When you drink water, think of its source." Obviously, to Wong, the source of success for a Chinese daughter is encouragement and benevolence from the larger society. As she indicates in the preface of the book: "We who did not choose our ancestry can be grateful for op- portunities more expansive in this country than in most others" (FCD xi). Wong has ample reasons to sing the praises of American opportunities and birthright. She was able to obtain support from the mainstream world at almost every critical stage of her life. Her education could not have been completed without the help of sympathetic white people; she was trusted by her white supervisor and welcomed by her colleagues while she worked at a navy shipyard during World War II; and, when she established her pottery business, her wares were purchased and appreciated highly by white Americans. Virtually all her victorious achievements—being class valedictorian, chosen to christen a Liberty Ship during the war, and even the publication of her personal story—resulted from the patronage of white Americans.

Wong's experience thus suggests that thanks to growing pro-Chinese sentiments, an American-born Chinese daughter now can achieve equality and self-respect in American society. As a Chinese American ceramicist, her pottery works have won numerous awards, been shown in various exhibitions, and been collected by more than twenty prestigious museums, including the Metropolitan Museum of Art in New York and the Smithsonian Institution in Washington, D.C. All these achievements illustrate that Chinese Americans have gradually been accepted as an integral part of American life. The social progress leads an American-born Chinese student in Wong's time to conclude optimistically: "[Earlier] hostility toward the Chinese has given way to a tolerant, kindly feeling, with instances of admiration and confidence in the daily intercourse among individuals."[37]

Of course, the more sympathetic attitude toward Chinese in the era during which Wong came of age does not mean that racial bias had disappeared. In her childhood, Wong encountered the presence of racial harassment at various times. She relates vividly how at one time, she was taunted by a white boy in school: " 'I've been waiting for a chance like this,' Richard said excitedly to Jade Snow. With malicious intent in his eyes, he burst forth, 'Chinky, Chinky, Chinaman' . . . Jade Snow decided that it was time to leave. As she went out of the doorway, a second eraser landed squarely on her back. She looked neither to the right nor left, but proceeded sedately down the stairs and out the front door. In a few minutes, her tormentor had caught up with her. Dancing around in glee, he chortled, 'Look at the eraser mark on the yellow Chinaman. Chinky, Chinky, no tickee, no washee, no shirtee!' " (FCD 68).

Although events such as this might cause furious responses from Chinese Americans today, Wong tried to cope with the situation rather than fighting back. Walking away placidly, she simply decided to "forgive" the white boy: "Jade Snow thought that he (Richard) was tiresome and ignorant. Everybody knew that the Chinese people had a superior culture. Her ancestors had created a great art heritage and had made inventions important to world civilization—the compass, gunpowder, paper, and a host of other essentials. She knew, too, that Richard's grades couldn't compare with her own, and his home training was obviously amiss. . . . They [white people] probably could not help their own insensibility. Mama said they hadn't even learned how to peel a clove of garlic the way the Chinese did" (FCD 68–69).

Such a calm and passive tolerance exemplifies how a "loyal-minority" woman willingly keeps quiet in the face of racial harassment in order to prove that she is civilized and harbors no anger or bitterness toward white

Americans. The attitude certainly constitutes a sharp contrast to that of many Chinese Americans today. However, although Wong's subdued tone and restrained manner might have reinforced the popular notion that the Chinese are a people lacking in normal assertiveness and temper, her behavior was not atypical for a Chinese American during the exclusion era. As one ethnic studies scholar points out, Chinese Americans were historically sustained throughout various ordeals by finding psychological comfort in the belief that "their ancestors had created a great and complex civilization when the inhabitants of the British Isles still painted their faces blue."[38] In this sense, Wong only followed an old practice advocated by Chinese Americans during the exclusion era and tried to tap "an inner resource" by thinking about her cultural superiority as this racial incident took place.

Wong's intention to construct a positive Chinese image seems to cause her to overidealize American life. Nevertheless, given that she has found more support and encouragement in her life and career from the mainstream world, it is understandable why she writes in this way. There is little doubt that as the "fifth daughter" born in a traditional Chinatown family, Wong owes her accomplishments more to the patronage of "American society" than to the Chinese cultural heritage. As she emphasizes, in traditional Chinese society where women are judged by their obedience to men, it is simply impossible for someone like her to rise to prominence. Wong underscores the "virulent misogyny" of Chinese tradition by pointing out that even in America's Chinatowns, women are still kept at the bottom of society: "She was trapped in a mesh of tradition woven thousands of miles away by ancestors who had no knowledge that someday one generation of their progeny might be raised in another culture" (FCD 110). Despite the Wong family's striking poverty, for example, her brother was cherished in the best Chinese tradition—he had his own room, kept a German Shepherd as a pet, was tutored by a Chinese scholar, and sent to a private college with full financial support from his parents. Such privileges were his birthright. As the only male child in the family, he was expected to carry on the Wong lineage and probably also return to China someday as a representative of the Wong clan to pay tribute to their ancestors' tombs, because according to traditional Chinese culture, only male children are considered the descendants of a family. In contrast, Wong and her sisters had to be content with whatever was left. When she asked her father to help pay for her college education, she received a stern lecture: "You are quite familiar by now with the fact that it is the sons who perpetuate our ancestral heritage by permanently bearing the Wong family name and transmitting it through their blood line, and therefore the sons must have priority over the daughters" (FCD 109).

Compared with such a hoary tradition, America appears to be a better world for a Chinese daughter such as Jade Snow Wong. The increasing gender equality in American society since the early twentieth century allows Chinese women in the United States to enjoy access to education, social activities, the right to choose their own husbands, and participation in the workforce. When Dr. Faith Sai Leong, an American-born Chinese daughter similar to Wong, began to set up her dental clinic in San Francisco in 1905, women in China were still forced to stay home with bound feet.[39] The traditional prejudice against women may also explain in part why Wong's talents have not been fully appreciated by the Chinese community. Despite the fact that her artistic achievement made her "a wonder in the eyes of the Western world," Wong's pottery works draw little interest from Chinatown residents: "Caucasians came from far and near to see her work, and Jade Snow sold all the pottery she could make.... But the Chinese did not come to buy one piece from her" (FCD 244). In retrospect, Wong feels fortunate that it is her father's failed dream to return to China that rendered her a different fate: "My father regretted that he had not become rich enough to retire during the depression thirties to his native Chung Shan district.... If he had returned with me and my siblings, I could never have had my independent career" (FCD x).

It should be noted that Wong's strong will to acquire social prominence is itself a product of acculturation and resembles the mentality and behavior of an American feminist rather than those of a "fifth Chinese daughter." According to Confucian doctrine, a woman of virtue is a woman without talent and ambition. The doctrine is based on the assumption that women are generally narrow-minded, shortsighted, and could not be cultivated—they are everything but intelligent and educable. Therefore, for their own benefit and for the sake of society's interests, they had better be humble and invisible. In her family and in the Chinatown community, Wong was repeatedly advised, kindly or contemptuously, that she should be a modest daughter who stayed home rather than an ambitious woman who mixed with "barbarians" in the mainstream world. Despite such "well-meant" advice, Wong early made up her mind that she would strive to win respect and honor as a solemn reply to male chauvinism: "In her bitterness, Jade Snow made up a solemn vow to God as she knelt in bedtime prayer. 'To make up for this neglect and prejudice, please help me to do my best in striving to be a person respected and honored ... when I grow up' " (FCD 93).

In other words, Wong pursued success by identifying with mainstream American culture. Her determination to challenge Chinese tradition is demonstrated conspicuously by her active participation in various programs sponsored by the larger society. When her essay on wartime absenteeism won top prize in a contest, she was given the honor of christening a Liberty Ship. The image of Wong striking the bow of a giant ocean freighter with a champagne bottle is surely symbolic. It must have been a rare and shocking sight in the eyes of the insular Chinatown old men because in traditional China, women were forbidden to touch a new ship before its maiden voyage. This taboo is rooted in a long-established superstition that maintains that female presence will bring a curse to a new ship and cause it misfortune.[40] Therefore, Wong's sending the giant ship to sea represents not only a personal honor but also an act of self-assertion and defiance against the weight of historical and societal injunctions against Chinese women.

Richly textured in content and ideals, *Fifth Chinese Daughter* also outshines most works by other Chinese American authors during the exclusion era in terms of its writing techniques. While the popularity of writings by Wong's contemporaries has waxed and waned, her work continues to be widely read. The enthusiastic reception by readers and critics alike of the most recent edition of *Fifth Chinese Daughter* attests to this fact.

Undoubtedly, Wong's choice of third-person narrative to tell her life story is a key factor enhancing the autobiography's popularity. Ironically, critics believe this is "a typical Chinese style" of autobiographical writing. This erroneous assumption is partly caused by Wong's own statement that "the third-person-singular style in which I told my story was rooted in Chinese literary form" (*FCD* vii). Wong's act of crediting her style to "Chinese habit" is rather misleading and is probably motivated by an intention to add an even more exotic flavor to her already highly colored personal narrative. Given the popular notion that "Orientals" are perpetual foreigners, her claim to writing a first-person-singular autobiography in a third-person "Chinese" style would surely help promote the book's sale. Yet, contrary to Wong's statement, the style has nothing to do with Chinese literary form since there is no such genre as autobiographical writing in the Chinese literary tradition. Until Western literature was introduced into China in the early 1900s, any attempts to write personal history were considered extremely egocentric—especially an autobiography by a young woman from a humble background. In reality, Wong's use of the third person singular reveals the astonishing influence of American autobiographical writings such as *The Education of Henry Adams*. Therefore, the style itself reflects the impact of mainstream American culture on Chinese American authors. That few critics are aware of this point shows that they tend to underestimate the degree of acculturation of American-born Chinese during the exclusion era.

As the first American-born Chinese author who gained international popularity, Wong's greatest accomplishment is her successful portrayal of the life of a Chinese daughter who realized her American dream through self-struggle in the later years of the exclusion era. It is true that Wong painted, albeit perhaps unconsciously, a portrait of a "model minority" for a mainstream audience's consumption—that is, she redefined her Chinese heritage to fit with certain expectations of the American reading public. Her popularity is in part based on the roles she described that are in line with the conventional images held by mainstream readers. For this reason, *Fifth Chinese Daughter* is sometimes criticized by Chinese Americans today. Frank Chin, for instance, called *Fifth Chinese Daughter* "part cook book" and "food pornography."[41] But Wong's personal narrative is also authentic and compelling in an understated way. As a Chinese American woman critic argues, though modest in tone, Wong's life story reveals the "inner fire" of a determined young Chinese woman growing up in the exclusion era, who endured all difficulties despite the odds, fought prejudice both within and outside the Chinese community, and achieved ultimate triumph.[42] Despite the tendency to overidealize American life and to filter her experiences to satisfy the tastes of mainstream readers, Wong delved into the issues indigenous to her historical and cultural milieu and created a new image of Chinese American women. While her portrayal of a hardworking and successful Chinese daughter may have contributed to the creation of a new or the strengthening of a conventional stereotype of the Chinese people, it is at least a step forward because it represented progress within the constraints of the historical circumstances of her day. The construction of Chinese American stereotypes began long before *Fifth Chinese Daughter* was published, and the "Oriental" women in popular American culture throughout the exclusion era inevitably appeared as either seductive dragon ladies or sensual sing-song girls. In comparison, nearly every aspect of Wong's heroine contrasts sharply with the luscious portrayal of stereotyped Chinese women; and the "fifth Chinese daughter" is closer to real Chinese American women who express a range of human emotions and qualities. While it may not be as powerful and profound as Kingston's "woman warrior," it is a serious and engaging account of the lives and minds of American-born Chinese growing up during the exclusion era.

In other words, changes can only come slowly and gradually, and even stereotypes have their values because not all of them have the same implications. Despite its weaknesses, the portrayal of Wong as an inspiring and successful Chinese daughter is a giant step forward in the "long march" of changing images of the Chinese in American society. In this sense, what Tiana (Thi Thanh Nga), a veteran Asian American actress and a close friend of Bruce Lee, says in her discussion of Asian stereotypes in movies, may help illustrate the significance of *Fifth Chinese Daughter*. In her eloquent argument for the movie *The World of Suzie Wong*, which is criticized by some Asian Americans as "sentimental, racist, and outdated," Tiana retorts: "Sentimental? Of course. Racist? You bet. Outdated? Like the horse and buggy. But sentimental, racist, and outdated as it was, *Suzie Wong* was a breaking through film in the long march from [Anna May] Wong to [John] Woo" because it "broke down the long-established taboo against presenting Asian-Caucasian love affairs on the screen."[43] This is perhaps why Wong's personal narrative is highly praised by most Chinese American critics today. As editors of the first Asian American anthology comment: "Struggle against being considered just another obedient child among her brothers and sisters, against racial prejudice visited upon her since childhood, against sexual discrimination that preferred the male off-spring, against parental authoritarianism, and finally against herself in an effort to find meaning for her own life—these are the tensions described in Jade Snow Wong's autobiographical novel."[44]

CONCLUSION

As is always the case in reading works by earlier Chinese American authors, one way to understand the substance and imagery of *Father and Glorious Descendent* and *Fifth Chinese Daughter* is to recognize the social and historical contexts of their time. Living in an era marked by an emphasis on Americanization and the rejection of "Oriental" values, Pardee Lowe and Jade Snow Wong could not foresee the awakening of Chinese American consciousness that followed the civil rights movement in the 1960s. Therefore, instead of taking their works out of historical context, we should view them as a mirror reflecting the process by which American-born Chinese evolved from a denial of self to self-fashioning their own identities in this critical phase of Chinese American history. Today, minority discourse and pan-Asian ethnicity seem nothing more than common sense, but in an era when the Chinese were denied even the right to enter the United States, the melting pot theory, exclusion, and alienation dominated the social consciousness of the Chinese in America.

More significantly, as their personal narratives and life stories demon-strate, what happened to Chinese immigrants in the exclusion era also greatly affected the lives of their American-born children. Despite their birthright as U.S. citizens and their enthusiastic embrace of American values and behavioral norms, American-born Chinese in those years were rebuffed and frustrated in their pursuit of the American dream in the same way as their immigrant parents experienced. Obviously, W.E.B. DuBois' well-known conclusion that the problem of twentieth-century America was the problem of "the color line" also applied to the experiences of Pardee Lowe, Jade Snow Wong, and other young people growing up Chinese American in the exclusion era.

Finally, as pioneers of "ABC" authors, Lowe and Wong broke new ground and their success paved the way for the rise of a new generation of

Chinese American writers. Maxine Hong Kingston, for example, praises Wong as the "Mother of Chinese American literature" and admits that Wong is the only Chinese American author she had read before she wrote *The Woman Warrior*. In fact, it was *Fifth Chinese Daughter* that inspired Kingston to start her literary career: "I found Jade Snow Wong's book myself in the library," she recalled years later, "and [I] was flabbergasted, helped, inspired, affirmed, made possible as a writer—for the first time I saw a person who looked like me as a heroine of a book, as a maker of a book."[45] Together with other "ABC" authors, Lowe and Wong brought the experiences of the American-born during the exclusion years to the public's attention, added a great deal to the understanding of Chinese American history, and gave rise to a new perspective on Chinese American life before the emergence of the Asian American movement in the 1960s. In this sense, the record of what U.S.-born Chinese Americans had to endure historically in their sensitively written personal stories is an important legacy for all Chinese Americans. Occupying a singular place in Chinese American literary history, the two representative autobiographical works of the exclusion era still appeal to us today.

Notes

PREFACE

1. Sucheng Chan, ed., *Entry Denied: Exclusion and the Chinese Community in America, 1882–1943* (Philadelphia: Temple University Press, 1991).
2. K. Scott Wong and Sucheng Chan, eds., *Claiming America: Constructing Chinese American Identities During the Exclusion Era* (Philadelphia: Temple University Press, 1998).
3. Erika Lee, *At America's Gates: Chinese Immigration During the Exclusion Era, 1882–1943* (Chapel Hill: University of North Carolina Press, 2003).
4. Madeline Y. Hsu, *Dreaming of Gold, Dreaming of Home: Transnationalism and Migration* (Stanford, Calif.: Stanford University Press, 2000).
5. Haiming Liu, *The Transnational History of a Chinese Family: Immigrant Letters, Family Business, and Reverse Migration* (New Brunswick, N.J.: Rutgers University Press, 2005).
6. Yong Chen, *Chinese San Francisco, 1850–1943: A Trans-Pacific Community* (Stanford, Calif.: Stanford University Press, 2000).
7. Shehong Chen, *Being Chinese, Becoming Chinese American* (Urbana: University of Illinois Press, 2002).
8. Xiao-huang Yin, *Chinese American Literature Since the 1850s* (Urbana: University of Illinois Press, 2000).

CHAPTER ONE

1. "Petition of the Chinese Six Companies to Prince Tsai Tao on His Visit to the United States," printed in *Chung Sai Yat Po*, May 2, 1910, translated by the U.S. Bureau of Immigration. File 52961/24-B, Subject Correspondence, Records of the U.S. Immigration and Naturalization Service, RG 85, National Archives, Washington, D.C. (hereafter cited as INS Subject Correspondence, National Archives). On the Chinese Six Companies, see Shih-shan Henry Tsai, *The Chinese Experience in America* (Bloomington: Indiana University Press, 1986), 46–47.
2. The 1882 Chinese Exclusion Act barred all Chinese laborers from entering the country for ten years and prohibited Chinese immigrants from becoming naturalized citizens. It expressly allowed only a few specific classes of Chinese—merchants, teachers, students, diplomats, and travelers—to continue to immigrate to the United States. Act of May 6, 1882, 22 Stat. 58.
3. Pre–exclusion era statistics are from Judy Yung, *Unbound Feet: A Social History of Chinese Women in San Francisco* (Berkeley and Los Angeles: University of California Press, 1995), 22. Because the government did not record Chinese

arrivals in a consistent manner over the sixty-one-year exclusion era, the figures that I cite are for immigrants only for 1882–1891 and for immigrants and returning citizens for 1894–1940. Statistics for the years 1892–93 and 1941–43 are not available. U.S. Bureau of Immigration, *Annual Report of the Commissioner-General of Immigration, 1898–1943* (Washington, D.C. Government Printing Office, 1898–1943); Helen Chen, "Chinese Immigration into the United States: An Analysis of Changes in Immigration Policies" (Ph.D. dissertation, Brandeis University, 1980), 181; Fu-ju Liu, "A Comparative Demographic Study of Native-Born and Foreign-Born Chinese Populations in the United States" (Ph.D. dissertation, University of Michigan, 1953), 223.

4. Sucheng Chan, *This Bittersweet Soil: The Chinese in California Agriculture, 1860–1910* (Berkeley and Los Angeles: University of California Press, 1986), 12; Sucheng Chan, *Asian Americans: An Interpretive History* (Boston: Twayne, 1991), 3–7.

5. George J. Sanchez explains the connection between imperialism and migration in "Race, Nation, and Culture in Recent Immigration Studies," *Journal of American Ethnic History* 18, no. 4 (Summer, 1999): 80.

6. More than 60 percent of the Chinese in the United States trace their roots to a small region of the Pearl River Delta that consists of the eight districts of Namhoi [Nanhai], Punyu [Panyu], and Shuntak [Shunde](collectively called Sam Yup [Sanyi], meaning three districts), Sunwui [Xinhui], Sunning [Xinning] (renamed Toisan [Taishan] in 1914), Hoiping [Haiping], and Yanping [Enping] (collectively called Sze Yup [Siyi], meaning four districts), and Heungsan [Xiangshan] (later renamed Chungsan [Zhongshan]), which is outside Sam Yup and Sze Yup. Scholars estimate that the vast majority of Chinese (over 70 percent) in nineteenth-century California were Toisan and other Sze Yup people. (In the previous place-names, the first transliteration is according to how the words are pronounced in the Cantonese dialect; their pronunciation in putonghua, within square brackets, is transliterated in pinyin.) Thomas W. Chinn, Him Mark Lai, and Philip C. Choy, eds., *A History of the Chinese in California: A Syllabus* (San Francisco: Chinese Historical Society of America, 1969), 2; Chan, *This Bittersweet Soil,* 17–18.

7. Yong Chen, *Chinese San Francisco, 1850–1943: A Trans-Pacific Community* (Stanford, Calif.: Stanford University Press, 2000), 12, 16–23.

8. Chan, *This Bittersweet Soil,* 27; Madeline Hsu, *Dreaming of Gold, Dreaming of Home: Transnationalism and Migration Between the United States and South China, 1882–1943* (Stanford, Calif.: Stanford University Press, 2000), 33; "Angel Island Immigration Station: Interviews with Chris Chow, Mr. Yuen, Ira and Ed Lee," Bancroft Library, University of California, Berkeley, transcript, 29–30.

9. Y. Chen, *Chinese San Francisco,* 23–38.

10. Interview with Mary Lee by author, February 20, 1990.

11. I borrow this phrase from J. S. Holliday, *The World Rushed In: The California Gold Rush Experience* (New York: Simon and Schuster, 1981).

12. Interview with Mr. Low by author, New York City, November 16, 1995. ("Mr. Low," without a first name or initial, was how this interviewee wished to be addressed.)

13. "Angel Island Immigration Station: Interviews with Chris Chow, Mr. Yuen, Ira and Ed Lee," Bancroft Library, University of California, Berkeley, transcript, 22.

14. Statement of Fong Ing Bong, September 28, 1907, File 10209/77, Chinese Arrival Investigation Case Files (hereafter cited as Chinese Arrival Files), Port of San Francisco, Records of the U.S. Immigration and Naturalization Service, RG 85, National Archives, Pacific-Sierra Region, San Bruno, California.

15. Interview with Wallace Lee by author, February 20, 1990.

16. Judy Yung, Genny Lim, and Him Mark Lai, "Summary of Interview with Jeong Foo Louie," (San Francisco, History of Chinese Detained on the Island [HOC DOI] Project, Asian American Studies Library, University of California, Berkeley, 1976).

17. Brett de Bary Nee and Victor Nee, *Longtime Californ': A Documentary Study of an American Chinatown* (New York: Pantheon Books, 1972), 16.

18. Marlon Kau Hom, "Some Cantonese Folksongs on the American Experience," *Western Folklore* 42 (April 1983): 128. See also Marlon Kau Hom, *Songs from Gold Mountain: Cantonese Rhymes from San Francisco Chinatown* (Berkeley and Los Angeles: University of California Press, 1987).

19. Lee Young Sing to Lee Wooey Hong, October 4, 1916, File 2, Box 1, Densmore Investigation Files, San Francisco District, Records of the U.S. Immigration and Naturalization Service, RG 85, National Archives, Pacific-Sierra Region, San Bruno, California (hereafter cited as Densmore Investigation Files, San Francisco).

20. A mou is a Chinese measurement for land. One mou equals one-sixth of an acre. Wong Ngum Yin (aka Wong Hock Won), "Composition on the Advantages and Disadvantages of America, from a Chinese Standpoint," enclosed in Inspector in Charge, San Francisco, to Commissioner-General of Immigration, October 29, 1906, File 13928, Chinese General Correspondence, Records of the U.S. Immigration and Naturalization Service, RG 85, National Archives, Washington, D.C. (hereafter cited as Chinese General Correspondence, National Archives).

21. Harold Bolce, Chinese Inspector, to Secretary of Commerce and Labor, May 29, 1905, File 53059/8, typescript, 44–46, INS Subject Correspondence, National Archives.

22. The occupations of the remaining 5 percent of workers are unknown. Sucheng Chan, "The Economic Life of the Chinese in California, 1850–1920," in *Early Chinese Immigrant Societies: Case Studies from North America and British Southeast Asia*, ed. Lee Tai To (Singapore: Heinemann Asia, 1988), 112. On the urban-rural composition of Chinese, see Ronald Takaki, *Strangers from a Different Shore: A History of Asian Americans* (Boston: Little, Brown, and Company, 1989), 239.

23. Interview with Mr. K. Chin and Mr. Low by author, November 16, 1995.

24. Paul C. Siu, ed. by John Kuo Wei Tchen, *The Chinese Laundryman: A Study in Social Isolation* (New York: New York University Press, 1987), 85.

25. File 26002/1–9, Chinese Arrival Files, San Francisco; Interview with Mary Lee by author, February 20, 1990.

26. Judy Yung, "Law Shee Low, Model Wife and Mother," in *Unbound Voices: A Documentary History of Chinese Women in San Francisco*, ed. Judy Yung (Berkeley and Los Angeles: University of California Press, 1999), 213–14.

27. "Angel Island Immigration Station: Interviews with Chris Chow, Mr. Yuen, Ira and Ed Lee," Bancroft Library, University of California, Berkeley, transcript, 29–30.

28. See Chapter 2 by Madeline Hsu in this volume for a brief discussion of one of the institutional mechanisms that enabled illegal Chinese immigrants, especially "paper sons," to enter the country.

29. U.S. Immigration Bureau, *Annual Reports, 1890, 1897–1905, 1913–1932*; U.S. Immigration and Naturalization Bureau, *Annual Reports, 1906–1912*, as cited in H. Chen, "Chinese Immigration," 206; Wen-hsien Chen, "Chinese Under Both Exclusion and Immigration Laws" (Ph.D. dissertation, University of Chicago, 1940), 206.

30. Yuen Tim Gong, translated by Marlon K. Hom, "A Gold Mountain Man's Memoir," *Chinese America: History and Perspectives* (1992), 211–37.

31. Siu, *The Chinese Laundryman*, 107.

32. See table entitled "Chinese Admitted by Class, 1894–1940," in Erika Lee, *At America's Gates: Chinese Immigration During the Exclusion Era, 1882–1943* (Chapel Hill: University of North Carolina Press, 2003), 101–102.

33. Data compiled by author and derived from a random sample survey of the immigration records of Chinese individuals who entered the United States through the port of San Francisco (1884–1941). Details of returns after visits to China can be found in the applicants' reentry and other processing documents. Chinese Arrival Files, San Francisco.

34. Arthur Lem to author, January 13, 1996.

35. Interview with Kaimon Chin by author, November 13, 1996.

36. As sociologist Evelyn Nakano Glenn explained, "many families adopted a strategy of long-term sojourning. Successive generations of men emigrated . . . to ensure loyalty to kin, young men were married off before leaving. Once in America, they were expected to send money to support not only wives and children but also parents, brothers, and other relatives." Evelyn Nakano Glenn, "Split Household, Small Producer and Dual Wage Earner: An Analysis of Chinese American Family Strategies," *Journal of Marriage and the Family* 45, no. 1 (1983): 38.

37. Nee and Nee, *Longtime Californ'*, 17.

38. Lee, *At America's Gates*, 92–96.

39. See table entitled, "Chinese Admitted by Sex, 1870–1960," in Lee, *At America's Gates*, 117–19.

40. Sucheng Chan, "The Exclusion of Chinese Women, 1875–1943," in *Entry Denied: Exclusion and the Chinese Community in America, 1882–1943*, ed. Sucheng Chan (Philadelphia: Temple University Press, 1991), 95, 97; Yung, *Unbound Feet*, 55–63.

41. U.S. government statistics for Chinese immigrant admissions are highly inconsistent. When categorized by sex, the U.S. Bureau of Immigration recorded 127,012 total Chinese immigrants (of whom 9,868 were women) admitted from 1882 to 1943. These figures do not include citizens returning to the United States.

When categorized by immigration status, the total number of Chinese admitted for the same period is recorded as 422,908, including Chinese in transit through the United States as well as U.S. citizens of Chinese descent. From 1910 to 1924, when the number of Chinese immigrants was broken down by both sex and immigration status, Chinese immigrant women were on average 9.4 percent of the total pool. Based on these calculations, the actual number of Chinese women (immigrants, U.S. citizens, and those in transit) who entered during the exclusion era was probably closer to forty thousand. See tables entitled "Immigrants Admitted" and "Summary of Chinese Seeking Admission to the U.S." in U.S. Bureau of Immigration, U.S. Department of Commerce, *Annual Reports of the Commissioner-General of Immigration, 1890, 1897–1932* (Washington, D.C.: Government Printing Office, 1890, 1897–1932) H. Chen, "Chinese Immigration," 181, 201, 206.

42. See table entitled, "Chinese Admitted by Sex, 1870–1960," in Lee, *At America's Gates*, 117–19.

43. This dependent status both mirrored and strengthened prevailing ideas about American gender roles and ideology in U.S. immigration laws in general. Immigrant women of all backgrounds were subject to the "likely to become a public charge" clause, and independent female immigrants were considered morally suspect. Donna Gabaccia, *From the Other Side: Women, Gender, and Immigration Life in the United States, 1820–1990* (Bloomington: Indiana University Press, 1994), 26.

44. File 10193, Chinese Arrival Files, Seattle, Washington, Records of the U.S. INS, RG 85, National Archives, Northwest Region, Seattle, Washington; Interview with Gladys Huie by author, September 9, 1993.

45. U.S. Bureau of Immigration, *Annual Report, 1910* and *1924* (Washington, D.C.: Government Printing Office, 1910 and 1924). One of the reasons for this range is the government's increased crackdown on illegal immigration, which was perpetuated mostly by males. See Lee, *At America's Gates*, 206.

46. Charles McClain, Jr., *In Search of Equality: The Chinese Struggle Against Discrimination in Nineteenth-Century America* (Berkeley and Los Angeles: University of California Press, 1994), 156–57, 93; Chan, "The Exclusion of Chinese Women."

47. Lucy Salyer, *Laws Harsh as Tigers: Chinese Immigrants and the Shaping of Modern Immigration Law* (Chapel Hill: University of North Carolina Press, 1995), 81–83.

48. *Fong Yue Ting* v. *United States*, 149 U.S. 698, 713 (1893); Salyer, *Laws Harsh as Tigers*, 47–58.

49. For Chinese diplomats and members of the elite, see K. Scott Wong, "Cultural Defenders and Brokers: Chinese Responses to the Anti-Chinese Movement," in *Claiming America: Constructing Chinese American Identities During the Exclusion Era*, ed. K. Scott Wong and Sucheng Chan (Philadelphia: Temple University Press, 1998), 8.

50. *San Francisco Morning Call*, September 14, 1892, 8.

51. Oscar Greenhalgh to Walter S. Chance, Mar. 16, 1899, File 52730/84, INS Subject Correspondence, National Archives.

52. Interview with Mr. Woo Gen, Jul. 24, 1924, Document 183, Survey of Race Relations: A Canadian-American Study of the Oriental on the Pacific Coast,

Hoover Institution on War, Revolution, and Peace, Stanford University [emphasis added].

53. See Files 52363/14, 52961/26-B, and 53620/115-C, INS Subject Correspondence, National Archives.

54. Wu Ting-fang to John Hay, Dec. 26, 1900, Notes from the Chinese Legation in the U.S. to the Department of State, Notes from Foreign Consuls, RG 59, National Archives, Washington, D.C.

55. See Files 54152/75, 55597/912, 54152/75, and 52961/24-B, INS Subject Correspondence, National Archives.

56. *Ju Toy* v. *United States,* 109 U.S. 253 (1905); Salyer, *Laws Harsh as Tigers,* 94–116.

57. Salyer, *Laws Harsh as Tigers,* 97–101, 139; Y. Chen, *Chinese San Francisco,* 148–61; Tsai, *The Chinese Experience,* 77–79.

58. From 1910 to 1940, an estimated 175,000 Chinese immigrants were processed and detained in the station's barracks. Designed to exclude, rather than admit, immigrants, Angel Island has been described by historian Him Mark Lai as representing a "half-open door [to America] at best." Him Mark Lai, " Island of Immortals: Chinese Immigrants and the Angel Island Immigration Station," *California History* 57, no. 1 (Spring 1978): 100. On Chinese immigrants' characterization of Angel Island as a prison, see Yung, "Law Shee Low," 216; Him Mark Lai, Genny Lim, and Judy Yung, *Island: Poetry and History of Chinese Immigrants on Angel Island* (Seattle: University of Washington Press, 1980), 66, 73, 75. For more on Angel Island, see Lee, *At America's Gates*; Nayan Shah, *Contagious Divides: Epidemics and Race in San Francisco's Chinatown* (Berkeley and Los Angeles: University of California Press, 2001); and Salyer, *Laws Harsh as Tigers.*

59. U.S. Department of Commerce and Labor, *Annual Report of the Commissioner-General of Immigration, 1910* (Washington, D.C.: Government Printing Office, 1910), 126.

60. Lee, *At America's Gates,* 124–29.

61. See various letters, Box 4, Customs Case File No. 3358d Related to Chinese Immigration, 1877–1891, Records of the U.S. Immigration and Naturalization Service, RG 85, National Archives, Washington, D.C. (hereafter cited as Customs Case File, National Archives).

62. Arthur Lem to author, Jan. 13, 1996.

63. All data compiled by author and derived from a random sample survey of 608 immigration records of Chinese individuals who entered the United States through the port of San Francisco, 1884–1941. Chinese Arrival Files, San Francisco.

64. Wong Gong Kim to Wong Teung Kim, June 18, 1917, Densmore Investigation Files, San Francisco.

65. Lee Young Sing to Lee Wooey Hong, Oct. 4, 1916, Densmore Investigation Files, San Francisco.

66. See testimony of Fong Tim, December 1, 1899, File 34240/8-19, Chinese Arrival Files. The district of "Ying Ping" referred to in Fong Tim's file was very likely a mistransliteration of Yanping [Enping].

67. See testimony of Wong Hong and Chew Dong Ngin, December 8, 1899, File 34240/8-19, Chinese Arrival Files, San Francisco.

68. Wong Ngum Yin to cousins of Yuen Wo, July 1906, in Inspector to CGI, Oct. 29, 1906, File 13928, Chinese General Correspondence, National Archives.

69. Siu, *The Chinese Laundryman*, 108.

70. W. Chen, "Chinese Under Both Exclusion and Immigration Laws," 402.

71. George Pippy to Treasury Secretary, July 24, 1899, File 624, Box 8, Chinese General Correspondence.

72. File 26002/1-9, Chinese Arrival Files, San Francisco; interview with Wallace Lee by author, February 20, 1990.

73. File 5-12-84/SS Oceanic, Chinese Arrival Files, San Francisco.

74. File 4098, Oct. 15, 1901, Chinese General Correspondence.

75. See letters from 1889 to 1891 to the Secretary of State and the Treasury Secretary, Customs Case File, National Archives.

76. File 9267/11, Chinese Arrival Files, San Francisco.

77. McConnell Jenkins to James Blaine, Jan. 3, 1890, Customs Case File (no file number), National Archives [emphasis added].

78. Acting Treasury Secretary to John H. Wise, Sept. 7, 1895, General Correspondence to the Office of the Collector, 1894–1928, Port of San Francisco, Records of the U.S. Bureau of Customs, RG 36, National Archives, Pacific-Sierra Region, San Bruno, California.

79. Frank B. Lenz to Charles Mehan, Jan. 25, 1915, File 14071/11-20, Chinese Arrival Files, San Francisco.

80. Ng Poon Chew to Samuel W. Backus, Jan. 26, 1915, File 14071/11-20, Chinese Arrival Files, San Francisco.

81. Peggy Pascoe, *Relations of Rescue: The Search for Moral Authority in the American West, 1874–1939* (New York: Oxford University Press, 1990), 78–78, 104, 106, 118, 167.

82. Yung, *Unbound Feet*, 66; Pascoe, *Relations of Rescue*, 96–98, 186–87.

83. Donaldina Cameron to Commissioner of Immigration, Jan. 26, 1916, File 14894/2-2, Chinese Arrival Files, San Francisco.

84. On legal challenges to the exclusion policy, see McClain, *In Search of Equality*. On Chinese use of the federal district courts in individual immigration cases, see Salyer, *Laws Harsh as Tigers*.

85. John Wise to Charles H. Page, n.d., 1895, General Correspondence from the Office of the Collector of Customs, 1869–1931, Port of San Francisco, Records of the U.S. Bureau of Customs, RG 36, National Archives, Pacific-Sierra Region, San Bruno, California.

86. Oscar Greenhalgh to Walter S. Chance, Mar. 11, 1899, File 52730/84, INS Subject Correspondence, National Archives.

87. W. Chen, "Chinese Under Both Exclusion and Immigration Laws," 428–29, 6.

88. All data compiled by author and derived from a random sample survey of 608 immigration records of Chinese individuals who entered the United States through the port of San Francisco, 1884–1941, Chinese Arrival Files, San Francisco.

89. Attorneys could examine only some of the evidence on which the inspector had based his decision to exclude, cited in Salyer, *Laws Harsh as Tigers*, 149.

90. See, for example, George McGowan in File 16288/14-15, Chinese Arrival Files, San Francisco.

91. John D. Nagle, "Comment on Proposed Chinese General Order No. 11," August, 1927, File 55597/912, INS Subject Correspondence.

92. McClain, *In Search of Equality*, 93, 336 n.43, 345–46 n.18.

93. Fong Wing to Samuel Backus, May 6, 1915, File 14315/4-8, Chinese Arrival Files, San Francisco.

94. O. L. Spaulding to Daniel Manning, November 2, 1885, Customs Case File (no file number), National Archives.

95. File 18703/13-5, Chinese Arrival Files, San Francisco.

96. See table entitled, "Admission Rates of Chinese Women and Men, 1910–1924," in Lee, *At America's Gates*, 142.

97. See table entitled, "Non-Chinese Immigrants and Non-Immigrant Aliens Debarred Under General Immigration Laws, 1908–1932," in Lee, *At America's Gates*, 144.

CHAPTER TWO

1. Thomas W. Chinn, Him Mark Lai, and Philip P. Choy, *A History of the Chinese in California: A Syllabus* (San Francisco: Chinese Historical Society of America, 1969), 18.

2. In 1907, an average of 1,390 large and small vessels with a combined tonnage of 98,707 entered or departed from Hong Kong harbor. This figure does not include large numbers of lighters, cargo boats, passenger boats, water boats, and fishing crafts of all kinds. According to Jung-fang Tsai, "This record exceeded that of any port in the world at that time." *Hong Kong in Chinese History: Community and Social Unrest in the British Colony, 1842–1913* (New York: Columbia University Press, 1993), 35.

3. C. P. Lo, *Hong Kong* (London: Bedhaven Press, 1992), 9.

4. Tsai, *Hong Kong in Chinese History*, 26.

5. K. C. Fok, *Lectures on Hong Kong History* (Hong Kong: Commercial Press, 1990), 100.

6. Lo, *Hong Kong*, 10–11. The opium trade did not end until 1909 when the British government adopted a policy to stop the use of opium in the United Kingdom, but the use of opium was not forbidden in Hong Kong until 1940.

7. Tsai, *Hong Kong in Chinese History*, 26.

8. G. William Skinner, *Chinese Society in Thailand: An Analytical History* (Ithaca, N.Y.: Cornell University Press, 1957), 43.

9. Tsai, *Hong Kong in Chinese History*, 24.

10. Chinn et al., *A History of the Chinese*, 18. Over the same period, records indicate that 24,041 Chinese returned to China from the United States.

11. Charles Denby, *China and Her People* (Boston: L. C. Page and Company, 1906), 2:110.

12. The earliest ships of this line were paddle steamers, which were replaced by steamships with screw propellers "as the demands of the traffic required." In 1902,

the Pacific Mail Steamship Company built new steam liners with 18,000 horse-power and a displacement of 18,000 tons. In 1903–04, the company purchased even larger ships, the *Mongolia* and the *Manchuria*, each with a displacement of 27,000 tons. Arnold Wright and H. A. Cartwright, *Twentieth-Century Impressions of Hongkong, Shanghai, and Other Treaty Ports of China: Their History, People, Commerce, Industries, and Resources* (London: Lloyd's Greater Britain Publishing, 1908), 203.

13. Robert Lee, "The Origins of Chinese Immigration to the United States, 1848–1882" in *The Life, Influence and the Role of the Chinese in the United States, 1776–1960*, ed. Chinese Historical Society of America (San Francisco: Chinese Historical Society of America, 1976), 188–89. Lee is citing advertisements that appeared in the *China Mail*, May 30, 1853, and the *California China Mail and Flying Dragon*, March 1, 1867.

14. Fok, *Lectures*, 104.

15. Tsai, *Hong Kong in Chinese History*, 25.

16. Tsai, *Hong Kong in Chinese History*, 25–26.

17. Tsai, *Hong Kong in Chinese History*, 26. Exports from the United States included flour, dried fish, and other commodities.

18. The advertisements of a gold shop and money shop dealing in remittances claimed to have started this line of business in the 1850s and 1860s: Shengyuan Yinhao, with branches in Taicheng and Hong Kong, claimed in a 1916 advertisement to have been in business for over sixty years, *Xinning Magazine* (1916 #9); Changsheng Goldshop in Hong Kong posted an advertisement in 1934 that also claimed to have been in the business of receiving letters and exchanging currency for over sixty years, *XNZZ* (1934 #25), second page of announcements section. (*Xinning Magazine* will be cited hereafter as *XNZZ*.)

19. "The Nam Pak Hong (Nanbeihang) Commercial Association of Hong Kong," *Journal of the Hong Kong Branch of the Royal Asiatic Society* 19 (1979): 218.

20. Fok, *Lectures*, 104.

21. Liu Zuoren claims that jinshanzhuang started between 1881 and 1890, but *Xinning Magazine* advertisements for such businesses date them back to the 1850s. See Liu Zuoren, "Jinshanzhuang de yanjiu" [Research on jinshanzhuang], *China Economist* 101 (Feb. 10, 1959): 21. In 1916, Shengyuan Yinhao, with branches in Taicheng and Hong Kong (the latter located at 109 Yong Le Street under the management of Liu Kongan), claimed a history of over sixty years, which would date jinshanzhuang remittance services back to the early 1850s. *XNZZ* (1916 #9), announcements in the back section. Changsheng Goldshop in Hong Kong, located at 52 Wing Lock Street, advertised itself as having been in operation as a receiving company for remittances for over sixty years (dating its service back to the 1870s). During that time it also offered the services of currency exchange, savings accounts, and security boxes. *XNZZ* (1934 #25), second page of the announcements section. Liu's article contains other inaccuracies. He describes the largest Chinese American import-export business as having forty-eight branches in the 1950s and operating under the name Zhongxing Company. The only business chain of this magnitude was the National Dollar Stores, founded and operated by Joe Shoong. However, the National Dollar Stores sold

primarily products manufactured in the United States, and not products imported from Hong Kong or China. See Liu, "Jinshanzhuang," 21. According to Elizabeth Sinn, who researched the history of Tung Wah Hospital, "California traders" were represented on its prestigious charitable board as early as 1869. Elizabeth Sinn, *Power and Charity: The Early History of the Tung Wah Hospital, Hong Kong* (Hong Kong: Oxford University Press, 1989), 273.

22. Tsai, *Hong Kong in Chinese History*, 26.

23. *Anglo-Chinese Directory of Hong Kong* (Hong Kong: Publicity Bureau for South China, 1922), 90–94. On pages 94–99, the directory also lists three firms doing business with Peru; three with Havana; eight with Japan; twenty with the Philippines; twenty-six with Tonkin, Annam, and Cochinchina (composing present-day Vietnam); ten with the Straits Settlements (exact locations not speci-fied); twenty-six with Singapore; ten with Penang; thirteen with Java, Surabaya, and Sandakan (in present-day Indonesia); two with India; and one with Spain. *The Chinese Commercial Directory* (Hong Kong: Chinese Commercial Directory Company, 1930), 392–433, lists forty-six businesses serving Singapore, six do-ing business between Singapore and Annam, another six between Singapore and Shantou, six in Penang, eleven in Java (Indonesia), fifteen in Japan, twenty-three in Manila, twenty-one in Annam, sixteen in the Straits Settlements, fifteen in Bangkok, two in Holland, four in Havana, and three in Calcutta (pp. 339–446).

24. These foodstuffs were preserved and prepared for shipping by companies like Zhangguang Yuan [Cheung Kwong Yuen], founded by Pun Wan Nam (Pan Wannan) in 1887. By 1917, Zhangguang Yuan was "one of the most important canning export houses of south China." Tsai, *Hong Kong in Chinese History*, 30–31. Also see W. Feldwick, ed., *Present Day Impressions of the Far East and Prominent and Progressive Chinese at Home and Abroad: The History, People, Commerce, Industries, and Resources of China, Hong Kong, Indo China, Malaya, and Netherlands India* (London: Globe Encyclopedia, 1917), 588; Wright and Cartwright, *Twentieth-Century Impressions*, 248; and Zheng Zican, *Xianggang Zhonghua shangye jiaotong renmin zhinanlu* [The Anglo-Chinese commercial directory of Hong Kong, 1915], 491.

25. Feldwick, *Present Day Impressions*, 558.

26. Tsai, *Hong Kong in Chinese History*, 26–27.

27. Southern California Chinese American Oral History Project (Los Angeles: UCLA Asian American Studies Center and the Chinese Historical So-ciety of Southern California, 1982), 19:15 (hereafter cited as SCCAOHP).

28. *XNZZ* (1919 #15) and (1927 #27).

29. See Bancroft Library Collections, Chinese Business Records, Placer County, California, 1884–1915, C–G 53–54.

30. Wright and Cartwright, *Twentieth-Century Impressions*, 133, 285–86. China complied with foreign pressures in 1896 and established a postal service modeled on western lines. Before that year, indigenous postal services consisted of the Imperial Government Courier Service and "native posting agencies," which adequately served the needs of Chinese within the country. Of the two, Wright and Cartwright considered the latter "[f]ar more obstructive to rapid progress.... These, also, have had a long life, but, unlike [the Imperial Government

Courier Service], they are wholly independent.... Their innumerable ramifications—fast couriers, or rapid 'post-boats,' as the style of country decides—extend to all connections which, with their slow ways, have for centuries answered the requirements of busy and thrifty communities." Wright and Cartwright worried in particular about a class of businesses that included jinshanzhuang. "These posting agencies are essentially shop associations, for the most part engaged also in other trades. The transmission of parcels, bank drafts, and sycee [cash] is the most lucrative part of their postal operations." The Imperial Postal Service that came into existence in 1896 wisely decided to supervise rather than displace the existing systems.

31. During the last half of the nineteenth century, the Qing rulers legalized the use of foreign silver coins. So, Mexican silver dollars came into common usage and would remain popular through the 1930s. Cantonese resisted Qing attempts to issue paper currency near the end of the Guangxu reign (1875–1907) even though they themselves did so after 1911 when the Republican government in Beijing issued new currency though the Communications Bank. In Guangdong, however, people clung to the two-tiered system of silver and copper coins—the currency in use in Taishan County. By the 1920s and 1930s, it was not uncommon for people to have U.S. dollars as well as Hong Kong bills lying around the house. Li Yiji, *Haiyan xiangtushi* [Local history of Haiyan] (Hong Kong: Yongde Yinwu, 1960), 37.

32. See Liu, "Jinshanzhuang," 21 and Lin Jinjia et al., "Jindai Guangdong qiaohui yanjiu" [Research into modern overseas Chinese remittances], *Dongnan Ya xuekan* [Southeast Asian Studies Magazine] 4 (1992), 48.

33. An example of business connections based on kinship or acquaintanceship can be found in the firm of Lisheng He in Hong Kong. In 1919, the new proprietor, Tan Wenbing, notified customers that with the death of his older cousin, Tan Wenyue, he would be taking over as manager but that the business would continue as before. He pointed out that Tan Wenyue's son, Ziju, would be going to Hong Kong to help out. Tan asked his customers, addressed as "each brother, kinsmen, and friend" who had accounts to write and explain their accounts. *XNZZ* (1919 #15), announcements section.

34. The Chens of Wah Ying Cheong were members of the Liangxing branch of the Chen clan living in Damei village. A minority of partners were relatives from the Zeng clan of nearby Shangge village. The Chen and Zeng clans worked well together. Interview with village elders of Damei village by author, July 31, 1995.

35. Wah Ying Cheong account books (Hong Kong: University of Hong Kong, Special Collections, unpublished materials, 1899–1937), accounts of transactions within China (1919).

36. *XNZZ* (1917 #25), announcements section and (1919 #15), announcements section.

37. *XNZZ* (1935 #27), 71–72.

38. Liu, "Jinshanzhuang," 22.

39. For example, the firm of Cheng Chang, based in Seattle, sent nineteen such packets to Wah Ying Cheong in 1919. The number of individual remittances

enclosed ranged from two to twenty. The large mailings occurred right before Chinese New Year. Wah Ying Cheong account books (1919), record of individual accounts.

40. By the twentieth century, jinshanzhuang ran something along the following lines. The largest jinshanzhuang employed as many as ten people but most had only four or five. Most were partnerships, not stock companies. Staff included a manager (*sili*), an accountant, and three or four service people. Liu, "Jinshanzhuang," 21.

41. *XNZZ* (1935 #6), 64–65.

42. *XNZZ* (1932 #24), front-page advertisements. One *li* was equal to one one-thousandth of a *tael*.

43. Wah Ying Cheong account books (1919), transactions with the interior. The yuan used throughout the account of Chen Kongzhao probably refers to Hong Kong dollars.

44. Wah Ying Cheong account books (1905, 1915, 1925, 1929, 1935), record of individual accounts.

45. Liu, "Jinshanzhuang," 22, and author's interview with Jiang Yongkang, 14 May 1994. Jiang started running a jinshanzhuang after World War II.

46. This practice was known as *zhengpi huigang*.

47. Estimates actually range on the higher side of 90 percent but because there are no actual statistics, it is possible only to cite guesses. Bureau of Immigration, *Annual Report 1909* (Washington, D.C.: Government Printing Office, 1909), 129. Commissioner North of San Francisco complained of this situation: "Thousands of Chinese persons have been declared by the courts and other appropriate authorities to be natives of the United States during the past fifteen years. Of this number I verily believe nearly 90 percent are fraud; but their cases have been adjudicated, and there is no gainsaying their present citizenship." SCCAOHP, 126:2 (95 percent); 45:9 (estimated 10 out of 11); 12:12–15 (estimated 90 percent).

48. See table 6 in Madeline Y. Hsu, *Dreaming of Gold, Dreaming of Home: Transnationalism and Migration Between the United States and South China, 1882–1943* (Stanford, Calif.: Stanford University Press, 2000), 76–77.

49. Jiang Yongkang, interview by author, May 13, 1994.

50. *XNZZ* 4 (1912). Liu also offered to inspect old immigration papers [*jiuzhi*] and tell people whether they were still valid (possibly with an eye to selling the proof of identity to somebody else wishing to go to the United States).

51. Liu, "Jinshanzhuang," 21.

52. Genny Lim, Judy Yung, and Him Mark Lai, "Interviews with Detainees at Angel Island Project" (San Francisco: History of Chinese Detained on the Island [HOC DOI] Project, Asian American Studies Library, University of California, Berkeley, 1976). See interview with Jeong Foo Louie conducted on Aug. 29, 1976.

53. *Taishan xian huaqiao zhi* [Gazetteer of Overseas Chinese from Taishan County] (Taishan: Taishan Xian Qiaowu Ban'gongshi [Taishan County Overseas Chinese Affairs Office], 1992), 341. The rest of its business consisted of dealing in medicines, dried seafood, dry goods, currency exchange, and acting as a posting agency.

54. Lin et al., "Jindai Guangdong," 54. After World War II, the two banks began working together. The occupation of Hong Kong by the Japanese during the war completely disrupted the activities of jinshanzhuang. This lapse enabled the two banks to win a larger share of the remittance business. In 1927, the Guangdong Postal Service had entered the fray by working with banks and money shops to establish the range of foreign and local services needed to handle remittances from beginning to end. In 1937 alone, the postal service handled 777,700 CNC dollars. See note 50.

55. Liu, "Jinshanzhuang," 21.

56. Yao Zengying, *Guangdong sheng de huaqiao huikuan* [Overseas Chinese remittances of Guangdong Province] (Shanghai: Commercial Press for the Academia Sinica, 1943), 42.

CHAPTER THREE

1. Lucie Cheng Hirata, "Free, Indentured, Enslaved: Chinese Prostitutes in Nineteenth-Century America," *Signs: Journal of Women in Culture and Society 5*, no. 1 (1979): 3–29, and Benson Tong, *Unsubmissive Women: Chinese Prostitutes in Nineteenth-Century San Francisco* (Norman: University of Oklahoma Press, 1994) focus entirely on prostitutes. Studies that discuss, but do not deal exclusively with, prostitution include Peggy Pascoe, *Relations of Rescue: The Search for Female Moral Authority in the American West, 1874–1939* (New York: Oxford University Press, 1990); Sucheng Chan, "The Exclusion of Chinese Women, 1870–1943," in *Entry Denied: Exclusion and the Chinese Community in America, 1882–1943*, ed. Sucheng Chan (Philadelphia: Temple University Press, 1991), 94–164; Judy Yung, *Unbound Feet: A Social History of Chinese Women in San Francisco* (Berkeley and Los Angeles: University of California Press, 1995); George A. Peffer, *If They Do Not Bring Their Women Here: Chinese Female Immigration Before Exclusion* (Urbana: University of Illinois Press, 1999); and Yong Chen, *Chinese San Francisco, 1850–1943: A Trans-Pacific Community* (Stanford, Calif.: Stanford University Press, 2000).

Studies that examine other aspects of the experiences of Chinese women in America, listed in chronological order by year of publication, include Judy Yung, "'A Bowlful of Tears': Chinese Women Immigrants on Angel Island," *Frontiers* 2, no. 2 (1977): 52–55; Lucie Cheng Hirata, "Chinese Immigrant Women in Nineteenth-Century California," in *Women of America: A History*, ed. Carol Ruth Berkin and Mary Beth Norton (Boston: Houghton Mifflin, 1979), 224–44; Vincent Tang, "Chinese Women Immigrants and the Two-Edged Sword of Habeas Corpus," in *The Chinese American Experience*, ed. Genny Lim (San Francisco: Chinese Historical Society of America and Chinese Cultural Foundation, 1984), 48–56; Asian American Studies Center, University of California, Los Angeles, and Chinese Historical Society of Southern California, eds., *Linking Our Lives: Chinese American Women of Los Angeles* (Los Angeles: Chinese Historical Society of Southern California, 1984); George A. Peffer, "Forbidden Families: Emigration Experiences of Chinese Women Under the Page Law, 1875–1882," *Journal of American Ethnic History* 6, no. 1 (1986): 28–47; David Beesley, "From Chinese

to Chinese American: Chinese Women and Families in a Sierra Nevada Town,"
California History (September 1988): 168–79, 206–7; Peggy Pascoe, "Gender Systems in Conflict: The Marriages of Mission-Educated Chinese American Women,
1874–1939," *Journal of Social History* 22, no. 4 (1989): 631–52; George A.
Peffer, "From Under the Sojourner's Shadow: A Historiographical Study of Chinese Female Immigration to America, 1852–1882," *Journal of American Ethnic History*
11, no. 3 (1992): 41–67; Huping Ling, "Chinese Merchants' Wives in the United
States, 1840–1945," in *Origins and Destinations: 41 Essays on Chinese America*,
ed. Chinese Historical Society of Southern California and Asian American Studies
Center, University of California, Los Angeles (Los Angeles: Chinese Historical Society of Southern California and Asian American Studies Center, University of California, Los Angeles, 1994), 79–92; Weili Ye, " '*Nu Liuxuesheng*':
The Story of American-Educated Chinese Women, 1880s–1920s," *Modern China*
20, no. 3 (1994): 315–46; Huping Ling, "A History of Chinese Female Students
in the United States, 1880s–1990s," *Journal of American Ethnic History* 16, no.
3 (1997): 81–109; Hua Liang, "Fighting for a New Life: Social and Patriotic
Activism of Chinese American Women in New York City, 1900 to 1945," *Journal of American Ethnic History* 17, no. 2 (1998): 22–38; Huping Ling, *Surviving on the Gold Mountain: A History of Chinese American Women and Their
Lives* (Albany: State University of New York Press, 1998); Huping Ling, "Family
and Marriage of Late-Nineteenth and Early-Twentieth Century Chinese Immi-
grant Women," *Journal of American Ethnic History* 19, no. 2 (2000): 43–63;
Yong Chen, "Remembering Ah Quin: A Century of Social Memory in a Chinese
American Family," *Oral History Review* 27, no. 1 (2000): 57–80; Xiaolan Bao,
*Holding Up More Than Half the Sky: Chinese Women Garment Workers in New
York City, 1948–1992* (Urbana: University of Illinois Press, 2001); Xiaojian Zhao,
Remaking Chinese America: Immigration, Family, and Community, 1940–1965
(New Brunswick, N.J.: Rutgers University Press, 2002); Xiaolan Bao, "Politi-
cizing Motherhood: Chinese Garment Workers' Campaign for Daycare Centers
in New York City, 1977–1982," in *Asian/Pacific Islander Women: A Histori-
cal Anthology*, ed. Shirley Hune and Gail M. Nomura (New York: New York
University Press, 2003), 286–300; Xiaolan Bao, "Revisiting New York's China-
town, 1900–1930," in *Remapping Asian American History*, ed. Sucheng Chan
(Walnut Creek, Calif.: AltaMira Press, 2003), 31–48; Erika Lee, "Exclusion Acts:
Chinese Women During the Chinese Exclusion Era, 1882–1943," in *Asian/Pacific
Islander American Women: A Historical Anthology*, ed. Shirley Hune and Gail
M. Nomura (New York: New York University Press, 2003), 77–89; George A.
Peffer, "Forgotten Families: The Development of the Chinese American Commu-
nity in San Francisco, 1860–1880," in *Remapping Asian American History*, ed.
Sucheng Chan (Walnut Creek, Calif.: AltaMira Press, 2003), 49–67; and Judy
Yung, " 'A Bowlful of Tears': Lee Puey You's Immigration Experience at Angel
Island," in *Asian/Pacific Islander Women: A Historical Anthology*, ed. Shirley
Hune and Gail M. Nomura (New York: New York University Press, 2003),
123–37.
    2. A vast majority of the "widowed or divorced" Chinese men and women
were widowed and not divorced. However, since census takers did write down

"divorced" in the marital status column for a small number of them, I combine the two categories in the tables.

3. Even though transnationalism is a trendy concept, scholars have recognized, either implicitly or explicitly, the transnational nature of Chinese families in the United States since the 1930s: Norman S. Hayner and Charles N. Reynolds, "Chinese Family Life in America," *American Sociological Review* 2, no. 5 (1937): 630–37; Peter S. Li, "Fictive Kinship, Conjugal Ties and Kinship Chain Among Chinese Immigrants in the United States," *Journal of Comparative Family Studies* 8, no. 1 (1977): 47–63; Evelyn Nakano Glenn, "Split Household, Small Producer and Dual Wage Earner: An Analysis of Chinese-American Family Strategies," *Journal of Marriage and the Family* (February 1983): 35–46; Haiming Liu, "The Trans-Pacific Family: A Case Study of Sam Chang's Family History," *Amerasia Journal* 18, no. 2 (1992): 1–34; Adam McKeown, "Transnational Chinese Families and Chinese Exclusion, 1875–1943," *Journal of American Ethnic Studies* 18, no. 2 (1999): 73–110; Madeline Y. Hsu, *Dreaming of Gold, Dreaming of Home: Transnationalism and Migration Between the United States and South China, 1882–1943* (Stanford, Calif.: Stanford University Press, 2000); and Erika Lee, *At America's Gates: Chinese Immigration During the Exclusion Era, 1882–1943* (Chapel Hill: University of North Carolina Press, 2003).

4. For an explanation of the discrepancies between the numbers in Tables 3.9A, 3.9B, 3.9C, 3.70A, 3.10B, and 3.10C and those in Tables 3.5A, 3.5B, 3.5C, 3.6A, 3.6B, and 3.6C, see Appendix C.

5. See Peffer, "Forgotten Families: The Development of the Chinese American Community."

6. Christian G. Fritz, "Due Process, Treaty Rights, and Chinese Exclusion, 1882–1943," in *Entry Denied: Exclusion and the Chinese Community in America, 1882–1943*, ed. Sucheng Chan (Philadelphia: Temple University Press, 1991), 25–56; and Lucy E. Salyer, *Laws Harsh as Tigers: Chinese Immigrants and the Shaping of Modern Immigration Law* (Chapel Hill: University of North Carolina Press, 1995).

CHAPTER THREE, APPENDIX B

1. Sucheng Chan, *This Bittersweet Soil: The Chinese in California Agriculture, 1860–1910* (Berkeley and Los Angeles: University of California Press, 1986).

CHAPTER FOUR

1. Thomas W. Chinn, H. Mark Lai, and Philip P. Choy, eds., *A History of the Chinese in California: A Syllabus* (San Francisco: Chinese Historical Society of America, 1969), 10.

2. Paul Buell and Christopher Muench, "Chinese Medical Recipes from Frontier Seattle," in *The Annals of the Chinese Historical Society of the Pacific Northwest* (1984), 101.

3. Charles Hillinger, *Hillinger's California: Stories from All 58 Counties* (Santa Barbara, Calif.: Capra Press, 1997), 25–26.

4. Liu Pei Chi [Liu Boji], *Meiguo huaqiao shi 1848–1911* [A history of the Chinese in the United States of America] (Taibei: *Xingzhangyuan Qiaowu Weiyuanhui*, 1976), 314. "Tang" refers to the Tang dynasty (618–907) while "Fan" means foreigners. Therefore, Tang Fan" refers to those physicians who treated Caucasians.

5. Chinn et al., eds., *A History of the Chinese*, 78.

6. A. W. Loomis, "Medical Art in the Chinese Quarter," *Overland Monthly* II (June 1869): 496.

7. Liu, *Meiguo huaqiao shi*, 343.

8. Item 1025 in Him Mark Lai, ed., *A History Reclaimed: An Annotated Bibliography of Chinese Language Materials on the Chinese of America* (Los Angeles: University of California, Los Angeles, Asian America Studies Center, 1986), 108.

9. Jacques Gernet, *Daily Life in China: On the Eve of the Mongol Invasion 1250–1276* (Stanford, Calif.: Stanford University Press, 1970), 172.

10. Charlott Furth, *A Flourishing Yin: Gender in China's Medical History, 960–1665* (Berkeley and Los Angeles: University of California Press, 1999), ch. 7.

11. Angela Ki Che Leung, "Medical Instruction and Popularization in Ming-Qing China," Late Imperial China 24, no. 1 (2003): 149.

12. Daniel Harrison Kulp, *Country Life in South China: The Sociology of Familism*, vol. 1, Phenix Village, Kwantung, China (1925; repr. Taibei: Cheng-wen, 1966), 60, 90–91.

13. Ralph C. Croizier, *Traditional Medicine in Modern China* (Cambridge, Mass.: Harvard University Press, 1968), 13, 19.

14. Croizier, *Traditional Medicine*, 34. Also see S. M. Hiller and J. A. Jewell, *Health Care and Traditional Medicine in China, 1800–1982* (London: Routledge and Kegan Paul, 1983); Richard Hyatt, *Chinese Herbal Medicine: Ancient Art and Modern Science* (New York: Schocken Books, 1978); and Paul D. Buell et al., *Chinese Medicine on the Golden Mountain: An Interpretive Guide* (Seattle, Wash.: Wing Luke Memorial Museum, 1984).

15. Li Jingwei and Li Zhizhong, *Zhongguo gudai yixue shi* [A history of medicine in ancient China] (Shijia zhuang, Hebei: Hebei kexue jishu chubanshe, 1990), ch. 10.

16. Yi-li Wu, "The Bamboo Grove Monastery and Popular Gynecology in Qing China," *Late Imperial China* 21, no.1 (2000): 41–76.

17. Buell and Muench, "Chinese Medical Recipes," 102.

18. John G. Kerr, *A Guide to the City and Suburbs of Canton* (Hong Kong: Kelly and Walsh, 1904).

19. Liu Shengyi and Song Dehua, *Lingnan jindai duiwai wenhua jiaoliu shi* [A history of modern Chinese and Western exchange in Lingnan] (Guangzhou: Guangdong renmin chubanshe, 1996), 71.

20. Liu and Song, *Lingnan*, 58, 247.

21. Liu and Song, *Lingnan*, 247–48.

22. "Zhong Mei yixuejie Jiujinshan jinian Meiguo Jiazhou shouwei huayi" [Pioneer Chinese doctor in California commemorated by the Chinese and American medical world in San Francisco], *Huasheng Bao* [Huasheng newspaper], Beijing, China, July 29, 2003.

23. Jonathan D. Spence, *Chinese Roundabout: Essays in History and Culture* (New York: Norton, 1992), 207, 211–14.

24. Henry S. Tsai, *The Chinese Experience of America* (Bloomington: Indiana University Press, 1986), 29.

25. Joan B. Trauner, "The Chinese as Medical Scapegoats in San Francisco, 1870–1905," *California History* 57, no. 1 (1978): 72.

26. Mary R. Coolidge, *Chinese Immigration* (1909; repr. New York: Arno Press), 415.

27. Coolidge, *Chinese Immigration*, 416.

28. For Chinese population percentage, see Chinn et al., *A History of the Chinese*, 22–23; and Sucheng Chan, *This Bittersweet Soil: The Chinese in California Agriculture, 1860–1910* (Berkeley and Los Angeles: University of California Press, 1986), 49. For hospital admission numbers, see Trauner, "The Chinese as Medical Scapegoats," 73, 82–83.

29. Trauner, "The Chinese as Medical Scapegoats," 82–83, 73.

30. Liu, *Meiguo huaqiao shi*, 84.

31. This section and some other parts of the chapter appeared earlier in Liu Haiming, "The Resilience of Ethnic Culture: Chinese Herbalists in the American Medical Profession," *Journal of Asian American Studies* 1, no. 2 (1998): 173–91.

32. Liu, *Meiguo huaqiao shi*, 314.

33. Stewart Culin, "Chinese Drug Stores in America," *American Journal of Pharmacy* (December 1887): 595.

34. William Tisdale, "Chinese Physicians in California," *Lippincott's Magazine* 63 (March 1899): 411–12.

35. Alexander McLeod, *Pigtails and Gold Dust: A Panorama of Chinese Life in Early Calfornia* (Caldwell, Idaho: Caxton Printers, 1947), 140–41.

36. Liu, *Meiguo huaqiao shi*, 415.

37. Raymond Lou, "The Chinese American Community of Los Angeles, 1870–1900: A Case of Resistance, Organization, and Participation" (Ph.D dissertation, University of California, Irvine, 1982), 44, 72.

38. Copies of such advertisements are in my possession.

39. Helen Zeese Papnikolas, *Toil and Rage in a New Land: The Greek Immigrants in Utah* (Salt Lake City: Utah Historical Society, 1974).

40. Tisdale, "Chinese Physicians," 412.

41. Arthur Chung interview, transcript, 1. The transcript is available at the Chinese Historical Society of Southern California (CHSSC).

42. Nellie Chung interview, tape 5, transcript, 9. The transcripts are available at CHSSC.

43. Rose Hum Lee, *The Chinese in the United States of America* (Hong Kong: Hong Kong University Press, 1960), 59.

44. Garding Lui, *Inside Los Angeles Chinatown* (no place: no publisher, 1948), 200.

45. Estelle Wong gave me copies of these calling cards.

46. Records of the Immigration and Naturalization Service—Los Angeles District Office: Segregated Chinese case files, no. 4935/6 [Cheung Tseng Gip], Box 108, Laguna Niguel branch of the National Archives and Records Administration.

47. Nellie Chung interview, tape 6, transcript, 3.

48. Louise Leong Larson, *Sweet Bamboo: A Saga of a Chinese American Family* (Los Angeles: Chinese Historical Society of Southern California, 1989), 21.

49. Jeffrey Barlow and Christine Richardson, *China Doctor of John Day* (Portland, Ore.: Bindord and Mort, 1979), 64–65.

50. William Mason, "The Chinese in Los Angeles," *Museum Alliance Quarterly* 6, no. 2 (1967): 16; and David Chan, "The Five Chinatowns of Los Angeles," *Bridge* 2 (1973): 41–45.

51. International Chinese Business Directory Co., *International Chinese Business Directory of the World for the Year 1913* (San Francisco: Author, 1913). See the section on Los Angeles.

52. Croizier, *Traditional Medicine*, 33.

53. Stanford Lyman, *The Asian in the West* (Las Vegas: University of Nevada System, 1970), 69.

54. Lui, *Inside Los Angeles Chinatown*, 201.

55. Tan Fuyuan, *The Science of Oriental Medicine: Diet and Hygiene* (Los Angeles: Foo and Wing Herb Co., 1897), 91.

56. Tom Leung, *Chinese Herbal Science* (Los Angeles: T. Leong Herb Co., 1928), 8.

57. Liu, *Meigui huaqiao shi*, 314; and Larson, *Sweet Bamboo*, 20.

58. Fong Wan, *Herb Lore* (Oakland, Calif.: Author, 1933), 177–78.

59. Haiming Liu, "The Trans-Pacific Family: A Case Study of Sam Changs Family History," *Amerasia Journal* 18, no. 2 (1992): 5–10.

60. Larson, *Sweet Bamboo*, 21.

61. Barlow and Richardson, *China Doctor*, 55–67.

62. McLeod, *Pigtails and Gold Dust*, 141.

63. Barlow and Richardson, *China Doctor*, 68.

64. William G. Rothstein, "The Botanical Movements," in *Other Healers: Unorthodox Medicine in America*, ed. Norman Gevitz (Baltimore: Johns Hopkins University Press, 1988), 32, 46.

65. Tan, *Science of Oriental Medicine*; Leong, *Chinese Herbal Science*; Fong Wan, *Herb Lore*; and Lui, *Inside Los Angeles Chinatown*.

66. Tan, *Science of Oriental Medicine*, 11.

67. Fong, *Herb Lore*, 15.

68. Buell and Muench, "Chinese Medical Recipes," 101.

69. Carey McWilliams, *Southern California: An Island on the Land* (Salt Lake City, Utah: Gibbs M. Smith, 1983), 258.

70. Barlow and Richardson, *China Doctor*, 1–2, 67.

71. Tan, *Science of Oriental Medicine*, 11.

72. Paul Chace has given me copies of these advertisements.

73. Fong, *Herb Lore*, 140.

74. Garding Lui, *Secrets of Chinese Physicians* (Los Angeles: B. N. Robertson, 1943), 104; and Fong, *Herb Lore*, 140.

75. Arthur Chung interview, tape 2, transcript, 12.

76. Nellie Chung interview, tape 5, transcript, 9.

77. Larson, *Sweet Bamboo*, 33, 135.

78. Barlow and Richardson, *China Doctor*, 65.

79. Records of the Immigration and Naturalization Service—Los Angeles District Office: Segregated Chinese case files, no. 4935/6.

80. Nellie Chung interview, tape 2, transcript, 1, 5.

81. Lucie Cheng et al., *Linking Our Lives: Chinese American Women of Los Angeles* (Los Angeles: Chinese Historical Society of Southern California, 1984), 84.

82. Larson, *Sweet Bamboo*, 167.

83. Fong, *Herb Lore*, 25.

84. Tan, *Science of Oriental Medicine*, 96.

85. Tisdale, "Chinese Physicians," 416.

86. Fong, *Herb Lore*, 35.

87. Fong, *Herb Lore*, 183.

88. Christopher Muench, "One Hundred Years of Medicine: The Ah-Fong Physicians of Idaho," in *Chinese Medicine on the Golden Mountain*, ed. Paul D. Buell et al., 70.

89. Larson, *Sweet Bamboo*, 72.

90. Larson, *Sweet Bamboo*, 72.

91. Arthur Chung interview, tape 2, transcript, 12.

92. Arthur Chung interview, tape 2, transcript, 12.

CHAPTER FIVE

1. Some had resided and worked in other places such as Cuba, Mexico, and Japan before coming to the United States.

2. Yong Chen, *Chinese San Francisco 1850–1943: A Trans-Pacific Community* (Stanford, Calif.: Stanford University Press, 2000), ch. 1.

3. Ping Chiu, *Chinese Labor in California, 1850–1880: An Economic Study* (Madison: Wisconsin Historical Society, 1967), 45, 72.

4. Gunther Barth, *Bitter Strength: A History of the Chinese in the US., 1850–1970* (Cambridge, Mass.: Harvard University Press, 1974), 196. According to Lucy M. Cohen, the approximately two thousand Chinese who went to work in the South were paid anywhere between twelve dollars (with board) to twenty dollars (without board) a month. See Lucy M. Cohen, *Chinese in the Post-Civil War South: A People Without a History* (Baton Rouge: Louisiana State University Press, 1984), 55, 85, 94.

5. June Mei, "Socioeconomic Origins of Emigration: Guangdong to California, 1850 to 1882," in *Labor Immigration Under Capitalism: Asian Workers in the United States Before World War II*, ed. Lucie Cheng and Edna Bonacich (Berkeley and Los Angeles: University of California Press, 1984), 240.

6. Ta Chen, *Emigrant Communities in South China: A Study of Overseas Migration and Its Influence on Standards of Living and Social Change* (New York: Institute of Pacific Relations, 1940), 85.

7. Paul C. P. Siu, *The Chinese Laundryman: A Study of Social Isolation* (New York: New York University Press, 1987), 118.

8. Sucheng Chan, "The Exclusion of Chinese Women," in *Entry Denied: Exclusion and the Chinese Community in America, 1882–1943*, ed. Sucheng Chan (Philadelphia: Temple University Press, 1991), 94–146.

9. The Scott Act of 1888, for example, arbitrarily annulled the return certificate of about twenty thousand Chinese immigrants.

10. See Jonathan D. Sarna, "From Immigrants to Ethnics: Toward a New Theory of 'Ethnicization,'" *Ethnicity* V (1978): 370–78; Humbert S. Nelli, *From Immigrants to Ethnics: The Italian Americans* (New York: Oxford University Press, 1983). Also see Oscar Handlin, *The Uprooted* (New York: Grosset and Dunlap, 1957), 186.

11. The Gentlemen's Agreement of 1907–1908, which was designed to end Japanese labor immigration to America, was the result of negotiations between Japan and the United States, whereas the United States ended Chinese immigration through unilateral action. Under the agreement, Japan would stop issuing passports to emigrant laborers, but those already in the United States could continue to bring over their parents, wives, and children. In exchange, San Francisco's school board had to rescind its 1906 attempt to send Japanese students to a segregated school. The agreement came about largely through the intervention of Theodore Roosevelt, who wanted to avoid offending Japan, a rising military and economic power in East Asia. See Roger Daniels, *Asian America: Chinese and Japanese in the United States since 1850* (Seattle: University of Washington Press, 1988), 119–23.

12. See the memorials to the Emperor by Xue Fucheng and Yi Kuang, in *Huagong chuguo shiliao huibian* [A compilation of historical documents concerning Chinese laborers overseas], ed. Chen Hansheng et al. (Beijing: Zhonghua shuju, 1985), vol. 1, part 1, 292–96. The first envoy was sent to Singapore in 1877, followed by another to the United States in 1878.

13. "The Suffering of Our Fellow Merchants," in *Fan mei huagong jinyue wenji* [A collection of the literature protesting against the American exclusion of Chinese laborers], ed. A Ying (Beijing: Zhonghua shuji, 1960), 546.

14. Lu Fangshang, ed., *Qingji huagong chuguo shiliao (1863–1910)* [Documents concerning the overseas emigration of Chinese laborers (1863–1910)] (Taibei: Zhongyang yanjiuyuan jindaishi yanjiusuo, 1995), 224.

15. These are based on U.S. census numbers.

16. List of correspondence, 1878–1880. The list is part of a series of diaries that Ah Quin wrote over the years, which are now in the San Diego Historical Society. Numerous people, including descendants of Ah Quin, have researched his experience.

17. Chen, *Emigrant Communities*, 85.

18. Siu, *The Chinese Laundryman*, 180.

19. Lo Hsiang-lin, *Liang Cheng de chushi meiguo* [Liang Cheng: Chinese minister in the United States] (Hong Kong: Zhongguo wenhua yanjiusuo, 1977), appendix II, 331.

20. *Chung Sai Yat Po* [Chinese-Western daily], July 26, 1908, the American news section.

21. In his *Coolies and Mandarins: China's Protection of Overseas Chinese During the Late Ch'ing Period (1851–1911)* (Singapore: Singapore University

Press, 1985), Yen Ching-Hwang discusses the diplomatic impetus for the Qing Court's change of policy and the establishment of Chinese envoys abroad from the perspective of international relations. See chapter 4, 180.

22. Lin Jinzhi and Zhuang Weiji, comps., *Jindai huaqiao touzi guonei qiye shi ziliao xuanji (Guangdong juan)* [Selected documents concerning modern overseas Chinese investments in Chinese industries (the volume on Guangdong)] (Fuzhou: Fujian renmin chubanshe, 1989), 160.

23. Lin and Zhuang, comps., *Jindai huaqiao touzi*, 167.

24. A comprehensive account of the history of the Xinning Railroad is found in Liu Yuzun, Cheng Luxi [Lucie Cheng], and Zheng Dehua, "Huaqiao, Xinning tielu yu Taishan" [overseas Chinese, Xinning Railroad, and Taishan], in *Huaqiao huaren lishi luncong* [Studies of overseas Chinese and ethnic Chinese], vol. 1, 62–80.

25. Chen invested in American railroads as well. He once loaned thirty thousand dollars to white Americans who were building railroads. See Zhang Yinhuan, *Sanzhou riji* [Journal of the journey to three continents] (n.p.: Jingdu yuedong xinguan, 1896), 3:16; 5:54; and 8:14. For more information about his experience in Seattle, where he resided for many years, and about his life in general, see Willard G. Jue, "Chin Gee-hee, Chinese Pioneer Entrepreneur in Seattle and Toishan," *The Annals of the Chinese Historical Society of the Pacific Northwest* (1983), 31–38.

26. See *Chung Sai Yat Po*, November 25, 1908.

27. "Memorial of the Commerce Department to the Emperor in 1906 requesting permission for Chen Yixi to start building the Xinning Railroad." Cited from Lin and Zhuang, comps., *Jindai huaqiao touzi*, 431.

28. Others have recognized "the role of emigrant capital and nationalism in the development of enterprises in the emigrant motherland." See Lucie Cheng and Liu Yuzun, with Zheng Dehua, "Chinese Emigration, the Sunning Railway and the Development of Toisan," *Amerasia* 9 no. 1 (Spring 1982): 60.

29. "Memorial of the Commerce Department to the Emperor" cited from Lin and Zhuang, comps., *Jindai huaqiao touzi*, 431.

30. According to Chen himself, constructing the railroad cost about three million dollars. See Xinning tielu gongsi [Xinning Railroad Company], "Shangban Guangdong Xinning tielu shiye guzhi tongjice" [Estimated property value of the private Guangdong Xinning railroad company] (1928), introduction.

31. Liu Pei Chi [Liu Boji], *Meiguo huaqiao yishi* [An anecdotal history of the Chinese in the U.S.A.] (Taibei: Liming wenhua shiye gufen youxian gongsi, 1984), 265.

32. Editorial in *Chung Sai Yat Po*, April 11, 1913.

33. Gloria Heyung Chun, *Of Orphans and Warriors: Inventing Chinese American Culture and Identity* (New Brunswick, N.J.: Rutgers University Press, 2000), 30.

34. Lin and Zhuang, comps., *Jindai huaqiao touzi*, 45.

35. Chun-Hsi Wu, *Dollars, Dependents and Dogma: Overseas Chinese Remittances to Communist China* (Stanford, Calif.: Hoover Institution on War, Revolution, and Peace, 1967), 81.

36. Liang Qichao, *Xindalu youji* [Journey to the new continent] (1904; repr. in Shen Yunlong, *Jindai zhongguo shiliao congkan* [Historical documents concerning modern China], Taibei: Wenhai chubanshe, 1967), 378–79.

37. Editorial in *Chung Sai Yat Po*, April 18, 1907.

38. *Chung Sai Yat Po*, July 4, 1907, the American news section.

39. L. Eve Armentrout Ma has discussed the activities of these political figures in the Americas before the 1911 Revolution in her *Revolutionaries, Monarchists, and Chinatowns* (Honolulu: University of Hawaii Press, 1990).

40. Leong Kai Cheu, "The Awakening of China," *The Independent* LV (May 28, 1903): 1268.

41. Its full name in Chinese was *Lumei huaqiao tongyi yiyuan jiugos zonghui* [the general fund-raising association of the Chinese in America to save China]. Its name in English was the China War Relief Association of America.

42. *Chung Sai Yat Po*, December 11, 1937.

43. See Him Mark Lai, *Cong huaqiao dao huaren: ershi shiji Meiguo huaren shehui fazhan shi* [From overseas Chinese to Chinese Americans: a social history of the Chinese in the United States in the twentieth century] (Hong Kong: Sanlian shudian youxian gongsi, 1992), 300.

44. Lai, *Cong huaqiao*, 300.

45. C. F. Remer, *Foreign Investments in China* (1933; repr., New York: H. Fertig, 1968), 220–21, 225.

46. Remer's own empirical data consisted mostly of records from eleven of the sixteen banks in Hong Kong that handled money overseas Chinese remitted to China in 1928, 1929, and 1930. A Chinese scholar, Yao Zengyin, who conducted extensive field studies in Hong Kong and Guangdong for five months in 1938, noted that Remer mistakenly believed that the sixteen banks in Hong Kong handled all Chinese remittances. In an article finished in 1938, Yao pointed out that a significant portion of the overseas remittance money evaded these banks in Hong Kong by taking other routes and using traditional Chinese financial institutions. According to Yao, the remittances that actually reached Guangdong Province alone amounted to 170 million Chinese dollars in that year. Based on the official exchange rate for June 1938, this was over US$31 million. See Yao Zengyin, *Guangdong sheng de huaqiao huikuan* [Overseas Chinese remittances to Guangdong Province] (Chongqing: Shangwu chubanshe, ca. 1943), 32–33, 41. For exchange rates, see Wu, *Dollars, Dependents and Dogma*, 186.

47. The average revenues of the Chinese central government from 1914 through 1930 was 358.46 million Chinese dollars. This is based on the figures for 1914, 1916, 1922, 1923, 1924, 1925, 1928, 1929, and 1930, which are cited in Hou Chi-Ming, *Foreign Investment and Economic Development in China, 1840–1937* (Cambridge, Mass.: Harvard University Press, 1964), 44. The figures do not include loans.

48. Huang Weici and Xu Xiaosheng, *Huaqiao dui zuguo kangzhan de gongxian* [The contributions of overseas Chinese to the motherland's war of resistance] (Guangdong: Guangdong renmin chubanshe, 1991), 60. Also see Wu, *Dollars, Dependents and Dogma*, 16.

49. Xia Chenghua, *Jindai Guangdong sheng qiaohui yanjiu, 1862–1949* [a study of remittances to Guangdong province in modern times, 1862–1949] (Singapore: Xinjiapo nanyang xuehui, 1992), 139.

50. Xia, *Jindai Guangdong sheng*, 141.

51. This is based on the estimates of overseas Chinese communities from the Chinese government in 1956, which put the size of Chinese America at more than 256,000. See Lin and Zhuang, comps., *Jindai huaqiao touzi*, 31–32.

52. Delber L. McKee writes in an essay on the 1905 boycott: "the tiny community in mainland America had temporarily acquired a special leverage with influential Chinese leaders and with groups both in and out of government." See "The Chinese Boycott of 1905–1906 Reconsidered: The Role of Chinese Americans," *Pacific Historical Review* 55, no. 2 (1986): 169.

53. He Zuo, comp., *1905 Fan Mei ai guo yundong* [the 1905 patriotic movement against the United States], *Jindaishi ziliao* [Documents concerning modern history] 1 (1956): 16.

54. Lu, ed., *Qingji huagong chuguo*, 224.

55. Xia, *Jingdai guangdong sheng*, 63.

56. See Lai, *Cong Huajiao*, 300.

57. According to the Overseas Chinese Commission in Taiwan, Chinese Americans contributed more than 290,000,000 U.S. dollars during the period. The number is cited from Huang and Xu, *Huaqiao dui zuguo kangzhan*, 59.

58. The limitations of the 1943 repeal are common knowledge. For example, it allowed only 105 Chinese per year (regardless of whether they were citizens of China or of other countries) to immigrate legally to the United States.

CHAPTER SIX

1. Portions of this chapter previously appeared in Shehong Chen, *Being Chinese, Becoming Chinese American* (Urbana: University of Illinois Press, 2002).

2. June Mei, "Socioeconomic Developments Among the Chinese in San Francisco, 1848–1906," in *Labor Immigration Under Capitalism: Asian Workers in the United States Before World War II*, ed. Lucie Cheng and Edna Bonacich (Berkeley and Los Angeles: University of California Press, 1984), 398.

3. Table 22: "Color or Race, for the United State: 1790 to 1930," U.S. Census Bureau, *Abstract of the 15th Census, 1930* (1930; repr., New York: Arno Press, 1976), 80.

4. Mei's analysis of the socioeconomic conditions of the Chinese in San Francisco at the turn of the century provides more details concerning the limits on economic opportunities that the Chinese American community faced. Mei, "Socioeconomic Developments," 378–97.

5. Ronald Takaki, *Strangers from a Different Shore: A History of Asian Americans* (New York: Penguin Books, 1990), 239. According to Takaki, 56 percent of the American Chinese population lived in urban areas in 1920 while by 1940 the percentage had increased to 71.

6. L. Eve Armentrout Ma, *Revolutionaries, Monarchists, and Chinatowns: Chinese Politics in the Americas and the 1911 Revolution* (Honolulu: University of Hawaii Press, 1990), 13.

7. Sucheng Chan, *Asian Americans: An Interpretive History* (Boston: Twayne, 1991), 34.

8. There were 56,596 Chinese born in China and 14,935 born in the United States. Table 25: "Nonwhite Races by Nativity, for the United States: 1930,"

Abstract of the 15th Census, 1930 (1930; repr., New York: Arno Press, 1976), 81.

9. Table 24: "Sex Distribution of Indian, Chinese, and Japanese Population in the United States, 1910," U.S. Census Bureau, *Abstract of the 13th Census, 1910* (1910; repr., New York: Arno Press, 1976), 99.

10. Him Mark Lai, Genny Lim, and Judy Yung, *Island: Poetry and History of Chinese Immigrants on Angel Island, 1910–1940* (Seattle: University of Washington Press, 1991), 84–86.

11. The Six Classics are *Book of Changes, Book of History, Book of Poetry, Book of Rites, Spring and Autumn Annals,* and *Book of Music.* In 1898, to preserve what he believed to be the best of China's cultural heritage, Kang Youwei proposed that Confucianism be established as China's state religion. See Kung-chuan Hsiao, *A Modern China and a New World: Kang Yu-wei, Reformer and Utopian, 1858–1927* (Seattle: University of Washington Press, 1975), 44–45, 532–34.

12. Liang Qichao met Kang Youwei for the first time in the fall of 1890. Thereafter Liang studied intermittently for four years at Kang's private school, *Wanmu Caotang,* in Guangzhou. It was during those four years that Liang's "intellectual foundation for his whole life was laid," according to Hao Chang, who studied Liang's development as an intellectual. Chang, *Liang Ch'i-ch'ao and Intellectual Transition in China, 1890–1907* (Cambridge, Mass.: Harvard University Press, 1971), 58–60.

13. Kang theorized that absolute monarchy was the lowest form of government while "the people's rule" or democracy, the highest form of government, could be achieved only in the future. According to him, the republican form of government in the United States and France was only a partial realization of the "people's rule." For China at the end of the nineteenth century, the appropriate form of government was, according to Kang and his followers, constitutional monarchy, a transitional form between absolute monarchy and democracy. Hsiao, *A Modern China and a New World,* 85–94.

14. The Baohuanghui-sponsored banking and investment programs were usually transnational cooperations attracting investments and participation from Chinese in Southeast Asia, Hong Kong, Europe, and North America. The two large programs in North America were the Compania Banking Chino Y Mexico and Zhenhua Company. The former, based in Mexico, dealt with real estate investment in Mexico and handled Baohuanghui's financial matters in North America. The latter made investments to develop natural resources in Guangxi Province in southern China. Him Mark Lai, *Cong huaqiao dao huaren: ershi shiji Meiguo huaren shehui fazhan shi* [From overseas Chinese to Chinese American: a social history of the Chinese in the United States in the twentieth century] (Hong Kong: Sanlian shudian youxian gongsi, 1992), 181–82. For the Compania Banking Chino Y Mexico and its real estate investment in Mexico, also see Leo M. Dambourges Jacques, "The Chinese Massacre in Torreon (Coahuila) in 1911," *Arizona and the West* 16 (1974): 235–36.

15. The Zhigongtang was an extension of a major secret society in China. The principal goal of this secret society was *fanqing fuming* (overthrow the Qing dynasty and restore the Ming dynasty). Its members were usually poor peasants

and outcasts in Chinese society. In the United States, members of the Zhigongtang were usually small businessmen and wageworkers. Their lower economic and social status and the political goal of the organization determined that they would be antiestablishment.

16. Ma, *Revolutionaries, Monarchists, and Chinatowns*, 59.

17. *Young China*, August 10, 1910.

18. According to Richard Smith, the cultural psychology in traditional China was characterized by "social conformity, consensus, collective responsibility, and...almost pathological fear of disorder." *China's Cultural Heritage: The Ch'ing Dynasty, 1644–1912* (Boulder, Colo.: Westview Press, 1983), xiii.

19. Corinne K. Hoexter, *From Canton to California: The Epic of Chinese Immigration* (New York: Four Winds Press, 1976), 153.

20. Hoexter, *From Canton to California*, 163.

21. By 1911, *Chung Sai Yat Po*'s readership went beyond Chinese Christians in the United States. In fact, it had become the most popular Chinese-language newspaper among Chinese in the United States, with a circulation of 3,500, while the figures for *Chinese World* and *Young China* (the latter was only a few months old) were 3,000 and 1,500, respectively. Emerson Daggett (supervisor), *History of Foreign Journalism in San Francisco* (San Francisco: United States Works Progress Administration, 1939), 49–57.

22. Hoexter, *From Canton to California*, 171.

23. *Chinese World*, October 16, 1911.

24. *Chung Sai Yat Po*, October 28, 1911.

25. Chien-nung Li, *The Political History of China, 1840–1928*, trans. and ed. Ssu-yu Teng and Jeremy Ingalls (Stanford, Calif.: Stanford University Press, 1956), 312–13.

26. *Young China*, October 30, 1911.

27. *Chung Sai Yat Po*, September 4, 1915; and *Young China*, November 11, 1915.

28. *Young China*, January 7, 1916.

29. *Young China*, January 5, 7, 25, and 28, 1916.

30. *Chung Sai Yat Po* editorialized on many American holidays such as Presidents' Day, Independence Day, Thanksgiving Day, and Christmas, praising and admiring the United States for its democratic institutions as well as its economic achievements. The paper persistently argued that the development of capitalism was essential for a China that aspired to be strong and modern.

31. *Chung Sai Yat Po*, January 27, 1916. The paper used the term "a conservative party" to refer to those who supported Yuan's restoration attempt.

32. *Chinese World*, March 3, 1916.

33. *Chung Sai Yat Po*, September 16, 1915.

34. *Young China*, October 25 and 29, 1915.

35. *Young China*, October 30, 31, November 11, 19, 30, and December 12, 1915.

36. *Young China*, December 11, 1915.

37. *Young China*, May 15 and 16, 1916; and *Chung Sai Yat Po*, May 27, 1916.

38. *Chinese World*, May 8, 1916; and *Young China*, May 15, 1916.

39. Guobiao Yang, Hanbiao Liu, and Anyao Yang, *Meiguo huaqiao shi* [A history of overseas Chinese in the United States] (Guangzhou: Guangdong gaojiao chubanshe, 1989), 484–85.

40. *Chinese World*, September 22, 1916.

41. *Chinese World*, September 22, 1916.

42. Theresa A. Sparks, *China Gold* (Fresno, Calif.: Academy Library Guild, 1954), 166.

43. Jade Snow Wong, *Fifth Chinese Daughter* (1950; repr., Seattle: University of Washington Press, 1995), 128.

44. Such ceremonies started in December 1913 when the new Chinese constitution failed to make Confucianism China's state religion. All Chinese schools, inside China and overseas, were encouraged to hold ceremonies to worship Confucius so that Confucianism could be carried from generation to generation through the educational channel.

45. *Chinese World*, September 23, 1916, October 6, 1923, and October 9 and 12, 1926.

46. Quoted in Sucheng Chan, "Race, Ethnic Culture, and Gender in the Construction of Identities Among Second-Generation Chinese Americans," in *Claiming America: Constructing Chinese American Identities During the Exclusion Era*, ed. K. Scott Wong and Sucheng Chan (Philadelphia: Temple University Press, 1998), 151.

47. *Chinese World*, June 29, 1920.

48. "Dr. Ng Poon Chew's View on Love and Marriage," Box 3, Ng Poon Chew Collection, Ethnic Studies Library, University of California at Berkeley.

49. Tse-tsung Chow, *The May Fourth Movement: Intellectual Revolution in Modern China* (Cambridge, Mass.: Harvard University Press, 1960), 46.

50. Chen, *New Youth*. Quoted in Chow, *The May Fourth Movement*, 59.

51. Chow, *The May Fourth Movement*, 45, 273–74.

52. *Chinese World*, January 8 and 9, 1919.

53. *Chinese World*, January 17, 1919.

54. *Chinese World*, November 22, December 8, 13, and 17, 1919.

55. Germany had a leasehold over Shandong. During World War I, the Beijing government, in order to secure financial support from Japan, had signed a secret agreement with Japan, giving Japan the right to station police and establish military garrisons in Jinan and Qingdao, two major cities in Shandong, as well as the right to build and manage railroads in that province. Great Britain, France, and Italy, in order to get Japan's naval assistance against Germany in the war, agreed secretly to support Japan's claims in Shandong. At the Versailles Peace Conference, these secret agreements became public and received the support of the American delegation led personally by President Woodrow Wilson.

56. *Chinese World*, May 5, 6, 9, 19, 20, and 30, 1919; and *Young China*, May 4, 5, 6, 31, and June 1, 1919.

57. *Chinese World*, March 12, 1920.

58. *Young China*, August 12, 1919.

59. *Chung Sai Yat Po*, October 15, 1919.

60. *Chung Sai Yat Po*, December 6, 1919.

61. Lai, *Cong huaqiao dao huaren*, 145–47.

62. *Chung Sai Yat Po*, March 24, 1922.

63. *Chung Sai Yat Po*, November 2, 1912.

64. *Chung Sai Yat Po*, July 10, 1912.

65. *Chung Sai Yat Po*, December 25, 1912.

66. *Chung Sai Yat Po*, May 5, 9, 31, June 2, August 5, September 26, 1913.

67. Thomas W. Chinn, "A Historian's Reflections on Chinese-American Life in San Francisco, 1919–1991" (an oral history conducted in 1990 and 1991 by Ruth Teiser, Regional Oral History Office, Bancroft Library, University of California, Berkeley, 1993), 25.

68. *Chung Sai Yat Po*, June 22, 1922.

69. Judy Yung documented a story of a widowed Chinese woman who sought help from the Chinatown YWCA in order to escape from her intolerable mother-in-law in the early 1920s. Judy Yung, *Unbound Feet: A Social History of Chinese American Women in San Francisco* (Berkeley and Los Angeles: University of California Press, 1995), 96–97.

70. Yung, *Unbound Feet*, 301, 96.

71. Yung, *Unbound Feet*, 80–82.

72. Chow, *The May Fourth Movement*, 324–25.

73. Peter Lin, *Christianity and China* (Taipei: Universal Light Publishing House, 1975). For an in-depth study of the anti-Christian movement of this period, see Ka-che Yip, *Religion, Nationalism, and Chinese Students: The Anti-Christian Movement of 1922–1927* (Bellingham: Center for East Asian Studies, Western Washington University, 1980).

74. *Chung Sai Yat Po*, May 13, 1922.

75. *Chung Sai Yat Po*, June 5, 1922.

76. *Ta Tung Yat Po*, April 18, 1922.

77. Xiaosheng Xu, *Huaqiao yu diyici guogong hezuo* [Overseas Chinese and the first Guomindang-Chinese Communist Party cooperation] (Guangzhou: Jinan daxue chubanshe, 1989), 41.

78. *Chinese World*, January 9, 1923.

79. *Chinese World*, June 27, 1923.

80. *Chung Sai Yat Po*, January 5, 1923.

81. *Chung Sai Yat Po*, May 17, 30, 31, June 4, 7, 18, 20, 29, July 6, 18, 19, 23, and 24, 1923.

82. Lucie Cheng, Yuzun Liu, and Dehua Zheng, "Chinese Emigration: The Sunning Railroad and the Development of Toisan," *Amerasia* 9, no. 1 (1982): 59–74. To all Chinese in the United States, Chen's financial success exemplified how capitalism was the best way for achieving individual and national development.

83. *Chung Sai Yat Po*, July 31, 1923; and Lai, *Cong huaqiao dao huaren*, 211. The information on the exchange rate between Chinese money and the United States dollar is from Jurgen Schneider, Oskar Schneider, and Markus A. Denzel, eds., *Wahrungen der Welt V: Asiatische und Australische Devisenkurse im 20. Jahrhundert* [Currencies of the World 5: Asian and Australian Exchange Rates in the Twentieth Century] (Stuttgart: Franz Steiner, 1994), 214.

84. *Chung Sai Yat Po*, July 31, 1923.

85. *Chung Sai Yat Po*, August 2, 1923.

86. *Chung Sai Yat Po*, August 8, 9, and 14, 1923.

87. *Young China*, April 10, 1924.

88. *Young China*, April 12, 1924.

89. *Chinese World*, August 19, 1924; and *Chung Sai Yat Po*, August 16, 1924.

90. *Chung Sai Yat Po*, August 26, 1924; and *Chinese World*, August 19, 1924.

91. *Young China*, October 12, 1924.

92. The British colonial authorities in Hong Kong threatened to order their navy to attack the Sun government's troops in the event of a military showdown. Li, *The Political History of China*, 465. The British also promised to help Chen Lianbo become "the Washington of China" by overthrowing the Sun government in Guangdong, which the British believed was leading China toward Communism unless it was crushed in time. Sheng Hu, *Imperialism and Chinese Politics* (Beijing: Beijing Foreign Language Press, 1955), 298–99.

93. *Chung Sai Yat Po*, September 1, 1924.

94. When Sun finally launched the Northern Expedition in September 1924, he apologized to the people in Guangdong. He said, "I have troubled many of my fellow elders and brothers in my native province by commanding several armies...and by asking all sorts of supplies.... The price of commodities is exorbitant and maintaining a livelihood for the people is increasingly difficult. The responsibility of revolution should be borne by the people of the whole nation; instead, a majority of responsibility has been taken by the people of Kwangtung (Guangdong). That is enough to make Cantonese people feel unjustly treated." Quoted in Li, *The Political History of China*, 463. Li Chien-nung stated that the Northern Expedition was launched in haste, mostly because Sun realized that the people in Guangdong, especially merchants, had developed ill feelings toward his government and army. So he ordered all his troops to leave the province, hoping to win back the sympathy and support of the people in Guangdong. Li, *The Political History of China*, 464.

CHAPTER SEVEN

1. The 1880 U.S. manuscript census listed more than a dozen Chinese teachers in San Francisco's Chinatown.

2. Victor Low, *The Unimpressible Race: A Century of Educational Struggle by the Chinese in San Francisco* (San Francisco: East/West Publishing, 1982), 62.

3. Liu Pei Chi [Liu Boji], *Meiguo huaqiao shi* [A history of the Chinese in the United States of America] (Taibei: Xingzhengyuan Qiaowu Weiyuanhui, 1976), 355–56.

4. Kongsun Lum, ed., *Hawaii Chinese in the Foreign Language School Case, a Memorial Publication* (Honolulu: Hawaii Chinese Educational Association and Chung Wah Chung Kung Hui, 1950), 31–32.

5. Wang Liming, *Qing mo de bianfa sixiang* [Reform ideology during the late Qing] *(1860–1898)* (Taibei: Chia Hsin Foundation, 1976), 8, 39; Wang Li, *Hanyu*

shigao [A draft history of the Chinese language] (Beijing: Kexue chubanshe, 1958) 528–37.

6. Li Huaxing, ed., *Minguo jiaoyushi* [History of education during the Republic] (Shanghai: Shanghai jiaoyu chubanshe, 1997), 77, 81.

7. Liang Qinggui, "A Report Transmitting the Register of Schools of Overseas Chinese in North America to the Ministry of Education, Second Year of the Xuantong Reign Era [1910]," *Chinese America: History and Perspectives 2000*, 49–53.

8. Du Zijing, "Zhongguo wenzi gaige yundong dashi nianpu" [Chronology of important events in the reform of the Chinese language], in *Zhongguo wenzi gaige wenti* [Issues in the reform of the Chinese language] (Beijing: Xinjianshe chubanshe, 1952), 139–53. Cited hereafter as Du, "Chronology of Important Events."

9. John De Francis, *The Chinese Language, Fact and Fantasy* (Honolulu: University of Hawaii Press, 1984), 230–31. Even before the founding of the People's Republic of China in 1949, there were individuals who felt that the Beijing-based national language (guoyu) had a bureaucratic taint; so, they favored putonghua or *dazhongyu*, incorporating features from various regional forms and various social levels. I first heard my mandarin teacher use the term while taking mandarin lessons in San Francisco's Chinatown around 1941. The term *putonghua* was officially defined, in 1955, in the People's Republic of China as the common speech of the Han nationality. Putonghua is not as rigidly or narrowly delimited as guoyu in its definition of a national standard.

10. Du, "Chronology of Important Events."

11. Du, "Chronology of Important Events."

12. Zhu Jingxian, *Huaqiao jiaoyu* [Education of overseas Chinese] (Taibei: Chung Hwa Book Co., 1973), 35, 348–55.

13. Liu Pei Chi [Liu Boji], *Meiguo huaqiao yi shi* [An anecdotal history of the Chinese in the U.S.A.] (Taibei: Liming wenhua shiye gufen youxian gongsi, 1984), 408.

14. According to the U.S. federal census, Chinese composed 23.1 and 18.4 percent of the Honolulu population in 1900 and 1910, respectively. The corresponding percentages for Chinese in San Francisco were 4.1 and 2.5, respectively.

15. "Tanshan Huaqiao" [Chinese of Hawaii] section, 60, and "Tanshan Huaqiao wenrenlu" [Biographies of notable Chinese in Hawaii] section, 79, in *Chinese of Hawaii*, ed. Dormant Chang and Min Hin Li (Honolulu: Overseas Penman Club, 1929).

16. Him Mark Lai, "Retention of the Ancestral Heritage: Chinese Schools in America Before World War II," *Chinese America: History and Perspectives 2000*, 10–31.

17. *Tanxiangshan Zhongshan Xuexiao di-ershisan zhounian, di shisan jie biye jinian tekan* [Hawaii's Chungshan School's 23rd anniversary publication](Honolulu: Chung Shan School, 1934), 232, 234. Cited hereafter as *Chung Shan School 23rd Anniversary Publication.*

18. Kum Pui Lai, *The Natural History of the Chinese Language School in Hawaii* (M.A. thesis in Sociology, University of Hawaii, 1935), 62–63.

19. *Chung Shan School 23rd Anniversary Publication*; "Jubu jishi" [Record of events in the drama department], in *Tanxiangshan Minglun Zhongxuexiao ershiwu zhounian jiniance* [Publication commemorating the 25th anniversary of Mun Lun School in Hawaii] (Honolulu: Mun Lun School, 1936), n.p. Cited hereafter as *Mun Lun School 25th Anniversary Publication*.

20. "Tanshan Huaqiao," in *Chinese of Hawaii*, Vol. II, ed. Chun Kwong Lau and Kum Pui Lai (Honolulu: Overseas Penman Club, 1936), 17–22.

21. Liu Pei Chi [Liu Boji], *Meiguo huaqiao shi xubian* [A History of the Chinese in the United States of America II] (Taibei: Liming wenhua shiye gufen youxian gongsi, 1981), 326. Cited hereafter as Liu, *A History of the Chinese II*.

22. *Chinese World*, January 5, 1915.

23. Liu, *A History of the Chinese II*, 327.

24. *Xiao* (San Francisco: Morning Bell School, 1922), 57, 68, 73, 81, 83, 84, 86, 88, 90.

25. Liu, *A History of the Chinese II*, 343–47.

26. *Yeong Wo School Publication* (San Francisco: Yeong Wo School, 1932), 13–17. Cited hereafter as *Yeong Wo School 1932 Publication*.

27. Liu, *A History of the Chinese II*, 328–29.

28. Liu, *A History of the Chinese II*, 349–54.

29. *Chung Shan School 23rd Anniversary Publication*.

30. "Xianren zaizhi jiaoyuan yilanbiao" [Table of current faculty members], in *Mun Lun School 25th Anniversary Publication*, n.p.

31. *Chung Shan School 23rd Anniversary Publication*, 236.

32. *Xiao*, 68.

33. Liu, *A History of the Chinese II*, 328.

34. *Huawen zazhi* [The Wah Mun miscellany] (Honolulu: Wah Mun School, 1915), no. 3; *Zhichen xiaoxue wenji* [Collected essays of the Jackson School] (Honolulu: Jackson School, 1917); *Xiao*.

35. *Chung Shan School 23rd Anniversary Publication*, 99–121, 131–39, 148–61, 172–77.

36. *Zhonghua xiaokan* [Chung Wah school publication] (San Francisco: Chinese Central High School, 1934), 58–80. Cited hereafter as *Chung Wah School 1934 Publication*.

37. *Meizhou Zhonghua Zhongxuexiao biyesheng jiniankan* [Chinese Central High School of America graduating students' commemorative publication] (San Francisco: Chinese Central High School, 1940), 68–95, cited hereafter as *Chinese Central High School 1940 Commemorative Publication*; *Shengmali Zhongxue biye tekan* (San Francisco: St. Mary's School, 1940), n.p. Cited hereafter as *St. Mary's School 1940 Publication*.

38. Zhang He, Muzhi, eds., *Zhongguo gudai mengshu jijin* [Collection of traditional beginners' readers] (Ji'nan: Shandong youyiu shushe, 1989), 1–14. Cited hereafter as *Collection of Traditional Beginner's Readers*. *Sanzijing*, *Biajiaxing*, *Qianziwen*, and *Youxueshi* were four texts frequently used by beginning students in Qing dynasty China. *Sanzijing* consisted of three characters per sentence. The work begins with the lines *ren zhi chu, xing ben shan* [when life begins, one's original character is good] and goes on to give a concise recitation of exemplary behavior in society. It is said that Wang Yinglin compiled the work during the Song

dynasty but it underwent a number of changes through the centuries. *Baijiaixing*, said to be first compiled during the Northern Song dynasty, gives 441 surnames (family or last names) arranged in groups consisting of four characters each, which is only a fraction of the estimated 3,000-plus surnames used in China today. *Qianziwen* was reputed to be the work of Zhou Xingsi of the Liang dynasty, who took a thousand characters from the calligraphy of Wang Xizhi and arranged them in rhymed groups of four. It is of interest to note that the first eighty characters beginning with *tiandi xuan huang* [the sky and earth are respectively black and yellow] were later used as symbols for spots in the Chinese lottery. In America, gaming houses in Nevada modified the Chinese lottery into Keno with numbers substituted for the Chinese characters.

39. *Xinbian mengxue baodian* [Newly compiled treasury of canons for beginning students] (Beijing: Zhongyang minzu daxue chubanshe, 1996), 122–42. *Shentong shi* [Poems for the child prodigy] is a series of poems with four lines of five characters each. The first few poems encourage students to study hard so that they can become officials to serve the empire. It is said to have been compiled by Wang Zhu, a child prodigy of the Song dynasty. However, a shortened and much revised version entitled *Youxueshi* was used during the Qing dynasty. The last two lines of the first poem, *wanban jie xiapin, weiyou dushu gao* [all the different things are of lower worth, it is only learning that is rated highest], are well known to many Chinese of the period.

40. *Collection of Traditional Beginners' Readers*, 72–109. This was a collection of essays that defined idiomatic terms for phenomena of the natural world and of society starting from the creation of heaven and earth and proceeding to geography, society, and human relationships. The work was originally compiled as *Youxue xuzhi* [What the beginning student should know] during the Ming dynasty. It was known also by other names such as *Chengyu kao* [Study of idioms] and *Gushi xunyuan* [Quest for the source of ancient affairs].

41. Hanyu dacidian editorial committee, *Hanyu dacidian* [Chinese Dictionary] (Hong Kong: Joint Publishing [H.K.] Company and Hanyu dacidian chubanshe, 1989), s.v. "Sishu." During the Southern Song dynasty, Zhu Xi edited and annotated *Lunyu* [Analects], the chapters entitled *Zhongyong* [The mean] and *Daxue* [Great learning] from the *Liji* [Record of rites], and *Mengzi* [Mencius] and named it *Sishu jiju jizhu* [Annotated collection of sentences from four books]. During the succeeding Yuan dynasty, the court decreed in 1113 that topics for the imperial examinations would be selected from the text of the *Sishu*, thus establishing the work as a required text for scholars who aimed to take the imperial examinations.

42. *Hanyu dacidian*, s.v. "Wujing," the five principal books of the Confucian school of philosophy as defined during the Han dynasty in 136 B.C. They consisted of *Shi* [Poetry], *Shu* [History], *Yi* [Changes], *Li* [Rites], and *Chunqiu* [Spring and autumn annals].

43. Liu, *A History of the Chinese II*, 356.

44. Kenneth Scott Latourette, *A History of Christian Missions in China* (London: Society for Promoting Christian Knowledge, 1929; repr. 1966 in Taibei by Ch'eng-wen Publishing), 413, 440, 451.

45. "Jiaokeshu de fakan gaikuang [A survey of the publication and distribution of textbooks], 1868–1919," in *Zhongguo jindai chuban shiliao, chubian* [Historical materials on modern China's publishing industry, 1st collection], comp. and annotated by Zhang Jinglu (Shanghai: Qunlian chubanshe, 1953), 219–53, cited hereafter as "Survey of the Publication and Distribution of Textbooks, 1868–1919"; Gu Changsheng, *Chuanjiaoshi yu jindai zhongguo* [Christian missionaries and modern China] (Shanghai: Shanghai renmin chubanshe, 1981), 238–39. *Jiaokeshu* is a Japanese loan word *kyōka-sho*. See Liu Zhengtan et al., *Hanyu wailaici cidian* [A dictionary of loan words and hybrid words in Chinese] (Shanghai: Shanghai cishu chubanshe, 1984). Cited hereafter as *Dictionary of Loan Words*.

46. "Jiaokeshu zhi fakan gaikuang: 1868–1918" [A survey of the publication of textbooks: 1868–1918], in *Zhongguo jindai chuban shiliao, chubian* [Historical materials on modern China's publishing industry, 1st collection], ed. Zhang Jinglu (Shanghai: Qunlian chubanshe, 1953), 219–53, cited hereafter as "Survey of the Publication and Distribution of Textbooks, 1868–1919"; Jiang Weiqiao, "Chuangban chuqi zhi Shangwu Yinshuguan yu Zhonghua Shuju" [Early period of the Commercial Press and Chung Hwa Book Company], in *Zhongguo xiandai chuban shiliao, ding bian* [Historical materials on modern China's publishing industry, 4th collection], ed. Zhang Jinglu (Beijing: Zhonghua shuju, 1959), 395–400; Latourette, *A History of Christian Missions*, 478. Commercial Press was founded by several Chinese who had learned the printing trade at Shanghai's Presbyterian Mission Press (Chinese name: Mei-Hua Shuguan). Its Chinese name, Shangwu Yinshuguan, was derived from the Chinese name of the Presbyterian Press.

47. "Survey of the Publication and Distribution of Textbooks, 1868–1919."

48. *Dictionary of Loan Words*, s.v. Two terms are Japanese loan words: *changshi* is from the Japanese *jōshiki*, *gongmin* is from *kōmin*.

49. Aesop's fables were translated by Lin Shu and published by Commercial Press in 1906.

50. Lai, *The Natural History of the Chinese Language School in Hawaii*, 63–64.

51. Lai, *The Natural History*, 64–65.

52. *Yeong Wo School 1932 Publication*, 39–49; *Chung Shan School 23rd Anniversary Publication*, 99–120; *Chung Wah School 1934 Publication*, 58–80; *Chinese Central High School 1940 Publication*, 68–59; *St. Mary's School 1940 Publication*, n.p. Following are samplings of titles of essays by students in the upper primary and high school grades:

Yeong Wo School: "Education and the Nation," "Reflection on the 1931 Commemoration of Double Ten [October 10—the national day of the Republic of China]," "Expounding on the Concept that One Realizes One's Inadequacies After Being Educated," "In Order to Learn One Must Set a Goal," "Preface to Launching a Fundraising Campaign to Establish a Library at Our School," "Expounding on the Idea That If One Did Not Learn a Skill When Young, One Will Regret It Later," "How Can We Chinese Exert Effort to Erase the Humiliation of Having Foreigners Ridicule Us as a Pan of Loose Sand, and as the Sick

Man of the East, and that Our Patriotism Lasts Only Five Minutes," "Expounding on the Importance of Agriculture," "A Discussion of Willpower," "On Xiang Yu of Chu" (On Xiang Yu was the defeated rival of Liu Bang, founder of the Han dynasty), "On National Humiliations," and "How Primary School Students Can Participate in the War of Resistance and National Salvation."

Chung Shan School: "After Reading 'The Foolish Old Man Moving the Mountain,'" "On National Calamity," "Outline of the Products of Hawaii," "Do Not Forget the National Calamity When Commemorating National Day," "Why We Should Study Chinese," "A Discourse on the First Emperor of Qin," "Discussion with a Friend on the Pineapple Industry of Hawaii," "Translating Hu Shi's Poem 'Climbing Up the Hill,'" "Morning at Waikiki," "Biography of the Father of the Nation, Sun Yat-sen," "A Discourse on National Salvation Through Improving Transportation," "The Real Meaning of Celebrating Double Ten," and "Discussion on the Resumption of Diplomatic Relations Between America and Russia."

Chinese Central High School: "Reflections on the Commemoration of the Anniversary of Loss of the Three Eastern provinces [Manchuria]," "On Ban Zhao," "Farewell Letter to My Classmates," "Proclamation on Raising Funds for the Relief of Flood Victims in the Ancestral Land," "On Filial Piety," "Activities During Summer Vacation," "Students Should Receive Military Training," "On Strikes," "On Liberty," "Biography of Columbus," "The Harmfulness of Flies," "On the Return Journey," "Diary of Participation in San Francisco's Second Rice Bowl Movement Selling Lapel Buttons," "Hike to Rattlesnake Camp," "Going Home on a Rainy Night," "The Latest Changes in the International Situation and the Far East," "Reading and Extracurricular Activities," "Circumstances and Aspirations," "Watching Fish," "On Composition," "Expounding on the Concept That Benefiting Others Would Be the Same as Benefiting Oneself," and "How to Be a Good Student."

St. Mary's School: "The Problem of Teaching Children," "Women of the New Era," "Overseas Chinese During the War of Resistance," "Sketches of the Graduating Students," "The Library of Our School," "Conducting the Commencement Ceremony During a Period of National Calamity," and "My Opinion Regarding Home Education of Chinese Families."

53. Lai, *The Natural History*, 67; *Chung Shan Annual* (Honolulu: Chung Shan School, 1936), 78–87; *Tanxiangshan Zhongshan Zhongxuexiao zhongxue shoujie biye jinian hao* [Publication commemorating the first high school graduating class of Chung Shan School of Hawaii] (Honolulu: Chung Shan School, 1937) 124–31.

CHAPTER EIGHT

1. Jade Snow Wong, *Fifth Chinese Daughter* (New York: Harper and Row, 1950), 68–69. The autobiography covers the author's life from 1922 to 1945. Parts of it were first published in 1945 in *Common Ground*, a California magazine.

2. Portions of this chapter have appeared in Xiao-huang Yin, *Chinese American Literature Since the 1850s* (Urbana: University of Illinois Press, 2000).

3. "ABC" is a neutral term used by Asian Americans to refer to a subgroup, American-born Chinese, within the Chinese American community, just as "OBC" refers to another subgroup, overseas-born Chinese. ABC is not a negative term unless it is used in a divisive and elitist way to distinguish American-born Chinese from recently arrived immigrants, often called "FOB" (fresh off the boat).

4. For more information on how U.S. immigration laws denied the entry of Chinese women, see Sucheng Chan, "The Exclusion of Chinese Women," in *Entry Denied: Exclusion and the Chinese Community in America, 1882–1943*, ed. Sucheng Chan (Philadelphia: Temple University Press, 1991), 94–146. Also see Judy Yung, *Unbound Feet: A Social History of Chinese Women in San Francisco* (Berkeley and Los Angeles: University of California Press, 1995).

5. Calculated from U.S. Census Bureau, *General Population Characteristics, 1900–1970* (Washington, D.C.: Government Printing Office, 1971).

6. Lee Chew, "The Life Story of a Chinaman," in *The Life Stories of Undistinguished Americans as Told by Themselves*, ed. Hamilton Holt (New York: Potts, 1906), 281–99.

7. Helen Zia, *Asian American Dreams: The Emergence of an American People* (New York: Farrar, Straus and Giroux, 2000), 9.

8. Calculated from *U.S. Census: General Population Characteristics, 1900–1970*.

9. Chinese immigrants who tried to enter the United States during the exclusion era on the false claim that they were offspring of American citizens were called "paper sons" (sons of U.S. citizens on paper only). For more discussions on this issue, see Xiao-huang Yin, *Chinese American Literatures Since the 1850s* (Urbana: University of Illinois Press, 2000), ch. 1, "Plea and Protest: The Voice of Early Chinese Immigrants," 11–52.

10. The mentality of America-born Chinese has undergone dramatic changes since the 1960s. The impact of the civil rights movement and the emergence of transpacific cultural, economic, and community networks have raised their interests in Chinese culture and China-related events. See Peter H. Koehn and Xiao-huang Yin, "Chinese American Transnationalism and U.S.-China Relations," in *The Expanding Roles of Chinese Americans in U.S.-China Relations: Transnational Networks and Trans-Pacific Interactions*, ed. Peter Koehn and Xiao-huang Yin (Armonk, N.Y.: M. E. Sharpe, 2002), xi–xl.

11. William Carlson Smith, *The Second Generation Oriental in America* (Honolulu: Institute of Pacific Relations, 1927), 5.

12. Parts of Lowe's personal stories appeared in journals and magazines as early as the 1930s. See Pardee Lowe, "Father's Robes of Immortality," *Atlantic Monthly* 162 (Dec. 1937): 785–92; and Pardee Lowe, "Letters of Hawk Sung," *Yale Review* 28 (Sept. 1938): 69–81.

13. Helen P. Bolman, "Notes: *Father and Glorious Descendant*," *Library Journal* 68, no. 7 (April 1, 1943), 287; R.L.B., "The Bookshelf: Meeting of the East and West," *Christian Science Monitor* (April 9, 1943), 12. Also see Elaine

H. Kim, *Asian American Literature: An Introduction to the Writings and Their Social Context* (Philadelphia: Temple University Press, 1982), 61.

14. For discussions of the changes in attitude on the part of average Americans toward China and the Chinese, see Harold R. Isaacs, *Scratches on Our Minds: American Views of China and India* (revised ed.; Armonk, N.Y.: M. E. Sharpe, 1980), 164–89.

15. Bolman, "Notes: *Father and Glorious Descendant*," 287. It is important to note the implications of "loyal minority groups" in Bolman's comment. By praising Chinese Americans as a "loyal minority group," she actually suggested that there were "disloyal minority groups" in America. It can be interpreted as her acceptance of the government's decision to confine Japanese Americans in internment camps during War World II.

16. Pardee Lowe rose to the rank of lieutenant colonel and was decorated with a Bronze Star for his service during World War II. He later served as the cultural attaché of the U.S. Embassy in Taiwan and also U.S.I.S. [United States Information Service] officer in the 1960s. More than one hundred boxes of his personal papers are stored at the Hoover Institution Archives at Stanford University.

17. Although the native-born accounted for about 10 percent of the Chinese American population at this time, their actual figure was much smaller. See my discussion earlier on this issue.

18. Pardee Lowe, *Father and Glorious Descendant* (Boston: Little, Brown and Company, 1943), 18. Subsequent page citations to *Father* appear in parentheses.

19. Bienvenido N. Santos, *The Man Who (Thought He) Looked Like Robert Taylor* (Quezon City, Philippines: New Day Publishers, 1983).

20. Malcolm X and Alex Haley, *The Autobiography of Malcolm X* (1965; repr. New York: Ballantine Books, 1973), 2–7, 40.

21. Corinne Hoexter, *From Canton to California: The Epic of Chinese Immigration* (New York: Four Winds Press, 1976), 252.

22. Smith, *The Second Generation Oriental*, 19.

23. Him Mark Lai, *Cong huaqiao dao huaren: ershi shiji Meiguo huaren shehui fazhan shi* [From overseas Chinese to Chinese Americans: a social history of the Chinese in the United States in the twentieth century] (Hong Kong: Sanlian shudian youxian gongsi, 1992), 158.

24. Keeping a queue was a cultural custom imposed on the Chinese by the Manchu, a nomadic tribe originating in Northeast China, after they conquered China and founded the Qing dynasty (1644–1911).

25. Smith, *The Second Generation Oriental*, 7.

26. Maxine Hong Kingston, *The Woman Warrior: Memoirs of a Girlhood Among Ghosts* (New York: Alfred Knopf, 1976), 76.

27. Emory Stephen Bogardus, *Immigration and Race Attitudes* (New York: D. C. Heath, 1928), 25–26; Betty Lee Sung, *Chinese American Intermarriage* (Staten Island, N.Y.: Center for Migration Studies, 1990), 1–19, 49–50, 87–99; Stanford Lyman, *Chinese Americans* (New York: Random House, 1974), 130.

28. Judith Judson, "Child of Two Cultures," *Washington Post*, July 2, 1989, D3.

29. The most recent paperback edition of *Fifth Chinese Daughter* was published by the University of Washington Press in 1989.

30. Jade Snow Wong, *Fifth Chinese Daughter* (Seattle: University of Washington Press, 1989), 161. Subsequent pages citations to *FCD* appear in parentheses.

31. For more discussions on this issue, see Fred Warren Riggs, *Pressures on Congress: A Study of the Repeal of Chinese Exclusion* (New York: Columbia University Press, 1950). Also see Isaacs, *Scratches on Our Minds*, 140–75.

32. Pearl S. Buck (1892–1973), who published several dozen books on China and the Chinese and won the Pulitzer Prize in 1935 and the Nobel Prize in 1938, made enormous contributions to "reshaping" the American image of the Chinese in the 1930s. Significantly, both Jade Snow Wong and Maxine Hong Kingston admit that Pearl Buck's writing had a positive impact on them. Wong admits that Buck's work on China "greatly enriched" her understanding of Chinese culture. (My interview with Jade Snow Wong in Wong Studio, San Francisco, February 5, 1991.) In the case of Kingston, she said during her visit to Taiwan in 1995: "When I started reading and writing...I was lucky to have Jade Snow Wong and Pearl S. Buck." Shan Te-hsing, "An Interview with Maxine Hong Kingston," *Tamkang Review* (Taipei) 27, no. 2 (Winter 1996), 253. For more discussions on how Pearl Buck's writing helped improve the Chinese image in popular American culture, see Peter J. Conn, *Pearl S. Buck: A Cultural Biography* (New York: Cambridge University Press, 1996).

33. My interview with Wong, February 5, 1991.

34. Jade Snow Wong, "Puritans from the Orient," in *The Immigrant Experience,* ed. Thomas C. Wheeler (New York: Penguin Books, 1971), 109.

35. Wong claimed she had never read any works by Chinese immigrant authors before she wrote *Fifth Chinese Daughter*. My interview with Wong, February 5, 1991.

36. Quoted in Ching-Chao Wu, "Chinatowns: A Study in Symbiosis and Assimilation" (Ph.D. dissertation, University of Chicago, 1928), 158. Also see Min Zhou, *Chinatown: The Socioeconomic Potential of an Urban Enclave* (Philadelphia: Temple University Press, 1992), 1–118.

37. Pearl Ng, "Writings on the Chinese in California" (M.A. thesis, University of California, Berkeley, 1939), 46–47.

38. Gerald W. Haslam, *Forgotten Pages of American Literature* (Boston: Houghton Mifflin, 1970), 80.

39. Lai, *Cong huaqiao dao huaren*, 158. Also see Yung, *Unbound Feet.*

40. The same taboo also forbids a female presence on occasions such as the first trip of a new cart. One telling example is that Xiangzi, the hero in Lao She's classic *Ruto xiangzi* [Rickshaw Boy, 1936], believed that the first customer on his newly purchased rickshaw cart "absolutely must not be a woman" because taking a female for the first ride would bring him misfortune and ruin his new cart. Lao She, *Ruto xiangzi* (1936; repr., Beijing: Renmin wenxu, 1994), 11.

41. Frank Chin, *The Chinaman Pacific & Frisco R.R. Co.* (Minneapolis, Minn.: Coffee House Press, 1988), 3.

42. Scarlet Chen, "The Asian Presence," *Belle Lettres: A Review of Books by Women* 6, no. 3 (Fall 1990): 22. Also see Amy Ling, *Between Worlds: Women Writers of Chinese Ancestry* (New York: Pergamon Press, 1990), 119–30.

43. Tiana (Thi Thanh Nga), "The Long March: From Wong to Woo: Asians in Hollywood," *Cineaste* 21, no. 4 (1995): 38.

44. Hsu Kai-yu and Helen Palubinskas, eds., *Asian-American Authors* (Boston: Houghton Mifflin, 1972), 24.

45. Quoted in Ling, *Between Worlds*, 120. Kingston also emphasized Wong's influence on her in my several interviews with her in the 1990s.

About the Contributors

SUCHENG CHAN is professor emerita of Asian American studies and global studies at the University of California, Santa Barbara. She received her Ph.D. from the University of California, Berkeley. Since she retired from teaching in 2001, she has published *Not Just Victims: Conversations with Cambodian Community Leaders in the United States* (2003), *Remapping Asian American History* (2003), *Survivors: Cambodian Refugees in the United States* (2004), and *In Defense of Asian American Studies: The Politics of Teaching and Program Building* (2005).

SHEHONG CHEN is associate professor of history at the University of Massachusetts, Lowell. She received her Ph.D. from the University of Utah and is the author of *Being Chinese, Becoming Chinese Americans* (2002); an occasional paper published by the Asian American Studies Institute at the University of Massachusetts, Boston; and a chapter in *Remapping Asian American History*. She is currently doing research on the history of her hometown in the People's Republic of China.

YONG CHEN is associate professor of history and was associate dean of graduate studies at the University of California, Irvine, from 1999 to 2004. He received his Ph.D. from Cornell University and is the author of *Chinese San Francisco, 1850–1943: A Transpacific Community* (2000) and articles in *Gastronomica: Journal of Food and Culture, Journal of Urban History, Journal of Asian American Studies, Oral History Review, Western Historical Quarterly,* and *Kexue shibao* [Science Times].

MADELINE HSU is associate professor of history at San Francisco State University. She received her Ph.D. from Yale University and is the author of *Dreaming of Gold, Dreaming of Home: Transnationalism and Migration Between the United States and South China, 1882–1943* (2000), which won the 2002 Association for Asian American Studies Outstanding Book in History award. Her articles have appeared in the *Journal of Asian Studies, Amerasia Journal, International Review of Social History,* and *China Review*. She is currently doing research on Taiwanese migration and exile.

HIM MARK LAI is an engineer by profession with a degree from the University of California, Berkeley. A historian by avocation, he taught the first college-level course in Chinese American history in the United States at San Francisco State University in 1969. The author of *Cong huaqiao dao huaren: ershi shiji Meiguo huaren shehui fazhan shi* [From overseas Chinese to Chinese Americans: a social history of the Chinese in the United States in the twentieth century] (1992) and *Becoming Chinese American: A History of Communities and Institutions* (2004), he has published dozens of journal articles and book chapters.

ERIKA LEE is associate professor of history at the University of Minnesota, Minneapolis. She received her Ph.D. from the University of California, Berkeley, and is the author of *At America's Gates: Chinese Immigrants During the Exclusion Era, 1882–1943* (2003), which won the 2004 Theodore Saloutos Book Award in Immigration History and the 2005 Association for Asian American Studies Outstanding Book in History award. Her articles have appeared in *Journal of American History* and *Journal of American Ethnic History*, as well as in edited books. She is currently doing research for a comparative study of Asian migration to the Americas.

HAIMING LIU is associate professor of ethnic and women's studies at California State Polytechnic University, Pomona. He received his Ph.D. from the University of California, Irvine, and is the author of *The Transnational History of a Chinese Family: Immigrant Letters, Family Business, and Reverse Migration* (2005). His articles have been published in *Amerasia Journal*, *Journal of Asian American Studies*, and *Journal of the History of Ideas*, as well as in edited books.

XIAO-HUANG YIN is professor and chair of the American studies program at Occidental College. He received his Ph.D. from Harvard University and is the author of *Chinese American Literature Since the 1850s* (2002) and coeditor with Peter H. Koehn of *The Expanding Roles of Chinese Americans in U.S.-China Relations: Transnational Networks and Trans-Pacific Interactions* (2002). His articles have appeared in *American Quarterly*, *Arizona Quarterly*, *Positions: The Journal of American-East Asian Relations*, and *Atlantic Monthly*, as well as in the *Los Angeles Times* and the *Boston Globe*.

Index

The names of firms, institutions, or organizations are indexed under the names of the cities or towns in which they were or are located. However, those organizations with branches in more than one location are indexed under their own headings.

1790 Naturalization Act/Law, 159, 176
1875 Page Act/Law, 211
1882 Chinese Exclusion Act/Law, 1, 5, 9, 17, 23, 31, 36–37, 60, 69, 159, 175, 178, 195, 211
1884 amendment to the Chinese Exclusion Act/Law, 36, 69
1888 Act of September 13, 36, 69
1888 Act of October 1 ("Scott Act"), 36, 60, 69, 175
1892 Geary Act/Law, 13, 175
  registration required by, 175
1913 Alien Land Act/Law, California, 159
1950 Trading with the Enemy Act/Law, 155

"ABC" (American-born Chinese), 213, 235–36. *See also* birthplace, American-born; Chinese American/s; United States, citizen/s; citizenship, native-born.
Aberdeen, Hong Kong, 24
accommodate or accommodation, 219
acculturate or acculturation, 210, 216, 219, 221, 223, 232–33
adapt or adaptation, 219
Aesop's Fables, 206
African American/s, 70, 217
age, 44, 65, 69–70
  distribution, 4
  gap. *See* marriage, age gap between spouses.
agency, ix–x, 1
agricultural counties. *See* California, agricultural counties.
agriculture or farming, 5, 25, 62. *See also* occupational categories, agricultural laborers; agriculturalists.

Ah Quin, 163
Ah Yaw, 163
Ah-Fong, C.K., 154
Alameda County, California, 40, 62
alienation, 219, 221, 223, 235
aliens, 2, 7. *See also* Chinese immigrant/s or immigration.
All-American Overseas Chinese Military Fund Raising Bureau, 181
Alpha (student wall bulletin), 199
Alpine County, California, 63
Amador County, California, 63
America. *See* United States.
American/s, ix, 3, 138, 174, 192–93, 208, 210, 213, 216–21, 223, 225, 227–28, 230–35
  creed, ideology, or values, ix, 174, 192–93, 217–18, 223
  culture or customs, xv, 3, 138, 193, 213, 217, 220–21, 232–33
  dream, xv, 216–18, 220, 223, 225, 233, 235
  history, 216, 221
  identity, 225
  society or life, 208, 210, 219, 221, 223, 227–28, 230–32, 234
  See also United States.
American-born or U.S.-born. *See* birthplace, American-born. *See also* Chinese Americans; United States, citizens; citizenship, native-born.
American Chinese. *See* Chinese immigrant/s or immigration.
American Indians, 149
American Medical Association, 154
American West. *See* United States, American West.
Americanization, 209, 213, 220, 235
American-ness, xiii, 157, 165, 215, 225

Americas, Chinese communities in the, 26, 60
Angel Island immigration station, 14, 17–21, 175
Anglo-American/s. *See* European American/s.
anti-Chinese actions, environment, or ideologies, 5, 9, 19, 145, 157, 159–61, 166, 171, 174–75, 178, 192, 195, 225. *See also* Chinese exclusion era; Chinese exclusion acts/laws; racism or racial discrimination or prejudice.
antimiscegenation laws, 214, 222
Asia, 26
    Central, 207
Asian American/s, x, 35, 137, 155, 211, 221, 234–36
    history or experience, x, 35, 137, 155, 211
    movement, 236
    studies, 211
Asian immigrant/s, 2. *See also* Chinese immigrant/s or immigration.
assimilate or assimilation, ix, x, 213, 215, 217, 219–21, 223
    theory, ix
Association to Save China, 170
At America's Gates, xi
Atlantic Ocean, 60
attorneys, lawyers, or legal services, xi, 7, 13–14, 16–21, 145
Auburn, California, 28
Augusta, Georgia, 14
Australia, xii, 25–26
autobiography or autobiographies, xv, 213–215, 219, 222–24, 226, 233, 235–36. *See also Father and Glorious Descendant; Fifth Chinese Daughter.*
Autobiography of Malcolm X, The, 217
Ayurvedic (Indian) medicine, 139

Backus, Samuel, 18
baihua (vernacular Chinese), xiv, 184, 196, 207
Baijiaxing (Surnames of the hundred families), 204
Baltimore, Maryland, 14, 22, 27
Bamboo Grove Monastery, Zhejiang Province, 140, 149
Bangkok, Thailand, 25–26
Bank of Canton, 29, 33

Bank of China, 29, 33
banking services, 22, 24, 28, 30, 33, 163
    Chinese, 24, 28, 33
    Western, 28
Baohuanghui, 176–78
    banking and investment programs of, 177
Baoshanghui, 176
Barlow, Jeffrey, 145, 150–51
Beijing, China, 147–48, 164, 167, 183, 197, 206
    Imperial Medical College, 139, 147–48
    University, 183
Being Chinese, Becoming Chinese Americans, xiii
Ben cao jing (pharmacopoeia), 139
birthplace, x, xii, xv, 1, 31, 38–50, 52, 65, 69–70, 152, 156, 167, 174–75, 182, 186–87, 211–15, 218–19, 221–26, 228, 230, 232–36
    American-born, U.S.-born, native/s, native-born, or second generation, x, xii, xv, 1, 31, 38–42, 44–49, 65, 69–70, 152, 167, 174, 182, 186–87, 211–15, 218–19, 221–26, 228, 230, 232–36; female/s, 38, 45–48, 182, 187, 214, 223–24, 226, 230, 232; male/s, 38–42, 45, 48–49, 222–23. *See also* "ABC;" Chinese American/s; United States, citizens; citizenship, native-born.
    China-born or immigrant/s, 38–43, 45–48, 50, 65, 69–70, 175, 182, 187; female/s, 38, 45–48, 182, 187; male/s, 38–42, 45, 48, 50. *See also* Chinese immigrant/s or immigration.
von Bismarck, Otto, 207
Board of Medical Examiners, 154
Boise, Idaho, 14
Bolce, Harold, 5
Bonaparte, Napoleon, 207
Boston, Massachusetts, 14, 22, 27, 29, 180, 211
British:
    colonial rule, 23–25, 191–92
    Isles, 231
    missionaries in China, 140
bubonic plague, 142
Buck, Pearl S., 226
Buddhist monks, 139

Buell, Paul, 137, 150
"Buffalo Bill" (William Cody), 216
Bureau of Immigration. *See* United States,
    Bureau of Immigration.
Burma, 25
business, small, 5. *See also* merchants;
    occupational categories, merchants;
    other businessmen.
Butte County, California, 62–63

Calaveras County, California, 63
Calgary, Alberta, 22, 27
California, xii, 3, 5, 22–23, 37–44, 46–47,
    49–51, 53–58, 62–64, 70–71, 137,
    150, 153, 157, 174, 195
    agribusiness, 64
    agricultural counties, xii, 37, 39–40,
        42–44, 46–47, 49–51, 53–56, 58, 62,
        70–71; Chinese population in, 39–40,
        43, 49, 51, 53, 55, 58, 70–71;
        female/s, 44, 47, 49, 51, 53, 55, 58,
        70–71; male/s; 39–40, 44, 47, 49, 51,
        53, 70–71
    educational code, 195
    gold rush, 3, 23, 39, 63, 137, 157, 174
    mining and mountain counties, xii, 37,
        39, 41, 43–44, 46–47, 50–51, 53–55,
        57–58, 62–63, 70–71; Chinese
        population in, 39–41, 43–44, 47,
        50–51, 53–55, 57–58, 70–71; female/s,
        44, 50–51, 53, 55, 58, 70–71; male/s,
        39, 41, 43, 50–51, 70–71
    Southern California Medical
        Association, 153
    State Medical Society, 150. *See also* San
        Francisco.
Cambridge, Massachusetts:
    Harvard Graduate School of Business
        Administration, 221–22, 224
Cameron, Donaldina, 18–19
Canada, xii, 22, 181, 196, 201
Canton. *See* Guangzhou.
Cantonese, xv, 3–4, 22, 26–27, 145, 162,
    202–04
capital, xiii, 157, 162, 164–65, 172, 175,
    190
    diasporic, 164; social and political
        significance of, 157
    flow of, from the United States to China,
        xiii, 162
capitalism, xiv, 2, 5, 22, 174, 192

Caucasian/s. *See* European American/s.
census of population, United States, xii,
    34–37, 39–40, 42–43, 52, 55–56,
    58–60, 62, 65, 68–69, 212
    information, 35–37, 55; reliability of,
        68–69
    manuscript, xii, 34–35, 37, 42–43,
        59–60, 68
    published, 35
    takers or enumerators, 35–36, 39, 52,
        56, 58, 65, 68
    See also United States, Bureau of the
        Census.
Central Pacific Railroad Co., 158, 190
Chan, Sucheng, xii
Chang, Sam, 144
changshi (common knowledge), 205
Chen Duxiu, 183–84
Chen Kongzhao, 30
Chen Lianbo, 191
Chen Qinjing, 31
Chen, Shehong, xiii–xiv
Chen Ta, 158, 163
Chen, Wen-hsien, 16, 19
Chen Yixi, 165–67, 189, 190
Chen, Yong, xiii, 2
Cheng, Holt, 141
Chew Dong Ngin, 15
Chew, Edward C., 218
Chicago, Illinois, 7, 22, 27–29, 158–59,
    163, 170, 181, 217
chidu (correspondence or letter writing),
    205
children. *See* family or families, children.
Chin, Cheung, 182–83
Chin, Frank, 234
Chin, Kaimon, 9
Chin Sing, 20–21
China, ix, xi–xv, 1–10, 13–14, 16, 18, 20,
    23–28, 31–33, 37–38, 45, 47–48,
    52–55, 57–60, 136–41, 148, 152,
    155–72, 174, 176–85, 187–209, 212,
    214–15, 217, 220–22, 226, 228, 231,
    232–33
    1898 Reform Movement (also known as
        One Hundred Days Reform), xiv,
        176–78, 197–98
    1911 Revolution, 6, 54, 161, 169–70,
        179–80, 206–07
    American/s in, 2–3, 140; missionaries, 3,
        140; trade, 2–3

China (*Continued*)
  Antireligious (anti-Christian) Movement,
    xiv, 187–88
  Air Force, 209
  boycott of American goods (1905),
    13–14, 161, 166, 169, 171
  British in, 140
  Communism or Communist/s in, 163,
    168
  cultural reform in, xiv
  diplomatic relations with the U.S.,
    severance of, 33
  diplomats representing, in the U.S., 14,
    164
  Duyin tongyi hui (Conference on the
    Unification of Pronunciation) (1905),
    196
  economy of, 2, 162, 164, 171–72, 184
  educational: reform, 197; system, 185,
    194, 196
  emigrant/s from, 5, 25, 32, 55, 157, 165
  emigrant communities, 158, 160,
    163–64, 166, 168, 172
  emigration from, 3–4, 24, 55, 58, 158,
    161–62
  European/s or Westerners in, 2, 164
  famine (1907), 169
  foreign or import-export trade, xii, 2,
    24, 26
  Guoyu tongyi choubeihui (Society for
    Preparing a Unification of the
    National Language), 196–97
  Guoyu yanjiuhui (National Language
    Research Association), 196
  Han dynasty, 207
  Hong Xian dynasty, 179–80
  imperial examination system, 196
  Japanese merchant/s in, 3
  Jiangnan Arsenal, 196
  language reform, xiv, 196, 202
  legislature of, 161
  literary reform, xiv, 184
  Marco Polo Bridge Incident (1937), 167
  May Fourth Movement, 54, 185,
    187–88
  Ming dynasty, 138, 161, 177
  Ministry of Education, 196; coeducation
    allowed by, 196
  missionaries in, 3, 140, 204
  New Culture Movement, xiv, 184–85,
    188
  Northern Expedition (1926–28), 189,
    192
  Office for the Education of Chinese
    Overseas, 197
  Opium War, first (1839–42), 195
  People's Republic of China, 33, 155
  petit bourgeoisie in, 191
  Qing dynasty, 138, 141, 161, 164,
    166–67, 177, 179, 189; court, 161,
    164, 166; government or officials,
    179; penal code article 225, 161.
    See also Manchu/s.
  Republic of China, 161, 170, 178–80
  revolutionary movement, xiv, 177–78,
    197–98
  Second Revolution, 179
  Shiyan jiaoyushe (Society for
    Experimental Education), 207
  Sino-Japanese War (1894–95), 195
  socioeconomic status in, 4, 163
  Song dynasty, 138, 206–07
  Tang dynasty, 148
  Tangren (Tang people), 137
  War of National Salvation Against
    Japanese Aggression (1937–45), also
    known as Sino-Japanese War
    (1937–45), 162, 167, 169–71, 203
  Western powers in, 166, 168
  See also Chinese Communist Party;
    Constitutionalist Party; Guomindang;
    Tongmenghui.
China-born. *See* birthplace, China-born;
  Chinese immigrant/s or immigration.
Chinatown/s, 5, 9, 14, 22, 29, 40, 137–38,
  142–45, 147, 175, 177, 180–83, 187,
  194, 200, 213, 216–18, 224, 226,
  228, 231–33.
  elite, 224. *See also* Chinese communities
    in the U. S.; San Francisco, Chinatown.
Chinese America, xiv–xv, 36, 45, 54–55,
  155–58, 160–63, 166, 168–72, 192,
  209, 211, 214
Chinese American/s, ix–x, xiii–xv, 33, 38,
  68, 155–74, 180, 186, 193, 208–12,
  215, 218, 223–31, 234–36
  historiography, x
  history or experience, x, xiv, 55, 156–58,
    160, 172, 192, 209, 211, 214, 223,
    235–36
  images or stereotypes of, changing,
    225–29, 231, 234

social status of, in China, xiii
texts, xv
See also birthplace, American-born;
   United States, citizen/s; citizenship,
   native-born.
Chinese American Citizens Alliance, 181,
   184
*Chinese American Literature Since the
   1850s*, xv
Chinese American Transnationalism, ix
Chinese Arrival Investigation Case Files, xi,
   8, 15, 45, 59–60, 69. *See also* United
   States, Bureau of Immigration.
Chinese Communist Party, 188
Chinese communities in the United States,
   ix–xi, xiii, 1, 13–14, 20–21, 26, 56,
   69, 137, 140, 142–43, 145, 147, 157,
   162, 169–70, 174, 179, 181, 186–87,
   196, 200–03, 211–13, 215, 218, 220,
   222, 224, 226, 232, 234
   institutional structure of, ix
   organizations in, 1, 13–14, 142, 181,
      200, 215–16
   See also Chinatown/s; San Francisco,
      Chinatown.
Chinese Consolidated Benevolent
   Association. *See* San Francisco,
   Chinese Consolidated Benevolent
   Association.
Chinese civilization, culture, ethics,
   heritage, moral standards, traditions
   or values, xiv, 9, 22, 38, 45, 53, 136,
   147–48, 152, 159, 175–76, 181–84,
   193–94, 198, 205–06, 208–09,
   212–14, 217–27, 231–32, 234
Chinese diaspora, 170–72. *See also*
   Americas, Chinese communities in the;
   Chinatown/s; Chinese communities in
   the U.S.; overseas Chinese; Southeast
   Asia, Chinese communities in.
Chinese exclusion era, x–xi, 1–2, 4, 7,
   9–10, 14, 16, 19, 23, 33, 53, 59, 68,
   151, 162, 175, 177, 204, 208–09,
   211–12, 214–18, 221–25, 231,
   233–36
Chinese exclusion acts/laws, ix, xi, xiv,
   1–2, 4–5, 9–10, 12–14, 17, 19–21, 23,
   31–32, 36–37, 42, 53, 58–59, 61,
   64–65, 172, 175, 194, 198, 201, 211,
   214–15, 217, 219, 222, 226
   enforcement of, ix, xi, 9, 12–14, 19, 58

exempt classes, 10, 31, 42, 65, 175
repeal of, 172, 214–15, 217
See also 1882 Chinese Exclusion
   Act/Law; 1884 amendment; Act of
   September 13, 1888; Act of October 1,
   1888; 1892 Geary Act/Law.
Chinese female migration. *See* Chinese
   immigrant/s or immigration, women/
   females.
Chinese foodstuffs, goods, groceries, or
   merchandise, xii, 22–23, 25–27
Chinese Herb Science, 149
Chinese immigrant/s or immigration, x–xii,
   xiv–xv, 1–10, 12–17, 19–21, 23, 25,
   33–61, 68–69, 136–38, 140–42, 148,
   156–59, 162, 165–66, 172–74,
   176–82, 184–95, 201–05, 209–17,
   221–22, 228–29, 235
   admission of, 12, 14
   ages of, 7
   children of, xii, xiv, 7, 10. *See also*
      birthplace, American-born;
      China-born; United States, citizen/s;
      citizenship.
   class composition of, 2, 7, 38, 45, 211
   consciousness of, xv, 156, 162, 173. *See
      also* ethnic consciousness or identity.
   cost of passage, 25
   demographic characteristics or
      composition of, 2, 7, 38–58, 211
   exempt-class, 6, 7, 49
   illegal, 2, 8, 218
   legal, 2
   lure of the United States, 2–4
   men/males, xi, 7, 9, 38–45
   merchants. *See* merchants.
   multigenerational, 7
   numbers, 1, 38–58
   occupations of, in China, 7; in the U.S.
      See employment, occupations, or
      work. *See also* laborers; laundrymen;
      merchants; occupational categories.
   "paper children," 212
   "paper daughters," 7, 212
   "paper sons," 7, 212
   patterns, xi, 12
   ratio of rejections, 14
   returning laborers, 7, 8, 13
   returning natives. *See* United States,
      citizen/s; citizenship, native-born.
   returning residents, 1, 6, 16–17, 19, 21

Chinese immigrant/s or immigration
  (*Continued*)
  "slots," 10
  socioeconomic class or status, xi, 7, 172,
    174
  sojourners or sojourning, ix, 4–5, 7, 9,
    12, 193–94
  strategies to defy exclusion laws, xi, 2,
    12, 15
  visits to China, 38, 49
  women/females, xi–xii, 6–7, 9–10, 17,
    21, 34–59, 61, 185–87; cultural
    constraints on emigration, 10;
    dependent status of, 10; traffickers in,
    56
  year of immigration, 36, 69
Chinese language, 68, 145, 152, 194–95,
  198–99, 204–10
Chinese-language newspapers, xiv, 14,
  177–78, 189–201. *See also Chinese
  World; Chung Sai Yat Po; Ta Tung Yat
  Po; Young China.*
Chinese Language Newspapers
  Association, 184
Chinese-language schools, xiv, 194–205,
  207–10, 220
  coeducation in, 199
  curriculum of, 195, 198–200, 205,
    209–10
  extracurricular activities in, xiv, 198–200
  in Honolulu, 195, 198–99, 201–03, 209;
    Chung Shan School, 198, 203, 209;
    Jackson School, 198, 202; Mun Lun
    School, 198–99, 201, 209; Wah Mun
    School, 198–99, 201–03
  in San Francisco, 195, 198–205, 207,
    209–10; Chinese Central High School,
    200, 203–04, 209; Chinese Public
    School, 200, 202; Daqing Qiaomin
    Xuetang (Great Qing Overseas
    Chinese School), 198–99; Daqing
    Shuyuan (Great Qing School), 195;
    Hip Wo School, 200; Morning Bell
    School, 199–200, 202; Nam Kue
    School, 200–02, 205, 207; St. Mary's
    School, 200, 204; Yeong Wo School,
    200, 203; Zhonghua Qiaomin Gongli
    Xuexiao (Overseas Chinese Public
    School), 199
  teachers in, xiv, 200–01
  textbooks used by, xiv, 198, 204–08, 210

Chinese-language sources, xi, xiii,
  xv–xvi
Chinese medicine, 138–40
  acupuncture, 139
  moxibustion, 139
  pharmacology, 139
  pulsology, 139
  See also herbalists or herbal
    doctors/physicians; herb stores; herbs
    or herbal medicine.
Chinese nationalism, 13, 157, 161–62,
  165–66, 168–69, 172, 176, 184, 188,
  192, 203, 208
Chinese New Year, 69, 178, 217
Chinese overseas. *See* overseas Chinese.
Chinese passenger lists, 59–60, 141
  arriving passengers, 59, 141
  departing passengers, 59
  in-transit passengers, 60
  women and girls, 59–60
Chinese San Francisco, xiii
Chinese Six Companies. *See* San Francisco,
  Chinese Consolidated Benevolent
  Association.
Chinese World, xiv, 177–85, 188–89,
  191
Chinese-ness, xiii, 156, 159, 165, 171–72
  political dimensions of, 171
Chinn, Thomas, 187
"Chonglou Courier Station," 32–33
Chonglou, Taishan District, Guangdong
  Province, 29, 33
Christian/ity, xiv, 3, 17–18, 174, 177, 182,
  185–88, 192, 204, 218, 221
  morals or values, 182
Chung, Arthur, 144, 154
Chung, Nellie Yee, 144, 151–52
Chung Sai Yat Po, xiv, 18, 167, 178–81,
  185–86, 188–91
Chung Shan District. *See* Zhongshan
  District.
Chung, Yick Hong, 144–45, 148, 151–52,
  154
citizenship. *See* United States, citizenship.
civil rights, 178
  movement. *See* United States, civil rights
  movement.
Claiming America, ix
cold war, 33
Colorado (name of ship), 25
Colusa County, California, 62

Comintern, 188
Communications Bank, 29
Communism or Communist/s, xiv–xv,
    189–90. *See also* China, Communism
    or Communists in; Chinese
    Communist Party.
Confucian classics, 196, 198
Confucian Society, 184
Confucianism, xiv, 174, 176, 181–86, 192,
    232
Confucius, 182
Constitutionalist Party, 169, 181,
    184
Contra Costa County, California, 62
Conwell, Russell, 158
Coolidge, Mary R., 142
Crozier, Ralph C., 139, 146
Cuba, 181

Daily Alta California, 22
Del Norte County, California, 62–63
democracy, ix, xv, 179–80, 183–84, 188,
    191, 218
Denby, Charles, 25
Denver, Colorado, 14
derivative citizens. *See* United States,
    citizenship, derivative.
Detroit, Michigan, 27, 181
Dewey, John, 183
*Dingzheng chudeng xiaoxue zuixin
    guowen jiaokeshu* (Lower primary
    schools new national readers, revised
    edition), 205
discrimination, ix, xiii, 12–14, 157, 160,
    177–79, 182, 193–94, 209–22, 227.
    See also racism or racial
    discrimination or prejudice.
    sexual, 231–32, 235
"Doc Lee," 148
domestic servants or workers, 5
Doushan, Taishan District, Guangdong
    Province, 29
    Yichang (company), 29
*Dreaming of Gold, Dreaming of
    Home*, xi
DuBois, W.E.B., 235
Duhu, Taishan District, Guangdong
    Province, 29
Dutch colonial rule, 25
Dutch Flat, California, 21, 28
    Wing On Wo, 27–28

earthquake. *See* San Francisco, 1906
    earthquake.
East Belleville, Alameda County, 215
East Las Vegas, New Mexico, 14
education:
    in China. *See* China, educational:
    reform; system
    in the U.S., 10.
Education of Henry Adams, The, 233
Eitel, E.J., 25
El Dorado County, California, 63
emigrants or emigration. *See* China,
    emigrants; emigration from.
Emperor Guang Xu, 176
Emperor Huang, 139
Emperor Yan, 139
employment, occupations, or work, xii,
    2–4, 9, 23, 33, 37, 40–41, 44, 56–57,
    63, 145, 155, 159, 175, 177, 218,
    224, 227
    of women, 10, 56–57
    opportunities, 5–6, 25, 44, 157, 167
    See also herbalists; laborers;
    laundrymen; merchants; miners or
    mining; occupational categories.
Empress Dowager Ci Xi, 177
England, 207
English language, 3, 21, 68, 143, 149, 152,
    187, 199, 209, 212
English-language newspapers, 144
English-language sources, x, xiii, xv–xvi
Enping District, Guangdong Province, 15,
    164
Entry Denied, ix–x
equality or equal rights, ix, xv, 179, 209,
    217–20, 230
ethnic:
    consciousness or identity, ix–x, xiii, 156,
    160, 162, 172–73, 213, 223, 225
    group/s, 159
    legacy, 223
    skill/s, 136
European American/s, Caucasian/s, or
    white/s, 17, 28, 58, 70, 142–45,
    149–51, 214, 221, 226, 229–32, 235
    women, 150–51, 221–22
European immigrant/s, x, 2, 8, 13
exclusion. *See* Chinese exclusion era;
    Chinese exclusion acts/laws.
exempt classes. *See* Chinese exclusion
    acts/laws, exempt classes.

Fairmont, Nebraska, 14
family or families, xii, 1–3, 5–7, 9, 13, 16,
    19, 21–23, 31, 36–38, 40–43, 50,
    54–56, 58, 65, 139, 144, 151–52, 158,
    164, 175, 182–83, 189, 194–95, 201,
    211–16, 221–22, 224–27, 229,
    231–32
  children, 38, 43
  clan/s, xii
  filial piety, 221
  formation, xii, 36–38, 41–42, 50, 55, 58,
    65; site/s of, 38, 42
  generation gap, 214
  life, 212, 221
  networks, xii
  primogeniture, 224
  relations, 36
  reunification, 9
  second generation. See birthplace,
    American-born.
  See also merchants, wives and children
    of; United States, citizens, wives and
    children of.
fanqing fuming (overthrow the Qing,
    restore the Ming), 177
Father and Glorious Descendant, xv,
    214–23, 235
female infanticide, 45
Fiddletown, Amador County, 137
  Chew Kee Herb Shop, 137
Fifth Chinese Daughter, xv, 182, 213–14,
    223–36
  recipient of Commonwealth Club Medal
    for Nonfiction, 224
  selection as Book of the Month, 224
  selection as Christian Herald Family
    Book, 224
Filipino/s, 217
First Opium War (1839–42). See China,
    Opium War, first.
Fong, Alice, 182
Fong Ing Bong, 4
Fong Sue Nom, 146
Fong Tim, 15–16
Fong Wan, 143, 147, 149–51, 153–54
Foo, Charley, 17–18
France, 179, 207
Fresno County, California, 62
Fritz, Christian, 61
Fujian Province, 33, 148

Fung Jong Yee, 137
Furth, Charlotte, 138

Gam Saan (Jinshan, meaning Gold
    Mountain), 2. See also "Gold
    Mountain."
Gam Saan haak (Jinshan ke, meaning Gold
    Mountain guest/s), 2–3, 6–7
Gee See [Shee], 17
gender, 10, 54, 65, 186, 196, 232
  equality, 186, 232
  propriety, 196
  relations, 54
  roles, 10
Germany, 184, 221
Gernet, Jacques, 138
Glenn County, California, 63
gold mining. See miners or mining.
"Gold Mountain," 2–4, 6, 15, 22, 157,
    174
"Gold Mountaineers," 167
gold rush. See California, gold rush.
gongmin (civics), 205
Good Earth, The, 226
Great Depression. See United States, Great
    Depression.
Greenhalgh, Oscar, 13
Guan Shuyi, 201
Guan Youzhang, 207
Guan Zhihuai, 207
Guangdong Province, xi, 2,4, 23, 27–32,
    139, 141, 158, 160, 165, 168–69,
    178, 189–90, 192, 201–03, 221
Guanghai, Taishan District, Guangdong
    Province, 29
Guangzhou (Canton), Guangdong
    Province, xv, 3, 6, 18, 22, 24, 140–41,
    148, 164–65, 188, 191–92, 201–02,
    207, 216
  Guanghua Hospital in, 141
  Merchants' Association, 191–92
  Ophthalmic Hospital in, 140
  Po-chi (Boji) Hospital in, 140–41
Guide to the City and Suburbs of Canton,
    A, 140
Guomindang (Kuomintang), 179, 181,
    188–91, 197, 199–203, 209
  Central Committee, 197
  Overseas Chinese Affairs Commission,
    197, 203

guowen (national readers), 205
guoyu (national language), xiv–xv, 196–97, 199–204
Guyamas, Mexico, 60

habeas corpus, writs of, 20, 60–61
Han Chinese, 177
Hangzhou, Zhejiang Province, 138
Hankou, Hubei Province, 206
Havana, Cuba, 28, 60
Hawaii/an, 60, 141, 198–99
Board of Health, 141
Hawn Mok (also known as Hong Ah Mock), 61
Hee, Jackson, 198
herb businesses or stores, 136–38, 142–43, 145, 147–48, 151–52, 155
Herb Lore, 149–51, 153
herbalists or herbal doctors/physicians, xiii, 137–38, 141–51, 153–55
  business of, xiii
  Caucasian patients of, xiii, 137, 144–45, 147, 149–51, 153
  Chinese patients of, xiii, 144, 147, 151
  discrimination against, xiii, 153–55
  Mexican patients of, 144
  "Tang doctors," 137
  "Tang-fan doctors," 137
  training of, xiii, 147–49
herbs or herbal medicine, xii–xiii, 26–27, 136–41, 145, 148–53, 155, 226
  as a transpacific practice or trade, xiii, 136
Hi Kowe, 165
Hillinger, Charles, 137
Hobart, Washington, 22, 27
Holmes, A.Z., 144–45
Hong Kong (Xianggang), xii, xv, 3, 7, 15, 22–32, 163, 190–92
  as center of international trade, 26, 28
  Bai'anlong Yinhao, 30
  British colonial government in, 191–92
  China Hong Nim Life Insurance Company, Ltd., 24
  Huaxin Ginseng Co., 32
  Liu Zanchen, 32
  Qinji Co., 31
  U.S. consulate in, 32
  Wah Ying Cheong, 29–31

Wu Chow Receiving Agency, Ltd., 24
  Yuen Fat Hong, 26
Hong Kong and Shanghai Banking Corporation, 191
Honolulu, Hawaii, 22, 27, 60, 141, 170, 195, 198–99, 201–03, 209
  Xueyi hui (Society for learning and the arts), 198.
  See also Chinese-language schools, in Honolulu.
Hopkins, Mark, 153
House Divided, A, 226
household composition, 36–37
  head of household, 36–37; female, 37–38
Houston, Texas, 22, 27
Hsu, Madeline Y., xi
Hu Shi, 183–84
Hua'nanchang, Taishan District, Guangdong Province, 30
Huang Kuan, 141
Huanghua Gang, Guangdong Province, 207
  Mausoleum of the Seventy-two Martyrs of the Revolution, 207
Huawen xuesheng (Chinese-language students), 198
Huawen xuesheng bao (Chinese-language students' newspaper), 198
Huawen zazhi (Chinese-language magazine), 198
Hubei Province, 165
Humboldt County, California, 62

Ichioka, Yuji, 35
Idaho, State Supreme Court of, 154
ideology or ideologies, xiv, 165, 174
immigration:
  authorities or officials, xi, 4–5, 7, 9, 13, 15–21, 32, 49, 59, 61, 64, 145, 212, 218; interrogation and detention by, 15, 19, 21, 32, 59
  laws, 1, 13, 178, 192, 201
  See also Chinese exclusion acts/laws; United States, Bureau of Immigration; commissioner-general of.
Imperial County, California, 62
imperialism, 188
  socialist, 189
India, 206
industrialization, 5

Ing Hay, 145, 148, 150
International Chinese Business Directory of the World, 146–47
international labor migration, 2
interracial marriage. *See* marriage, interracial.
investments. *See* remittances, investments.
Inyo County, California, 63

Japan, 155, 160, 162, 167, 169–71, 179, 181, 184–85, 195–96, 201, 203, 206
    invasion of China, 155, 162, 167, 169–71, 203
    Meiji Restoration (1868), 195, 206
    Twenty-one Demands (on China), 179
Japanese, 144, 195
Java, Indonesia, 25
Jenkins, McConnell, 18
Jeong Foo Louie, 4
Jersey City, New Jersey, 14
Jiang Weiqiao, 205
Jiang Yongkang, 32
jiaokeshu (textbooks), 204
Jiebao, 164
Jing-Zhang Railroad, 167
Jinping mei (Golden vase plum), 226
jinshanzhuang (Gold Mountain firms), xi–xii, 22–23, 26–33, 163
jiubahang (ninety-eight percent firms), 26
jobs. *See* employment, occupations, or work.
Joffe, Adolf, 188
John Day, Oregon, 148, 150
judicial courts or system. *See* United States, judicial system.

Kang Youwei, 176
Kao Man-hua, 26
Kennah, Henry C., 20
Kern County, California, 62
Kerr, John, 140–41
kinship networks or kinsmen, xi, 1, 14–16, 21–23, 26, 29, 32, 228
King Solomon, 217
Kings County, California, 62
Kingston, Maxine Hong, 221, 224, 234, 236
Knights Ferry, Stanislaus County, 17–18
Kobe, Japan, 26
Kong Chin Young, 201
Kong Rong, 206

Korea, 206
Kulp, Daniel, 139
Kuomintang. *See* Guomindang.
Kung Yick village, Taishan District, Guangdong Province, 4
Kwoo River, 221

labor brokers, contractors, or recruiters, 5, 23, 25–26, 158
laborers, 2, 5, 7, 9, 31, 42, 60, 159, 162–63, 175, 177, 190
    wives of, 175
Lai, Him Mark, xiv, 170
Lake County, California, 62
language barrier, 68
Larson, Louise Leung, 154
Lassen County, California, 63
laundries, 5, 64, 145, 155, 175
laundryman or laundrymen, 6–7, 17–18, 43, 46, 64, 67, 163, 211, 212
Law Shee Low, 6, 187
Lee, Bruce, 234
Lee Chew, 211
Lee Chi Yet, 4, 6, 17
Lee, Erika, xi, 59
Lee Fook, 16
Lee Kan, 18–19
Lee, Rose Hum, 144
Lee, Sue Ben, 18
Lee, Virginia Chin-lan, 214
Lee Yan Phou, 228
Lee Young Sing, 5, 15
Lem, Arthur, 9, 15
Lenz, Frank B., 18
Leong Cum, 17
Leong, Faith Sai, 232
Leong, Gilbert, 27
Leung, Angela K.C., 138
Leung, Taft, 152
Leung, Tom, 144–45, 147–52, 154
letters, xii, 4–5, 28, 30, 33, 34. *See also* postal services.
Lewiston, Idaho, 17
Li Hongzhang, 165
Li Po Tai (Li Putai), 143, 153
Li Rongyao, 147
Liang Qichao, 161, 169, 176
Liang Qinggui, 196, 198
Liang yao zhaozhi (food and drug labels), 138
Liberty Ship, 229, 233

Life magazine, 226
Lin Sen, 202
Lincoln, Abraham, 207
Lippincott's Magazine, 143
Little, Brown and Co., 214
Liu, Haiming, xii
Liu Pei Chi (Liu Boji), 137, 143, 166
Liu Zuoren, 33
Logansport, Indiana, 18
Los Angeles (city), California, 14, 17, 22, 27, 29, 143–47, 149–52, 154, 164
    Bow Sui Tong, 146
    Chan, H.T., physician, 146
    Chinese Herb Co., 146
    Chinese Medical Co., 146
    Chinese Tea and Herb Co., 146
    Dai Sang Tong, Drugs, 146
    Din Au Tong, Drugs, 146
    Foo and Wing Herb Co., Medicines, 146
    Gee Ning Tong, Drugs, 146
    Hong Wo Tong, Drugs, 146
    Kam Brothers and Co., physicians, 146
    Leung Herb Co., 154
    Lum Wing Yue Chinese Tea and Herb Co., 146
    Mon Yick Tong, Drugs, 146
    Mon Yuen Tong, Drugs, 146
    Po Sang, Drugs, 146
    Po Sow Tong, Drugs, 146
    Quan Tong, Herb Co., 146
    Suey Gee Tong and Co., Drugs, 146
    Sun Kam Lee and Co., Teas, 146
    Tom She Bin and Sons, physicians, 146
    Wah Young Herb Co., Drugs, 146
    Wing On Tong, Drugs, 146
    Wong Company Sanitarium, 146
    Yee Sing and Co., Drugs, 146
    Yick Yuen Tong, Drugs, 146
    Young Woo Tong, Drugs, 146
Los Angeles County, California, 62, 156
Los Angeles Times, 150, 153
Lou, Raymond, 144
Louie, Stella, 152
Louis XIV, 207
Lowe, Pardee, xv, 213–25, 235–36
Lui, Garding, 147, 149–51

Macao (Aomen), Guangdong Province, 24–25
Madera County, California, 61
Malay Peninsula, 25

Malcolm X (Malcolm Little, also known as El-Hajj Malik El-Shabazz), 217
male chauvinism, 232
Man (Who Thought) He Looked Like Robert Taylor, The, 217
"mandarin," xv
Manchu/s, 177, 222. *See also* China, Qing dynasty.
    anti-Manchuism, 177
Manchuria, 189
Manila, the Philippines, 25, 29
manufacturing, 5. *See also* employment, occupations, or work.
manuscript census. *See* census of population, United States, manuscript.
Marin County, California, 62
Mariposa County, California, 63
marital status, 37–49, 51–59, 64–65, 69–70
    China-born, 37–49, 51, 53–59; females, 37, 45–49, 52–59; married with resident husbands, 45–49, 53–58, 64, 69–70; married without resident husbands, 37, 45–46, 48, 55, 57; single, 37, 45, 47–48, 55–56, 58; widowed or divorced, 37, 45–46, 48; males, 37, 39–42, 44, 49, 51, 59, 69; married, total number, 37, 39–42; married with resident wives, 41–44, 49, 51, 69–70; married without resident wives, 42; widowed or divorced, 39–41
    U.S.-born, 38–49, 52–55, 64, 69–70; females, 42, 45–49, 52–55, 64, 69–70; married with resident husbands, 45–49, 52–55, 64, 69–70; married without resident husbands, 45; single, 45–48; widowed or divorced, 45; males, 38–44, 49, 51, 69; married, total number, 39–41; married with resident wives, 41–44, 49, 51, 69–70; married without resident wives, 42; widowed or divorced, 39–41
    See also marriage.
marriage, xii, 39–58, 64, 69–70, 186, 214, 221–22
    age at marriage, 36, 52, 70
    age gap between spouses, 48–53
    betrothal of children, 52
    comparative advantage of China-born men, 48

marriage (*Continued*)
  "coresident spouses," 48, 50–51
  divorced men, 39–41
  divorced women, 37, 45–46, 48
  interracial, 214, 222
  median age at marriage, 53, 55, 57
  non-Chinese spouses, 70
  number of years married, 36, 52, 70
  "presently married men," 37
  "presently married women," 52
  rate/s of, xii, 37, 41–44
  "resident husbands," 37, 45–49, 52–58,
    64, 69–70
  "resident wives," 41–44, 49, 51, 69–70
  single men, 39–41, 49
  single women, 37, 45–48, 55–56, 58
  type of couple, 48–51, 53, 55; type I:
    China-born husband with China-born
    wife, 48–51, 55; type II: China-born
    husband with U.S.- born wife, 48–51,
    53; type III: U.S.-born husband with
    China-born wife, 48–51; type IV:
    U.S.-born husband with U.S.-born
    wife, 48–51
  widows, 37
  widowers, 39–41
  See also marital status
Marshall, Thomas R., 216
Mazatlan, Mexico, 60
McLeod, Alexander, 143, 148
McGowan, George, 21
McWilliams, Carey, 150
medical knowledge of the Chinese,
  136–40
Melbourne, Australia, 28
"melting pot." *See* assimilation.
Memphis, Tennessee, 14
Mendocino County, California, 62
Merced County, California, 62
merchants, xii, 2, 7, 9, 12, 16, 18–19, 22,
  27, 31, 37, 41–44, 64, 66, 141, 145,
  151, 165–66, 171, 174, 212, 215,
  226
  wives and children of, xii, 3, 7, 10,
    12–13, 17–19, 31, 151
Mexican immigrants, 8, 70, 144
Mexico, xii, 26, 60, 181
Millian, Jerome, 17
miners or mining, 3, 5, 9, 23, 40–41, 57,
  65, 137, 165
  camps, 57

counties. *See* California, mining and
  mountain counties.
  deep shaft, 23
  hydraulic, 23
Minneapolis, Minnesota, 22
minority:
  discourse, 235
  paradigm, ix
missionaries, 140, 195. *See also* China,
  missionaries in.
"model minority," 225, 227, 234
Modoc County, California, 63
Mongolia, 189
Mono County, California, 63
Montana, 144
Monterey County, California, 62
Montreal, Quebec, 22, 27, 29
Morrison, Robert, 140
Moy Sau Bik, 10
Muench, Christopher, 137, 150
multicultural/ism, x

Nafu, Taishan District, Guangdong
  Province, 29
Nagle, John D., 20
nanbeihang (north-south firms), 26
Nanjing, China, 197, 206
Nanyang (Southern ocean), 197
Napa County, California, 62
National Protection Army, 180–81
National Salvation Association, 185
nationalism. *See* Chinese nationalism.
naturalized citizens. *See* United States,
  citizenship, naturalized.
Nee, Brett de Bary, 9
Nee, Victor, 9
Nevada, 63
Nevada County, California, 63
New Brunswick, New Jersey, 14
New England, 221
"New Society" village, Guangdong
  Province, 221
New World, 159–60, 163, 197, 201
New York City, New York, 5, 9, 14, 22,
  27–30, 159, 170, 180, 183, 186, 211,
  230
  Chinatown, 5
  Columbia University, 183
  Metropolitan Museum of Art, 230
New Youth (magazine), 183
New Zealand, 29

Newark, New Jersey, 22, 27
Ng Poon Chew (Wu Panzhao), xiv, 18,
    177–78, 183, 218
Ningyang Railroad. See Xinning/Ningyang
    Railroad.
non-Chinese, 136
Norfolk, Virginia, 14
North America, xii, xiv, 22–23, 25–27,
    158, 161, 176, 181, 196–97, 202
Noyce, J.S., 18
Nüzhen armies, 207

Oakland, California, 40, 143, 147, 149,
    153, 186
    Mills College, 225, 228
occupational categories, 37–38, 41–44,
    63–67
    agents and supervisors, 41–43, 67
    agricultural laborers, 65
    agriculturalists, 43, 65
    clerks and shop assistants, 41–42, 44, 66
    cooks, 43, 64–65, 67
    entrepreneurs, 64, 66. See also
        merchants.
    factory workers, 41–42, 66
    fishermen, 65
    laundrymen. See laundryman or
        laundrymen.
    merchants. See merchants.
    miners. See miners or mining.
    nonagricultural workers, 42, 60, 67
    other businessmen, 41–44, 64, 66
    other personal service providers, 67
    primary producers and extractors, 65
    professionals, 41–42, 44, 65
    skilled artisans, 5, 41–42, 44, 64, 66
    students, 65, 67
occupations. See employment, occupations,
    or work.
opium, 24, 142, 189
    smoking, 142, 189
    trade, 24
Opium War. See China, Opium War, first.
oppressed groups or oppression, ix. See
    also racism or racial discrimination or
    prejudice.
oral history or histories, xi, 35
Orange County, California, 62
Oregon, 63, 145, 148, 187
"Orientals," 213, 233–35
Osaka, Japan, 29

Overland Monthly, 128
overseas Chinese, xi–xii, 22–28, 33, 157,
    161–62, 164–65, 168–72, 197, 207
    communities, 24, 26–27
    education of. See Chinese-language
        schools.
    trade networks established by, 22
Overseas Chinese Corps of Volunteers, 181

Pacific Coast, 178, 216, 221
Pacific Mail Steamship Company, 3,
    14–16, 25
    detention shed operated by, 14, 16
Pacific Ocean, xi, xiv, 3, 7, 22–23, 27,
    55, 57, 60, 156, 159, 162, 166, 174,
    193
pan-Asian ethnicity, 235
"paper children." See Chinese immigrants,
    "paper children."
"paper daughters." See Chinese
    immigrants, "paper daughters."
"paper sons." See Chinese immigrants,
    "paper sons."
Panama, 60
Pardee, George C., 216
Park, Robert E., 212
Parker, Peter, 140–41
Peace Planning Society, 179
Pearl River, Guangdong Province, 222
Pearl River Delta, Guangdong Province, 2,
    4, 24, 160, 162–64, 167, 201
Peffer, George A., 56, 68
Penang, Malaysia, 24
Peoria, Illinois, 14
"perpetual foreigners," 233
Peru, 60
Peter the Great, 207
Philadelphia, Pennsylvania, 22, 27, 143
Philippines, 25
pinyin system. See transliteration.
Pittsburgh, Pennsylvania, 27
Placer County, California, 62–63
Plumas County, California, 63
pluralism, x
Poon Lung Cheng village, Taishan district,
    Guangdong Province, 4
Port Townsend, Washington, 60
Portland, Oregon, 22, 27, 29, 150, 181
postal service, xii, 22, 28–29, 33, 163
prejudice. See racism or racial
    discrimination or prejudice.

prostitutes or prostitution, 9, 17–18,
34–35, 56–58
Prussia, 207
published census. *See* census of population,
United States, published.
Puget Sound, Washington, 60
putonghua (common language) xv, 3, 196

Qianziwen (Thousand characters essay),
204
Qingdao, Shandong Province, 181
Qiu Jin, 207

race, xv, 213
relations, 160
"racial uniform," 212, 217
racism or racial discrimination or
prejudice, xiii, xv, 33, 149, 153,
158–59, 162, 166, 172, 175, 182,
213, 218–19, 223, 230, 234–35.
See also anti-Chinese activities,
environment, or ideologies; Chinese
exclusion acts/laws.
railroads or railroad construction, 5, 9, 25,
165. *See also* Xinning/ Ningyang
Railroad.
Rangoon, Burma, 29
religious freedom, 188
Remer, C.F., 170–71
remittance/s, xii, 7, 22, 28, 30–31, 33,
157–58, 162–65, 167–70, 172
charitable donations, 157, 162
family-oriented, 164, 169, 172
as investment/s, 157, 162, 164–65,
167–69, 172–73
Remondino, P.C., 153
republicanism, xiv, 174, 179–81, 192, 196
resistance, ix–x, 1
restaurants, 5, 155
reverse assimilation, xiii, 136
Richardson, Christine, 145, 150–51
Riordan, Thomas, 20
Riverside County, California, 18, 62
Rochester, New York, 14
Roosevelt, Alice, 216
Roosevelt, Theodore, 13
ru yi (scholar-doctor), 148
Russia, 207

Sacramento (city), California, 28, 154
Hall-Luhrs and Co., 28
Sacramento County, California, 62
Sacramento Valley, California, 62

Salt Lake City, Utah, 144
Salyer, Lucy, 61
Sam Yup (Sanyi-Three Districts), 202
San Benito County, California, 62
San Bernardino County, California, 62
San Diego (city), California, 22, 27, 29,
216
San Diego County, California, 62
San Francisco (city and county), California,
xii, 3, 5, 9, 13–20, 22–23, 25, 27–55,
57–58, 60, 62, 69–71, 137–38,
142–43, 147, 159, 161, 165, 169–71,
178, 180–82, 184–87, 192, 194–95,
197, 199–205, 207, 209, 216, 218,
224–25, 232
1906 earthquake, 40, 43–44, 50, 55, 169
Board of Education, 195
Board of Supervisors, 142
Chinatown, 9, 14, 40, 137–38, 142–43,
182, 186–87, 195, 197, 204–05, 216,
224
Chinese Chamber of Commerce, 20,
138, 184, 192
Chinese Church Alliance, 181, 184
Chinese consulate or consul general, 13,
19–20, 142, 147, 161
Chinese Historical Society of America,
138
Chinese-language schools. *See*
Chinese-language schools, in San
Francisco.
Chinese population in, 39–44, 47–50,
54, 58, 69–71; females, 44, 47–50, 52,
54, 58, 70–71; males, 30–43, 48–50,
70–71
Commonwealth Club, 224
Customs House, 23, 25
Customs Reform Society, 186
Donghua (Tung Wah) Dispensary, 142
Flip Flap Flop (club), San Francisco, 200
Junior College, 225
Kwang Sick Co., 28
Morning Bell Theatrical Society, 199
Nam Hoy Fook Yum Tong, 200
Presbyterian Church school, 178
Presbyterian Mission Home, 18
public school, segregated Chinese, 195
Song Loy Co., 138
Theological Seminary, 178
Vifee Vofee (club), 200
San Francisco Bay, 14, 40, 55, 216
San Francisco Bay area, 62, 153, 215

San Joaquin County, California, 62
San Joaquin Valley, California, 62
San Luis Obispo County, California, 62
San Mateo County, California, 62
Sanba village, Taishan District, Guangdong
    Province, 28
sanda zhengce (three major policies), 188
sanmin zhuyi (three people's principles),
    188, 200
Santa Barbara County, California, 62
Santa Clara County, California, 62
Santa Cruz County, California, 63
Santos, Bienvenido N., 217
Sanzijing (Trimetrical classics), 204
Schell, A.S., 17–18
science, xiv, 183, 188, 204, 206
Science of Oriental Medicine, The, 147,
    149, 153
Seattle, Washington, 13, 22, 27–28, 60,
    140, 165, 182, 186, 216
    Wah Chung Co., 140
second generation. *See* birthplace,
    American-born.
Secrets of Chinese Physicians, 149
Septima (name of ship), 141
Shandong Province, 184–85
Shanghai, China, 162, 204–06
    Commercial Press, 204–05
Shantou, Guangdong Province, 24–26
Shasta County, California, 63
Shen Bao, 141
Shen Nong (Emperor Yan), 139
Shenck, Paul, 154
shi yi (hereditary doctor), 148
Shiqi, Zhongshan District, Guangdong
    Province, 202
shipbuilding and shipping companies or
    industries, 23–26
    Western ships or shipping companies,
    24–25
Shisu (Four books), 204
Shiyan guowen jaiokeshu (Experimental
    national-language textbooks), 207
shuike (water guest/s), 28
Sierra County, California, 63
Sierra Nevada mountains, 57
Sima Guang, 206
Singapore, 24–26, 28–29
Sino-Japanese War. *See* China,
    Sino-Japanese War (1894–95); War of
    National Salvation Against Japanese
    Aggression (1937–45).

Sino-U.S. relations, 33
Siskiyou County, California, 63
Siu, Paul C.P., 6–7, 16, 163
smallpox, 142
social Darwinism, 161
social/socioeconomic status, 41–42. *See
    also* Chinese immigrants,
    socioeconomic class or status.
Solano County, California, 63
Sonoma County, California, 63
Sons, 226
South America, 161
South Seas. *See* Southeast Asia.
Southeast Asia, 4, 25–26, 158, 161, 197,
    201
    Chinese communities in, 26, 197, 201
Soviet Union. *See* Union of Soviet Socialist
    Republics.
Spanish colonial rule, 25
Spence, Jonathan D., 141
Springfield, Massachusetts, 14
Stanford, California:
    University, 222, 224
Stanford, Leland, 153
Stanislaus County, California, 63
steamships, 3, 6
    fare/s, 6
    routes of, 3
Stidger, Jason, 20
Stidger, Oliver P., 20
Straits Settlements, 24
Su Wu, 207
Sumatra, Indonesia, 25
Sun Yat-sen, xiv–xv, 169–70, 177–78,
    188–91, 198, 200, 207. *See also sanda
    zhengce*; *sanmin zhuyi*.
Sutter County, California, 63
Sweet Bamboo, 154
Sze Yup (Siyi-Four Districts), 202

Ta Tung Yat Po, 177, 181, 188
Tacoma, Washington, 60
Taft, Helen, 216
Taft, William Howard, 13
Taishan (Toisan) City, Guangdong
    Province, 29
    Baochang Money Shop, 29
    Wansheng Hao, 29
    Yu Lianhe's Zhengji Porcelain Store, 29
Taishan (Toisan) District, Guangdong
    Province, xi, 4, 27–30, 164–68
taishi (Chinese-style armchair), 222

Taiwan, 156
Tan Fuyuan, 144, 147, 149–50, 153
Tangmei village, Taishan District,
    Guangdong Province, 30
Taoist priests, 139
Tehachepi Mountains, California, 62
Tehama County, California, 62
Tennessee, 70
Thailand, 26
Thi Thanh Nga (Tiana), 234
This Bittersweet Soil, 63, 68
Tianjin, China, 206
Time magazine, 226
Ting Ching village, Guangdong Province,
    15
Tisdale, William, 144, 153
Tokyo, Japan, 177,
Tongmenghui, 177
Toronto, Ontario, 22
trade, global networks of, 23
transliteration, xv–xvi, 61
    pinyin system, xv
transnational/ism, ix–x, xii–xiii, 33, 60,
    137, 144, 156–57, 159–60, 163, 165,
    167, 172
    Chinese American, xiii, 33, 156, 160
*Transnational History of a Chinese Family,
    The*, xii
transpacific, ix, 6, 14, 25, 38, 136, 138,
    157, 160, 162, 168, 172, 183
Trinity County, California, 63
Tsai, Jung-fang, 26
Tsai, Shih-shan Henry, 141
Tulare County, California, 62–63
Tuolumne County, California, 63

"Uncle Tomism," 219
Union of Soviet Socialist Republics,
    188–89
United States, ix–xiii, xv, 1–10, 12–15,
    17–27, 30–34, 36–38, 42, 44–45,
    47–49, 52, 54–59, 61–63, 69, 136–37,
    139, 141–43, 147–49, 151, 153–61,
    163, 165–66, 170–75, 177–79, 181,
    184, 186, 189–91, 194, 196–97, 201,
    204, 209–15, 217, 219, 222, 226–27,
    231–32, 235
    American West, 5, 27, 155, 158
    Army, 215
    Bureau of the Census, 37, 62–63, 147,
    212

Bureau of Immigration, 5, 17–20, 32,
    212; commissioner-general of, 14. *See
    also* immigration authorities or
    officials.
civil rights movement, 213, 235
citizen/s, 1–2, 7–8, 10, 12–13, 17,
    20–21, 31–32, 45, 48–49, 186, 212,
    235; female, 12; wives and children of,
    12, 31. *See also* birthplace,
    American-born.
citizenship, 32, 159, 178, 217, 219;
    derivative, 31–32, 212; native-born,
    1–2, 7–8, 10, 13, 17, 20–21, 31, 212,
    219; naturalized, 159, 172, 175, 217
Congress, 23, 31, 155, 184, 214
diplomatic relations with China,
    severance of, 33
East Coast, 143
Great Depression, 6, 33, 170, 227, 232
judicial system, 12, 19, 21, 61; 153;
    circuit court/s of appeals, 61; district
    court/s, 61; officials of, 61; Supreme
    Court, 13
postal service, 171
Treasury Department, 19–20
U.S.-born. *See* birthplace,
    American-born; United States,
    citizen/s; United States, native-born.

Vancouver, British Columbia, 22, 27, 29
Ventura County, California, 63
Versailles Peace Conference, 184
Victoria, British Columbia, 22, 27, 29, 60

Washington, D.C., 27, 161, 195
    Chinese legation in, 161, 195
    Smithsonian Institution, 230
Washington, George, 207
Way, A.C., 154
welfare, Chinese attitude toward, 227
Wen Yanbo, 206
wenyan (literary language), xiv, 184, 196,
    202–04, 207
West River valley, Guangdong Province,
    24
Western:
    bank/s, 167
    culture/s, 22
    doctors, 142–43, 150, 153
    expansionism, 174. *See also* capitalism.
    medicine, 140–41, 150

nation/s or societies/society, 136, 161, 196
Wheatland, California, 28
When I Was a Boy in China, 228
White, Thomas, 154
white/s. *See* European American/s.
"Wild Bill Hickok" (William Hickok), 216
Wilhelm I, 207
Wilson, Woodrow, 13, 180, 216
Winnipeg, Manitoba, 22
Wise, John, 19
witness/es, 7, 20, 145
Wo Tsun Yuen, (Hu Junxiao), 143
Woman Warrior, The, 224, 236
women, Chinese. *See* Chinese immigrants, women/females; birthplace, China-born, females; U.S.-born, females.
women's:
history, 34–35
liberation movement, xiv, 183
rights, 199
Wong, Anna May, 235
Wong, Bing Woo, 152
Wong Gong Kim, 15
Wong Hong, 15–16
Wong, Jade Snow, xv, 182, 213–14, 223–36
Wong, K. Scott, x
Wong Lan Fong, 3, 6, 17
Wong Let, 18
Wong Ngum Yin, 5, 16
Wong Quong Ken, 15
Woo Gen, 13
Woo, John, 235
work. *See* employment, occupation, or work.
World of Suzie Wong, The, 234–35
World War I, 218
World War II, 5, 155, 158, 170, 172–73, 194, 208, 210, 212, 215, 223, 225, 229
Worley, Alfred, 21
Wu Bingjian (also known as Howqua), 141
Wu Chun-hsi, 169
Wu Panzhao. *See* Ng Poon Chew.
Wu Ting-fang, 13
Wu, Yi-li, 140
Wujing (Five classics), 204

Xia Chenghua, 171
Xialang, Taishan District, Guangdong Province, 29
Xiamen, Fujian Province, 25
xiaozhang (principal), 196
Xinning District. *See* Taishan District.
Xinning zhazi, 27
Xinning/Ningyang Railroad, 165–68, 189–90
"three no" policy of, 166–67
Xiongnu, 207
xiushen (moral character), 205
Xue Fucheng, 164
Xuesheng yuebao (Students' monthly), 199
xuetang (school), 196–97
xuexiao (school), 196
xunchengma (city-circuit horses), 28

Yan Row, 163
Yangzi River, China, 169, 206
Yee Pai, 152
Yeong Wo Association, 200
Yi bu sanshi, bo fu qi yao (if a doctor does not have three generations in medicine, do not take his remedies), 148
Yin, Xiao-huang, xv
Yolo County, California, 63
Young China, 177, 179, 181–82, 188, 190–91
Young, Jin, 17–18
Young Men's Christian Association (YMCA), 18, 186–87
Young Women's Christian Association (YWCA), 186–87
Youxue qionglin (Jade forest of learning for children), 204
Youxue shi (Poems for the young student), 204
Yuan Shikai, 179–81
Yuba County, California, 28, 62–63
Yue Fei, 207
Yuen Tim Gong, 7
Yung Hen, 13
Yung, Judy, 18
yutiwen (vernacular written Chinese), xiv, 196–97, 202–04

Zhang Bingchang, 165
Zhang Liang, 207
Zhang Qian, 207

Zhang Zhidong, 164–65

Zhangjiakou, Hebei Province, 167

Zheng Yun (also known as Wan Chang or Yum Sinn Chang), 201

Zhigongtang, 177, 181

Zhongguo dili (geography of China), 205

Zhongguo lishi (history of China), 205

Zhongshan District, Guangdong Province, 141, 202, 232

Zhuang Yu, 205

Zhudong, Taishan District, Guangdong Province, 30

zhuyin fuhao (Chinese phonetic symbols), 197

zhuyin zimu (Chinese phonetic alphabet), 196–97